Congressional Directories

Standard Version

Organized by state delegation, the popular Standard Version offers biographical data for each Member of Congress and includes current color photos, phone, fax and room numbers, web site and e-mail addresses (where available), district offices, and key staff. Committee and subcommittee rosters include room, phone and fax numbers, web site addresses, and staff directors.

Actual size: 4" x 9"

Alpha Version

The Alpha Version includes all the information featured in the Standard Version. Photos are in black and white and information about Members of the Senate and the House of Representatives are arranged in alphabetical order rather than by the state they represent. This is an ideal format for many congressional directory users!

Actual size: 4" x 9"

Condensed Version

If you prefer a smaller, less expensive directory without photos, the Condensed Version offers Members' name, party, district, term, phone, fax and room numbers, web site addresses and key staff. Committee rosters include room and phone numbers plus names of majority and minority staff directors. Also included are Senate/House leadership, telephone numbers of important congressional offices and national party organizations, a schedule for the 109th Congress, a map of Capitol Hill and more!

Actual size: $3^{1}/_{2}$" x $6^{3}/_{4}$"

CAPITOL ADVANTAGE PRODUCTS

Qty.	Product	Total Price
_____	***Standard Congressional Directories*** ☐ 109th/1st Session ☐ 109th/2nd Session	
_____	***Alpha Congressional Directories*** ☐ 109th/1st Session ☐ 109th/2nd Session	
_____	***Condensed Congressional Directories*** ☐ 109th/1st Session ☐ 109th/2nd Session	
	VA residents/orgs. add 5% sales tax	
	Subtotal	
	TOTAL	

PRICING INFORMATION

Qty.	Standard	Alpha	Condensed
Single	$17.95	$17.95	$12.95
2-5	16.95	16.95	12.25
6-25	15.95	15.95	11.50

Over 25 copies…call for prices

Orders of 100+ can be personalized with your name, logo and inserts!

Call for details and special rates

PAYMENT/BILLING INFORMATION

☐ Payment enclosed. *Make check payable to Capitol Advantage Publishing.*

Please bill: ☐ MasterCard   ☐ VISA   ☐ AMEX

(All orders billed prior to shipping)

Card # _____ Exp. Date _____

Name on card: _____

Signature: _____

SEND ORDER TO:

Name _____

Organization _____

Address _____

City _____ State ____ ZIP _____

Phone _____ E-mail _____

CAPITOL ADVANTAGE®

PO Box 2018 • Merrifield, VA 22116-2018
703-550-9500 • Toll Free 877-827-3321 • Fax 703-550-0406
capitoladvantage.com

Table of Contents

Key Websites 1

Key Telephone Numbers and Addresses 2

Congressional Schedule 3

Communicating With Congress
    Tips on Writing to a Member 4
    Sending E-mail to Congress 4
    Suggestions for a Personal Visit 5
    The Roles of Congressional Staff 6
    How a Bill Becomes Law 7
    Guide to Using This Book 8

The White House 9

The Cabinet 10

Selected Agencies 12

The Supreme Court 15

State Governors 16

State Governors Re-election Schedule 24

Senate Leadership and Officers 25

Senate Re-election Schedule 26

Alphabetized Guide to the Senate 27

Senate Committees and Subcommittees 47

House of Representatives Party Breakdown 63

House of Representatives Leadership and Officers 64

Alphabetized Guide to the House of Representatives 65

Selected Congressional Caucus Information 139

House Committees and Subcommittees 143

Joint Committees 168

State Legislature Information 169

Legislative Glossary 172

State Maps .... Appendix

Map of Capitol Hill .... Fold-Out

Information in directory corrected to March 18, 2005

© Copyright 2005. Capitol Advantage Publishing
P.O. Box 2018, Merrifield, VA 22116-2018, 703-550-9500

Key Websites

EXECUTIVE
The White House .... www.whitehouse.gov

JUDICIARY
Supreme Court of the United States .... www.supremecourtus.gov

LEGISLATIVE
US House of Representatives .... www.house.gov
Clerk of the House .... clerk.house.gov
Currently on the House
  Floor clerk.house.gov/floorsummary/floor.php3
US Senate .... www.senate.gov
US Senate Calendar
  of Business .... www.gpoaccess.gov/calendars/senate
THOMAS .... thomas.loc.gov
Congressional Information .... congress.org
Congressional Record .... www.gpoaccess.gov/crecord

OTHER GOVERNMENT RESOURCES
Federal Election Commission .... www.fec.gov
Federal Register .... www.archives.gov/federal_register
Government Printing Office .... www.gpoaccess.gov
The Library of Congress .... www.loc.gov
FirstGov .... www.firstgov.com
US Census Bureau .... www.census.gov

POLITICAL PARTIES
Democratic National Committee .... www.democrats.org
Senate Democratic Conference .... democrats.senate.gov
Democratic Senatorial Campaign Committee ...... www.dscc.org
House Democratic Caucus .... democrats.house.gov
Democratic Congressional
  Campaign Committee .... www.dccc.org
Republican National Committee .... www.rnc.org
Senate Republican Conference .... src.senate.gov
National Republican Senatorial Committee .... www.nrsc.org
House Republican Conference .... www.gop.gov
National Republican Congressional Committee .. www.nrcc.org

MEDIA
ABC News .... abcnews.go.com
CBS News .... www.cbsnews.com
CNN .... www.cnn.com
C-SPAN .... www.c-span.org
Fox News Channel .... foxnews.com
The Hill .... www.hillnews.com
Los Angeles Times .... www.latimes.com
NBC News .... www.msnbc.com
The New York Times .... www.nytimes.com
Roll Call .... www.rollcall.com
USA TODAY .... www.usatoday.com
The Wall Street Journal .... www.wsj.com
The Washington Post .... www.washingtonpost.com
The Washington Times .... www.washingtontimes.com

Key Telephone Numbers and Addresses

US Capitol Switchboard 202-224-3121
Architect of the Capitol 202-228-1793
Congressional Budget Office 202-226-2600
Congressional Record Index (GPO) 202-512-0275
Congressional Research Service 202-707-5700
Federal Register 202-741-6000
Library of Congress 202-707-5000
Office of Special Services 202-224-4048
Postal Operations, House 202-225-3856
Postal Operations, Senate 202-224-5353
Senate and House Bill Status 202-225-1772

Senate Offices (Room/Phone Numbers):
  Document Room SH-B04/202-224-7860
  Cloak Room .... (R) 202-224-6191, (D) 202-224-4691
  Floor Information .... (R) 202-224-8601, (D) 202-224-8541
  Press Gallery S-316/202-224-0241
  Addresses: *Street addresses are Washington, DC 20510*
  SD .... Dirksen Building .... 1st & C Sts., NE
  SH .... Hart Building .... 2nd & C Sts., NE
  SR .... Russell Building .... 1st & C Sts., NE
  S .... US Capitol

House Offices (Room/Phone Numbers):
  Document Room B106 CHOB/202-226-5200
  Cloak Room .... (R) 202-225-7350, (D) 202-225-7330
  Floor Information .... (R) 202-225-7430, (D) 202-225-7400
  Press Gallery H-315/202-225-3945
  Addresses: *Street addresses are Washington, DC 20515*
  Three digit room numbers are located in:
  CHOB .... Cannon House Office Bldg.
                                    1st St. & Independence Ave., SE
  Four digit room numbers beginning with 1 are located in:
  LHOB .... Longworth House Office Bldg.
                                    Independence & New Jersey Aves., SE
  Four digit room numbers beginning with 2 are located in:
  RHOB .... Rayburn House Office Bldg.
                                    Independence Ave. & S. Capitol St., SW
  Other Buildings:
  FHOB .... Ford House Office Bldg.
                                    300 D St., SW
  H .... US Capitol
  ALOC .... Adams Bldg., Library of Congress
                                    101 Independence Ave., SE

Party information:
Democratic National Committee 202-863-8000
Democratic Congressional Campaign Committee 202-863-1500
Democratic Senatorial Campaign Committee 202-224-2447
Democratic Governors' Association 202-772-5600
Republican National Committee 202-863-8500
National Republican Congressional Committee 202-479-7000
National Republican Senatorial Committee 202-675-6000
Republican Governors Association 202-662-4140

Congressional Schedule

109th Congress / First Session

	House	**Senate**
First Business Day	Jan. 4	Jan. 4
Republican Retreat	Jan. 27-29	Jan. 27-29
Democrat Retreat	Feb. 3-5	TBA
Presidents' Day District Work Period	Feb. 21-25	Feb. 21-25
Spring District Work Period	March 21-April 1	March 21-April 1
District Work Period	—	May 2-6
Memorial Day District Work Period	May 30-June 3	May 30-June 3
Independence Day District Work Period	July 4-8	July 4-8
Summer District Work Period	Aug. 1-Sept. 5	Aug. 1-Sept. 5
Target Adjournment	Sept. 30	Sept. 30

Important Dates - 2005

Martin Luther King, Jr. Day	Monday, Jan. 17
Presidents' Day	Monday, Feb. 21
Easter	Sunday, March 27
Passover	Sunday, April 24
Memorial Day	Monday, May 30
Independence Day	Monday, July 4
Labor Day	Monday, Sept. 5
Patriot Day	Sunday, Sept. 11
Rosh Hashanah	Tuesday, Oct. 4
Columbus Day	Monday, Oct. 10
Yom Kippur	Thursday, Oct. 13
Veterans Day	Friday, Nov. 11
Thanksgiving	Thursday, Nov. 24
Christmas	Sunday, Dec. 25
Chanukah	Monday, Dec. 26

Communicating With Congress

TIPS ON WRITING TO A MEMBER

The letter is the most popular choice of communication with a congressional office. If you decide to write a letter, this list of helpful suggestions will improve the effectiveness of the letter.

Addressing Correspondence:

- **To a Senator...**
    The Honorable (Full Name)
    United States Senate
    Washington, DC 20510
    Dear Senator ____(Last Name)____ :

- **To a Representative...**
    The Honorable (Full Name)
    House of Representatives
    Washington, DC 20515
    Dear Mr./Mrs./Ms. ____(Last Name)____ :

Note: When writing to the Chair of a Committee or the Speaker of the House, it is proper to address him/her as:

> Dear Mr. Chairman or Madam Chairwoman:
> or Dear Mr. Speaker:

Purpose of Your Letter:

- Your purpose for writing should be stated in the first paragraph of the letter. If the letter pertains to a specific piece of legislation, identify it accordingly, e.g., House bill: H.R. ____, Senate bill: S.____.

- Be courteous, to the point, and include key information, using examples to support your position.

- Address only one issue in each letter; and, if possible, keep the letter to one page.

SENDING E-MAIL TO CONGRESS

When addressing an e-mail to a Member of Congress, follow the same suggestions as for a printed letter. For the subject line of your e-mail, identify your message by topic or bill number. The body of your message should use this format:

> Your Name
> Address
> City, State ZIP
>
> Dear (Title) (Last Name),

Many Members now have web forms rather than public e-mail addresses. If there is no e-mail address listed in this book, visit the Member's web site or http://congress.org to send your message through the Internet.

Communicating With Congress

SUGGESTIONS FOR A PERSONAL VISIT

Meeting with a Member of Congress, or congressional staff, is a very effective way to convey a message about a specific issue or legislative matter. Below are some suggestions to consider when planning a visit to a congressional office.

Plan Your Visit Carefully: Be clear about what it is you want to achieve; determine in advance which Member or committee staff you need to meet with to achieve your purpose.

Make an Appointment: When attempting to meet with a Member, contact the Appointment Secretary/Scheduler. Explain your purpose and who you represent. It is easier for congressional staff to arrange a meeting if they know what you wish to discuss and your relationship to the area or interests represented by the Member.

Be Prompt and Patient: When it is time to meet with a Member, be punctual and be patient. It is not uncommon for a Congressman or Congresswoman to be late, or to have a meeting interrupted due to the Member's crowded schedule. If interruptions do occur, be flexible. When the opportunity presents itself, continue your meeting with a Member's staff.

Be Prepared: Whenever possible, bring to the meeting information and materials supporting your position. Members are required to take positions on many different issues. In some instances, a Member may lack important details about the pros and cons of a particular matter. It is therefore helpful to share with the Member information and examples that demonstrate clearly the impact or benefits associated with a particular issue or piece of legislation.

Be Political: Members of Congress want to represent the best interests of their district or state. Whenever possible, demonstrate the connection between what you are requesting and the interests of the Member's constituency. If possible, describe for the Member how you or your group can be of assistance to him/her. When it is appropriate, remember to ask for a commitment.

Be Responsive: Be prepared to answer questions or provide additional information in the event the Member expresses interest or asks questions. Follow up the meeting with a thank-you letter that outlines the different points covered during the meeting, and send along any additional information and materials requested.

Communicating With Congress

THE ROLES OF CONGRESSIONAL STAFF

Each Member of Congress has staff to assist him/her during a term in office. To be most effective in communicating with Congress, it is helpful to know the titles and principal functions of key staff.

Commonly used titles and job functions:

Administrative Assistant (AA) or **Chief of Staff (CoS):** The AA reports directly to the Member of Congress. He/she usually has overall responsibility for evaluating the political outcomes of various legislative proposals and constituent requests. The AA is usually the person in charge of overall office operations, including the assignment of work and the supervision of key staff.

Legislative Director (LD), Senior Legislative Assistant (Sr LA), or **Legislative Counsel (LC):** The LD is usually the staff person who monitors the legislative schedule and makes recommendations regarding the pros and cons of particular issues. In some congressional offices there are several LAs and responsibilities are assigned to staff with particular expertise in specific areas. For example, depending on the responsibilities and interests of the Member, an office may include a different LA for health issues, environmental matters, taxes, etc.

Press Secretary (Press) or **Communications Director (Comm Dir):** The Press Secretary's responsibility is to build and maintain open and effective lines of communication between the Member, his/her constituency, and the general public. The Press Secretary is expected to know the benefits, demands, and special requirements of both print and electronic media, and how to most effectively promote the Member's views or position on specific issues.

Appointment Secretary (Appt), Personal Secretary, or **Scheduler (Sch):** The Appointment Secretary is usually responsible for allocating a Member's time among the many demands that arise from congressional responsibilities, staff requirements, and constituent requests. The Appointment Secretary may also be responsible for making necessary travel arrangements, arranging speaking dates, visits to the district, etc.

Caseworker: The Caseworker is the staff member usually assigned to help with constituent requests by preparing replies for the Member's signature. The Caseworker's responsibilities may also include helping resolve problems constituents present in relation to federal agencies, e.g., Social Security and Medicare issues, veteran's benefits, passports, etc. There are often several Caseworkers in a congressional office.

Other Staff Titles: Other titles used in a congressional office may include: Executive Assistant, Legislative Correspondent, Executive Secretary, Office Manager, and Receptionist.

Communicating With Congress

HOW A BILL BECOMES LAW

1. Introduction of Legislation
There are two basic types of legislation: bills and resolutions. Bills are used to create public policy. There are three types of resolutions – joint, concurrent, and simple – that can be used to appropriate money or express a sentiment of Congress. Constitutional amendments originate in Congress as joint resolutions.

Ideas for bills can come from anyone, although only a Member of Congress can introduce legislation. All bills are assigned an identifying number. Those introduced in the House begin with H.R., and those in the Senate begin with S. Legislation appropriating money must originate in the House.

2. Committee Action
Once legislation is introduced, it is referred to the committee that has jurisdiction over its subject. A bill may be sent to a single committee (single referral), several committees at once (multiple or joint referral), from one committee to another (sequential referral), or different parts of a bill may be sent to different committees (split referral).

Because most of the work done on a bill is at the committee level, committees have a great deal of power to decide which bills will receive the most attention. The more support a bill has, especially from congressional or committee leadership or from the President, the greater its chance of receiving consideration.

3. Subcommittee Action
After it receives a bill, a committee will generally refer it to the proper subcommittee. Subcommittees have a more narrow focus than committees. Three main steps occur at this stage:

- Hearings. Witnesses are called to testify about the merits and shortcomings of a piece of legislation. Questions from committee members and testimony of witnesses are generally prepared in advance to support a particular position on a bill.
- Mark Up. At this stage, committee members may offer their own views on a bill and suggest amendments. Amendments do not have to be related to the subject of the overall bill at this stage.
- Reporting Out. When the mark up is complete, a final draft of the legislation is voted on for approval. If a majority supports the bill, it is "reported out." If the legislation does not receive majority support, the bill dies.

After a subcommittee reports out legislation, the full committee will go through the same consideration process. If the committee approves a bill, it is reported out to the full House or Senate.

4. Publication of a Written Report
After a committee votes to report a bill, the committee chair instructs the committee staff to prepare a report on the bill. This report describes the intent of the legislation, its impact on existing laws and programs, and views of dissenting members.

5. Floor Action
Next, legislation is placed on the House or Senate calendar for debate by the full chamber.

In the House, the Rules Committee sets the terms of debate. This Committee may place limits on the time for debate or on the number and type of amendments that may be offered. If the Committee does not place a rule on a bill, there is little chance of it being debated, and the bill dies. Once a bill comes to the floor, supporters and opponents are given a chance to speak. Any amendments offered on the floor must be germane, or related to the main subject of the legislation.

Communicating With Congress

The Senate places fewer restrictions on debate. The terms of debate are often set by a Unanimous Consent Agreement, which is approved by party leaders. Any Senator may filibuster, or speak against a particular piece of legislation, for as long as he or she wishes. A filibuster may only be ended by invoking cloture, which requires that 60 Senators vote to end debate.

When debate concludes in either chamber, a vote takes place to approve or defeat a bill.

6. Conference Committee
Bills may originate in one chamber, and upon passage, move to the opposite chamber to repeat the approval process. Often, however, similar bills work their way through both the House and Senate at the same time. Both chambers must pass identical bills in order for the legislation to be sent to the President for approval, so the House and Senate will form a conference committee to reconcile any differences between their bills. Both chambers may instruct their conferees on acceptable compromises. Once differences are resolved and a conference report is generated, both chambers must once again vote to approve the legislation.

7. Action by the President
The President has four choices upon receiving legislation. He may:
- sign the bill into law;
- veto the bill and send it back to Congress with suggestions for reconsideration;
- take no action while Congress is in session, in which case the bill will become law in ten days;
- take no action and let the bill die after Congress has adjourned for the session. This is called a "pocket veto."

8. Overriding a Veto
If the President vetoes a bill, Congress may override his decision. A two-thirds vote in both chambers is required to overturn a veto.

Guide To Using This Book

Member Photo	**Name (Party-District/State)** **Phone Number** Address Term/Last Election % Fax Number E-mail Address Website Address **Staff Title** .... *Staff Name* **Staff Title** ..... *Staff Name* **Staff Title** .... *Staff Name* **Staff Title** ..... *Staff Name* **Bio:** Birthdate Birthplace; Religion; Highest Degree Achieved, School, Year; Military Service; Previous Profession; Marital Status, Spouse's Name **Comm.:** Committee Assignments **Dist. Offices:** City, Phone Number

Commonly used staff titles:

AA:	Administrative Assistant	**LD:**	Legislative Director
AD:	Administrative Director	**OpD:**	Operations Director
Appt:	Appointment Secretary	**PD:**	Policy Director
Comm Dir:	Communications Director	**Press:**	Press Secretary
CoS:	Chief of Staff	**Sch:**	Scheduler
Dep CoS:	Deputy Chief of Staff	**Sr LA:**	Senior Legislative Assistant
EA:	Executive Assistant	**Sr PA:**	Senior Policy Advisor
LC :	Legislative Counsel		

The White House

1600 Pennsylvania Ave., NW
Washington, DC 20500
202-456-1414

Office of the President

The President – George W. Bush	456-1414

Office of the Vice President

*The Vice President – Richard B. Cheney	456-9000
Chief of Staff to the Vice President – Lewis Libby	456-9000

Office of the Chief of Staff

*Chief of Staff – Andrew H. Card, Jr.	456-6798

Office of the First Lady

The First Lady – Laura Bush	456-7064
Chief of Staff to the First Lady – Andrea Ball	456-7064
Press Secretary to the First Lady – Susan Dryden Whitson	456-6313

Executive Offices of the President

Advance, Director of – Todd Beyer	456-5309
Appointments and Scheduling – Melissa Bennett	456-5323
Cabinet Affairs – Heidi Marques Smith	456-2572
Communications Director – Nicole Devenish	456-2640
Counsel to the President – Harriet Miers	456-2632
Deputy Chief of Staff & Senior Advisor to the President – Karl Rove	456-2369
Domestic Policy Council – Claude Allen	456-5594
*Environmental Protection Agency – Stephen L. Johnson (acting)	564-4700
Faith-Based and Community Initiatives – James Towey	456-6708
Intergovernmental Affairs – Ruben Barrales	456-2896
Legislative Affairs – Candi Wolff	456-2230
*Management and Budget – Joshua Bolten	395-4840
Military Office – Mark Fox (acting)	757-2151
*National Drug Control Policy – John P. Walters	395-6700
National Economic Council – Allan B. Hubbard	456-2800
National Security Advisor – Stephen Hadley	456-9491
Political Affairs – Sara Taylor	456-1125
Presidential Personnel – Dina Powell	456-7060
Press Secretary – Scott McClellan	456-2673
Public Liaison – Lezlee Westine	456-2380
Science and Technology Policy – John H. Marburger III	456-7116
*US Trade Representative – Peter Allgeier (acting)	395-6890
White House Management & Administration – Linda Gambatesa	456-5400

*CABINET RANK

Area code for all numbers is 202

The Cabinet

Department of Agriculture 202-720-3631
Secy. Mike Johanns   www.usda.gov
1400 Independence Ave., SW
Washington, DC 20250

Director of Communications
Matt Raymond (acting) 202-720-4623

Department of Commerce 202-482-2112
Secy. Carlos M. Gutierrez   www.commerce.gov
1401 Constitution Ave., NW
Washington, DC 20230

Director of Public Affairs
Vacant 202-482-4883

Department of Defense 703-692-7100
Secy. Donald H. Rumsfeld www.defenselink.mil
1000 Defense Pentagon
Washington, DC 20301-1000

Principal Deputy Secretary of Public Affairs
Lawrence Di Rita 703-697-9312

Department of Education 202-401-3000
Secy. Margaret Spellings   www.ed.gov
400 Maryland Ave., SW
Washington, DC 20202

Director of Public Affairs
D.J. Nordquist (acting) 202-401-3026

Department of Energy 202-586-6210
Secy. Samuel W. Bodman   www.energy.gov
1000 Independence Ave., SW
Washington, DC 20585

Director of Public Affairs
Anne Womack Kolton 202-586-4940

**Department of Health and
  Human Services** 202-690-7000
Secy. Mike Leavitt   www.dhhs.gov
200 Independence Ave., SW
Washington, DC 20201

Assistant Secretary for Public Affairs
Kevin Keane 202-690-7850

**Department of Homeland
  Security** 202-282-8000
Secy. Michael Chertoff   www.dhs.gov
Nebraska Ave. Center, NW
Washington, DC 20528

Assistant Secretary for Public Affairs
Brian Besanceney (acting) 202-282-8010

The Cabinet *(cont'd)*

**Department of Housing and
   Urban Development** **202-708-0417**
Secy. Alphonso Jackson   www.hud.gov
451 7th St., SW
Washington, DC 20410

Assistant Secretary for Public Affairs
Cathy MacFarlane 202-708-0980

Department of the Interior **202-208-7351**
Secy. Gale A. Norton   www.doi.gov
1849 C St., NW
Washington, DC 20240

Director of Communications
Tina Kreisher 202-208-6416

Department of Justice **202-514-2001**
Atty. Gen. Alberto R. Gonzales www.usdoj.gov
950 Pennsylvania Ave., NW
Washington, DC 20530

Director, Office of Public Affairs
Tasia Scolinos 202-616-2777

Department of Labor **202-693-6000**
Secy. Elaine L. Chao   www.dol.gov
200 Constitution Ave., NW
Washington, DC 20210

Assistant Secretary for Public Affairs
Lisa Kruska 202-693-4676

Department of State **202-647-4000**
Secy. Condoleezza Rice   www.state.gov
2201 C St., NW
Washington, DC 20520

Assistant Secretary for Public Affairs
Richard Boucher 202-647-6607

Department of Transportation **202-366-1111**
Secy. Norman Y. Mineta   www.dot.gov
400 7th St., SW
Washington, DC 20590

Director of Public Affairs
Robert Johnson 202-366-4570

Department of the Treasury **202-622-1100**
Secy. John W. Snow   www.ustreas.gov
1500 Pennsylvania Ave., NW
Washington, DC 20220

Assistant Secretary for Public Affairs
Rob Nichols 202-622-2920

Department of Veterans Affairs .. **202-273-4800**
Secy. Jim Nicholson   www.va.gov
810 Vermont Ave., NW
Washington, DC 20420

*Assistant Secretary for Public and
Intergovernmental Affairs*
Cynthia R. Church 202-273-5750

Selected Agencies

Alcohol and Tobacco Tax and Trade Bureau 202-927-5000
1310 G St., NW, Washington, DC 20220
www.ttb.gov

Bureau of Customs and Border Protection 202-354-1000
1300 Pennsylvania Ave., NW, Washington, DC 20229
www.cbp.gov

Bureau of the Census 301-763-2135
4700 Silver Hill Rd., Suitland, MD 20746
www.census.gov

Centers for Medicare and Medicaid Services 410-786-3000
7500 Security Blvd., Baltimore, MD 21244
cms.hhs.gov

Central Intelligence Agency 703-482-0623
Central Intelligence Agency, Washington, DC 20505
www.cia.gov

Commission on Civil Rights 202-376-7700
624 9th St., NW, Washington, DC 20425
www.usccr.gov

Consumer Product Safety Commission 301-504-7923
4330 East-West Hwy., Bethesda, MD 20814
www.cpsc.gov

Corporation for National and Community Service 202-606-5000
1201 New York Ave., NW, Washington, DC 20525
www.cns.gov

Drug Enforcement Administration 202-307-1000
2401 Jefferson Davis Hwy., Alexandria, VA 22301
www.dea.gov

Environmental Protection Agency 202-272-0167
1200 Pennsylvania Ave., NW, Washington, DC 20460
www.epa.gov

Equal Employment Opportunity Commission 202-663-4900
1801 L St., NW, Washington, DC 20507
www.eeoc.gov

Export-Import Bank of the US 202-565-3946
811 Vermont Ave., NW, Washington, DC 20571
www.exim.gov

Farm Credit Administration 703-883-4000
1501 Farm Credit Dr., McLean, VA 22102
www.fca.gov

Federal Aviation Administration 202-267-3111
800 Independence Ave., SW, Washington, DC 20591
www.faa.gov

Federal Bureau of Investigation 202-324-3000
935 Pennsylvania Ave., NW, Washington, DC 20535
www.fbi.gov

Federal Communications Commission 202-418-1000
445 12th St., SW, Washington, DC 20554
www.fcc.gov

Federal Deposit Insurance Corporation 202-736-0000
550 17th St., NW, Washington, DC 20429
www.fdic.gov

Federal Election Commission 202-694-1000
999 E St., NW, Washington, DC 20463
www.fec.gov

Selected Agencies

Federal Emergency Management Agency **202-566-1600**
500 C St., SW, Washington, DC 20472
www.fema.gov

Federal Highway Administration **202-366-0650**
400 7th St., SW, Washington, DC 20590
www.fhwa.dot.gov

Federal Railroad Administration **202-493-6000**
1120 Vermont Ave., NW, Washington, DC 20590
www.fra.dot.gov

Federal Reserve System **202-452-3000**
20th St. & Constitution Ave., NW, Washington, DC 20551
www.federalreserve.gov

Federal Trade Commission **202-326-2222**
600 Pennsylvania Ave., NW, Washington, DC 20580
www.ftc.gov

Federal Transit Administration **202-366-4040**
400 7th St., SW, Washington, DC 20590
www.fta.dot.gov

Food and Drug Administration **301-827-2410**
5600 Fishers Ln., Rockville, MD 20857
www.fda.gov

General Services Administration **202-501-0800**
1800 F St., NW, Washington, DC 20405
www.gsa.gov

Government Accountability Office **202-512-3000**
441 G St., NW, Washington, DC 20548
www.gao.gov

Government Printing Office **202-512-0000**
732 N. Capitol St., NW, Washington, DC 20401
www.gpo.gov

Internal Revenue Service **202-622-5000**
1111 Constitution Ave., NW, Washington, DC 20224
www.irs.gov

International Monetary Fund **202-623-7000**
700 19th St., NW, Washington, DC 20431
www.imf.org

International Trade Commission **202-205-2000**
500 E St., SW, Washington, DC 20436
www.usitc.gov

National Aeronautics and Space Administration ... **202-358-0000**
300 E St., SW, Washington, DC 20546
www.nasa.gov

National Endowment for the Arts **202-682-5400**
1100 Pennsylvania Ave., NW, Washington, DC 20506
www.arts.gov

National Endowment for the Humanities **202-606-8400**
1100 Pennsylvania Ave., NW, Washington, DC 20506
www.neh.gov

National Highway Traffic Safety Administration ... **202-366-0123**
400 7th St., SW, Washington, DC 20590
www.nhtsa.gov

National Institutes of Health **301-496-4000**
9000 Rockville Pk., Bethesda, MD 20892
www.nih.gov

Selected Agencies

National Park Service **202-208-6843**
1849 C St., NW, Washington, DC 20240
www.nps.gov

National Science Foundation **703-292-5111**
4201 Wilson Blvd., Arlington, VA 22230
www.nsf.gov

**National Telecommunications and Information
Administration** **202-482-7002**
1401 Constitution Ave., NW, Washington, DC 20230
www.ntia.doc.gov

National Transportation Safety Board **202-314-6000**
490 L'Enfant Plz., SW, Washington, DC 20594
www.ntsb.gov

Occupational Safety and Health Administration ... **202-693-2000**
200 Constitution Ave., NW, Washington, DC 20210
www.osha.gov

Office of Personnel Management **202-606-1800**
1900 E St., NW, Washington, DC 20415
www.opm.gov

Peace Corps **202-692-2000**
1111 20th St., NW, Washington, DC 20526
www.peacecorps.gov

Pension Benefit Guaranty Corporation **202-326-4000**
1200 K St., NW, Washington, DC 20005
www.pbgc.gov

Securities and Exchange Commission **202-942-8088**
450 5th St., NW, Washington, DC 20549
www.sec.gov

Small Business Administration **202-205-6600**
409 3rd St., SW, Washington, DC 20416
www.sba.gov

Smithsonian Institution **202-357-2627**
1000 Jefferson Dr., SW, Washington, DC 20560
www.si.edu

Social Security Administration **410-965-3120**
6401 Security Blvd., Baltimore, MD 21235
www.ssa.gov

Surface Transportation Board **202-565-1500**
1925 K St., NW, Washington, DC 20423
www.stb.dot.gov

Surgeon General **301-443-4000**
5600 Fishers Ln., Rockville, MD 20857
www.surgeongeneral.gov

Transportation Security Administration **866-289-9673**
601 S. 12th St., Arlington, VA 22202
www.tsa.gov

US Citizenship and Immigration Services **800-375-5283**
20 Massachusetts Ave., NW, Washington, DC 20529
www.uscis.gov

US Fish and Wildlife Service **202-208-4717**
1849 C St., NW, Washington, DC 20242
www.fws.gov

US Postal Service **202-268-2000**
475 L'Enfant Plz., SW, Washington, DC 20260
www.usps.gov

The Supreme Court

United States Supreme Court Building
1 First St., NE
Washington, DC 20543
202-479-3000

Chief Justice

William H. Rehnquist
  Nominated Chief Justice by President Reagan, 1986
  Nominated Associate Justice by President Nixon, 1971
  b. 10/1/24 Milwaukee, WI; LLB Stanford Univ., 1952; USAF, 43-46; widowed

Associate Justices

John Paul Stevens
  Nominated by President Ford, 1975
  b. 4/20/20 Chicago, IL; JD Northwestern Univ., 1947; USN, 1942-45; m. Maryan

Sandra Day O'Connor
  Nominated by President Reagan, 1981
  b. 3/26/30 El Paso, TX; LLB Stanford Univ., 1952; m. John

Antonin Scalia
  Nominated by President Reagan, 1986
  b. 3/11/36 Trenton, NJ; LLB Harvard Univ., 1960; m. Maureen

Anthony M. Kennedy
  Nominated by President Reagan, 1988
  b. 7/23/36 Sacramento, CA; LLB Harvard Univ., 1961; CAARNG, 1961; m. Mary

David H. Souter
  Nominated by President Bush, 1990
  b. 9/17/39 Melrose, MA; LLB Harvard Univ., 1966; single

Clarence Thomas
  Nominated by President Bush, 1991
  b. 6/23/48 Pin Point, GA; JD Yale Univ., 1974; m. Virginia

Ruth Bader Ginsburg
  Nominated by President Clinton, 1993
  b. 3/15/33 Brooklyn, NY; LLB Columbia Univ., 1959; m. Martin

Stephen G. Breyer
  Nominated by President Clinton, 1994
  b. 8/15/38 San Francisco, CA; LLB Harvard Univ., 1964; m. Joanna

*Ginsburg, Souter, Thomas, Breyer (standing)
Scalia, Stevens, Rehnquist, O'Connor, Kennedy (seated)*

State Governors

ALABAMA
www.alabama.gov

Bob Riley (R)   **334-242-7100**
Next Election: 2006   1st Term/49.2%   Fax: 334-353-0004
Bio: b. 10/3/44 Clay Co., AL; Baptist; BA Univ. of AL, 1965; Businessman; m. Patsy

State Capitol, 600 Dexter Ave., Montgomery, AL 36130

ALASKA
www.state.ak.us

Frank H. Murkowski (R)   **907-465-3500**
Next Election: 2006   1st Term/56%   Fax: 907-465-3532
Bio: b. 3/28/33 Seattle, WA; Catholic; BA Seattle Univ., 1955; USCG, 1955-56; Banker; m. Nancy

PO Box 110001, Juneau, AK 99811-0001

Washington Office: 202-624-5858

ARIZONA
www.az.gov

Janet Napolitano (D)   **602-542-4331**
Next Election: 2006   1st Term/46%   Fax: 602-542-1381
Bio: b. 11/29/57 Pittsburgh, PA; Methodist; JD Univ. of VA, 1983; Attorney; single

1700 W. Washington St., Phoenix, AZ 85007

Washington Office: 202-220-1396

ARKANSAS
www.arkansas.gov

Mike Huckabee (R)   **501-682-2345**
Next Election: 2006   3rd Term/53%   Fax: 501-682-3597
Bio: b. 8/24/55 Hope; Southern Baptist; BA Ouachita Baptist Univ., 1975; Communications Executive, Pastor; m. Janet

State Capitol, Rm. 250, Little Rock, AR 72201

Washington Office: 202-220-1340

CALIFORNIA
www.ca.gov

Arnold Schwarzenegger (R)   **916-445-2841**
Next Election: 2006   1st Term/48.7%   Fax: 916-445-4633
E-mail: governor@governor.ca.gov
Bio: b. 7/30/47 Thal, Styria, Austria; Catholic; BA Univ. of WI - Superior, 1980; Actor, Businessman; m. Maria Shriver

State Capitol Bldg., Sacramento, CA 95814

Washington Office: 202-624-5270

COLORADO
www.colorado.gov

Bill Owens (R)   **303-866-2471**
Next Election: 2006   2nd Term/63%   Fax: 303-866-2003
E-mail: governorowens@state.co.us
Bio: b. 10/22/50 Fort Worth, TX; Roman Catholic; MPA Univ. of TX, 1975; Public Official; m. Frances

136 State Capitol, Denver, CO 80203-1792

Washington Office: 202-624-7865

State Governors

CONNECTICUT   www.ct.gov

M. Jodi Rell (R)   **860-566-4840**
Next Election: 2006   1st Term   Fax: 860-524-7395
E-mail: governor.rell@po.state.ct.us
Bio: b. 6/16/46 Norfolk, VA; Protestant; Western CT St. Univ.; Public Official; m. Lou

210 Capitol Ave., Hartford, CT 06106
Washington Office: 202-347-4535

DELAWARE   www.delaware.gov

Ruth Ann Minner (D)   **302-744-4101**
Next Election: 2008   2nd Term/59%   Fax: 302-739-2775
Bio: b. 1/17/35 Milford, DE; Methodist; Attended DE Tech.; Public Official, Business Owner; widowed

Tatnall Bldg., William Penn St., 2nd Fl., Dover, DE 19901
Washington Office: 202-624-7724

FLORIDA   www.myflorida.com

Jeb Bush (R)   **850-488-4441**
Next Election: 2006   2nd Term/56%   Fax: 850-487-0801
E-mail: jeb@myflorida.com
Bio: b. 2/11/53 Midland, TX; Roman Catholic; BA Univ. of TX, 1974; Businessman; m. Columba

The Capitol, 400 S. Monroe St., Tallahassee, FL 32399
Washington Office: 202-624-5885

GEORGIA   www.georgia.gov

Sonny Perdue (R)   **404-656-1776**
Next Election: 2006   1st Term/51%   Fax: 404-656-5947
Bio: b. 12/20/46 Perry, GA; Baptist; DVM Univ. of GA, 1971; USAF, 1971-74; Small Business Owner; m. Mary

203 State Capitol, Atlanta, GA 30334
Washington Office: 202-624-3681

HAWAII   www.hawaii.gov

Linda Lingle (R)   **808-586-0034**
Next Election: 2006   1st Term/51%   Fax: 808-586-0006
Bio: b. 6/4/53 St. Louis, MO; Jewish; BA CA St. Univ., 1975; Public Official, Political Activist; single

State Capitol, Executive Chambers, Honolulu, HI 96813

IDAHO   www.idaho.gov

Dirk Kempthorne (R)   **208-334-2100**
Next Election: 2006   2nd Term/56%   Fax: 208-334-2175
Bio: b. 10/29/51 San Diego, CA; Methodist; BA Univ. of ID, 1975; Public Affairs Manager; m. Patricia

700 W. Jefferson St., 2nd Fl., Boise, ID 83720-0034
Washington Office: 202-434-8045

State Governors

ILLINOIS
www.illinois.gov

Rod R. Blagojevich (D)   217-782-0244
Next Election: 2006   1st Term/52%   Fax: 217-524-4049
Bio: b. 12/10/56 Chicago, IL; Eastern Orthodox; JD Pepperdine Univ., 1983; Attorney; m. Patricia

207 Statehouse, Springfield, IL 62706
Washington Office: 202-624-7760

INDIANA
www.in.gov

Mitchell Daniels (R)   317-232-4567
Next Election: 2008   1st Term/53%   Fax: 317-232-3443
Bio: b. 4/7/49 Monogahela, PA; Presbyterian; JD Georgetown Univ., 1979; Government Aide, Business Executive; m. Cheri

Statehouse Rm. 206, Indianapolis, IN 46204

IOWA
www.iowa.gov

Thomas J. Vilsack (D)   515-281-5211
Next Election: 2006   2nd Term/53%   Fax: 515-281-6611
Bio: b. 12/13/50 Pittsburgh, PA; Catholic; JD Union Univ., 1975; Attorney; m. Christie

State Capitol, Des Moines, IA 50319-0001
Washington Office: 202-624-5442

KANSAS
www.accesskansas.org

Kathleen Sebelius (D)   785-296-3232
Next Election: 2006   1st Term/53%   Fax: 785-296-7973
Bio: b. 5/15/48 Cincinnati, OH; Catholic; MPA Univ. of KS, 1977; Public Official; m. Gary

Capitol, 300 SW 10th Ave., Ste. 212S,
Topeka, KS 66612-1590
Washington Office: 202-715-2923

KENTUCKY
www.kentucky.gov

Ernie Fletcher (R)   502-564-2611
Next Election: 2007   1st Term/55%   Fax: 502-564-2517
Bio: b. 11/12/52 Mount Sterling, KY; Baptist; MD Univ. of KY, 1984; USAF, 1974-79; Physician; m. Glenna

700 Capitol Ave., Ste. 100, Frankfort, KY 40601
Washington Office: 202-220-1350

LOUISIANA
www.louisiana.gov

Kathleen Babineaux Blanco (D)   225-342-0991
Next Election: 2007   1st Term/52%   Fax: 225-342-7099
Bio: b. 12/15/42 New Iberia, LA; Catholic; BS Univ. of LA, 1964; Teacher, Consultant; m. Raymond

PO Box 94004, Baton Rouge, LA 70804-9004
Washington Office: 202-434-4795

State Governors

MAINE
www.maine.gov

John Elias Baldacci (D)   **207-287-3531**
Next Election: 2006   1st Term/47%   Fax: 207-287-1034
E-mail: governor@maine.gov
Bio: b. 1/30/55 Bangor, ME; Catholic; BA Univ. of ME, 1986; Restaurateur; m. Karen

1 State House Station, Augusta, ME 04333

MARYLAND
www.maryland.gov

Robert L. Ehrlich (R)   **410-974-3901**
Next Election: 2006   1st Term/52%   Fax: 410-974-3275
E-mail: governor@gov.state.md.us
Bio: b. 11/25/57 Baltimore, MD; Methodist; JD Wake Forest Univ., 1982; Attorney; m. Kendel

State House, 100 State Circle, Annapolis, MD 21401
Washington Office: 202-624-1430

MASSACHUSETTS
www.mass.gov

Mitt Romney (R)   **617-725-4005**
Next Election: 2006   1st Term/50%   Fax: 617-727-9725
Bio: b. 3/12/47 Detroit, MI; Mormon; MBA & JD Harvard Univ., 1975; Business Executive; m. Ann

State House, Rm. 360, Boston, MA 02133
Washington Office: 202-624-7713

MICHIGAN
www.michigan.gov

Jennifer M. Granholm (D)   **517-373-3400**
Next Election: 2006   1st Term/51%   Fax: 517-335-6863
Bio: b. 2/5/59 Vancouver, Canada; Catholic; JD Harvard Univ., 1987; Attorney; m. Daniel Granholm Mulhern

PO Box 30013, Lansing, MI 48909
Washington Office: 202-624-5840

MINNESOTA
www.state.mn.us

Tim Pawlenty (R)   **651-296-3391**
Next Election: 2006   1st Term/44%   Fax: 651-296-2089
E-mail: tim.pawlenty@state.mn.us
Bio: b. 11/27/60 St. Paul, MN; Lutheran; JD Univ. of MN, 1986; Attorney; m. Mary

130 State Capitol, 75 MLK Jr. Blvd., St. Paul, MN 55155
Washington Office: 202-624-5308

MISSISSIPPI
www.mississippi.gov

Haley Barbour (R)   **601-359-3150**
Next Election: 2007   1st Term/53%   Fax: 601-359-3741
Bio: b. 10/22/47 Yazoo City, MS; Presbyterian; JD Univ. of MS, 1973; Lobbyist; m. Marsha

PO Box 139, Jackson, MS 39205

State Governors

MISSOURI   www.missouri.gov

Matt Blunt (R)   **573-751-3222**
Next Election: 2008   1st Term/51%   Fax: 573-751-4458
E-mail: mogov@mail.state.mo.us
Bio: b. 11/20/70 Strafford, MO; Baptist; BS US Naval Acad., 1993; USN, 1993-98; Public Official, Development & Research Manager; m. Melanie

Missouri Capitol Bldg., Rm. 216, Jefferson City, MO 65101

MONTANA   www.montana.gov

Brian Schweitzer (D)   **406-444-3111**
Next Election: 2008   1st Term/50%   Fax: 406-444-5529
E-mail: governor@mt.gov
Bio: b. 9/5/55 Havre, MT; Catholic; MS MT St. Univ., 1980; Farmer, Rancher; m. Nancy Hupp

State Capitol, Helena, MT 59620-0801

NEBRASKA   www.nebraska.gov

David Heineman (R)   **402-471-2244**
Next Election: 2006   1st Term   Fax: 402-471-6031
Bio: b. 5/12/48 Falls City, NE; Not Stated; US Military Acad.; USA, 1970-75; Public Official; m. Sally Ganem

PO Box 94848, Lincoln, NE 68509-4848

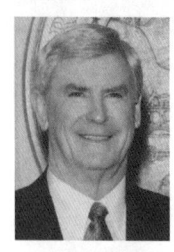

NEVADA   www.nv.gov

Kenny Guinn (R)   **775-684-5670**
Next Election: 2006   2nd Term/68%   Fax: 775-684-5683
Bio: b. 8/24/36 Exeter, CA; Non-denominational; PhD UT St. Univ., 1970; Bank Chair, College President; m. Dema

Capitol Bldg., Carson City, NV 89701
Washington Office: 202-624-5405

NEW HAMPSHIRE   www.nh.gov

John Lynch (D)   **603-271-2121**
Next Election: 2006   1st Term/51%   Fax: 603-271-8788
Bio: b. 11/25/52 Waltham, MA; Roman Catholic; JD Georgetown Univ.; Businessman; m. Susan

State House, 25 Capitol St., Concord, NH 03301

NEW JERSEY   www.newjersey.gov

Richard J. Codey (D)   **609-292-6000**
Next Election: 2005   1st Term   Fax: 609-777-2922
Bio: b. 11/27/46 Orange, NJ; Roman Catholic; BA Fairleigh Dickinson Univ.; Insurance Executive; m. Mary Jo Rolli

PO Box 001, Trenton, NJ 08625
Washington Office: 202-638-0631

State Governors

NEW MEXICO   www.state.nm.us

Bill Richardson (D)   **505-476-2200**
Next Election: 2006   1st Term/55%   Fax: 505-476-2226
Bio: b. 11/15/47 Pasadena, CA; Catholic; MA Tufts Univ., 1971; Public Official; m. Barbara Flavin

State Capitol, Rm. 400, Santa Fe, NM 87501
Washington Office: 202-220-1348

NEW YORK   www.state.ny.us

George E. Pataki (R)   **518-474-8390**
Next Election: 2006   3rd Term/49%   Fax: None
Bio: b. 6/24/45 Peekskill, NY; Catholic; JD Columbia Univ., 1970; Attorney; m. Libby

Executive Chamber, State Capitol, Albany, NY 12224
Washington Office: 202-434-7100

NORTH CAROLINA   www.ncgov.com

Michael F. Easley (D)   **919-733-4240**
Next Election: 2008   2nd Term/52%   Fax: 919-733-2120
Bio: b. 3/23/50 Nash Co., NC; Catholic; JD NC Central Univ., 1976; Public Official; m. Mary

20301 Mail Service Ctr., Raleigh, NC 27699-0301
Washington Office: 202-624-5830

NORTH DAKOTA   www.discovernd.com

John Hoeven (R)   **701-328-2200**
Next Election: 2008   2nd Term/71%   Fax: 701-328-2205
E-mail: governor@state.nd.us
Bio: b. 3/13/57 Bismarck, ND; Catholic; MBA Northwestern Univ., 1981; Bank President; m. Mical

600 E. Boulevard Ave., Dept. 101,
Bismarck, ND 58505-0001
Washington Office: 202-347-6607

OHIO   www.ohio.gov

Bob Taft (R)   **614-466-3555**
Next Election: 2006   2nd Term/58%   Fax: 614-466-9354
Bio: b. 1/8/42 Boston, MA; Methodist; JD Univ. of Cincinnati, 1976; Public Official; m. Hope

77 S. High St., 30th Fl., Columbus, OH 43215-6117
Washington Office: 202-624-5844

OKLAHOMA   www.ok.gov

Brad Henry (D)   **405-521-2342**
Next Election: 2006   1st Term/43.3%   Fax: 405-521-3353
Bio: b. 7/10/63 Shawnee, OK; Baptist; JD Univ. of OK, 1988; Attorney; m. Kimberley

2300 N. Lincoln Blvd., Rm. 212,
Oklahoma City, OK 73105

State Governors

OREGON
www.oregon.gov

Ted Kulongoski (D)   **503-378-4582**
Next Election: 2006   1st Term/49%   Fax: 503-378-6827
Bio: b. 11/5/40 Washington Co., MO; Catholic; JD Univ. of MO, 1970; USMC, 1960-63; Attorney; m. Mary Oberst

160 State Capitol, 900 Court St., Salem, OR 97301-4047

PENNSYLVANIA
www.state.pa.us

Edward G. Rendell (D)   **717-787-2500**
Next Election: 2006   1st Term/53%   Fax: 717-772-8284
Bio: b. 1/5/44 New York, NY; Jewish; JD Villanova Univ., 1968; USAR, 1968-74; Attorney, Instructor; m. Marjorie

225 Main Capitol Bldg., Harrisburg, PA 17120
Washington Office: 202-638-3730

RHODE ISLAND
www.ri.gov

Donald L. Carcieri (R)   **401-222-2080**
Next Election: 2006   1st Term/55%   Fax: 401-222-8096
Bio: b. 12/16/42 East Greenwich, RI; Roman Catholic; BA Brown Univ., 1965; Businessman; m. Suzanne Owren

State House, Rm. 115, Providence, RI 02903
Washington Office: 202-624-3605

SOUTH CAROLINA
www.myscgov.com

Mark C. Sanford (R)   **803-734-2100**
Next Election: 2006   1st Term/53%   Fax: 803-734-5167
Bio: b. 5/28/60 Fort Lauderdale, FL; Episcopal; MBA Univ. of VA, 1988; USAR, 2002-present; Businessman; m. Jenny

PO Box 12267, Columbia, SC 29211
Washington Office: 202-624-7784

SOUTH DAKOTA
www.state.sd.us

M. Michael Rounds (R)   **605-773-3212**
Next Election: 2006   1st Term/57%   Fax: 605-773-5844
Bio: b. 10/24/54 Huron, SD; Catholic; BS SD St. Univ., 1977; Insurance Executive; m. Jean Vedvei

500 E. Capitol Ave., Pierre, SD 57501

TENNESSEE
www.tennessee.gov

Phil Bredesen (D)   **615-741-2001**
Next Election: 2006   1st Term/51%   Fax: 615-532-9711
E-mail: phil.bredesen@state.tn.us
Bio: b. 11/21/43 Shortsville, NY; Presbyterian; BS Harvard Univ., 1967; Businessman; m. Andrea

State Capitol, Nashville, TN 37243-0001

State Governors

TEXAS   www.texas.gov

Rick Perry (R)   **512-463-2000**
Next Election: 2006   2nd Term/58%   Fax: 512-463-1849
Bio: b. 3/4/50 Paint Creek, TX; United Methodist; BS TX A&M Univ., 1972; USAF, 1972-77; Rancher; m. Anita

PO Box 12428, Austin, TX 78711-2428
Washington Office: 202-638-3927

UTAH   www.utah.gov

Jon Huntsman, Jr. (R)   **801-538-1000**
Next Election: 2008   1st Term/57%   Fax: 801-538-1528
Bio: b. 3/26/60 Palo Alto, CA; Mormon; BA Univ. of PA; Business Executive, Public Official; m. Mary Kaye

East Office Bldg., Ste. E220, Salt Lake City, UT 84114

VERMONT   www.vermont.gov

James H. Douglas (R)   **802-828-3333**
Next Election: 2006   2nd Term/45%   Fax: 802-828-3339
Bio: b. 6/21/51 Springfield, MA; United Church of Christ; AB Middlebury Col., 1972; Public Official; m. Dorothy

109 State St., Pavilion, Montpelier, VT 05609-0101

VIRGINIA   www.virginia.gov

Mark R. Warner (D)   **804-786-2211**
Next Election: 2005   1st Term/52%   Fax: 804-371-6351
Bio: b. 12/15/54 Indianapolis, IN; Presbyterian; JD Harvard Univ., 1980; Businessman; m. Lisa

State Capitol, 3rd Fl., Richmond, VA 23219
Washington Office: 202-783-1769

WASHINGTON   www.access.wa.gov

Christine O. Gregoire (D)   **360-902-4111**
Next Election: 2008   1st Term/49%   Fax: 360-753-4110
Bio: b. 3/24/47 Auburn, WA; Catholic; JD Gonzaga Univ., 1977; Public Official; m. Mike

PO Box 40002, Olympia, WA 98504-0002

WEST VIRGINIA   www.wv.gov

Joe Manchin III (D)   **304-558-2000**
Next Election: 2008   1st Term/63%   Fax: 304-342-7025
E-mail: governor@wvgov.org
Bio: b. 8/24/47 Farmington, WV; Catholic; BS WV Univ., 1970; Business Owner; m. Gayle

1900 Kanawha Blvd., East, Charleston, WV 25305

State Governors

WISCONSIN   www.wisconsin.gov

Jim Doyle (D)   **608-266-1212**
Next Election: 2006   1st Term/45%   Fax: 608-267-8983
Bio: b. 11/23/45 Washington, DC; Catholic; JD Harvard Univ., 1972; Attorney; m. Jessica

115 E. State Capitol, Madison, WI 53702
Washington Office: 202-624-5870

WYOMING   www.wyoming.gov

Dave Freudenthal (D)   **307-777-7434**
Next Election: 2006   1st Term/50%   Fax: 307-632-3909
E-mail: governor@state.wy.us
Bio: b. 10/12/1950 Thermopolis, WY; Episcopal; JD Univ. of WY, 1980; Attorney; m. Nancy

State Capitol, Rm. 124, Cheyenne, WY 82002

State Governors Re-election Schedule

2005 Gubernatorial Races

Richard J. Codey (D-NJ)*   Mark R. Warner (D-VA)*

2006 Gubernatorial Races

John Elias Baldacci (D-ME)
Rod R. Blagojevich (D-IL)
Phil Bredesen (D-TN)
Jeb Bush (R-FL)*
Felix Perez Camacho (R-GU)
Donald L. Carcieri (R-RI)
James H. Douglas (R-VT)#
Jim Doyle (D-WI)
Robert L. Ehrlich (R-MD)
Dave Freudenthal (D-WY)
Jennifer M. Granholm (D-MI)
Kenny Guinn (R-NV)*
David Heineman (R-NE)
Brad Henry (D-OK)
Mike Huckabee (R-AR)*
Dirk Kempthorne (R-ID)*
Ted Kulongoski (D-OR)
Linda Lingle (R-HI)
John Lynch (D-NH)#

Frank H. Murkowski (R-AK)
Janet Napolitano (D-AZ)
Bill Owens (R-CO)*
George E. Pataki (R-NY)
Tim Pawlenty (R-MN)
Sonny Perdue (R-GA)
Rick Perry (R-TX)
M. Jodi Rell (R-CT)
Edward G. Rendell (D-PA)
Bill Richardson (D-NM)
Bob Riley (R-AL)
Mitt Romney (R-MA)
M. Michael Rounds (R-SD)
Mark C. Sanford (R-SC)
Arnold Schwarzenegger (R-CA)
Kathleen Sebelius (D-KS)
Bob Taft (R-OH)*
Charles Turnbull (D-VI)
Thomas J. Vilsack (D-IA)

2007 Gubernatorial Races

Haley Barbour (R-MS)   Ernie Fletcher (R-KY)
Kathleen Babineaux Blanco (D-LA)

2008 Gubernatorial Races

Anibal Acevedo-Vila (PDP-PR)
Matt Blunt (R-MO)
Mitchell Daniels (R-IN)
Michael F. Easley (D-NC)*
Christine O. Gregoire (D-WA)
John Hoeven (R-ND)*

Jon Huntsman (R-UT)
Joe Manchin (D-WV)
Ruth Ann Minner (D-DE)*
Brian Schweitzer (D-MT)
Togiola T.A. Tulafono (D-AS)

* = Open seat. Incumbent term limited/not seeking re-election.
 # = Two-year term.

Senate Leadership and Officers

Area code for all numbers is 202

President .... Richard B. Cheney, Vice President

Assistant to the Vice President
for Legislative Affairs
Office: S-212

Brenda Becker
Phone: 224-2424

President Pro Tempore .... Ted Stevens (R-AK)
Office: S-237
Phone: 224-1034

Majority Leader .... Bill Frist (R-TN)
Chief of Staff
Office: S-230

Eric Ueland
Phone: 224-3135

Majority Whip .... Mitch McConnell (R-KY)
Chief of Staff
Office: S-208

Kyle Simmons
Phone: 224-2708

**Republican Policy Committee
Chair** .... Jon Kyl (R-AZ)
Staff Director
Office: SR-347

Lawrence Willcox
Phone: 224-2946

Republican Conference Chair .... Rick Santorum (R-PA)
Staff Director
Office: SH-405

Mark Rodgers
Phone: 224-2764

Minority Leader .... Harry Reid (D-NV)
Chief of Staff
Office: S-221

Susan McCue
Phone: 224-5556

Minority Whip .... Richard J. Durbin (D-IL)
Chief of Staff
Office: SD-332

Ed Greelegs
Phone: 224-2152

**Democratic Policy Committee
Chair** .... Byron Dorgan (D-ND)
Staff Director
Office: SH-419

Chuck Cooper
Phone: 224-3232

Democratic Conference Chair ...... Harry Reid (D-NV)
Chief of Staff
Office: S-221

Susan McCue
Phone: 224-5556

Secretary of the Senate .... Emily J. Reynolds
Office: S-312
Phone: 224-3622

Sergeant at Arms .... Bill Pickle
Office: S-151
Phone: 224-2341

Majority Secretary .... David J. Schiappa
Office: S-337
Phone: 224-3835

Minority Secretary .... Martin P. Paone
Office: S-309
Phone: 224-3735

Parliamentarian .... Alan Frumin
Office: S-133
Phone: 224-6128

Assistant Secretary .... Mary Suit Jones
Office: S-312
Phone: 224-2114

Chaplain .... Dr. Barry C. Black
Office: S-332
Phone: 224-2510

Senate Re-election Schedule

Up for Re-election in 2006

Daniel K. Akaka (D-HI)
George Allen (R-VA)
Jeff Bingaman (D-NM)
Conrad Burns (R-MT)
Robert C. Byrd (D-WV)
Maria Cantwell (D-WA)
Thomas R. Carper (D-DE)
Lincoln D. Chafee (R-RI)
Hillary Rodham Clinton (D-NY)
Kent Conrad (D-ND)
Jon S. Corzine (D-NJ)
Mark Dayton (D-MN)
Mike DeWine (R-OH)
John Ensign (R-NV)
Dianne Feinstein (D-CA)
Bill Frist (R-TN)
Orrin G. Hatch (R-UT)
Kay Bailey Hutchison (R-TX)
James M. Jeffords (I-VT)
Edward M. Kennedy (D-MA)
Herbert H. Kohl (D-WI)
Jon L. Kyl (R-AZ)
Joseph I. Lieberman (D-CT)
Trent Lott (R-MS)
Richard G. Lugar (R-IN)
Ben Nelson (D-NE)
Bill Nelson (D-FL)
Rick Santorum (R-PA)
Paul S. Sarbanes (D-MD)
Olympia J. Snowe (R-ME)
Debbie A. Stabenow (D-MI)
Jim Talent (R-MO)
Craig Thomas (R-WY)

Up for Re-election in 2008

Lamar Alexander (R-TN)
Wayne Allard (R-CO)
Max Baucus (D-MT)
Joseph R. Biden, Jr. (D-DE)
Saxby Chambliss (R-GA)
Thad Cochran (R-MS)
Norm Coleman (R-MN)
Susan M. Collins (R-ME)
John Cornyn (R-TX)
Larry E. Craig (R-ID)
Elizabeth Dole (R-NC)
Pete V. Domenici (R-NM)
Richard J. Durbin (D-IL)
Michael B. Enzi (R-WY)
Lindsey O. Graham (R-SC)
Chuck Hagel (R-NE)
Tom Harkin (D-IA)
James M. Inhofe (R-OK)
Tim Johnson (D-SD)
John F. Kerry (D-MA)
Mary Landrieu (D-LA)
Frank R. Lautenberg (D-NJ)
Carl Levin (D-MI)
Mitch McConnell (R-KY)
Mark Pryor (D-AR)
Jack Reed (D-RI)
Pat Roberts (R-KS)
John D. Rockefeller IV (D-WV)
Jeff Sessions (R-AL)
Gordon Smith (R-OR)
Ted Stevens (R-AK)
John E. Sununu (R-NH)
John W. Warner (R-VA)

Up for Re-election in 2010

Evan Bayh (D-IN)
Robert Bennett (R-UT)
Christopher S. Bond (R-MO)
Barbara Boxer (D-CA)
Sam Brownback (R-KS)
Jim Bunning (R-KY)
Richard Burr (R-NC)
Tom Coburn (R-OK)
Mike Crapo (R-ID)
Jim DeMint (R-SC)
Christopher J. Dodd (D-CT)
Byron L. Dorgan (D-ND)
Russ Feingold (D-WI)
Charles E. Grassley (R-IA)
Judd Gregg (R-NH)
Daniel K. Inouye (D-HI)
Johnny Isakson (R-GA)
Patrick J. Leahy (D-VT)
Blanche L. Lincoln (D-AR)
Mel Martinez (R-FL)
John McCain (R-AZ)
Barbara A. Mikulski (D-MD)
Lisa Murkowski (R-AK)
Patty Murray (D-WA)
Barack Obama (D-IL)
Harry Reid (D-NV)
Ken Salazar (D-CO)
Charles E. Schumer (D-NY)
Richard C. Shelby (R-AL)
Arlen Specter (R-PA)
John R. Thune (R-SD)
David Vitter (R-LA)
George V. Voinovich (R-OH)
Ron Wyden (D-OR)

SENATORS

Daniel K. Akaka (D-HI)   202-224-6361
SH-141   3rd Term/73%   Fax: 202-224-2126
E-mail: senator@akaka.senate.gov
Website: akaka.senate.gov
AA .... *James Sakai* **LD** .... *Melissa Hampe*
Appt .... *Pat Hill* **Press** ..... *Donalyn Dela Cruz*
Bio: b. 9/11/24 Honolulu, HI; Congregationalist; MEd Univ. of HI, 1966; USA, 1945-47; School Principal; m. Millie
Comm.: Armed Services; Energy & Natural Resources; Homeland Security & Governmental Affairs; Veterans' Affairs (Rnk. Mem.); Indian Affairs; Select Ethics
Dist. Offices: Honolulu, 808-522-8970; Hilo, 808-935-1114

Lamar Alexander (R-TN)   202-224-4944
SH-302   1st Term/54%   Fax: 202-228-3398
Website: alexander.senate.gov
CoS .... *Tom Ingram* **LD** .... *Vacant*
Appt ...... *Bonnie Sansonetti* **Press** .... *Alexia Poe*
Bio: b. 7/3/40 Maryville, TN; Presbyterian; JD NYU Law School, 1965; Public Official; m. Honey
Comm.: Budget; Energy & Natural Resources; Foreign Relations; Health, Education, Labor & Pensions; Special Aging
Dist. Offices: Nashville, 615-736-5129; Knoxville, 865-545-4253; Memphis, 901-544-4224; Chattanooga, 423-752-5337; Jackson, 731-423-9344; Blountville, 423-325-6240

Wayne Allard (R-CO)   202-224-5941
SD-521   2nd Term/51%   Fax: 202-224-6471
Website: allard.senate.gov
CoS .... *Sean Conway* **LD** .... *Cory Gardner*
Sch .... *Alison Monroe* **Press** ...... *Angela de Rocha*
Bio: b. 12/2/43 Ft. Collins, CO; Protestant; DVM CO St. Univ., 1968; Veterinarian; m. Joan
Comm.: Appropriations; Banking, Housing & Urban Affairs; Budget
Dist. Offices: Englewood, 303-220-7414; Loveland, 970-461-3530; Colorado Springs, 719-634-6071; Pueblo, 719-545-9751; Grand Junction, 970-245-9553; Durango, 970-375-6311

George Allen (R-VA)   202-224-4024
SR-204   1st Term/52%   Fax: 202-224-5432
Website: allen.senate.gov
CoS .... *Dick Wadhams* **LD** .... *Paul Unger*
Sch .... *Carlos Munoz* **CD** .... *John Reid*
Bio: b. 3/8/52 Whittier, CA; Presbyterian; JD Univ. of VA, 1977; Attorney; m. Susan
Comm.: Commerce, Science & Transportation; Energy & Natural Resources; Foreign Relations; Small Business & Entrepreneurship
Dist. Offices: Richmond, 804-771-2221; Roanoke, 540-772-4236; Abingdon, 276-676-2646; Virginia Beach, 757-518-1674; Herndon, 703-435-0039; Southside, 804-347-2587

Max Baucus (D-MT)   202-224-2651
SH-511   5th Term/63%   Fax: 202-224-4700
Website: baucus.senate.gov
CoS .... *Jim Messina* **LD** .... *Sara Roberts*
Appt .... *Farrar Johnston* **Press** .... *Sara Kuban*
Bio: b. 12/11/41 Helena, MT; United Church of Christ; LLB Stanford Univ., 1967; Attorney; m. Wanda
Comm.: Agriculture, Nutrition & Forestry; Environment & Public Works; Finance (Rnk. Mem.); Joint Taxation
Dist. Offices: Billings, 406-657-6790; Helena, 406-449-5480; Missoula, 406-329-3123; Kalispell, 406-756-1150; Bozeman, 406-586-6104; Butte, 406-782-8700; Great Falls, 406-761-1574

SENATORS

Evan Bayh (D-IN)   202-224-5623
SR-463   2nd Term/62%   Fax: 202-228-1377
Website: bayh.senate.gov
CoS .... *Tom Sugar* **LD** .... *Charlie Salem*
Sch .... *Sarah Rozensky* **CD** .... *Dan Pfeiffer*
Bio: b. 12/26/55 Shirkieville, IN; Episcopal; JD Univ. of VA, 1982; Attorney; m. Susan
Comm.: Armed Services; Banking, Housing & Urban Affairs; Small Business & Entrepreneurship; Select Intelligence; Special Aging
Dist. Offices: Indianapolis, 317-554-0750; Evansville, 812-465-6500; Ft. Wayne, 260-426-3151; Jeffersonville, 812-218-2317; Hammond, 219-852-2763; South Bend, 574-236-8302

Robert Bennett (R-UT)   202-224-5444
SD-431   3rd Term/68%   Fax: 202-228-1168
Website: bennett.senate.gov
CoS .... *Chip Yost* **LD** .... *Mark Morrison*
Sch .... *Roxane Taylor* **CD** ...... *Mary Jane Collipriest*
Bio: b. 9/18/33 Salt Lake City, UT; Mormon; BS Univ. of UT, 1957; USANG, 1957-60; Management Consultant; m. Joyce
Comm.: Appropriations; Banking, Housing & Urban Affairs; Homeland Security & Governmental Affairs; Rules & Administration; Joint Economic (Vice Chair)
Dist. Offices: Salt Lake City, 801-524-5933; St. George, 435-628-5514; Ogden, 801-625-5676; Provo, 801-379-2525; Cedar City, 435-865-1335

Joseph R. Biden, Jr. (D-DE)   202-224-5042
SR-201   6th Term/58%   Fax: 202-224-0139
Website: biden.senate.gov
CoS .... *Danny O'Brien* **LD** .... *Jane Woodfin*
Sch .... *Michelle Smith* **CD** .... *Norm Kurz*
Bio: b. 11/20/42 Scranton, PA; Catholic; JD Syracuse Univ., 1968; Attorney; m. Jill
Comm.: Foreign Relations (Rnk. Mem.); Judiciary
Dist. Offices: Wilmington, 302-573-6345; Milford, 302-424-8090

Jeff Bingaman (D-NM)   202-224-5521
SH-703   4th Term/62%   Fax: 202-224-2852
E-mail: senator_bingaman@bingaman.senate.gov
Website: bingaman.senate.gov
CoS .... *Stephen Ward* **LD** .... *Trudy Vincent*
EA .... *Virginia White* **Press** .... *Jude McCartin*
Bio: b. 10/3/43 El Paso, TX; Methodist; JD Stanford Univ., 1968; USAR, 1968-74; Attorney; m. Anne
Comm.: Energy & Natural Resources (Rnk. Mem.); Finance; Health, Education, Labor & Pensions; Joint Economic
Dist. Offices: Santa Fe, 505-988-6647; Roswell, 505-622-7113; Las Cruces, 505-523-6561; Albuquerque, 505-346-6601; Las Vegas, 505-454-8824

Christopher S. "Kit" Bond (R-MO)   202-224-5721
SR-274   4th Term/56%   Fax: 202-224-8149
Website: bond.senate.gov
CoS .... *Julie Dammann* **LD** .... *Brian Klippenstein*
Sch .. *Kathleen Youngblood* **CD** .... *Rob Ostrander*
Bio: b. 3/6/39 St. Louis, MO; Presbyterian; LLB Univ. of VA, 1963; Attorney; m. Linda
Comm.: Appropriations; Environment & Public Works; Small Business & Entrepreneurship; Select Intelligence
Dist. Offices: Jefferson City, 573-634-2488; Springfield, 417-864-8258; Cape Girardeau, 573-334-7044; St. Louis, 314-725-4484; Kansas City, 816-471-7141

SENATORS

Barbara Boxer (D-CA)   202-224-3553
SH-112   3rd Term/58%   Fax: 415-956-6701
Website: boxer.senate.gov
CoS .... *Karen Olick* **LD** .... *Matthew Baumgart*
Sch .... *Michael Weiss* **CD** .... *David Sandretti*
Bio: b. 11/11/40 Brooklyn, NY; Jewish; BA Brooklyn Col., 1962; Journalist; m. Stewart
Comm.: Commerce, Science & Transportation; Environment & Public Works; Foreign Relations
Dist. Offices: San Francisco, 415-403-0100; Los Angeles, 213-894-5000; San Diego, 619-239-3884; Fresno, 559-497-5109; San Bernardino, 909-888-8525; Sacramento, 916-448-2787

Sam Brownback (R-KS)   202-224-6521
SH-303   3rd Term/69%   Fax: 202-228-1265
Website: brownback.senate.gov
CoS .... *Rob Wasinger* **LD** .... *Glen Chambers*
Sch .... *Sally Berwick* **CD** .... *Brian Hart*
Bio: b. 9/12/56 Garnett, KS; Catholic; JD Univ. of KS, 1982; Attorney; m. Mary
Comm.: Appropriations; Judiciary; Joint Economic
Dist. Offices: Topeka, 785-233-2503; Pittsburg, 620-231-6040; Overland Park, 913-492-6378; Wichita, 316-264-8066; Garden City, 620-275-1124

Jim Bunning (R-KY)   202-224-4343
SH-316   2nd Term/51%   Fax: 202-228-1373
Website: bunning.senate.gov
CoS .... *Jon Deuser* **LD** .... *Kim Taylor*
Sch .... *Amy Davis* **Press** .... *Mike Reynard*
Bio: b. 10/23/31 Southgate, KY; Catholic; BS Xavier Univ., 1953; Pro Baseball Player, Investment Broker; m. Mary
Comm.: Banking, Housing & Urban Affairs; Budget; Energy & Natural Resources; Finance
Dist. Offices: Ft. Wright, 859-341-2602; Hazard, 606-435-2390; Hopkinsville, 270-885-1212; Lexington, 859-219-2239; Louisville, 502-582-5341; Owensboro, 270-689-9085

Conrad Burns (R-MT)   202-224-2644
SD-187   3rd Term/51%   Fax: 202-224-8594
Website: burns.senate.gov
CoS .... *Clark Johnson* **LD** .... *Ric Molen*
Sch .... *Angela Schulze* **Press** .... *Jennifer O'Shea*
Bio: b. 1/25/35 Gallatin, MO; Lutheran; Attended Univ. of MO; USMC, 1955-57; Broadcaster; m. Phyllis
Comm.: Appropriations; Commerce, Science & Transportation; Energy & Natural Resources; Small Business & Entrepreneurship; Special Aging
Dist. Offices: Billings, 406-252-0550; Butte, 406-723-3277; Bozeman, 406-586-4450; Helena, 406-449-5401; Great Falls, 406-452-9585; Glendive, 406-365-2391; Missoula, 406-728-3003; Kalispell, 406-257-3360

Richard Burr (R-NC)   202-224-3154
SR-217   1st Term/52%   Fax: 202-228-2981
Website: burr.senate.gov
CoS ... *Alicia Peterson-Clark* **LD** .... *Chris Joyner*
Sch .... *Parker White* **CD** .... *Doug Heye*
Bio: b. 11/30/55 Charlottesville, VA; Methodist; BA Wake Forest Univ., 1978; Businessman; m. Brooke
Comm.: Energy & Natural Resources; Health, Education, Labor & Pensions; Veterans' Affairs; Indian Affairs
Dist. Office: Winston-Salem, 800-685-8916

SENATORS

Robert C. Byrd (D-WV)   202-224-3954
SH-311   8th Term/78%   Fax: 202-228-0002
Website: byrd.senate.gov
CoS .... *Barbara Videnieks* **LD** .... *Jane Mellow*
Sch .... *Martha Anne McIntosh* **Press** .... *Tom Gavin*
Bio: b. 11/20/17 North Wilkesboro, NC; Baptist; JD American Univ., 1963; Attorney; m. Erma
Comm.: Appropriations (Rnk. Mem.); Armed Services; Budget; Rules & Administration
Dist. Office: Charleston, 304-342-5855

Maria Cantwell (D-WA)   202-224-3441
SH-717   1st Term/49%   Fax: 202-228-0514
Website: cantwell.senate.gov
CoS .... *Kurt Beckett* **LD** .... *Mary Frances Repko*
Sch .... *Denielle Crutchfield* **CD** .... *Angela Becker-Dippmann*
Bio: b. 10/13/58 Indianapolis, IN; Catholic; BA Miami Univ. of OH, 1981; Businesswoman; single
Comm.: Commerce, Science & Transportation; Energy & Natural Resources; Small Business & Entrepreneurship; Indian Affairs
Dist. Offices: Seattle, 206-220-6400; Spokane, 509-353-2507; Vancouver, 360-696-7838; Richland, 509-946-8106; Everett, 425-303-0114; Tacoma, 253-572-2281

Thomas R. Carper (D-DE)   202-224-2441
SH-513   1st Term/56%   Fax: 202-228-2190
Website: carper.senate.gov
CoS .... *Jonathon Jones* **LD** .... *Sheila Murphy*
Appt .... *Patricia Guarnieri* **CD** .... *Bill Ghent*
Bio: b. 1/23/47 Beckley, WV; Presbyterian; MBA Univ. of DE, 1975; USN, 1968-73; USNR, 1973-92; Public Official; m. Martha Stacy
Comm.: Banking, Housing & Urban Affairs; Environment & Public Works; Homeland Security & Governmental Affairs; Special Aging
Dist. Offices: Dover, 302-674-3308; Georgetown, 302-856-7690; Wilmington, 302-573-6291

Lincoln D. Chafee (R-RI)   202-224-2921
SR-141A   1st Term/57%   Fax: 202-228-2853
Website: chafee.senate.gov
CoS .... *David Griswold* **LD** .... *Deb Brayton*
Sch .... *Betty Dudik* **Press** ...... *Stephen Hourahan*
Bio: b. 3/26/53 Warwick, RI; Episcopal; BA Brown Univ., 1975; Blacksmith, Businessman; m. Stephanie
Comm.: Environment & Public Works; Foreign Relations; Homeland Security & Governmental Affairs
Dist. Offices: Providence, 401-453-5294; Newport, 401-845-0700

Saxby Chambliss (R-GA)   202-224-3521
SR-416   1st Term/53%   Fax: 202-224-0103
Website: chambliss.senate.gov
CoS .... *Krister Holladay* **LD** .... *Alex Shively*
Appt .... *Mary Beth Farr* **CD** .... *Angie Lundberg*
Bio: b. 11/10/43 Warrenton, NC; Episcopal; JD Univ. of TN, 1968; Attorney; m. Julianne
Comm.: Agriculture, Nutrition & Forestry (Chair); Armed Services; Rules & Administration; Select Intelligence; Joint Printing
Dist. Offices: Atlanta, 770-763-9090; Macon, 478-476-0788; Moultrie, 229-985-2112; Savannah, 912-232-3657; Augusta, 706-738-0302

SENATORS

Hillary Rodham Clinton (D-NY)   202-224-4451
SR-476   1st Term/55%   Fax: 202-228-0282
Website: clinton.senate.gov
CoS ...... *Tamera S. Luzzatto* **LD** .... *Laurie Rubiner*
Sch .... *Eric Woodard* **CD** .... *Lorrie McHugh*
Bio: b. 10/26/47 Chicago, IL; Methodist; JD Yale Univ., 1973; Public Official; m. Bill
Comm.: Armed Services; Environment & Public Works; Health, Education, Labor & Pensions; Special Aging
Dist. Offices: New York, 212-688-6262; Albany, 518-431-0120; Syracuse, 315-448-0470; Buffalo, 716-854-9725; Hartsdale, 914-725-9294; Lowville, 315-376-6118; Rochester, 585-263-6250; Melville, 631-249-2825

Tom Coburn (R-OK)   202-224-5754
SR-172   1st Term/53%   Fax: 202-224-6008
Website: coburn.senate.gov
AD .... *John Denning* **LD** .... *Roland Foster*
Sch .... *Courtney Cox* **CD** .... *John Hart*
Bio: b. 3/14/48 Casper, WY; Baptist; MD Univ. of OK, 1983; Physician; m. Carolyn
Comm.: Homeland Security & Governmental Affairs; Judiciary; Indian Affairs
Dist. Offices: Tulsa, 918-581-7651; Oklahoma City, 405-231-4941; Lawton, 580-357-9878

Thad Cochran (R-MS)   202-224-5054
SD-113   5th Term/85%   Fax: 202-224-9450
Website: cochran.senate.gov
CoS .... *Mark Keenum* **LD** .... *Blake Thompson*
Appt .... *Doris Wagley* **Press** .... *Jenny Manley*
Bio: b. 12/7/37 Pontotoc, MS; Baptist; JD Univ. of MS, 1965; USN, 1959-61; Attorney; m. Rose
Comm.: Agriculture, Nutrition & Forestry; Appropriations (Chair); Rules & Administration; Joint Library; Joint Printing
Dist. Offices: Jackson, 601-965-4459; Oxford, 662-236-1018; Gulfport, 228-867-9710

Norm Coleman (R-MN)   202-224-5641
SH-320   1st Term/50%   Fax: 202-224-1152
Website: coleman.senate.gov
CoS .... *Erich Mische* **LD** .... *Jeff Harrison*
Sch ...... *Danielle Chauncey* **CD** .... *Tom Steward*
Bio: b. 8/17/49 Brooklyn, NY; Jewish; JD Univ. of IA, 1976; Attorney; m. Laurie
Comm.: Agriculture, Nutrition & Forestry; Foreign Relations; Homeland Security & Governmental Affairs; Small Business & Entrepreneurship
Dist. Offices: St. Paul, 651-645-0323; Mankato, 507-625-6800

Susan M. Collins (R-ME)   202-224-2523
SD-461   2nd Term/59%   Fax: 202-224-2693
Website: collins.senate.gov
CoS .... *Steve Abbott* **LD** .... *Jim Dohoney*
EA .... *Alana Weinstein* **CD** .... *Jen Burita*
Bio: b. 12/7/52 Caribou, ME; Catholic; BA St. Lawrence Univ., 1975; Businesswoman; single
Comm.: Armed Services; Homeland Security & Governmental Affairs (Chair); Special Aging
Dist. Offices: Bangor, 207-945-0417; Augusta, 207-622-8414; Biddeford, 207-283-1101; Lewiston, 207-784-6969; Caribou, 207-493-7873; Portland, 207-780-3575

SENATORS

Kent Conrad (D-ND)   202-224-2043
SH-530   4th Term/61%   Fax: 202-224-7776
Website: conrad.senate.gov
CoS .... *Bob Van Heuvelen* **LD** .... *Tom Mahr*
Appt .... *Geri Gaginis* **CD** .... *Chris Thorne*
Bio: b. 3/12/48 Bismarck, ND; Unitarian; MBA George Washington Univ., 1975; Personnel Director; m. Lucy
Comm.: Agriculture, Nutrition & Forestry; Budget (Rnk. Mem.); Finance; Indian Affairs
Dist. Offices: Bismarck, 701-258-4648; Fargo, 701-232-8030; Grand Forks, 701-775-9601; Minot, 701-852-0703

John Cornyn (R-TX)   202-224-2934
SH-517   1st Term/55%   Fax: 202-228-2856
Website: cornyn.senate.gov
CoS .... *Pete Olson* **LD** .... *Beth Jafari*
Sch .... *Molly Simpson* **CD** .... *Don Stewart*
Bio: b. 2/2/52 Houston, TX; Church of Christ; LLM Univ. of VA, 1995; Attorney; m. Sandy
Comm.: Armed Services; Budget; Judiciary; Small Business & Entrepreneurship; Joint Economic
Dist. Offices: Austin, 512-469-6034; Dallas, 972-239-1310; Houston, 713-572-3337; San Antonio, 210-224-7485; Harlingen, 956-423-0162; Lubbock, 806-472-7533; Tyler, 903-593-0902

Jon S. Corzine (D-NJ)   202-224-4744
SH-502   1st Term/50%   Fax: 202-228-2197
Website: corzine.senate.gov
CoS .... *Heather Howard* **LD** ...... *Roger Hollingsworth*
Sch .... *Alison Brosnan* **Press** .... *Allyn Brooks-Lasure*
Bio: b. 1/1/47 Willey's Station, IL; Church of Christ; MBA Univ. of Chicago, 1973; USMCR, 1969-75; Businessman; div.
Comm.: Banking, Housing & Urban Affairs; Budget; Energy & Natural Resources; Select Intelligence
Dist. Offices: Newark, 973-645-3030; Barrington, 856-757-5353

Larry E. Craig (R-ID)   202-224-2752
SH-520   3rd Term/65%   Fax: 202-228-1067
Website: craig.senate.gov
CoS .... *Mike Ware* **LD** .... *Brooke Roberts*
Sch .... *Katie Palmer* **Press** .... *Dan Whiting*
Bio: b. 7/20/45 Council, ID; Methodist; BA Univ. of ID, 1969; USARNG, 1970-72; Rancher; m. Suzanne
Comm.: Appropriations; Energy & Natural Resources; Veterans' Affairs (Chair); Special Aging
Dist. Offices: Boise, 208-342-7985; Coeur d'Alene, 208-667-6130; Lewiston, 208-743-0792; Pocatello, 208-236-6817; Twin Falls, 208-734-6780; Idaho Falls, 208-523-5541

Mike Crapo (R-ID)   202-224-6142
SD-239   2nd Term/Unc.   Fax: 202-228-1375
Website: crapo.senate.gov
CoS .... *John Hoehne* **LD** .... *Ken Flanz*
Sch .... *Mary Klappa* **CD** .... *Susan Wheeler*
Bio: b. 5/20/51 Idaho Falls, ID; Mormon; JD Harvard Univ., 1977; Attorney; m. Susan
Comm.: Agriculture, Nutrition & Forestry; Banking, Housing & Urban Affairs; Budget; Finance; Indian Affairs
Dist. Offices: Boise, 208-334-1776; Pocatello, 208-236-6775; Idaho Falls, 208-522-9779; Coeur d'Alene, 208-664-5490; Lewiston, 208-743-1492; Caldwell, 208-455-0360; Twin Falls, 208-734-2515

SENATORS

Mark Dayton (D-MN)   202-224-3244
SR-123   1st Term/49%   Fax: 202-228-2186
Website: dayton.senate.gov
CoS .... *Jack Danielson* **LD** .... *Chani Wiggins*
Sch .... *Britta Gustafson* **CD** .... *Chris Lisi*
Bio: b. 1/26/47 Minneapolis, MN; Presbyterian; BA Yale Univ., 1969; Private Investor, Public Official; single
Comm.: Agriculture, Nutrition & Forestry; Armed Services; Homeland Security & Governmental Affairs; Rules & Administration; Joint Printing
Dist. Offices: Ft. Snelling, 612-727-5220; Biwabik, 218-865-4480; East Grand Forks, 218-773-1110

Jim DeMint (R-SC)   202-224-6121
SR-340   1st Term/54%   Fax: 202-228-5143
Website: demint.senate.gov
CoS .... *Bret Bernhardt* **LD** .... *Matt Hoskins*
Sch .... *Katy Taylor* **CD** .... *Wesley Denton*
Bio: b. 9/2/51 Greenville, SC; Presbyterian; MBA Clemson Univ., 1981; Business Owner; m. Debbie
Comm.: Commerce, Science & Transportation; Environment & Public Works; Special Aging; Joint Economic
Dist. Offices: Greenville, 864-233-5366; Charleston, 843-727-4525

Mike DeWine (R-OH)   202-224-2315
SR-140   2nd Term/60%   Fax: 202-224-6519
Website: dewine.senate.gov
CoS .... *Laurel Pressler* **LD** .... *Paul Palagyi*
Sch .... *Lindsey Schauer* **CD** .... *Mike Dawson*
Bio: b. 1/5/47 Springfield, OH; Catholic; JD OH Northern Univ., 1972; Attorney; m. Fran
Comm.: Appropriations; Health, Education, Labor & Pensions; Judiciary; Select Intelligence
Dist. Offices: Columbus, 614-469-5186; Cincinnati, 513-763-8260; Cleveland, 216-522-7272; Toledo, 419-259-7536; Marietta, 740-373-2317; Xenia, 937-376-3080

Christopher J. Dodd (D-CT)   202-224-2823
SR-448   5th Term/66%   Fax: 202-224-1083
Website: dodd.senate.gov
CoS .... *Sheryl Cohen* **LD** .... *Shawn Maher*
Appt .... *Cape Boyd* **CD** .... *Marvin Fast*
Bio: b. 5/27/44 Willimantic, CT; Catholic; JD Univ. of Louisville, 1972; USA, 1969-75; Attorney; m. Jackie Clegg
Comm.: Banking, Housing & Urban Affairs; Foreign Relations; Health, Education, Labor & Pensions; Rules & Administration (Rnk. Mem.); Joint Library
Dist. Office: Wethersfield, 860-258-6940

Elizabeth Dole (R-NC)   202-224-6342
SD-555   1st Term/54%   Fax: 202-224-1100
Website: dole.senate.gov
CoS .... *Greg Gross* **LD** .... *Scott Quesenberry*
Sch .... *Amanda Dawson* **CD** .... *Lindsay Taylor*
Bio: b. 7/29/36 Salisbury, NC; Methodist; JD Harvard Univ., 1965; Public Official; m. Robert
Comm.: Armed Services; Banking, Housing & Urban Affairs; Special Aging
Dist. Offices: Raleigh, 919-856-4630; Salisbury, 704-633-5011; Hendersonville, 828-698-3747; Greenville, 252-329-1093

SENATORS

Pete V. Domenici (R-NM)   **202-224-6621**
SH-328   6th Term/65%   Fax: 202-228-3261
Website: domenici.senate.gov
CoS .... *Steve Bell* **LD** .... *Edward G. Hild*
Sch .... *Elizabeth Harvey* **Press** .... *Chris Gallegos*
Bio: b. 5/7/32 Albuquerque, NM; Catholic; JD Univ. of Denver, 1958; Attorney; m. Nancy
Comm.: Appropriations; Budget; Energy & Natural Resources (Chair); Homeland Security & Governmental Affairs; Indian Affairs
Dist. Offices: Albuquerque, 505-346-6791; Roswell, 505-623-6170; Santa Fe, 505-988-6511; Las Cruces, 505-526-5475

Byron L. Dorgan (D-ND)   **202-224-2551**
SH-322   3rd Term/68%   Fax: 202-224-1193
E-mail: senator@dorgan.senate.gov
Website: dorgan.senate.gov
CoS .... *Bernie Toon* **LD** .... *Elizabeth Gore*
Sch .... *Christy Beach* **CD** .... *Barry Piatt*
Bio: b. 5/14/42 Dickinson, ND; Lutheran; MBA Univ. of Denver, 1966; Public Official; m. Kim
Comm.: Appropriations; Commerce, Science & Transportation; Energy & Natural Resources; Indian Affairs (Vice Chair)
Dist. Offices: Bismarck, 701-250-4618; Grand Forks, 701-746-8972; Fargo, 701-239-5389; Minot, 701-852-0703

Richard J. Durbin (D-IL)   **202-224-2152**
SD-332   2nd Term/60%   Fax: 202-228-0400
Website: durbin.senate.gov
CoS .... *Ed Greelegs* **LD** .... *Tom Faletti*
Appt ..... *Andrea Del'Aguila* **Press** .... *Joe Shoemaker*
Bio: b. 11/21/44 East St. Louis, IL; Catholic; JD Georgetown Univ., 1969; Attorney; m. Loretta
Comm.: Appropriations; Judiciary; Rules & Administration; Minority Whip
Dist. Offices: Chicago, 312-353-4952; Springfield, 217-492-4062; Marion, 618-998-8812

John Ensign (R-NV)   **202-224-6244**
SR-364   1st Term/55%   Fax: 202-228-2193
Website: ensign.senate.gov
CoS .... *Scott Bensing* **LD** .... *Pam Thiessen*
Sch .... *Jim Shepard* **CD** .... *Jack Finn*
Bio: b. 3/25/58 Roseville, CA; Christian; DVM CO St. Univ., 1985; Veterinarian; m. Darlene
Comm.: Armed Services; Budget; Commerce, Science & Transportation; Health, Education, Labor & Pensions; Veterans' Affairs
Dist. Offices: Las Vegas, 702-388-6605; Reno, 775-686-5770; Carson City, 775-885-9111

Michael B. Enzi (R-WY)   **202-224-3424**
SR-379A   2nd Term/73%   Fax: 202-228-0359
Website: enzi.senate.gov
CoS ..... *Flip McConnaughey* **LD** .... *Randi Reid*
Sch .... *Christen Petersen* **Press** .... *Coy Knobel*
Bio: b. 2/1/44 Bremerton, WA; Presbyterian; MBA Univ. of Denver, 1968; WYARNG, 1967-73; Accounting Manager, Computer Programmer; m. Diana
Comm.: Banking, Housing & Urban Affairs; Budget; Health, Education, Labor & Pensions (Chair); Small Business & Entrepreneurship
Dist. Offices: Gillette, 307-682-6268; Cheyenne, 307-772-2477; Casper, 307-261-6572; Cody, 307-527-9444; Jackson, 307-739-9507

SENATORS

Russ Feingold (D-WI)   202-224-5323
SH-506   3rd Term/55%   Fax: 202-224-2725
Website: feingold.senate.gov
CoS .... *Mary Irvine* **LD** .... *Paul Weinberger*
Sch .... *Margaret Whiting* **Press** .... *Trevor Miller*
Bio: b. 3/2/53 Janesville, WI; Jewish; JD Harvard Univ., 1979; Attorney; m. Mary
Comm.: Budget; Foreign Relations; Judiciary; Special Aging
Dist. Offices: Middleton, 608-828-1200; Wausau, 715-848-5660; La Crosse, 608-782-5585; Milwaukee, 414-276-7282; Green Bay, 920-465-7508

Dianne Feinstein (D-CA)   202-224-3841
SH-331   3rd Term/56%   Fax: 202-228-3954
Website: feinstein.senate.gov
CoS .... *Mark Kadesh* **LD** .... *Peter Cleveland*
Sch .... *Alexis Wilson* **CD** .... *Howard Gantman*
Bio: b. 6/22/33 San Francisco, CA; Jewish; BA Stanford Univ., 1955; Public Official; m. Richard Blum
Comm.: Appropriations; Energy & Natural Resources; Judiciary; Rules & Administration; Select Intelligence
Dist. Offices: San Francisco, 415-393-0707; Fresno, 559-485-7430; Los Angeles, 310-914-7300; San Diego, 619-231-9712

Bill Frist (R-TN)   202-224-3344
SH-509   2nd Term/65%   Fax: 202-228-1264
Website: frist.senate.gov
CoS .... *Andrea Becker* **LD** .... *Jim Hippe*
Sch .... *Lee Anne Akers* **Press** .... *Elie Tiechman*
Bio: b. 2/22/52 Nashville, TN; Presbyterian; MD Harvard Univ., 1978; Surgeon; m. Karyn
Comm.: Finance; Health, Education, Labor & Pensions; Rules & Administration; Majority Leader
Dist. Offices: Nashville, 615-352-9411; Memphis, 901-683-1910; Knoxville, 865-637-4180; Chattanooga, 423-756-2757; Jackson, 731-424-9655; Kingsport, 423-323-1252

Lindsey O. Graham (R-SC)   202-224-5972
SR-290   1st Term/55%   Fax: 202-224-3808
Website: lgraham.senate.gov
CoS .... *Richard Perry* **LD** .... *Jen Olson*
Appt .... *Ellen Bradley* **Press** .... *Wes Hickman*
Bio: b. 7/9/55 Pickens Co., SC; Baptist; JD Univ. of SC, 1981; USAF, 1982-88; SCANG, 1989-95; USAFR, 1995-present; Attorney; single
Comm.: Armed Services; Budget; Judiciary; Veterans' Affairs
Dist. Offices: Greenville, 864-250-1417; Mt. Pleasant, 843-849-3887; Columbia, 803-933-0112; Florence, 843-669-1505; Rock Hill, 803-366-2828; Seneca, 864-888-3330

Charles E. Grassley (R-IA)   202-224-3744
SH-135   5th Term/70%   Fax: 202-224-6020
Website: grassley.senate.gov
CoS .... *Ken Cunningham* **LD** .... *Kolan Davis*
Sch .... *Leah Shimp* **CD** .... *Jill Kozeny*
Bio: b. 9/17/33 New Hartford, IA; Baptist; MA Univ. of Northern IA, 1956; Farmer; m. Barbara Ann
Comm.: Agriculture, Nutrition & Forestry; Budget; Finance (Chair); Judiciary; Joint Taxation (Vice Chair)
Dist. Offices: Des Moines, 515-288-1145; Davenport, 563-322-4331; Cedar Rapids, 319-363-6832; Sioux City, 712-233-1860; Council Bluffs, 712-322-7103; Waterloo, 319-232-6657

SENATORS

Judd Gregg (R-NH)   202-224-3324
SR-393   3rd Term/66%   Fax: 202-224-4952
E-mail: mailbox@gregg.senate.gov
Website: gregg.senate.gov
CoS .... *Vas Christopoulos* **LD** .... *Vacant*
Appt .... *Sheila Dukes* **Press** .... *Erin Rath*
Bio: b. 2/14/47 Nashua, NH; Congregationalist; LLM Boston Univ., 1975; Attorney; m. Kathleen
Comm.: Appropriations; Budget (Chair); Health, Education, Labor & Pensions
Dist. Offices: Concord, 603-225-7115; Berlin, 603-752-2604; Manchester, 603-622-7979; Portsmouth, 603-431-2171

Chuck Hagel (R-NE)   202-224-4224
SR-248   2nd Term/83%   Fax: 202-224-5213
Website: hagel.senate.gov
CoS .... *Lou Ann Linehan* **LD** .... *Jill Konz*
Sch .... *Lindsay Hamilton* **CD** .... *Mike Buttry*
Bio: b. 10/4/46 North Platte, NE; Episcopal; BA Univ. of NE - Omaha, 1971; USA, 1967-68; Investment Company President; m. Lilibet
Comm.: Banking, Housing & Urban Affairs; Foreign Relations; Rules & Administration; Select Intelligence
Dist. Offices: Omaha, 402-758-8981; Lincoln, 402-476-1400; Scottsbluff, 308-632-6032; Kearney, 308-236-7602

Tom Harkin (D-IA)   202-224-3254
SH-731   4th Term/54%   Fax: 202-224-9369
Website: harkin.senate.gov
CoS .... *Brian Ahlberg* **LD** .... *None*
Appt .... *Todd Batta* **Press** .... *Allison Dobson*
Bio: b. 11/19/39 Cumming, IA; Catholic; JD Catholic Univ., 1972; USN, 1962-67; USNR, 1968-70; Attorney; m. Ruth
Comm.: Agriculture, Nutrition & Forestry (Rnk. Mem.); Appropriations; Health, Education, Labor & Pensions; Small Business & Entrepreneurship
Dist. Offices: Des Moines, 515-284-4574; Cedar Rapids, 319-365-4504; Davenport, 563-322-1338; Dubuque, 563-582-2130; Sioux City, 712-252-1550

Orrin G. Hatch (R-UT)   202-224-5251
SH-104   5th Term/66%   Fax: 202-224-6331
Website: hatch.senate.gov
CoS .... *Patricia Knight* **LD** .... *Jace Johnson*
Sch .... *Ruth Montoya* **CD** .... *Adam Elggren*
Bio: b. 3/22/34 Pittsburgh, PA; Mormon; JD Univ. of Pittsburgh, 1962; Attorney; m. Elaine
Comm.: Finance; Health, Education, Labor & Pensions; Judiciary; Select Intelligence; Joint Taxation
Dist. Offices: Salt Lake City, 801-524-4380; Ogden, 801-625-5672; Provo, 801-375-7881; Cedar City, 435-586-8435; St. George, 435-634-1795

Kay Bailey Hutchison (R-TX)   202-224-5922
SR-284   3rd Term/65%   Fax: 202-224-0776
Website: hutchison.senate.gov
CoS .... *Lindsey Parham* **LD** .... *Harley Walsh*
Sch .... *Bethany Smith* **Press** .... *Chris Paulitz*
Bio: b. 7/22/43 La Marque, TX; Episcopal; JD Univ. of TX, 1967; Attorney, Journalist, Bank Executive, Small Business Owner; m. Ray
Comm.: Appropriations; Commerce, Science & Transportation; Rules & Administration; Veterans' Affairs
Dist. Offices: Dallas, 214-361-3500; Houston, 713-653-3456; San Antonio, 210-340-2885; Austin, 512-916-5834; Abilene, 325-676-2839; Harlingen, 956-425-2253

SENATORS

James M. Inhofe (R-OK)   202-224-4721
SR-453   3rd Term/57%   Fax: 202-228-0380
Website: inhofe.senate.gov
CoS .... *Glenn Powell* **LD** .... *Aloysius Hogan*
Sch .... *Wendi Price* **CD** .... *Danny Finnerty*
Bio: b. 11/17/34 Des Moines, IA; Presbyterian; BA Univ. of Tulsa, 1973; USA, 1954-56; Insurance Executive; m. Kay
Comm.: Armed Services; Environment & Public Works (Chair)
Dist. Offices: Tulsa, 918-748-5111; Oklahoma City, 405-608-4381; McAlester, 918-426-0933; Enid, 580-234-5105

Daniel K. Inouye (D-HI)   202-224-3934
SH-722   8th Term/73%   Fax: 202-224-6747
Website: inouye.senate.gov
AA .... *Patrick DeLeon* **LD** .... *Marie Blanco*
Sch .... *Jessica Lee* **Press** .... *Mike Yuen*
Bio: b. 9/7/24 Honolulu, HI; Methodist; JD George Washington Univ., 1952; USA, 1943-47; Attorney; m. Margaret
Comm.: Appropriations; Commerce, Science & Transportation (Rnk. Mem.); Rules & Administration; Indian Affairs; Joint Printing
Dist. Offices: Honolulu, 808-541-2542; Hilo, 808-935-0844; Wailuku, 808-242-9702; Kaunakakai, 808-560-3653; Lihue, 808-245-4611; Kealakekua, 808-935-0844; Mililani, 808-847-5761

Johnny Isakson (R-GA)   202-224-3643
SR-120   1st Term/58%   Fax: 202-228-0724
Website: isakson.senate.gov
CoS .... *Heath Garrett* **Dep CoS** .... *Chris Carr*
Sch .... *Tempe Landrum* **CD** .... *Joan Kirchner*
Bio: b. 12/28/44 Atlanta, GA; Methodist; BBA Univ. of GA, 1966; USANG, 1966-72; Real Estate Executive; m. Dianne
Comm.: Environment & Public Works; Health, Education, Labor & Pensions; Small Business & Entrepreneurship; Veterans' Affairs
Dist. Office: Atlanta, 404-347-2202

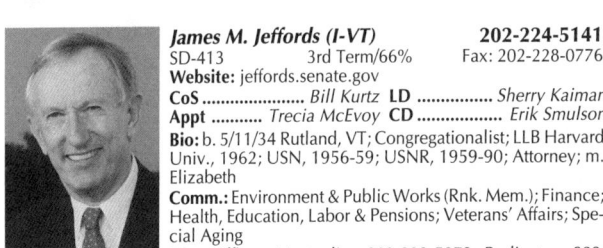

James M. Jeffords (I-VT)   202-224-5141
SD-413   3rd Term/66%   Fax: 202-228-0776
Website: jeffords.senate.gov
CoS .... *Bill Kurtz* **LD** .... *Sherry Kaiman*
Appt .... *Trecia McEvoy* **CD** .... *Erik Smulson*
Bio: b. 5/11/34 Rutland, VT; Congregationalist; LLB Harvard Univ., 1962; USN, 1956-59; USNR, 1959-90; Attorney; m. Elizabeth
Comm.: Environment & Public Works (Rnk. Mem.); Finance; Health, Education, Labor & Pensions; Veterans' Affairs; Special Aging
Dist. Offices: Montpelier, 802-223-5273; Burlington, 802-658-6001; Rutland, 802-773-3875

Tim Johnson (D-SD)   202-224-5842
SH-136   2nd Term/50%   Fax: 202-228-5765
Website: johnson.senate.gov
CoS .... *Drey Samuelson* **LD** .... *Todd Stubbendieck*
Sch .... *Sonja Dean* **CD** .... *Julianne Fisher*
Bio: b. 12/28/46 Canton, SD; Lutheran; JD Univ. of SD, 1975; Attorney; m. Barbara
Comm.: Appropriations; Banking, Housing & Urban Affairs; Budget; Energy & Natural Resources; Indian Affairs; Select Ethics (Vice Chair)
Dist. Offices: Sioux Falls, 605-332-8896; Aberdeen, 605-226-3440; Rapid City, 605-341-3990

SENATORS

Edward M. Kennedy (D-MA)   202-224-4543
SR-317   8th Term/73%   Fax: 202-224-2417
Website: kennedy.senate.gov
CoS .... *Danica Petroshius* **LD** .... *Carey Parker*
Appt .... *Scott Fay* **Press** .... *Melissa Wagoner*
Bio: b. 2/22/32 Boston, MA; Catholic; LLB Univ. of VA, 1959; USA, 1951-53; Attorney; m. Victoria
Comm.: Armed Services; Health, Education, Labor & Pensions (Rnk. Mem.); Judiciary; Joint Economic
Dist. Office: Boston, 617-565-3170

John F. Kerry (D-MA)   202-224-2742
SR-304   4th Term/81%   Fax: 202-224-8525
Website: kerry.senate.gov
CoS .... *David McKean* **LD** .... *George Abar*
Sch .... *Julie Wirkkala* **Press** .... *April Boyd*
Bio: b. 12/11/43 Denver, CO; Catholic; JD Boston Col., 1976; USN, 1966-70; Attorney; m. Teresa Heinz Kerry
Comm.: Commerce, Science & Transportation; Finance; Foreign Relations; Small Business & Entrepreneurship (Rnk. Mem.)
Dist. Offices: Boston, 617-565-8519; Springfield, 413-785-4610; Worcester, 508-831-7380; Fall River, 508-677-0522

Herbert H. Kohl (D-WI)   202-224-5653
SH-330   3rd Term/62%   Fax: 202-224-9787
Website: kohl.senate.gov
CoS .... *Paul Bock* **LD** .... *Kate Sparks*
Sch .... *Arlene Branca* **CD** .... *Lynn Becker*
Bio: b. 2/7/35 Milwaukee, WI; Jewish; MBA Harvard Univ., 1958; USAR, 1958-64; Pro Basketball Team Owner; single
Comm.: Appropriations; Judiciary; Special Aging (Rnk. Mem.)
Dist. Offices: Milwaukee, 414-297-4451; Madison, 608-264-5338; Eau Claire, 715-832-8424; Appleton, 920-738-1640; La Crosse, 608-796-0045

Jon L. Kyl (R-AZ)   202-224-4521
SH-730   2nd Term/79%   Fax: 202-224-2207
Website: kyl.senate.gov
CoS .... *Tim Glazewski* **LD** .... *Elizabeth Maier*
Sch .... *Jill Cernok* **Press** .... *Andrew Wilder*
Bio: b. 4/25/42 Oakland, NE; Presbyterian; LLB Univ. of AZ, 1966; Attorney; m. Caryll
Comm.: Finance; Judiciary
Dist. Offices: Phoenix, 602-840-1891; Tucson, 520-575-8633

Mary Landrieu (D-LA)   202-224-5824
SH-724   2nd Term/52%   Fax: 202-224-9735
Website: landrieu.senate.gov
CoS ... *Norma Jane Sabiston* **LD** .... *Jason Matthews*
Sch .... *Amy Cenicola* **Press** .... *Adam Sharp*
Bio: b. 11/23/55 Arlington, VA; Catholic; BA LA St. Univ., 1977; Businesswoman, Public Official; m. Frank Snellings
Comm.: Appropriations; Energy & Natural Resources; Small Business & Entrepreneurship
Dist. Offices: New Orleans, 504-589-2427; Baton Rouge, 225-389-0395; Shreveport, 318-676-3085; Lake Charles, 337-436-6650

SENATORS

Frank R. Lautenberg (D-NJ)   202-224-3224
SH-324   4th Term/54%   Fax: 202-228-4054
Website: lautenberg.senate.gov
CoS .... *Tim Yehl* **LD** .... *Gray Maxwell*
Appt .... *Ellen Nedrow* **Press** .... *Alex Formuzis*
Bio: b. 1/23/24 Paterson, NJ; Jewish; BS Columbia Univ., 1949; USA, 1942-46; Businessman; m. Bonnie Englebardt
Comm.: Commerce, Science & Transportation; Environment & Public Works; Homeland Security & Governmental Affairs
Dist. Offices: Newark, 973-639-8700; Camden, 856-338-8922

Patrick J. Leahy (D-VT)   202-224-4242
SR-433   6th Term/71%   Fax: 202-224-3479
Website: leahy.senate.gov
CoS .... *Luke Albee* **LD** .... *John Dowd*
Sch .... *Kevin McDonald* **Press** .... *David Carle*
Bio: b. 3/31/40 Montpelier, VT; Catholic; JD Georgetown Univ., 1964; Attorney; m. Marcelle
Comm.: Agriculture, Nutrition & Forestry; Appropriations; Judiciary (Rnk. Mem.)
Dist. Offices: Burlington, 802-863-2525; Montpelier, 802-229-0569

Carl Levin (D-MI)   202-224-6221
SR-269   5th Term/61%   Fax: 202-224-1388
Website: levin.senate.gov
CoS .... *David Lyles* **LD** .... *Rich Arenberg*
Sch .... *Alison Warner* **Press** .... *Tara Andringa*
Bio: b. 6/28/34 Detroit, MI; Jewish; JD Harvard Univ., 1959; Attorney; m. Barbara
Comm.: Armed Services (Rnk. Mem.); Homeland Security & Governmental Affairs; Small Business & Entrepreneurship; Select Intelligence
Dist. Offices: Detroit, 313-226-6020; Saginaw, 989-754-2494; Lansing, 517-377-1508; Grand Rapids, 616-456-2531; Warren, 586-573-9145; Escanaba, 906-789-0052; Traverse City, 231-947-9569

Joseph I. Lieberman (D-CT)   202-224-4041
SH-706   3rd Term/63%   Fax: 202-224-9750
Website: lieberman.senate.gov
CoS .... *Clarine Nardi Riddle* **LD** .... *Bill Bonvillian*
Sch .... *Melissa Winter* **CD** .... *Matt Gobush*
Bio: b. 2/24/42 Stamford, CT; Jewish; JD Yale Univ., 1967; Attorney; m. Hadassah
Comm.: Armed Services; Environment & Public Works; Homeland Security & Governmental Affairs (Rnk. Mem.); Small Business & Entrepreneurship
Dist. Office: Hartford, 860-549-8463

Blanche L. Lincoln (D-AR)   202-224-4843
SD-355   2nd Term/56%   Fax: 202-228-1371
Website: lincoln.senate.gov
CoS .... *Kelly Bingel* **LD** .... *Jim Stowers*
Appt .... *Megan Robertson* **Press** .... *Drew Goesl*
Bio: b. 9/30/60 Helena, AR; Episcopal; BA Randolph-Macon Women's Col., 1982; Homemaker; m. Steve
Comm.: Agriculture, Nutrition & Forestry; Finance; Special Aging
Dist. Offices: Little Rock, 501-375-2993; Ft. Smith, 479-782-9215; Texarkana, 870-774-3106; Jonesboro, 870-910-6896

SENATORS

Trent Lott (R-MS)   202-224-6253
SR-487   3rd Term/66%   Fax: 202-224-2262
E-mail: senatorlott@lott.senate.gov
Website: lott.senate.gov
CoS .... *William Gottshall* **LD** .... *Jim Sartucci*
Sch .... *Hardy Lott* **CD** .... *Susan Irby*
Bio: b. 10/9/41 Grenada, MS; Southern Baptist; JD Univ. of MS, 1967; Attorney; m. Patricia
Comm.: Commerce, Science & Transportation; Finance; Rules & Administration (Chair); Select Intelligence; Joint Library; Joint Printing (Chair); Joint Taxation
Dist. Offices: Jackson, 601-965-4644; Gulfport, 228-863-1988; Pascagoula, 228-762-5400; Oxford, 662-234-3774

Richard G. Lugar (R-IN)   202-224-4814
SH-306   5th Term/67%   Fax: 202-228-0360
E-mail: senator_lugar@lugar.senate.gov
Website: lugar.senate.gov
CoS .... *Marty Morris* **LD** .... *Chris Geeslin*
Sch .... *Justin Ailes* **Press** .... *Andy Fisher*
Bio: b. 4/4/32 Indianapolis, IN; Methodist; MA Oxford Univ., 1956; USN, 1957-60; Businessman; m. Charlene
Comm.: Agriculture, Nutrition & Forestry; Foreign Relations (Chair)
Dist. Offices: Indianapolis, 317-226-5555; Jeffersonville, 812-288-3377; Ft. Wayne, 260-422-1505; Valparaiso, 219-548-8035; Evansville, 812-465-6313

Mel Martinez (R-FL)   202-224-3041
SH-317   1st Term/49%   Fax: 202-228-5171
Website: martinez.senate.gov
CoS .... *John Little* **LD** .... *Tripp Baird*
Sch .... *Christina Voliva* **CD** .... *Kerry Feehery*
Bio: b. 10/23/46 Sagua La Grande, Cuba; Catholic; JD FL St. Univ., 1973; Attorney, Public Official; m. Kitty
Comm.: Banking, Housing & Urban Affairs; Energy & Natural Resources; Foreign Relations; Special Aging
Dist. Office: Orlando, 407-254-2573

John McCain (R-AZ)   202-224-2235
SR-241   4th Term/77%   Fax: 202-228-2862
Website: mccain.senate.gov
CoS .... *Mark Salter* **LD** .... *Ann Begeman*
Sch .... *Ellen Cahill* **Press** .... *Andrea Jones*
Bio: b. 8/29/36 Panama Canal Zone; Episcopal; BS US Naval Acad., 1958; USN, 1958-81; Naval Officer; m. Cindy Lou
Comm.: Armed Services; Commerce, Science & Transportation; Indian Affairs (Chair)
Dist. Offices: Phoenix, 602-952-2410; Tempe, 480-897-6289; Tucson, 520-670-6334

Mitch McConnell (R-KY)   202-224-2541
SR-361A   4th Term/64%   Fax: 202-224-2499
Website: mcconnell.senate.gov
CoS .... *Billy Piper* **LD** .... *Billy Piper*
Sch .... *Karen Willard* **CD** .... *Robert Steurer*
Bio: b. 2/20/42 Sheffield, AL; Baptist; JD Univ. of KY, 1967; Public Official; m. Elaine Chao
Comm.: Agriculture, Nutrition & Forestry; Appropriations; Rules & Administration; Majority Whip
Dist. Offices: Louisville, 502-582-6304; Lexington, 859-224-8286; London, 606-864-2026; Paducah, 270-442-4554; Ft. Wright, 859-578-0188; Bowling Green, 270-781-1673

SENATORS

Barbara A. Mikulski (D-MD)   202-224-4654
SH-503   4th Term/65%   Fax: 202-224-8858
Website: mikulski.senate.gov
CoS .... *Julia Frifield* **LD** .... *Dennis Kelleher*
Sch .... *Shannon Kula* **Press** .... *Amy Hagovsky*
Bio: b. 7/20/36 Baltimore, MD; Catholic; MSW Univ. of MD, 1965; Social Worker; single
Comm.: Appropriations; Health, Education, Labor & Pensions; Select Intelligence
Dist. Offices: Baltimore, 410-962-4510; Annapolis, 410-263-1805; Greenbelt, 301-345-5517; Salisbury, 410-546-7711; Hagerstown, 301-797-2826

Lisa Murkowski (R-AK)   202-224-6665
SH-709   2nd Term/49%   Fax: 202-224-5301
Website: murkowski.senate.gov
CoS .... *Tom Daffron* **LD** .... *Isaac Edwards*
Appt .... *Kristen Daimler* **CD** .... *Kristin Pugh*
Bio: b. 5/22/57 Ketchikan, AK; Catholic; JD Willamette Col., 1985; Attorney; m. Verne Martell
Comm.: Energy & Natural Resources; Environment & Public Works; Foreign Relations; Indian Affairs
Dist. Offices: Anchorage, 907-271-3735; Fairbanks, 907-456-0233; Juneau, 907-586-7400; Kenai, 907-283-5808; Ketchikan, 907-225-6880; Wasilla, 907-376-7665; Bethel, 907-543-1639

Patty Murray (D-WA)   202-224-2621
SR-173   3rd Term/55%   Fax: 202-224-0238
Website: murray.senate.gov
CoS .... *Rick Desimone* **LD** .... *Ben McMakin*
Sch .... *Sheila Babb* **Press** .... *Mike Spahn*
Bio: b. 10/11/50 Bothell, WA; Catholic; BA WA St. Univ., 1972; Educator; m. Rob
Comm.: Appropriations; Budget; Health, Education, Labor & Pensions; Veterans' Affairs
Dist. Offices: Seattle, 206-553-5545; Vancouver, 360-696-7797; Spokane, 509-624-9515; Yakima, 509-453-7462; Everett, 425-259-6515; Tacoma, 253-573-3636

Ben Nelson (D-NE)   202-224-6551
SH-720   1st Term/51%   Fax: 202-228-0012
Website: bennelson.senate.gov
CoS .... *Tim Becker* **LD** .... *Amy Tejral*
Sch .... *Melanie Rogge* **CD** .... *David DiMartino*
Bio: b. 5/17/41 McCook, NE; Methodist; JD Univ. of NE, 1970; Attorney; m. Diane
Comm.: Agriculture, Nutrition & Forestry; Armed Services; Commerce, Science & Transportation; Rules & Administration
Dist. Offices: Lincoln, 402-441-4600; Omaha, 402-391-3411; Chadron, 308-430-0587; Scottsbluff, 308-631-7614

Bill Nelson (D-FL)   202-224-5274
SH-716   1st Term/51%   Fax: 202-228-2183
Website: billnelson.senate.gov
CoS .... *Peter J. Mitchell* **LD** .... *Dan Shapiro*
Sch .... *Katie Platt* **CD** .... *Dan McLaughlin*
Bio: b. 9/29/42 Miami, FL; Protestant; JD Univ. of VA, 1968; USA, 1968-70; USAR, 1965-68, 1970-71; Attorney; m. Grace
Comm.: Armed Services; Budget; Commerce, Science & Transportation; Foreign Relations; Special Aging
Dist. Offices: Orlando, 407-872-7161; Tallahassee, 850-942-8415; Tampa, 813-225-7040; Coral Gables, 305-536-5999; West Palm Beach, 561-514-0189; Jacksonville, 904-346-4500; Davie, 954-693-4851; Ft. Myers, 239-334-7760

SENATORS

Barack Obama (D-IL)   202-224-2854
SH-713   1st Term/70%   Fax: 202-228-5417
Website: obama.senate.gov
CoS .... *Pete Rouse* **LD** .... *Chris Lu*
Sch .... *Mike Robertson* **CD** .... *Robert Gibbs*
Bio: b. 8/4/61 Honolulu, HI; United Church of Christ; JD Harvard Univ., 1991; Attorney, Lecturer; m. Michelle
Comm.: Environment & Public Works; Foreign Relations; Veterans' Affairs
Dist. Offices: Chicago, 312-886-3506; Springfield, 217-492-5089; Marion, 618-997-2402

Mark Pryor (D-AR)   202-224-2353
SD-257   1st Term/54%   Fax: 202-228-0908
Website: pryor.senate.gov
CoS .... *Bob Russell* **LD** .... *Walter Pryor*
Appt .... *Shiloh Dillon* **CD** .... *Rodell Mollineau*
Bio: b. 1/10/63 Fayetteville, AR; Christian; JD Univ. of AR, 1988; Public Official; m. Jill
Comm.: Commerce, Science & Transportation; Homeland Security & Governmental Affairs; Small Business & Entrepreneurship; Select Ethics
Dist. Office: Little Rock, 501-324-6336

Jack Reed (D-RI)   202-224-4642
SH-728   2nd Term/78%   Fax: 202-224-4680
Website: reed.senate.gov
CoS .... *Neil Campbell* **LD** .... *Elyse Wasch*
Sch .... *Rosanne Haroian* **Press** .... *Greg McCarthy*
Bio: b. 11/12/49 Providence, RI; Catholic; JD Harvard Univ., 1982; USA, 1967-79; Attorney; eng.
Comm.: Armed Services; Banking, Housing & Urban Affairs; Health, Education, Labor & Pensions; Joint Economic
Dist. Offices: Cranston, 401-943-3100; Providence, 401-528-5200

Harry Reid (D-NV)   202-224-3542
SH-528   4th Term/61%   Fax: 202-224-7327
Website: reid.senate.gov
CoS .... *Susan McCue* **Dep CoS** .... *Kai Anderson*
Sch .... *Callie Fuselier* **Press** .... *Tessa Hafen*
Bio: b. 12/2/39 Searchlight, NV; Mormon; JD George Washington Univ., 1964; Attorney; m. Landra
Comm.: Appropriations; Minority Leader
Dist. Offices: Las Vegas, 702-388-5020; Reno, 775-686-5750; Carson City, 775-882-7343

Pat Roberts (R-KS)   202-224-4774
SH-109   2nd Term/Unc.   Fax: 202-224-3514
Website: roberts.senate.gov
CoS .... *Jackie Cottrell* **LD** .... *Keith Yehle*
Sch .... *Maggie Ward* **Press** .... *Sarah Little*
Bio: b. 4/20/36 Topeka, KS; Methodist; BS KS St. Univ., 1958; USMC, 1958-62; Journalist; m. Franki
Comm.: Agriculture, Nutrition & Forestry; Armed Services; Health, Education, Labor & Pensions; Select Ethics; Select Intelligence (Chair)
Dist. Offices: Overland Park, 913-451-9343; Topeka, 785-295-2745; Wichita, 316-263-0416; Dodge City, 620-227-2244

SENATORS

John D. Rockefeller IV (D-WV)   202-224-6472
SH-531   4th Term/63%   Fax: 202-224-7665
E-mail: senator@rockefeller.senate.gov
Website: rockefeller.senate.gov
CoS .... Kerry Ates   **LD** .... Ellen Doneski
Sch .... Beth Powers   **CD** .... Wendy Morigi
Bio: b. 6/18/37 New York, NY; Presbyterian; BA Harvard Univ., 1961; College President; m. Sharon
Comm.: Commerce, Science & Transportation; Finance; Veterans' Affairs; Select Intelligence (Vice Chair); Joint Taxation
Dist. Offices: Charleston, 304-347-5372; Beckley, 304-253-9704; Fairmont, 304-367-0122; Martinsburg, 304-262-9285

Ken Salazar (D-CO)   202-224-5852
SH-702   1st Term/51%   Fax: 202-228-5036
Website: salazar.senate.gov
CoS .... Ken Lane   **LD** .... Denis McDonough
Sch .... Joan Padilla   **Press** .... Cody Wertz
Bio: b. 3/2/55 San Luis Valley, CO; Catholic; JD Univ. of MI, 1981; Attorney, Farmer, Small Business Owner; m. Hope
Comm.: Agriculture, Nutrition & Forestry; Energy & Natural Resources; Veterans' Affairs
Dist. Office: Denver, 303-455-7600

Rick Santorum (R-PA)   202-224-6324
SD-511   2nd Term/52%   Fax: 202-228-0604
Website: santorum.senate.gov
CoS .... Wayne Palmer   **LD** .... Zack Moore
EA .... Ramona Ely   **Press** .... Christine Shott
Bio: b. 5/10/58 Winchester, VA; Catholic; JD Dickinson Univ., 1986; Attorney; m. Karen
Comm.: Agriculture, Nutrition & Forestry; Banking, Housing & Urban Affairs; Finance; Rules & Administration; Special Aging
Dist. Offices: Pittsburgh, 412-562-0533; Philadelphia, 215-864-6900; Harrisburg, 717-231-7540; Scranton, 570-344-8799; Erie, 814-454-7114; Allentown, 610-770-0142; Altoona, 814-946-7023; Coudersport, 814-274-9773

Paul S. Sarbanes (D-MD)   202-224-4524
SH-309   5th Term/63%   Fax: 202-224-1651
Website: sarbanes.senate.gov
CoS .... Julie Kehrli   **LD** .... Jonathan Davidson
Sch .... Elise Gillette   **Press** .... Jesse Jacobs
Bio: b. 2/3/33 Salisbury, MD; Greek Orthodox; LLB Harvard Univ., 1960; Attorney; m. Christine
Comm.: Banking, Housing & Urban Affairs (Rnk. Mem.); Budget; Foreign Relations; Joint Economic
Dist. Offices: Baltimore, 410-962-4436; Silver Spring, 301-589-0797; Cumberland, 301-724-0695; Bryans Road, 301-283-0947; Salisbury, 410-860-2131

Charles E. Schumer (D-NY)   202-224-6542
SH-313   2nd Term/71%   Fax: 202-228-3027
Website: schumer.senate.gov
CoS .... David Hantman   **LD** .... Polly Trottenberg
Appt .... Kristen Brandt   **Press** .... Semonti Mustaphi
Bio: b. 11/23/50 Brooklyn, NY; Jewish; JD Harvard Univ., 1974; Public Official; m. Iris Weinshall
Comm.: Banking, Housing & Urban Affairs; Finance; Judiciary; Rules & Administration; Joint Library
Dist. Offices: New York, 212-486-4430; Buffalo, 716-846-4111; Rochester, 585-263-5866; Albany, 518-431-4070; Binghamton, 607-772-6792; Syracuse, 315-423-5471; Red Hook, 914-285-9741; Melville, 631-753-0978

SENATORS

Jeff Sessions (R-AL)   202-224-4124
SR-335   2nd Term/59%   Fax: 202-224-3149
Website: sessions.senate.gov
CoS .... *Rick Dearborn* **LD** .... *Alan Hanson*
Sch .... *Stormie Janzen* **Press** .... *Mike Brumas*
Bio: b. 12/24/46 Hybart, AL; Methodist; JD Univ. of AL, 1973; USAR, 1973-86; Attorney; m. Mary
Comm.: Armed Services; Budget; Health, Education, Labor & Pensions; Judiciary; Joint Economic
Dist. Offices: Montgomery, 334-244-7017; Birmingham, 205-731-1500; Mobile, 251-414-3083; Huntsville, 256-533-0979

Richard C. Shelby (R-AL)   202-224-5744
SH-110   4th Term/68%   Fax: 202-224-3416
E-mail: senator@shelby.senate.gov
Website: shelby.senate.gov
CoS .... *Louis Tucker* **LD** .... *Shannon Hines*
Appt .... *Anne Caldwell* **Press** .... *Virginia Davis*
Bio: b. 5/6/34 Birmingham, AL; Presbyterian; LLB Univ. of AL, 1963; Attorney; m. Annette
Comm.: Appropriations; Banking, Housing & Urban Affairs (Chair); Special Aging
Dist. Offices: Tuscaloosa, 205-759-5047; Mobile, 251-694-4164; Montgomery, 334-223-7303; Birmingham, 205-731-1384; Huntsville, 256-772-0460

Gordon Smith (R-OR)   202-224-3753
SR-404   2nd Term/56%   Fax: 202-228-3997
Website: gsmith.senate.gov
CoS .... *John Easton* **LD** .... *Rob Epplin*
Sch .... *Sue Keenom* **CD** .... *Chris Matthews*
Bio: b. 5/25/52 Pendleton, OR; Mormon; JD Southwestern Univ., 1979; Frozen Food Company Executive, Attorney; m. Sharon
Comm.: Commerce, Science & Transportation; Energy & Natural Resources; Finance; Indian Affairs; Special Aging (Chair)
Dist. Offices: Portland, 503-326-3386; Pendleton, 541-278-1129; Medford, 541-608-9102; Eugene, 541-465-6750; Bend, 541-318-1298

Olympia J. Snowe (R-ME)   202-224-5344
SR-154   2nd Term/69%   Fax: 202-224-1946
Website: snowe.senate.gov
CoS .... *John Richter* **LD** .... *Ginny Worrest*
EA .... *Lindsey Ledwin* **CD** .... *Antonia Ferrier*
Bio: b. 2/21/47 Augusta, ME; Greek Orthodox; BA Univ. of ME, 1969; Public Official; m. John R. McKernan, Jr.
Comm.: Commerce, Science & Transportation; Finance; Small Business & Entrepreneurship (Chair); Select Intelligence
Dist. Offices: Portland, 207-874-0883; Auburn, 207-786-2451; Augusta, 207-622-8292; Bangor, 207-945-0432; Biddeford, 207-282-4144; Presque Isle, 207-764-5124

Arlen Specter (R-PA)   202-224-4254
SH-711   5th Term/53%   Fax: 202-228-1229
E-mail: arlen_specter@specter.senate.gov
Website: specter.senate.gov
CoS .... *David Brog* **LC** .... *Mark Heilbrun*
Sch .... *Julie Clark* **CD** .... *Scott Hoeflich*
Bio: b. 2/12/30 Wichita, KS; Jewish; LLB Yale Univ., 1956; USAF, 1951-53; Attorney; m. Joan
Comm.: Appropriations; Judiciary (Chair); Veterans' Affairs
Dist. Offices: Philadelphia, 215-597-7200; Erie, 814-453-3010; Allentown, 610-434-1444; Wilkes Barre, 570-826-6265; Harrisburg, 717-782-3951; Pittsburgh, 412-644-3400; Scranton, 570-346-2006

SENATORS

Debbie A. Stabenow (D-MI)   202-224-4822
SH-133   1st Term/49%   Fax: 202-228-0325
Website: stabenow.senate.gov
CoS .... *Sander Lurie* **LD** .... *Noushin Jahanian*
Appt .... *Sally Cluthe* **CD** .... *Dave Lemmon*
Bio: b. 4/29/50 Gladwin, MI; Methodist; MSW MI St. Univ., 1975; Training Consultant; m. Tom Athans
Comm.: Agriculture, Nutrition & Forestry; Banking, Housing & Urban Affairs; Budget
Dist. Offices: East Lansing, 517-203-1760; Traverse City, 231-929-1031; Flint, 810-720-4172; Detroit, 313-961-4330; Grand Rapids, 616-975-0052; Marquette, 906-228-8756

Ted Stevens (R-AK)   202-224-3004
SH-522   7th Term/79%   Fax: 202-224-2354
Website: stevens.senate.gov
CoS .... *George Lowe* **LD** .... *Karina Waller*
Sch .... *DeLynn Henry* **Press** .... *Courtney Schikora*
Bio: b. 11/18/23 Indianapolis, IN; Episcopal; LLB Harvard Univ., 1950; USAF, 1943-46; Attorney; m. Catherine
Comm.: Appropriations; Commerce, Science & Transportation (Chair); Homeland Security & Governmental Affairs; Rules & Administration; Joint Library (Vice Chair); President Pro Tempore
Dist. Offices: Anchorage, 907-271-5915; Fairbanks, 907-456-0261; Juneau, 907-586-7400; Kenai, 907-283-5808; Ketchikan, 907-225-6880; Wasilla, 907-376-7665; Bethel, 907-543-1639

John E. Sununu (R-NH)   202-224-2841
SR-111   1st Term/51%   Fax: 202-228-4131
E-mail: mailbox@sununu.senate.gov
Website: sununu.senate.gov
CoS .... *Paul J. Collins, Jr.* **LD** .... *Jamie Burnett*
Appt .... *Sheri M. Keniston* **CD** .... *Barbara Riley*
Bio: b. 9/10/64 Boston, MA; Catholic; MBA Harvard Univ., 1991; Engineer, Chief Financial Officer; m. Kitty
Comm.: Banking, Housing & Urban Affairs; Commerce, Science & Transportation; Foreign Relations; Joint Economic
Dist. Offices: Manchester, 603-647-7500; Portsmouth, 603-430-9560; Berlin, 603-752-6074; Claremont, 603-542-4872

Jim Talent (R-MO)   202-224-6154
SR-493   1st Term/50%   Fax: 202-228-1518
Website: talent.senate.gov
CoS .... *Mark Strand* **LD** .... *Brett Thompson*
Sch .... *Cortney Brown* **CD** .... *Rich Chrismer*
Bio: b. 10/18/56 Des Peres, MO; Presbyterian; JD Univ. of Chicago, 1981; Attorney, Public Official; m. Brenda
Comm.: Agriculture, Nutrition & Forestry; Armed Services; Energy & Natural Resources; Special Aging
Dist. Offices: St. Louis, 314-432-5211; Kansas City, 816-421-1639; Cape Girardeau, 573-651-0964; Jefferson City, 573-636-1070; Springfield, 417-831-2735

Craig Thomas (R-WY)   202-224-6441
SD-307   2nd Term/74%   Fax: 202-224-1724
Website: thomas.senate.gov
CoS .... *Shawn Whitman* **LD** .... *Bryn Stewart*
Sch .... *Kathi Wise* **Press** .... *Cameron Hardy*
Bio: b. 2/17/33 Cody, WY; Methodist; BS Univ. of WY, 1955; USMC, 1955-59; Businessman; m. Susan
Comm.: Agriculture, Nutrition & Forestry; Energy & Natural Resources; Finance; Indian Affairs; Select Ethics
Dist. Offices: Casper, 307-261-6413; Cheyenne, 307-772-2451; Rock Springs, 307-362-5012; Riverton, 307-856-6642; Sheridan, 307-672-6456

SENATORS

John R. Thune (R-SD)   202-224-2321
SR-383   1st Term/51%   Fax: 202-228-5429
Website: thune.senate.gov
CoS .... *Matt Zabel* **LD** .... *Bob Taylor*
Sch .... *Summer Pitlick* **Press** .... *Alex Conant*
Bio: b. 1/7/61 Pierre, SD; Protestant; MBA Univ. of SD, 1984; Association Executive; m. Kimberley
Comm.: Armed Services; Environment & Public Works; Small Business & Entrepreneurship; Veterans' Affairs
Dist. Offices: Sioux Falls, 605-334-9596; Rapid City, 605-348-7551; Aberdeen, 605-225-8823

David Vitter (R-LA)   202-224-4623
SH-516   1st Term/51%   Fax: 202-228-5061
Website: vitter.senate.gov
CoS .... *Kyle Ruckert* **LD** .... *Evelyn Fortier*
Sch .... *Kathryn Fulton* **CD** .... *Mac Abrams*
Bio: b. 5/3/61 New Orleans, LA; Catholic; JD Tulane School of Law, 1988; Professor, Attorney; m. Wendy
Comm.: Commerce, Science & Transportation; Environment & Public Works; Small Business & Entrepreneurship
Dist. Office: Metairie, 504-589-2753

George V. Voinovich (R-OH)   202-224-3353
SH-524   2nd Term/64%   Fax: 202-228-1382
Website: voinovich.senate.gov
CoS .... *Aric Newhouse* **LD** .... *Phil Park*
Appt .... *Angie Youngen* **CD** .... *Scott Milburn*
Bio: b. 7/15/36 Cleveland, OH; Catholic; JD OH St. Univ., 1961; Public Official; m. Janet
Comm.: Environment & Public Works; Foreign Relations; Homeland Security & Governmental Affairs; Select Ethics (Chair)
Dist. Offices: Columbus, 614-469-6697; Cleveland, 216-522-7095; Cincinnati, 513-684-3265; Toledo, 419-259-3895; Gallipolis, 740-441-6410

John W. Warner (R-VA)   202-224-2023
SR-225   5th Term/Unc.   Fax: 202-224-6295
Website: warner.senate.gov
CoS .... *Susan Magill* **LD** .... *Ann Loomis*
Appt .... *Anna Reilly* **CD** .... *John Ullyot*
Bio: b. 2/18/27 Washington, DC; Episcopal; LLB Univ. of VA, 1953; USN, 1945-46; USMC, 1950-52; USMCR, 1952-62; Attorney; m. Jeanne Vander Myde
Comm.: Armed Services (Chair); Environment & Public Works; Homeland Security & Governmental Affairs; Select Intelligence (Ex Officio)
Dist. Offices: Midlothian, 804-739-0247; Norfolk, 757-441-3079; Abingdon, 276-628-8158; Roanoke, 540-857-2676

Ron Wyden (D-OR)   202-224-5244
SD-230   3rd Term/64%   Fax: 202-228-2717
Website: wyden.senate.gov
CoS .... *Josh Kardon* **LD** .... *Carole Grunberg*
Sch .... *Sallie Derr* **CD** .... *Carol Guthrie*
Bio: b. 5/3/49 Wichita, KS; Jewish; JD Univ. of OR, 1974; Legal Services Executive, Seniors Advocate; div.
Comm.: Budget; Energy & Natural Resources; Finance; Select Intelligence; Special Aging
Dist. Offices: Portland, 503-326-7525; Eugene, 541-431-0229; Bend, 541-330-9142; LaGrande, 541-962-7691; Medford, 541-858-5122; Salem, 503-589-4555

Senate Committees and Subcommittees

AGRICULTURE, NUTRITION AND FORESTRY

Phone: (202) 224-2035—Room: SR-328A—Fax: 224-1725
http://agriculture.senate.gov

Republicans (11)
Saxby Chambliss, GA, *Chair**
Richard G. Lugar, IN
Thad Cochran, MS
Mitch McConnell, KY
Pat Roberts, KS
Jim Talent, MO
Craig Thomas, WY
Rick Santorum, PA
Norm Coleman, MN
Mike Crapo, ID
Charles E. Grassley, IA

Democrats (9)
Tom Harkin, IA, *Rnk. Mem.**
Patrick J. Leahy, VT
Kent Conrad, ND
Max Baucus, MT
Blanche L. Lincoln, AR
Debbie A. Stabenow, MI
Ben Nelson, NE
Mark Dayton, MN
Ken Salazar, CO

Maj. Staff Dir.:
Martha Scott Poindexter
224-2035, SR-328A

Min. Staff Dir. & Chief Counsel:
Mark Halverson
224-2035, SR-328A

*Ex officio members on all subcommittees.

Agriculture, Nutrition and Forestry Subcommittees

Forestry, Conservation and Rural Revitalization
224-2035/SR-328A/Fax: 224-9287
Rep: Crapo, *Chair;* Lugar; Cochran; Talent; Thomas; Coleman
Dem: Lincoln, *Rnk. Mem.;* Leahy; Nelson; Dayton; Salazar
Maj. Staff Dir.: Martha Scott Poindexter, 224-2035, SR-328A
Min. Staff Dir.: Mark Halverson, 224-2035, SR-328A

Marketing, Inspection and Product Promotion
224-2035/SR-328A/Fax: 224-9287
Rep: Talent, *Chair;* McConnell; Thomas; Roberts; Grassley; Lugar
Dem: Baucus, *Rnk. Mem.;* Nelson; Salazar; Conrad; Stabenow
Maj. Staff Dir.: Martha Scott Poindexter, 224-2035, SR-328A
Min. Staff Dir.: Mark Halverson, 224-2035, SR-328A

Production and Price Competitiveness
224-2035/SR-328A/Fax: 224-9287
Rep: McConnell, *Chair;* Cochran; Roberts; Santorum; Coleman; Grassley
Dem: Conrad, *Rnk. Mem.;* Dayton; Baucus; Leahy; Lincoln
Maj. Staff Dir.: Martha Scott Poindexter, 224-2035, SR-328A
Min. Staff Dir.: Mark Halverson, 224-2035, SR-328A

Research, Nutrition and General Legislation
224-2035/SR-328A/Fax: 224-9287
Rep: Santorum, *Chair;* Lugar; Crapo; Cochran; McConnell; Roberts
Dem: Leahy, *Rnk. Mem.;* Stabenow; Lincoln; Baucus; Nelson
Maj. Staff Dir.: Martha Scott Poindexter, 224-2035, SR-328A
Min. Staff Dir.: Mark Halverson, 224-2035, SR-328A

APPROPRIATIONS

Phone: (202) 224-7363—Room: S-128 Capitol—Fax: 228-0248
http://appropriations.senate.gov

Republicans (15)
Thad Cochran, MS, *Chair**
Ted Stevens, AK
Arlen Specter, PA
Pete V. Domenici, NM
Christopher S. Bond, MO
Mitch McConnell, KY
Conrad Burns, MT
Richard C. Shelby, AL
Judd Gregg, NH
Robert Bennett, UT
Larry E. Craig, ID
Kay Bailey Hutchison, TX
Mike DeWine, OH
Sam Brownback, KS
Wayne Allard, CO

Democrats (13)
Robert C. Byrd, WV, **Rnk. Mem.***
Daniel K. Inouye, HI
Patrick J. Leahy, VT
Tom Harkin, IA
Barbara A. Mikulski, MD
Harry Reid, NV
Herbert H. Kohl, WI
Patty Murray, WA
Byron L. Dorgan, ND
Dianne Feinstein, CA
Richard J. Durbin, IL
Tim Johnson, SD
Mary Landrieu, LA

Maj. Staff Dir.:
Keith Kennedy
224-7363, S-128 Capitol

Min. Staff Dir.:
Terrence Sauvain
224-7200, S-146A Capitol

*Ex officio members on all subcommittees of which they are not regular members.

Appropriations Subcommittees

Agriculture, Rural Development and Related Agencies
224-5270/SD-188/Fax: 224-9087

Rep: Bennett, *Chair;* Cochran; Specter; Bond; McConnell; Burns; Craig; Brownback
Dem: Kohl, *Rnk. Mem.;* Harkin; Dorgan; Feinstein; Durbin; Johnson; Landrieu
Maj. Clerk: John Ziolkowski, 224-5270, SD-188
Min. Clerk: Galen Fountain, 224-8090, SH-123

Commerce, Justice and Science
224-7277/S-146A Capitol/Fax: 228-0587

Rep: Shelby, *Chair;* Gregg; Stevens; Domenici; McConnell; Hutchison; Brownback; Bond
Dem: Mikulski, *Rnk. Mem.;* Inouye; Leahy; Kohl; Murray; Harkin; Dorgan
Maj. Clerk: Katherine Hennessey, 224-7277, S-146A Capitol
Min. Clerk: Lila Helms, 224-7270, SH-123

Defense
224-7255/SD-119/Fax: 224-4402

Rep: Stevens, *Chair;* Cochran; Specter; Domenici; Bond; McConnell; Shelby; Gregg; Hutchison; Burns
Dem: Inouye, *Rnk. Mem.;* Byrd; Leahy; Harkin; Dorgan; Durbin; Reid; Feinstein; Mikulski
Maj. Clerk: Sid Ashworth, 224-7255, SD-119
Min. Clerk: Charles Houy, 224-7293, SD-117

District of Columbia
224-7643/S-128 Capitol

Rep: Brownback, *Chair;* DeWine; Allard
Dem: Landrieu, *Rnk. Mem.;* Durbin
Maj. Staff Dir.: Mary Dietrich, 224-7643, S-128 Capitol
Min. Clerk: Kate Eltrich, 224-6933, SH-123

Energy and Water Development
224-7260/SD-127/Fax: 224-6835

Rep: Domenici, *Chair;* Cochran; McConnell; Bennett; Burns; Craig; Bond; Hutchison; Allard
Dem: Reid, *Rnk. Mem.;* Byrd; Murray; Dorgan; Feinstein; Johnson; Landrieu; Inouye
Maj. Clerk: Scott O'Malia, 224-7260, SD-127
Min. Clerk: Drew Willison, 224-0335, SD-156

Appropriations Subcommittees

Homeland Security
224-7337/SD-188/Fax: 228-0248
Rep: Gregg, *Chair;* Cochran; Stevens; Specter; Domenici; Shelby; Craig; Bennett; Allard
Dem: Byrd, *Rnk. Mem.;* Inouye; Leahy; Mikulski; Kohl; Murray; Reid; Feinstein
Maj. Clerk: Rebecca Davies, 224-7337, SD-188
Min. Clerk: Chip Walgren, 224-6280, SD-196

Interior and Related Agencies
224-7257/SD-132/Fax: 228-4532
Rep: Burns, *Chair;* Stevens; Cochran; Domenici; Bennett; Gregg; Craig; Allard
Dem: Dorgan, *Rnk. Mem.;* Byrd; Leahy; Reid; Feinstein; Mikulski; Kohl
Maj. Clerk: Bruce Evans, 224-7257, SD-132
Min. Clerk: Peter Keifhaber, 228-0774, SD-160

Labor, Health and Human Services, Education and Related Agencies
224-7216/SD-184/Fax: 228-2321
Rep: Specter, *Chair;* Cochran; Gregg; Craig; Hutchison; Stevens; DeWine; Shelby
Dem: Harkin, *Rnk. Mem.;* Inouye; Reid; Kohl; Murray; Landrieu; Durbin
Maj. Clerk: Bettilou Taylor, 224-7216, SD-184
Min. Staff Dir.: Ellen Murray, 224-7288, SH-123

Legislative Branch
224-7238/SD-127
Rep: Allard, *Chair;* Cochran; DeWine
Dem: Durbin, *Rnk. Mem.;* Johnson
Maj. Clerk: Carolyn Apostolou, 224-7238, SD-127
Min. Staff Dir.: Drew Willison, 224-0335, SD-156

Military Construction and Veterans Affairs
224-3378/SD-140/Fax: 228-5795
Rep: Hutchison, *Chair;* Burns; Craig; DeWine; Brownback; Allard; McConnell
Dem: Feinstein, *Rnk. Mem.;* Inouye; Johnson; Landrieu; Byrd; Murray
Maj. Clerk: Dennis Ward, 224-3378, SD-140
Min. Clerk: Christina Evans, 224-3088, SH-123

State, Foreign Operations and Related Programs
224-5095/SD-142/Fax: 224-2255
Rep: McConnell, *Chair;* Specter; Gregg; Shelby; Bennett; Bond; DeWine; Brownback
Dem: Leahy, *Rnk. Mem.;* Inouye; Harkin; Mikulski; Durbin; Johnson; Landrieu
Maj. Clerk: Paul Grove, 224-5095, SD-142
Min. Clerk: Tim Rieser, 224-8202, SH-123

Transportation, Treasury, the Judiciary and Housing and Urban Development
224-4869/SD-133/Fax: 224-4401
Rep: Bond, *Chair;* Shelby; Specter; Bennett; Hutchison; DeWine; Brownback; Stevens; Domenici; Burns
Dem: Murray, *Rnk. Mem.;* Byrd; Mikulski; Reid; Kohl; Durbin; Dorgan; Leahy; Harkin
Maj. Clerk: Paul Doerrer, 224-4869, SD-133
Min. Clerk: Peter Rogoff, 224-7281, SD-144

ARMED SERVICES

Phone: (202) 224-3871—Room: SR-228—Fax: 228-0037
http://armed-services.senate.gov

Republicans (13)
John W. Warner, VA, *Chair**
John McCain, AZ
James M. Inhofe, OK
Pat Roberts, KS
Jeff Sessions, AL
Susan M. Collins, ME
John Ensign, NV
Jim Talent, MO
Saxby Chambliss, GA
Lindsey O. Graham, SC
Elizabeth Dole, NC
John Cornyn, TX
John R. Thune, SD

Democrats (11)
Carl Levin, MI, *Rnk. Mem.**
Edward M. Kennedy, MA
Robert C. Byrd, WV
Joseph I. Lieberman, CT
Jack Reed, RI
Daniel K. Akaka, HI
Bill Nelson, FL
Ben Nelson, NE
Mark Dayton, MN
Evan Bayh, IN
Hillary Rodham Clinton, NY

Maj. Staff Dir.:
Judy Ansley
224-3871, SR-228

Min. Staff Dir.:
Richard DeBobes
224-3871, SR-228

*Ex officio members on all subcommittees.

Armed Services Subcommittees

Airland
224-3871/SR-228/Fax: 228-0037

Rep: McCain, *Chair;* Inhofe; Sessions; Ensign; Talent; Chambliss; Graham; Dole
Dem: Lieberman, *Rnk. Mem.;* Reed; Akaka; Nelson (FL); Dayton; Bayh; Clinton
Maj. Prof. Staff Mems.: Thomas MacKenzie, Bruce Hock, 224-3871, SR-228
Min. Prof. Staff Mems.: Dan Cox, Creighton Greene, 224-3871, SR-228

Emerging Threats and Capabilities
224-3871/SR-228/Fax: 228-0037

Rep: Cornyn, *Chair;* Roberts; Collins; Ensign; Talent; Graham; Dole; Thune
Dem: Reed, *Rnk. Mem.;* Kennedy; Byrd; Nelson (FL); Nelson (NE); Bayh; Clinton
Maj. Prof. Staff Mems.: Chuck Alsup, Lynn Rusten, 224-3871, SR-228
Min. Prof. Staff Mems.: Evelyn Farkas, Phil Monahan, 224-3871, SR-228

Personnel
224-3871/SR-228/Fax: 228-0037

Rep: Graham, *Chair;* McCain; Collins; Chambliss; Dole
Dem: Nelson (NE), *Rnk. Mem.;* Kennedy; Lieberman; Akaka
Maj. Prof. Staff Mem.: Dick Walsh, 224-3871, SR-228
Min. Prof. Staff Mem.: Gary Leeling, 224-3871, SR-228

Readiness and Management Support
224-3871/SR-228/Fax: 228-0037

Rep: Ensign, *Chair;* McCain; Inhofe; Roberts; Sessions; Chambliss; Cornyn; Thune
Dem: Akaka, *Rnk. Mem.;* Byrd; Nelson (FL); Nelson (NE); Dayton; Bayh; Clinton
Maj. Prof. Staff Mems.: Bill Greenwalt, Joe Sixeas, 224-3871, SR-228
Min. Prof. Staff Mem.: Mike McCord, 224-3871, SR-228

SeaPower
224-3871/SR-228/Fax: 228-0037

Rep: Talent, *Chair;* McCain; Collins; Chambliss
Dem: Kennedy, *Rnk. Mem.;* Lieberman; Reed
Maj. Prof. Staff Mems.: Bruce Hock, Thomas MacKenzie, 224-3871, SR-228
Min. Prof. Staff Mem.: Creighton Greene, 224-3871, SR-228

Armed Services Subcommittees

Strategic Forces
224-3871/SR-228/Fax: 228-0037
Rep: Sessions, *Chair;* Inhofe; Roberts; Graham; Cornyn; Thune
Dem: Nelson (FL), *Rnk. Mem.;* Byrd; Reed; Nelson (NE); Dayton
Maj. Prof. Staff Mems.: Rob Soofer, Kristine Spinicki, 224-3871, SR-228
Min. Prof. Staff Mems.: Madelyn Creedon, Richard Fieldhouse, 224-3871, SR-228

BANKING, HOUSING AND URBAN AFFAIRS

Phone: (202) 224-7391—Room: SD-534—Fax: 224-5137
http://banking.senate.gov

Republicans (11)
Richard C. Shelby, AL, *Chair**
Robert Bennett, UT
Wayne Allard, CO
Michael B. Enzi, WY
Chuck Hagel, NE
Rick Santorum, PA
Jim Bunning, KY
Mike Crapo, ID
John E. Sununu, NH
Elizabeth Dole, NC
Mel Martinez, FL

Democrats (9)
Paul S. Sarbanes, MD,
*Rnk. Mem.**
Christopher J. Dodd, CT
Tim Johnson, SD
Jack Reed, RI
Charles E. Schumer, NY
Evan Bayh, IN
Thomas R. Carper, DE
Debbie A. Stabenow, MI
Jon S. Corzine, NJ

Maj. Staff Dir.:
Kathy Casey
224-7391, SD-534

Min. Staff Dir.:
Steven Harris
224-7391, SD-534

*Ex officio members on all subcommittees of which they are not regular members.

Banking, Housing and Urban Affairs Subcommittees

Economic Policy
224-7391/SD-534/Fax: 224-5137
Rep: Bunning, *Chair;* Shelby
Dem: Schumer, *Rnk. Mem.*
Maj. Staff Dir.: Steve Patterson, 224-4343, SH-316
Min. Staff Dir.: Carmencita Whonder, 224-6542, SH-313

Financial Institutions
224-7391/SD-534/Fax: 224-5137
Rep: Bennett, *Chair;* Allard; Santorum; Sununu; Martinez; Hagel; Bunning; Crapo
Dem: Johnson, *Rnk. Mem.;* Carper; Dodd; Reed; Stabenow; Bayh
Maj. Staff Dir.: Mike Nielsen, 224-5444, SD-431
Min. Staff Dir.: Naomi Camper, 224-5842, SH-136

Housing and Transportation
224-7391/SD-534/Fax: 224-5137
Rep: Allard, *Chair;* Santorum; Dole; Enzi; Bennett; Martinez; Shelby
Dem: Reed, *Rnk. Mem.;* Stabenow; Corzine; Dodd; Carper; Schumer
Maj. Prof. Staff Mem.: Tewana Wilkerson, 224-5941, SD-525
Min. Prof. Staff Mem.: Didem Nisanci, 224-4642, SH-728

International Trade and Finance
224-7391/SD-534/Fax: 224-5137
Rep: Crapo, *Chair;* Hagel; Enzi; Sununu; Dole
Dem: Bayh, *Rnk. Mem.;* Johnson; Corzine
Maj. Staff Dir.: Vacant, 224-6142, SD-239
Min. Prof. Staff Mem.: Catherine Cruz Wojtasik, 224-5623, SR-463

Securities and Investment
224-7391/SD-534/Fax: 224-5137
Rep: Hagel, *Chair;* Enzi; Sununu; Martinez; Bennett; Bunning; Crapo; Dole; Allard; Santorum
Dem: Dodd, *Rnk. Mem.;* Johnson; Reed; Schumer; Bayh; Stabenow; Corzine; Carper
Maj. Staff Dir.: Joe Cwiklinski , 224-4224, SR-248
Min. Staff Dir.: Alex Sternhell, 224-7391, SD-534

BUDGET

Phone: (202) 224-0642—Room: SD-624—Fax: 224-4835
http://budget.senate.gov

Republicans (12)
Judd Gregg, NH, *Chair*
Pete V. Domenici, NM
Charles E. Grassley, IA
Wayne Allard, CO
Michael B. Enzi, WY
Jeff Sessions, AL
Jim Bunning, KY
Mike Crapo, ID
John Ensign, NV
John Cornyn, TX
Lamar Alexander, TN
Lindsey O. Graham, SC

Democrats (10)
Kent Conrad, ND, *Rnk. Mem.*
Paul S. Sarbanes, MD
Patty Murray, WA
Ron Wyden, OR
Russ Feingold, WI
Tim Johnson, SD
Robert C. Byrd, WV
Bill Nelson, FL
Debbie A. Stabenow, MI
Jon S. Corzine, NJ

Maj. Staff Dir.:
Scott Gudes
224-0642, SD-624

Min. Staff Dir.:
Mary Naylor
224-0642, SD-624

NO SUBCOMMITTEES

COMMERCE, SCIENCE AND TRANSPORTATION

Phone: (202) 224-5115—Room: SD-508—Fax: 224-1259
http://commerce.senate.gov

Republicans (12)
Ted Stevens, AK, *Chair**
John McCain, AZ
Conrad Burns, MT
Trent Lott, MS
Kay Bailey Hutchison, TX
Olympia J. Snowe, ME
Gordon Smith, OR
John Ensign, NV
George Allen, VA
John E. Sununu, NH
Jim DeMint, SC
David Vitter, LA

Democrats (10)
Daniel K. Inouye, HI,
  Rnk. Mem.*
John D. Rockefeller IV, WV
John F. Kerry, MA
Byron L. Dorgan, ND
Barbara Boxer, CA
Bill Nelson, FL
Maria Cantwell, WA
Frank R. Lautenberg, NJ
Ben Nelson, NE
Mark Pryor, AR

Maj. Staff Dir.:
Lisa Sutherland
224-1251, SR-255

Min. Staff Dir.:
Margaret Cummisky
224-0411, SD-560

*Ex officio members on all subcommittees.

Commerce, Science and Transportation Subcommittees
Assignments to be announced.

Aviation
224-5115/SD-508/Fax: 224-1259
Rep: Burns, *Chair;* TBA
Dem: Rockefeller, *Rnk. Mem.;* TBA
Maj. Sr. Counsel: Chris Bertrum, 224-5115, SD-508
Min. Sr. Counsel: Sam Whitehorn, 224-9000, SD-516

Consumer Affairs, Product Safety, and Insurance
224-5115/SD-508/Fax: 224-1259
Rep: Allen, *Chair;* TBA
Dem: Pryor, *Rnk. Mem.;* TBA
Maj. Sr. Counsel: Bill Bailey, 224-5184, SH-428
Min. Sr. Counsels: James Assey, Rachel Welch, 224-9340, SD-510

Commerce, Science and Transportation Subcommittees

Disaster Prevention and Prediction
224-5115/SD-508/Fax: 224-1259
Rep: DeMint, *Chair;* TBA
Dem: Nelson (NE), *Rnk. Mem.;* TBA
Maj. Sr. Counsel: Vacant, 224-5115, SD-508
Min. Chief Counsel: Vacant, 224-0411, SD-560

Fisheries and the Coast Guard
224-5115/SD-508/Fax: 224-1259
Rep: Snowe, *Chair;* TBA
Dem: Cantwell, *Rnk. Mem.;* TBA
Maj. Prof. Staff Mem.: Andrew Minkiewicz, 224-8172, SH-227
Min. Sr. Counsel: Margaret Spring, 224-4912, SH-425

Global Climate Change and Impacts
224-5115/SD-508/Fax: 224-1259
Rep: Vitter, *Chair;* TBA
Dem: Lautenberg, *Rnk. Mem.;* TBA
Maj. Prof. Staff Mem.: Vacant, 224-5115, SD-508
Min. Prof. Staff Mem.: Vacant, 224-0411, SD-560

Science and Space
224-5115/SD-508/Fax: 224-1259
Rep: Hutchison, *Chair;* TBA
Dem: Nelson (FL), *Rnk. Mem.;* TBA
Maj. Sr. Staff Mem.: Floyd DesChamps, 224-8172, SH-227
Min. Prof. Staff Mem.: Jean Toal Eisen, 224-0415, SD-566

Surface Transportation and Merchant Marine
224-5115/SD-508/Fax: 224-1259
Rep: Lott, *Chair;* TBA
Dem: Inouye, *Rnk. Mem.;* TBA
Maj. Prof. Staff Mem.: Chris Bertrum, 224-5115, SD-508
Min. Chief Counsel: David Strickland, 224-0411, SD-560

Technology, Innovation, and Competitiveness
224-5115/SD-508/Fax: 224-1259
Rep: Ensign, *Chair;* TBA
Dem: Kerry, *Rnk. Mem.;* TBA
Maj. Prof. Staff Mem.: Vacant, 224-5115, SD-508
Min. Prof. Staff Mem.: Vacant, 224-0411, SD-560

Trade, Tourism, and Economic Development
224-5115/SD-508/Fax: 224-1259
Rep: Smith, *Chair;* TBA
Dem: Dorgan, *Rnk. Mem.;* TBA
Maj. Prof. Staff Mem.: Vacant, 224-5115, SD-508
Min. Prof. Staff Mem.: Vacant, 224-0411, SD-560

ENERGY AND NATURAL RESOURCES

Phone: (202) 224-4971—Room: SD-364—Fax: 224-6163
http://energy.senate.gov

Republicans (12)
Pete V. Domenici, NM, ***Chair****
Larry E. Craig, ID
Craig Thomas, WY
Lamar Alexander, TN
Lisa Murkowski, AK
Richard Burr, NC
Mel Martinez, FL
Jim Talent, MO
Conrad Burns, MT
George Allen, VA
Gordon Smith, OR
Jim Bunning, KY

Democrats (10)
Jeff Bingaman, NM, ***Rnk. Mem.****
Daniel K. Akaka, HI
Byron L. Dorgan, ND
Ron Wyden, OR
Tim Johnson, SD
Mary Landrieu, LA
Dianne Feinstein, CA
Maria Cantwell, WA
Jon S. Corzine, NJ
Ken Salazar, CO

Maj. Staff Dir.:
Alex Flint
224-4971, SD-364

Min. Staff Dir.:
Bob Simon
224-4103, SD-312

*Ex officio members on all subcommittees.

Energy and Natural Resources Subcommittees

Energy
224-4971/SD-364/Fax: 224-6163
Rep: Alexander, *Chair;* Burr, *Vice Chair;* Martinez; Talent; Allen; Bunning; Murkowski; Craig; Thomas; Burns
Dem: Dorgan, *Rnk. Mem.;* Akaka; Johnson; Landrieu; Feinstein; Cantwell; Corzine; Salazar
Maj. Staff Dir.: Alex Flint, 224-4971, SD-364
Min. Staff Dir.: Bob Simon, 224-4103, SD-312

National Parks
224-4971/SD-364/Fax: 224-6163
Rep: Thomas, *Chair;* Alexander, *Vice Chair;* Allen; Burr; Martinez; Smith
Dem: Akaka, *Rnk. Mem.;* Wyden; Landrieu; Corzine; Salazar
Maj. Staff Dir.: Alex Flint, 224-4971, SD-364
Min. Staff Dir.: Bob Simon, 224-4103, SD-312

Public Lands and Forests
224-4971/SD-364/Fax: 224-6163
Rep: Craig, *Chair;* Burns, *Vice Chair;* Thomas; Talent; Smith; Alexander; Murkowski; Allen
Dem: Wyden, *Rnk. Mem.;* Akaka; Dorgan; Johnson; Landrieu; Feinstein; Cantwell
Maj. Staff Dir.: Alex Flint, 224-4971, SD-364
Min. Staff Dir.: Bob Simon, 224-4103, SD-312

Water and Power
224-4971/SD-364/Fax: 224-6163
Rep: Murkowski, *Chair;* Smith, *Vice Chair;* Craig; Burr; Martinez; Burns; Bunning; Talent
Dem: Johnson, *Rnk. Mem.;* Dorgan; Wyden; Feinstein; Cantwell; Corzine; Salazar
Maj. Staff Dir.: Alex Flint, 224-4971, SD-364
Min. Staff Dir.: Bob Simon, 224-4103, SD-312

ENVIRONMENT AND PUBLIC WORKS

Phone: (202) 224-6176—Room: SD-410—Fax: 224-5167
http://epw.senate.gov

Republicans (10)
James M. Inhofe, OK, **Chair***
John W. Warner, VA
Christopher S. Bond, MO
George V. Voinovich, OH
Lincoln D. Chafee, RI
Lisa Murkowski, AK
John R. Thune, SD
Jim DeMint, SC
Johnny Isakson, GA
David Vitter, LA

**Maj. Staff Dir. &
Chief Counsel:**
Andrew Wheeler
224-6176, SD-410

Democrats (7)
Max Baucus, MT
Joseph I. Lieberman, CT
Barbara Boxer, CA
Thomas R. Carper, DE
Hillary Rodham Clinton, NY
Frank R. Lautenberg, NJ
Barack Obama, IL

Independent (1)
James M. Jeffords, VT,
Rnk. Mem.*

Min. Staff Dir.:
Ken Connolly
224-8832, SD-456

*Ex officio members on all subcommittees.

Environment and Public Works Subcommittees

Clean Air, Climate Change and Nuclear Safety
224-6176/SD-410/Fax: 224-5167
Rep: Voinovich, *Chair;* Bond; DeMint; Isakson; Vitter
Dem: Carper, *Rnk. Mem.;* Lieberman; Lautenberg; Obama
Maj. Staff Dir.: Brian Mormino, 224-6176, SD-415
Min. Prof. Staff Mem.: Chris Miller, 224-8832, SD-456

Environment and Public Works Subcommittees

Fisheries, Wildlife and Water
224-6176/SD-410/Fax: 224-5167
Rep: Chafee, *Chair;* Warner; Murkowski; DeMint; Vitter
Dem: Clinton, *Rnk. Mem.;* Lieberman; Lautenberg; Obama
Maj. Staff Dir.: Christy Plummer, 224-6228, SD-415
Min. Prof. Staff Mem.: Jo-Ellen Darcy, 224-8832, SD-456

Superfund and Waste Management
224-6176/SD-410/Fax: 224-5167
Rep: Thune, *Chair;* Isakson; Warner; Bond
Dem: Boxer, *Rnk. Mem.;* Baucus; Lautenberg
Maj. Staff Dir.: David Schweitert, 224-6176, SD-415
Min. Prof. Staff Mem.: Malcolm Woolf, 224-8832, SD-456

Transportation and Infrastructure
224-6176/SD-410/Fax: 224-5167
Rep: Bond, *Chair;* Warner; Voinovich; Chafee; Murkowski; Thune
Dem: Baucus, *Rnk. Mem.;* Lieberman; Boxer; Carper; Clinton
Maj. Staff Dir.: Ellen Stein, 224-6176, SD-415
Min. Prof. Staff Mem.: Kathy Ruffalo, 224-8832, SD-456

FINANCE

Phone: (202) 224-4515—Room: SD-219—Fax: 228-0554
http://finance.senate.gov

Republicans (11)
Charles E. Grassley, IA, ***Chair*****
Orrin G. Hatch, UT
Trent Lott, MS
Olympia J. Snowe, ME
Jon L. Kyl, AZ
Craig Thomas, WY
Rick Santorum, PA
Bill Frist, TN
Gordon Smith, OR
Jim Bunning, KY
Mike Crapo, ID

Democrats (8)
Max Baucus, MT, ***Rnk. Mem.****
John D. Rockefeller IV, WV
Kent Conrad, ND
Jeff Bingaman, NM
John F. Kerry, MA
Blanche L. Lincoln, AR
Ron Wyden, OR
Charles E. Schumer, NY

Independent (1)
James M. Jeffords, VT

Maj. Staff Dir.:
Kolan Davis
224-4515, SD-219

Min. Staff Dir.:
Russ Sullivan
224-5315, SD-219

*Ex officio members on all subcommittees of which they are not regular members.

Finance Subcommittees

Health Care
224-4515/SD-219/Fax: 228-0554
Rep: Hatch, *Chair;* Snowe; Frist; Kyl; Thomas; Santorum; Bunning
Dem: Rockefeller, *Rnk. Mem.;* Bingaman; Kerry; Wyden
Ind: Jeffords
Maj. Staff Dir.: Kolan Davis, 224-4515, SD-219
Min. Staff Dir.: Russ Sullivan, 224-5315, SD-219

International Trade
224-4515/SD-219/Fax: 228-0554
Rep: Thomas, *Chair;* Crapo; Lott; Smith; Bunning; Hatch; Snowe; Frist
Dem: Bingaman, *Rnk. Mem.;* Baucus; Rockefeller; Conrad; Wyden; Schumer
Maj. Staff Dir.: Kolan Davis, 224-4515, SD-219
Min. Staff Dir.: Russ Sullivan, 224-5315, SD-219

Long-Term Growth and Debt Reduction
224-4515/SD-219/Fax: 228-0554
Rep: Smith, *Chair;* Grassley
Dem: Kerry, *Rnk. Mem.*
Maj. Staff Dir.: Kolan Davis, 224-4515, SD-219
Min. Staff Dir.: Russ Sullivan, 224-5315, SD-219

Finance Subcommittees

Social Security and Family Policy
224-4515/SD-219/Fax: 228-0554

Rep: Santorum, *Chair;* Grassley; Bunning; Frist; Lott; Kyl; Smith; Crapo
Dem: Conrad, *Rnk. Mem.;* Rockefeller; Bingaman; Kerry; Lincoln
Ind: Jeffords
Maj. Staff Dir.: Kolan Davis, 224-4515, SD-219
Min. Staff Dir.: Russ Sullivan, 224-5315, SD-219

Taxation and IRS Oversight
224-4515/SD-219/Fax: 228-0554

Rep: Kyl, *Chair;* Lott; Hatch; Snowe; Crapo; Thomas; Santorum
Dem: Baucus; Conrad; Lincoln; Schumer
Ind: Jeffords, *Rnk. Mem.*
Maj. Staff Dir.: Kolan Davis, 224-4515, SD-219
Min. Staff Dir.: Russ Sullivan, 224-5315, SD-219

FOREIGN RELATIONS

Phone: (202) 224-4651—Room: SD-446—Fax: 224-0836
http://foreign.senate.gov

Republicans (10)
Richard G. Lugar, IN, *Chair**
Chuck Hagel, NE
Lincoln D. Chafee, RI
George Allen, VA
Norm Coleman, MN
George V. Voinovich, OH
Lamar Alexander, TN
John E. Sununu, NH
Lisa Murkowski, AK
Mel Martinez, FL

Democrats (8)
Joseph R. Biden, Jr., DE, *Rnk. Mem.**
Paul S. Sarbanes, MD
Christopher J. Dodd, CT
John F. Kerry, MA
Russ Feingold, WI
Barbara Boxer, CA
Bill Nelson, FL
Barack Obama, IL

Maj. Staff Dir.:
Ken Myers
224-4651, SD-450

Min. Staff Dir.:
Antony Blinken
224-3953, SD-439

*Ex officio members on all subcommittees of which they are not regular members.

Foreign Relations Subcommittees

African Affairs
224-4651/SD-450/Fax: 228-1608

Rep: Martinez, *Chair;* Alexander; Coleman; Sununu; Murkowski
Dem: Feingold, *Rnk. Mem.;* Sarbanes; Dodd; Obama
Maj. Prof. Staff Mem.: Carl Meacham, 224-4651, SD-450
Min. Prof. Staff Mem.: Heather Flynn, 224-3953, SD-439

East Asian and Pacific Affairs
224-4651/SD-450/Fax: 228-1608

Rep: Murkowski, *Chair;* Alexander; Hagel; Chafee; Allen
Dem: Kerry, *Rnk. Mem.;* Biden; Feingold; Obama
Maj. Prof. Staff Mem.: Keith Luse, 224-4651, SD-450
Min. Prof. Staff Mem.: Frank Jannuzi, 224-3953, SD-439

European Affairs
224-4651/SD-450/Fax: 228-1608

Rep: Allen, *Chair;* Voinovich; Murkowski; Hagel; Chafee
Dem: Biden, *Rnk. Mem.;* Sarbanes; Dodd; Feingold
Maj. Prof. Staff Mem.: Ken Myers, 224-4651, SD-450
Min. Prof. Staff Mem.: Mike Haltzel, 224-3953, SD-439

International Economic Policy, Export and Trade Promotion
224-4651/SD-450/Fax: 228-1608

Rep: Hagel, *Chair;* Alexander; Murkowski; Martinez; Voinovich
Dem: Sarbanes, *Rnk. Mem.;* Dodd; Kerry; Obama
Maj. Prof. Staff Mem.: Keith Luse, 224-4651, SD-450
Min. Prof. Staff Mem.: Diana Ohlbaum, 224-3953, SD-439

Foreign Relations Subcommittees

International Operations and Terrorism
224-4651/SD-450/Fax: 228-1608
Rep: Sununu, *Chair;* Voinovich; Allen; Coleman; Alexander
Dem: Nelson, *Rnk. Mem.;* Biden; Kerry; Boxer
Maj. Prof. Staff Mem.: Patrick Garvey, 224-4651, SD-450
Min. Prof. Staff Mem.: Caroline Tess, 224-3953, SD-439

Near Eastern and South Asian Affairs
224-4651/SD-450/Fax: 228-1608
Rep: Chafee, *Chair;* Hagel; Coleman; Voinovich; Sununu
Dem: Boxer, *Rnk. Mem.;* Sarbanes; Nelson; Obama
Maj. Prof. Staff Mem.: Ken Myers, 224-4651, SD-450
Min. Prof. Staff Mem.: Puneet Talwar, 224-3953, SD-439

Western Hemisphere, Peace Corps and Narcotics Affairs
224-4651/SD-450/Fax: 228-1608
Rep: Coleman, *Chair;* Chafee; Allen; Martinez; Sununu
Dem: Dodd, *Rnk. Mem.;* Kerry; Boxer; Nelson
Maj. Prof. Staff Mem.: Carl Meacham, 224-4651, SD-450
Min. Prof. Staff Mem.: Janice O'Connell, 224-3953, SD-439

HEALTH, EDUCATION, LABOR AND PENSIONS

Phone: (202) 224-5375—Room: SD-428—Fax: 224-6510
http://labor.senate.gov

Republicans (11)
Michael B. Enzi, WY, *Chair**
Judd Gregg, NH
Bill Frist, TN
Lamar Alexander, TN
Richard Burr, NC
Johnny Isakson, GA
Mike DeWine, OH
John Ensign, NV
Orrin G. Hatch, UT
Jeff Sessions, AL
Pat Roberts, KS

Democrats (8)
Edward M. Kennedy, MA, *Rnk. Mem.**
Christopher J. Dodd, CT
Tom Harkin, IA
Barbara A. Mikulski, MD
Jeff Bingaman, NM
Patty Murray, WA
Jack Reed, RI
Hillary Rodham Clinton, NY

Independent (1)
James M. Jeffords, VT

Maj. Staff Dir.:
Katherine McGuire
224-6770, SH-835

Min. Staff Dir. & Chief Counsel:
Michael Myers
224-0767, SD-644

*Ex officio members on all subcommittees of which they are not regular members.

Health, Education, Labor and Pensions Subcommittees

Bioterrorism and Public Health Preparedness
224-5375/SD-428/Fax: 225-6510
Rep: Burr, *Chair;* Gregg; Frist; Alexander; DeWine; Ensign; Hatch; Roberts
Dem: Kennedy, *Rnk. Mem.;* Dodd; Harkin; Mikulski; Bingaman; Murray; Reed
Maj. Staff Dir.: Steve Northrup, 224-5375, SH-725
Min. Staff Dir.: David Bowen, 224-9243, SH-113

Education and Early Childhood Development
228-4312/SH-833
Rep: Alexander, *Chair;* Gregg; Burr; Isakson; DeWine; Ensign; Hatch; Sessions
Dem: Dodd, *Rnk. Mem.;* Harkin; Bingaman; Murray; Reed; Clinton
Ind: Jeffords
Maj. Staff Dir.: Beth Buhlman, 228-4312, SH-833
Min. Staff Dir.: Roberto Rodriguez, 224-5630, SH-404

Health, Education, Labor and Pensions Subcommittees

Employment and Workplace Safety
224-2315/SH-608/Fax: 224-3533
Rep: Isakson, *Chair;* Alexander; Burr; Ensign; Sessions; Roberts
Dem: Murray, *Rnk. Mem.;* Dodd; Harkin; Mikulski
Ind: Jeffords
Maj. Staff Dir.: Glee Smith, 224-2315, SH-608
Min. Staff Dir.: David Bowen, 224-7675, SH-527

Retirement Security and Aging
224-7229/SH-615/Fax: 228-0934
Rep: DeWine, *Chair;* Isakson; Hatch; Sessions; Roberts
Dem: Mikulski, *Rnk. Mem.;* Bingaman; Clinton
Ind: Jeffords
Maj. Staff Dir.: Lauren Fuller, 224-7229, SH-615
Min. Staff Dir.: Ellen-Marie Whelan, 224-9243, SH-113

HOMELAND SECURITY AND GOVERNMENTAL AFFAIRS

Phone: (202) 224-4751—Room: SD-340—Fax: 224-9603
http://hsgac.senate.gov

Republicans (9)
Susan M. Collins, ME, *Chair**
Ted Stevens, AK
George V. Voinovich, OH
Norm Coleman, MN
Tom Coburn, OK
Lincoln D. Chafee, RI
Robert Bennett, UT
Pete V. Domenici, NM
John W. Warner, VA

Democrats (7)
Joseph I. Lieberman, CT,
Rnk. Mem.*
Carl Levin, MI
Daniel K. Akaka, HI
Thomas R. Carper, DE
Mark Dayton, MN
Frank R. Lautenberg, NJ
Mark Pryor, AR

Maj. Staff Dir.:
Michael Bopp
224-4751, SD-340

Min. Staff Dir. & Counsel:
Joyce Rechtschaffen
224-2627, SH-604

*Ex officio members on all subcommittees.

Homeland Security and Governmental Affairs Subcommittees

Federal Financial Management, Government Information and International Security
224-2254/SH-446/Fax: 228-3796
Rep: Coburn, *Chair;* Stevens; Voinovich; Chafee; Bennett; Domenici; Warner
Dem: Carper, *Rnk. Mem.;* Levin; Akaka; Dayton; Lautenberg
Maj. Staff Dir.: Chris Gacek, 224-2254, SH-446
Min. Staff Dir.: Sheila Murphy, 224-7155, SD-326

Oversight of Government Management, the Federal Workforce and the District of Columbia
224-3682/SH-442/Fax: 228-0454
Rep: Voinovich, *Chair;* Stevens; Coleman; Coburn; Chafee; Bennett; Domenici; Warner
Dem: Akaka, *Rnk. Mem.;* Levin; Carper; Dayton; Lautenberg; Pryor
Maj. Staff Dir.: Andrew Richardson, 224-3682, SH-442
Min. Staff Dir.: Richard Kessler, 224-5538, SD-326

Permanent Subcommittee on Investigations
224-3721/SR-199/Fax: 224-1972
Rep: Coleman, *Chair;* Stevens; Coburn; Chafee; Bennett; Domenici; Warner
Dem: Levin, *Rnk. Mem.;* Akaka; Carper; Dayton; Lautenberg; Pryor
Maj. Staff Dir.: Raymond V. Shepard, 224-3721, SR-199
Min. Staff Dir.: Elise J. Bean, 224-9505, SR-199

JUDICIARY

Phone: (202) 224-5225—Room: SD-224—Fax: 224-9102
http://judiciary.senate.gov

Republicans (10)
Arlen Specter, PA, *Chair**
Orrin G. Hatch, UT
Charles E. Grassley, IA
Jon L. Kyl, AZ
Mike DeWine, OH
Jeff Sessions, AL
Lindsey O. Graham, SC
John Cornyn, TX
Sam Brownback, KS
Tom Coburn, OK

Democrats (8)
Patrick J. Leahy, VT, *Rnk. Mem.**
Edward M. Kennedy, MA
Joseph R. Biden, Jr., DE
Herbert H. Kohl, WI
Dianne Feinstein, CA
Russ Feingold, WI
Charles E. Schumer, NY
Richard J. Durbin, IL

Maj. Staff Dir. & Chief Counsel:
David Brog
224-5225, SD-224

Min. Staff Dir. & Chief Counsel:
Bruce Cohen
224-7703, SD-152

*Ex officio members on all subcommittees of which they are not regular members.

Judiciary Subcommittees

Administrative Oversight and the Courts
224-7572/SD-G66/Fax: 228-0545
Rep: Sessions, *Chair;* Specter; Grassley; Kyl
Dem: Schumer, *Rnk. Mem.;* Feinstein; Feingold
Maj. Chief Counsel: William Smith, 224-7572, SD-G66
Min. Chief Counsel: Preet Bharara, 224-6542, SH-313

Antitrust, Competition Policy and Consumer Rights
224-9494/SD-161/Fax: 228-0463
Rep: DeWine, *Chair;* Specter; Hatch; Grassley; Graham; Brownback
Dem: Kohl, *Rnk. Mem.;* Leahy; Biden; Feingold; Schumer
Maj. Chief Counsel: Pete Levitas, 224-9494, SD-161
Min. Chief Counsel: Jeffrey Miller, 224-3406, SH-308

Constitution, Civil Rights and Property Rights
224-5225/SD-224/Fax: 224-9102
Rep: Brownback, *Chair;* Specter; Graham; Cornyn; Coburn
Dem: Feingold, *Rnk. Mem.;* Kennedy; Feinstein; Durbin
Maj. Chief Counsel: Vacant, 224-5225, SD-224
Min. Chief Counsel: Bob Schiff, 224-5573, SH-807

Corrections and Rehabilitation
224-5225/SD-224/Fax: 224-9102
Rep: Coburn, *Chair;* Specter; Sessions; Cornyn; Brownback
Dem: Durbin, *Rnk Mem.;* Leahy; Biden; Feingold
Maj. Chief Counsel: Vacant, 224-5225, SD-224
Min. Chief Counsel: Vacant, 224-5225, SD-224

Crime and Drugs
224-5972/SR-290/Fax: 224-3808
Rep: Graham, *Chair;* Grassley; Kyl; DeWine; Sessions; Coburn
Dem: Biden, *Rnk Mem.;* Kohl; Feinstein; Feingold; Schumer
Maj. Chief Counsel: James Galyean, 224-5972, SR-290
Min. Chief Counsel: Neil MacBride, 224-0558, SH-305

Immigration, Border Security and Citizenship
224-7840/SD-139/Fax: 224-9102
Rep: Cornyn, *Chair;* Grassley; Kyl; DeWine; Sessions; Brownback; Coburn
Dem: Kennedy, *Rnk Mem.;* Biden; Feinstein; Feingold; Schumer; Durbin
Maj. Chief Counsel: James Ho, 224-7840, SD-139
Min. Chief Counsel: James Flug, 224-7878, SD-520

Judiciary Subcommittees

Intellectual Property
224-5225/SD-224/Fax: 224-9102

Rep: Hatch, *Chair;* Kyl; DeWine; Graham; Cornyn; Brownback; Coburn
Dem: Leahy, *Rnk Mem.;* Kennedy; Biden; Feinstein; Kohl; Durbin
Maj. Chief Counsel: Vacant, 224-5225, SD-224
Min. Chief Counsel: Vacant, 224-5225, SD-224

Terrorism, Technology and Homeland Security
224-6791/SH-325/Fax: 228-0542

Rep: Kyl, *Chair;* Hatch; Grassley; Cornyn; DeWine; Sessions; Graham
Dem: Feinstein; *Rnk. Mem.;* Kennedy; Biden; Kohl; Feingold; Durbin
Maj. Chief Counsel: Stephen Higgins, 224-6791, SH-325
Min. Chief Counsel: Steve Cash, 224-4933, SH-815

RULES AND ADMINISTRATION

· Phone: (202) 224-6352—Room: SR-305—Fax: 228-2401
http://rules.senate.gov

Republicans (10)
Trent Lott, MS, **Chair**
Ted Stevens, AK
Mitch McConnell, KY
Thad Cochran, MS
Rick Santorum, PA
Kay Bailey Hutchison, TX
Bill Frist, TN
Saxby Chambliss, GA
Robert Bennett, UT
Chuck Hagel, NE

Democrats (8)
Christopher J. Dodd, CT, **Rnk. Mem.**
Robert C. Byrd, WV
Daniel K. Inouye, HI
Dianne Feinstein, CA
Charles E. Schumer, NY
Mark Dayton, MN
Richard J. Durbin, IL
Ben Nelson, NE

Maj. Staff Dir.:
Susan Wells
224-6352, SR-305

Min. Staff Dir.:
Kennie Gill
224-6351, SR-479

NO SUBCOMMITTEES

SMALL BUSINESS AND ENTREPRENEURSHIP

Phone: (202) 224-5175—Room: SR-428A—Fax: 224-4885
http://sbc.senate.gov

Republicans (10)
Olympia J. Snowe, ME, **Chair**
Christopher S. Bond, MO
Conrad Burns, MT
George Allen, VA
Norm Coleman, MN
John R. Thune, SD
Johnny Isakson, GA
David Vitter, LA
Michael B. Enzi, WY
John Cornyn, TX

Democrats (8)
John F. Kerry, MA, **Rnk. Mem.**
Carl Levin, MI
Tom Harkin, IA
Joseph I. Lieberman, CT
Mary Landrieu, LA
Maria Cantwell, WA
Evan Bayh, IN
Mark Pryor, AR

Maj. Staff Dir. & Chief Counsel:
Wes Coulam
224-5175, SR-428A

Min. Staff Dir. & Chief Counsel:
Kevin Wheeler
224-5175, SR-428A

NO SUBCOMMITTEES

VETERANS' AFFAIRS

Phone: (202) 224-9126—Room: SR-412—Fax: 224-8908
http://veterans.senate.gov

Republicans (8)
Larry E. Craig, ID, *Chair*
Arlen Specter, PA
Kay Bailey Hutchison, TX
Lindsey O. Graham, SC
Richard Burr, NC
John Ensign, NV
John R. Thune, SD
Johnny Isakson, GA

**Maj. Staff Dir. &
Chief Counsel:**
Lupe Wissel
224-9126, SR-412

Democrats (5)
Daniel K. Akaka, HI, *Rnk. Mem.*
John D. Rockefeller IV, WV
Patty Murray, WA
Barack Obama, IL
Ken Salazar, CO

Independent (1)
James M. Jeffords, VT

Min. Staff Dir.:
Davelyn Kalipi
224-2074, SH-116

NO SUBCOMMITTEES

INDIAN AFFAIRS

Phone: (202) 224-2251—Room: SH-836—Fax: 228-2589
http://indian.senate.gov

Republicans (8)
John McCain, AZ, *Chair*
Craig Thomas, WY
Lisa Murkowski, AK
Tom Coburn, OK
Pete V. Domenici, NM
Gordon Smith, OR
Mike Crapo, ID
Richard Burr, NC

Maj. Staff Dir.:
Jeanne Bumpus
224-2251, SH-836

Democrats (6)
Byron L. Dorgan, ND, *Vice Chair*
Daniel K. Inouye, HI
Kent Conrad, ND
Daniel K. Akaka, HI
Tim Johnson, SD
Maria Cantwell, WA

Min. Staff Dir.:
Sara Garland
224-2251, SH-836

NO SUBCOMMITTEES

SELECT COMMITTEE ON ETHICS

Phone: (202) 224-2981—Room: SH-220—Fax: 224-7416
http://ethics.senate.gov

Republicans (3)
George V. Voinovich, OH,
 Chair
Pat Roberts, KS
Craig Thomas, WY

Staff Dir. & Chief Counsel
Robert Walker
224-2981, SH-220

Democrats (3)
Tim Johnson, SD, *Vice Chair*
Daniel K. Akaka, HI
Mark Pryor, AR

NO SUBCOMMITTEES

SELECT COMMITTEE ON INTELLIGENCE

Phone: (202) 224-1700—Room: SH-211—Fax: 224-1772
http://intelligence.senate.gov

Republicans (9)
Pat Roberts, KS, *Chair*
Orrin G. Hatch, UT
Mike DeWine, OH
Christopher S. Bond, MO
Trent Lott, MS
Olympia J. Snowe, ME
Chuck Hagel, NE
Saxby Chambliss, GA
John W. Warner, VA, Ex Officio

Democrats (7)
John D. Rockefeller IV, WV, *Vice Chair*
Carl Levin, MI
Dianne Feinstein, CA
Ron Wyden, OR
Evan Bayh, IN
Barbara A. Mikulski, MD
Jon S. Corzine, NJ

Maj. Staff Dir.:
William Duhnke
224-1700, SH-211

Min. Staff Dir.:
Andrew Johnson
224-1700, SH-211

Bill Frist (R-TN) and Harry Reid (D-NV) serve as ex officio members.

NO SUBCOMMITTEES

SPECIAL COMMITTEE ON AGING

Phone: (202) 224-5364—Room: SD-G31—Fax: 224-8660
http://aging.senate.gov

Republicans (11)
Gordon Smith, OR, *Chair*
Richard C. Shelby, AL
Susan M. Collins, ME
Jim Talent, MO
Elizabeth Dole, NC
Mel Martinez, FL
Larry E. Craig, ID
Rick Santorum, PA
Conrad Burns, MT
Lamar Alexander, TN
Jim DeMint, SC

Democrats (8)
Herbert H. Kohl, WI, *Rnk. Mem.*
Russ Feingold, WI
Ron Wyden, OR
Blanche L. Lincoln, AR
Evan Bayh, IN
Thomas R. Carper, DE
Bill Nelson, FL
Hillary Rodham Clinton, NY

Independent (1)
James M. Jeffords, VT

Maj. Staff Dir.:
Catherine Finley
224-5364, SD-G31

Min. Staff Dir.:
Julie Cohen
224-5364, SD-G31

NO SUBCOMMITTEES

House of Representatives Party Breakdown

Alabama	5 Rep./2 Dem.
Alaska	1 Rep.
Arizona	6 Rep./2 Dem.
Arkansas	1 Rep./3 Dem.
California	20 Rep./33 Dem
Colorado	4 Rep./3 Dem.
Connecticut	3 Rep./2 Dem.
Delaware	1 Rep.
Florida	18 Rep./7 Dem.
Georgia	7 Rep./6 Dem.
Hawaii	2 Dem.
Idaho	2 Rep.
Illinois	9 Rep./10 Dem.
Indiana	7 Rep./2 Dem.
Iowa	4 Rep./1 Dem.
Kansas	3 Rep./1 Dem.
Kentucky	5 Rep./1 Dem.
Louisiana	5 Rep./2 Dem.
Maine	2 Dem.
Maryland	2 Rep./6 Dem.
Massachusetts	10 Dem.
Michigan	9 Rep./6 Dem.
Minnesota	4 Rep./4 Dem.
Mississippi	2 Rep./2 Dem.
Missouri	5 Rep./4 Dem.
Montana	1 Rep.
Nebraska	3 Rep.
Nevada	2 Rep./1 Dem.
New Hampshire	2 Rep.
New Jersey	6 Rep./7 Dem.
New Mexico	2 Rep./1 Dem.
New York	9 Rep./20 Dem.
North Carolina	7 Rep./6 Dem.
North Dakota	1 Dem.
Ohio	12 Rep./6 Dem.
Oklahoma	4 Rep./1 Dem.
Oregon	1 Rep./4 Dem.
Pennsylvania	12 Rep./7 Dem.
Rhode Island	2 Dem.
South Carolina	4 Rep./2 Dem.
South Dakota	1 Dem.
Tennessee	4 Rep./5 Dem.
Texas	21 Rep./11 Dem.
Utah	2 Rep./1 Dem.
Vermont	1 Ind
Virginia	8 Rep./3 Dem.
Washington	3 Rep./6 Dem.
West Virginia	1 Rep./2 Dem.
Wisconsin	4 Rep./4 Dem.
Wyoming	1 Rep.

House of Representatives Leadership and Officers

Area code for all numbers is 202

Speaker .... **J. Dennis Hastert (R-14th IL)**
Chief of Staff   Scott Palmer
Office: H-232   Phone: 225-0600

Majority Leader .... **Tom DeLay (R-22nd TX)**
Chief of Staff   Tim Berry
Office: H-107   Phone: 225-4000

Majority Whip .... **Roy Blunt (R-7th MO)**
Chief of Staff   Brian Gaston
Office: H-329   Phone: 225-0197

Republican Conference Chair .... **Deborah Pryce (R-15th OH)**
Chief of Staff   Kathryn Lehman
Office: 202A CHOB   Phone: 225-5107

Republican Policy Chair .... **John B. Shadegg (R-3rd AZ)**
Exec. Director   Elise Finley
Office: 2471 RHOB   Phone: 225-6168

Minority Leader .... **Nancy Pelosi (D-8th CA)**
Chief of Staff   George Crawford
Office: H-204   Phone: 225-0100

Minority Whip .... **Steny Hoyer (D-5th MD)**
Chief of Staff   Cory Alexander
Office: H-306   Phone: 225-3130

Democratic Caucus Chair .... **Robert Menendez (D-13th NJ)**
Exec. Director   Andrew Kauders
Office: 1420 LHOB   Phone: 226-3210

Assistant Minority Leader .... **John Spratt (D-5th SC)**
Chief of Staff   Ellen Buchanan
Office: 1401 LHOB   Phone: 225-5501

Clerk of the House .... **Jeff Trandahl**
Office: H-154   Phone: 225-7000

Chief Administrative Officer .... **James M. Eagen III**
Office: HB-30   Phone: 225-6900

Sergeant at Arms .... **Wilson Livingood**
Office: H-124   Phone: 225-2456

Parliamentarian .... **John V. Sullivan**
Office: H-209   Phone: 225-7373

Inspector General .... **Steven A. McNamara**
Office: 385 FHOB   Phone: 226-1250

Chaplain .... **Father Daniel Coughlin**
Office: HB-25   Phone: 225-2509

REPRESENTATIVES

Neil Abercrombie (D-1st/HI)   202-225-2726
1502 LHOB   9th Term/61%   Fax: 202-225-4580
E-mail: neil.abercrombie@mail.house.gov
Website: www.house.gov/abercrombie
CoS .... *Amy Asselbaye* **LD** .... *Tom Wanley*
Appt .... *Laura Flores* **Press** .... *Michael Slackman*
Bio: b. 6/26/38 Buffalo, NY; Not Stated; PhD Univ. of HI, 1974; Consultant, Lecturer; m. Nancie Caraway
Comm.: Armed Services; Resources
Dist. Office: Honolulu, 808-541-2570

Gary L. Ackerman (D-5th/NY)   202-225-2601
2243 RHOB   12th Term/71%   Fax: 202-225-1589
Website: www.house.gov/ackerman
CoS .... *Jedd Moskowitz* **LD** .... *Howard Diamond*
Appt .... *Lisa Baranello* **Press** .... *Jordan Goldes*
Bio: b. 11/19/42 Brooklyn, NY; Jewish; BA Queens Col., 1965; Educator, Newspaper Publisher; m. Rita
Comm.: Financial Services; International Relations
Dist. Office: Bayside, 718-423-2154

Robert B. Aderholt (R-4th/AL)   202-225-4876
1433 LHOB   5th Term/75%   Fax: 202-225-5587
Website: aderholt.house.gov
CoS .... *Hood Harris* **LD** .... *Mark Dawson*
Sch .... *Tiffany Noel* **CD** .... *Wade Newton*
Bio: b. 7/22/65 Haleyville, AL; Congregationalist; JD Samford Univ., 1990; Municipal Court Judge; m. Caroline
Comm.: Appropriations
Dist. Offices: Jasper, 205-221-2310; Cullman, 256-734-6043; Gadsden, 256-546-0201; Decatur, 256-350-4093

Todd Akin (R-2nd/MO)   202-225-2561
117 CHOB   3rd Term/65%   Fax: 202-225-2563
Website: www.house.gov/akin
CoS ..... *Rob Schwarzwalder* **LD** .... *Vacant*
Appt .... *Tressa Merola* **Press** .... *Steve Taylor*
Bio: b. 7/5/47 New York, NY; Christian; MDiv Covenant Seminary, 1985; USA, 1972-80; Engineer, Businessman; m. Lulli
Comm.: Armed Services; Science; Small Business
Dist. Offices: St. Louis, 314-590-0029; St. Charles, 636-949-6826

Rodney Alexander (R-5th/LA)   202-225-8490
316 CHOB   2nd Term/59%   Fax: 202-225-5639
Website: www.house.gov/alexander
CoS .... *Royal Alexander* **LD** .... *None*
Sch .... *Jonathan Johnson* **Press** .... *Adam Terry*
Bio: b. 12/5/46 Bienville, LA; Baptist; Attended LA Tech Univ.; Insurance Agent; m. Nancy
Comm.: Appropriations
Dist. Offices: Alexandria, 318-445-0818; Monroe, 318-322-3500

Thomas H. Allen (D-1st/ME)   202-225-6116
1127 LHOB   5th Term/60%   Fax: 202-225-5590
E-mail: rep.tomallen@mail.house.gov
Website: tomallen.house.gov
CoS .... *Peter Wiley* **LD** .... *Todd Stein*
Sch .... *Jolene Chonko* **Press** .... *Mark Sullivan*
Bio: b. 4/16/45 Portland, ME; Protestant; JD Harvard Univ., 1974; Policy Consultant; m. Diana
Comm.: Budget; Energy & Commerce
Dist. Offices: Portland, 207-774-5019; Saco, 207-283-8054

REPRESENTATIVES

Robert E. Andrews (D-1st/NJ)   202-225-6501
2439 RHOB   8th Term/75%   Fax: 202-225-6583
Website: www.house.gov/andrews
CoS .... None   LD .... Robert Knotts
Sch .... Helene Brooks   **Press** .... Bill Caruso
Bio: b. 8/4/57 Camden, NJ; Episcopal; JD Cornell Univ., 1982; Professor; m. Camille
Comm.: Armed Services; Education & the Workforce
Dist. Offices: Haddon Heights, 856-546-5100; Woodbury, 856-546-5100

Joe Baca (D-43rd/CA)   202-225-6161
328 CHOB   4th Term/66%   Fax: 202-225-8671
Website: www.house.gov/baca
CoS .... Linda Macias   LD .... Ben Firschein
Appt .... Erica Woodward   **Press** .... Joanne Peters
Bio: b. 1/23/47 Belen, NM; Catholic; BA CA St. Univ. - Los Angeles, 1971; USA, 1966-68; Travel Agency Owner; m. Barbara
Comm.: Agriculture; Financial Services
Dist. Office: San Bernardino, 909-885-2222

Spencer Bachus (R-6th/AL)   202-225-4921
442 CHOB   7th Term/Unc.   Fax: 202-225-2082
Website: bachus.house.gov
CoS .... Larry Lavender   LD .... Jason Reese
Sch .... Lucy King   **Press** .... Jason Goggins
Bio: b. 12/28/47 Birmingham, AL; Baptist; JD Univ. of AL, 1972; USARNG, 1969-71; Attorney; m. Linda
Comm.: Financial Services; Judiciary; Transportation & Infrastructure
Dist. Offices: Birmingham, 205-969-2296; Northport, 205-333-9894; Clanton, 205-280-0704

Brian Baird (D-3rd/WA)   202-225-3536
1421 LHOB   4th Term/62%   Fax: 202-225-3478
Website: www.house.gov/baird
CoS .... Lisa Boyd   LD .... Ivan Kaplan
Sch ...... Andrew Dohrmann   **Press** .... Sundance Banks
Bio: b. 3/7/56 Chama, NM; Protestant; PhD Univ. of WY, 1984; Professor; m. Rachel Nugent
Comm.: Budget; Science; Transportation & Infrastructure
Dist. Offices: Vancouver, 360-695-6292; Olympia, 360-352-9768

Richard H. Baker (R-6th/LA)   202-225-3901
341 CHOB   10th Term/72%   Fax: 202-225-7313
Website: baker.house.gov
AA .... Paul Sawyer   LD .... Scott Canady
Sch .... Lynn Ann Kirk   **Press** .... Michael DiResto
Bio: b. 5/22/48 New Orleans, LA; Methodist; BA LA St. Univ., 1971; Real Estate Broker; m. Kay
Comm.: Financial Services; Transportation & Infrastructure; Veterans' Affairs
Dist. Office: Baton Rouge, 225-929-7711

Tammy Baldwin (D-2nd/WI)   202-225-2906
1022 LHOB   4th Term/63%   Fax: 202-225-6942
Website: tammybaldwin.house.gov
CoS .... Bill Murat   LD .... Kris Pratt
Sch .... Maureen Hekmat   **Press** .... Jerilyn Goodman
Bio: b. 2/11/62 Madison, WI; Not Stated; JD Univ. of WI - Madison, 1989; Attorney; dp Lauren Azar
Comm.: Energy & Commerce
Dist. Offices: Madison, 608-258-9800; Beloit, 608-362-2800

REPRESENTATIVES

J. Gresham Barrett (R-3rd/SC)   202-225-5301
1523 LHOB   2nd Term/Unc.   Fax: 202-225-3216
Website: www.house.gov/barrett
CoS .... *Lance Williams* **LD** .... *Sandra Campbell*
Sch .... *Darrell Scott* **Press** .... *Colleen Mangone*
Bio: b. 2/14/61 Westminster, SC; Baptist; BS The Citadel, 1983; USA, 1983-87; Small Business Owner; m. Natalie
Comm.: Budget; Financial Services; International Relations
Dist. Offices: Anderson, 864-224-7401; Greenwood, 864-223-8251; Aiken, 803-649-5571

John Barrow (D-12th/GA)   202-225-2823
226 CHOB   1st Term/52%   Fax: 202-225-3377
Website: www.house.gov/barrow
CoS .... *Roman Levit* **Sr LA** .... *Aaron Schmidt*
Appt .... *Ashley Jones* **Press** .... *Harper Lawson*
Bio: b. 10/31/55 Athens, GA; Baptist; JD Harvard Univ., 1979; Attorney; m. Victoria Pentlarge
Comm.: Agriculture; Education & the Workforce; Small Business
Dist. Office: Athens, 706-613-3232

Roscoe Bartlett (R-6th/MD)   202-225-2721
2412 RHOB   7th Term/68%   Fax: 202-225-2193
Website: www.bartlett.house.gov
CoS .... *Bud Otis* **LD** .... *John Biddison*
Sch .... *Barbara Calligan* **Press** .... *Lisa Lyons Wright*
Bio: b. 6/3/26 Moreland, KY; Seventh-day Adventist; PhD Univ. of MD, 1952; Professor, Scientist; m. Ellen
Comm.: Armed Services; Science; Small Business
Dist. Offices: Frederick, 301-694-3030; Westminster, 410-857-1115; Cumberland, 301-724-3105; Hagerstown, 301-797-6043

Joe Barton (R-6th/TX)   202-225-2002
2109 RHOB   11th Term/66%   Fax: 202-225-3052
Website: joebarton.house.gov
CoS .... *Heather Couri* **LD** .... *Theresa Lavery*
Sch .... *Linda Gillespie* **Press** .... *Brooks Landgraf*
Bio: b. 9/15/49 Waco, TX; Methodist; MS Purdue Univ., 1973; Engineer; m. Terri
Comm.: Energy & Commerce (Chair)
Dist. Offices: Arlington, 817-543-1000; Ennis, 817-543-1000

Charles Bass (R-2nd/NH)   202-225-5206
2421 RHOB   6th Term/59%   Fax: 202-225-2946
E-mail: cbass@mail.house.gov
Website: www.house.gov/bass
CoS .... *Darwin Cusack* **LD** .... *Tad Furtado*
Sch .... *Margo Shideler* **Press** .... *Margo Shideler*
Bio: b. 1/8/52 Boston, MA; Episcopal; AB Dartmouth Col., 1974; Businessman; m. Lisa
Comm.: Energy & Commerce
Dist. Offices: Concord, 603-226-0249; Nashua, 603-889-8772; Littleton, 603-444-1271; Keene, 603-358-4094

Melissa L. Bean (D-8th/IL)   202-225-3711
512 CHOB   1st Term/52%   Fax: 202-225-7830
E-mail: congresswomanmelissabean@mail.house.gov
Website: www.house.gov/bean
CoS .... *John Gonzalez* **LD** .... *Elizabeth Hart*
Sch .... *Jessica Woolley* **CD** .... *Brian Herman*
Bio: b. 1/22/62 Chicago, IL; Serbian Orthodox; BA Roosevelt Univ., 2002; Business Owner; m. Alan
Comm.: Financial Services; Small Business
Dist. Office: Palatine, 847-358-9160

REPRESENTATIVES

Bob Beauprez (R-7th/CO)   **202-225-2645**
504 CHOB   2nd Term/55%   Fax: 202-225-5278
Website: www.house.gov/beauprez
CoS .... *Sean Murphy* **LD** .... *Marc Scheessele*
EA .... *Jean Carbutt* **Press** .... *Jordan Stoick*
Bio: b. 9/22/48 Lafayette, CO; Catholic; BS Univ. of CO, 1970; Farmer, Bank Owner; m. Claudia
Comm.: Ways & Means
Dist. Offices: Wheat Ridge, 303-940-5821; Aurora, 303-343-3707

Xavier Becerra (D-31st/CA)   **202-225-6235**
1119 LHOB   7th Term/81%   Fax: 202-225-2202
Website: becerra.house.gov
CoS .... *Krista Atteberry* **LD** .... *Debra Dixon*
Sch .... *Michael Nielsen* **Press** .... *Cindy Panuco*
Bio: b. 1/26/58 Sacramento, CA; Catholic; JD Stanford Univ., 1984; Attorney; m. Carolina Reyes
Comm.: Ways & Means
Dist. Office: Los Angeles, 213-483-1425

Shelley Berkley (D-1st/NV)   **202-225-5965**
439 CHOB   4th Term/66%   Fax: 202-225-3119
Website: www.house.gov/berkley
CoS .... *Richard Urey* **LD** .... *Heather Urban*
Sch .... *Joanne Jensen* **CD** .... *David Cherry*
Bio: b. 1/20/51 New York, NY; Jewish; JD Univ. of San Diego, 1976; Hotel Executive; m. Larry Lehrner
Comm.: International Relations; Transportation & Infrastructure; Veterans' Affairs
Dist. Office: Las Vegas, 702-220-9823

Howard L. Berman (D-28th/CA)   **202-225-4695**
2221 RHOB   12th Term/71%   Fax: 202-225-3196
E-mail: howard.berman@mail.house.gov
Website: www.house.gov/berman
CoS .... *Gene Smith* **LD** .... *Doug Campbell*
Appt .... *Nancy Milburn* **Press** .... *Gene Smith*
Bio: b. 4/15/41 Los Angeles, CA; Jewish; LLB UCLA, 1965; Attorney; m. Janis
Comm.: International Relations; Judiciary
Dist. Office: Van Nuys, 818-994-7200

Marion Berry (D-1st/AR)   **202-225-4076**
2305 RHOB   5th Term/67%   Fax: 202-225-5602
Website: www.house.gov/berry
CoS .... *Thad Huguley* **LD** .... *Chad Causey*
Sch .... *Jen Waller* **CD** .... *Andrew Nannis*
Bio: b. 8/27/42 Bayou Meto, AR; Methodist; BS Univ. of AR - Little Rock, 1965; Farmer, Pharmacist; m. Carolyn
Comm.: Appropriations
Dist. Offices: Jonesboro, 870-972-4600; Cabot, 501-843-3043; Mountain Home, 870-425-3510

Judy Biggert (R-13th/IL)   **202-225-3515**
1317 LHOB   4th Term/65%   Fax: 202-225-9420
Website: judybiggert.house.gov
CoS .... *Kathy Lydon* **LD** .... *Paul Doucette*
Appt .... *Dean Franks* **Press** .... *Melissa Guido*
Bio: b. 8/15/37 Chicago, IL; Episcopal; JD Northwestern Univ., 1963; Attorney; m. Rody
Comm.: Education & the Workforce; Financial Services; Science; Standards of Official Conduct
Dist. Office: Willowbrook, 630-655-2052

REPRESENTATIVES

Michael Bilirakis (R-9th/FL)   202-225-5755
2408 RHOB   12th Term/Unc.   Fax: 202-225-4085
Website: www.house.gov/bilirakis
CoS .... *Rebecca Hyder* **LD** .... *Sarah Owen*
Sch .... *Doug Menorca* **CD** .... *Christy Stefadouros*
Bio: b. 7/16/30 Tarpon Springs, FL; Greek Orthodox; JD Univ. of FL, 1963; USAF, 1951-55; Attorney; m. Evelyn
Comm.: Energy & Commerce (Vice Chair); Veterans' Affairs (Vice Chair)
Dist. Offices: Palm Harbor, 727-773-2871; Tampa, 813-960-8173

Rob Bishop (R-1st/UT)   202-225-0453
124 CHOB   2nd Term/68%   Fax: 202-225-5857
Website: www.house.gov/robbishop
CoS .... *Scott Parker* **LD** .... *Justin Harding*
Appt .... *Jennifer Griffith* **Press** .... *Scott Parker*
Bio: b. 7/13/51 Kaysville, UT; Church of Jesus Christ of Latter-day Saints; BA Univ. of UT, 1974; Educator, Public Official; m. Jeralynn
Comm.: Rules
Dist. Offices: Ogden, 801-625-0107; Salt Lake City, 801-468-3570

Sanford Bishop, Jr. (D-2nd/GA)   202-225-3631
2429 RHOB   7th Term/67%   Fax: 202-225-2203
Website: www.house.gov/bishop
CoS .... *Phyllis Hallmon* **LD** .... *Roger Manno*
Sch .... *Martina Morgan* **CD** .... *Jennifer Hoelzer*
Bio: b. 2/4/47 Mobile, AL; Baptist; JD Emory Univ., 1971; USA, 1969-71; Attorney; m. Vivian
Comm.: Appropriations
Dist. Offices: Albany, 229-439-8067; Dawson, 229-995-3991; Valdosta, 229-247-9705; Columbus, 706-320-9477

Tim Bishop (D-1st/NY)   202-225-3826
1133 LHOB   2nd Term/56%   Fax: 202-225-3143
Website: www.house.gov/timbishop
CoS .... *Sean Sweeney* **LD** .... *Vacant*
Appt ..... *Rosemary Manesis* **Press** .... *Brian Farber*
Bio: b. 6/1/50 Southampton, NY; Catholic; MPA Long Island Univ., 1981; College Provost; m. Kathy
Comm.: Education & the Workforce; Transportation & Infrastructure
Dist. Offices: Coram, 631-696-6500; Southampton, 631-259-8450

Marsha Blackburn (R-7th/TN)   202-225-2811
509 CHOB   2nd Term/Unc.   Fax: 202-225-3004
Website: www.house.gov/blackburn
CoS .... *Steve Brophy* **LD** .... *Mike Platt*
Sch .... *Josh Mullen* **CD** .... *Ryan Loskarn*
Bio: b. 6/6/52 Laurel, MS; Presbyterian; BS MS St. Univ., 1973; Retail Marketing; m. Chuck
Comm.: Energy & Commerce
Dist. Offices: Memphis, 901-382-5811; Clarksville, 931-503-0391; Franklin, 615-591-5161

Earl Blumenauer (D-3rd/OR)   202-225-4811
2446 RHOB   6th Term/71%   Fax: 202-225-8941
Website: blumenauer.house.gov
CoS .... *Mariia Zimmerman* **LD** .... *James Koski*
Sch .... *Jackie Lynn Ray* **Press** .... *Kathie Eastman*
Bio: b. 8/16/48 Portland, OR; Not Stated; JD Lewis and Clark Col., 1976; Attorney; m. Margaret Kirkpatrick
Comm.: International Relations; Transportation & Infrastructure
Dist. Office: Portland, 503-231-2300

REPRESENTATIVES

Roy Blunt (R-7th/MO)   202-225-6536
217 CHOB   5th Term/70%   Fax: 202-225-5604
E-mail: blunt@mail.house.gov
Website: www.blunt.house.gov
CoS .... *Brian Gaston* **LD** .... *Neil Bradley*
Sch .... *Richard Eddings* **CD** .... *Burson Taylor*
Bio: b. 1/10/50 Niangua, MO; Baptist; MA SW MO St. Univ., 1972; University President; m. Abigail
Comm.: Energy & Commerce; Majority Whip
Dist. Offices: Springfield, 417-889-1800; Joplin, 417-781-1041

Sherwood L. Boehlert (R-24th/NY)   202-225-3665
2246 RHOB   12th Term/57%   Fax: 202-225-1891
Website: www.house.gov/boehlert
CoS .... *Dean D'Amore* **LD** .... *Deirdre Walsh*
EA .... *John Konkus* **Press** .... *Sam Marchio*
Bio: b. 9/28/36 Utica, NY; Catholic; BS Utica Col., 1961; USA, 1956-58; Congressional Aide; m. Marianne
Comm.: Science (Chair); Transportation & Infrastructure
Dist. Offices: Utica, 315-793-8146; Auburn, 315-255-0649; Cortland, 607-758-3918

John A. Boehner (R-8th/OH)   202-225-6205
1011 LHOB   8th Term/69%   Fax: 202-225-0704
Website: johnboehner.house.gov
CoS .... *Mike Sommers* **LD** .... *Jaclyn Madden*
Appt .... *Kelly Cayer* **Press** .... *Don Seymour*
Bio: b. 11/17/49 Cincinnati, OH; Catholic; BS Xavier Univ., 1977; USN, 1968; Businessman; m. Debbie
Comm.: Agriculture (Vice Chair); Education & the Workforce (Chair)
Dist. Offices: West Chester, 513-779-5400; Troy, 937-339-1524

Henry Bonilla (R-23rd/TX)   202-225-4511
2458 RHOB   7th Term/69%   Fax: 202-225-2237
Website: www.house.gov/bonilla
CoS .... *Marc Lubin* **LD** .... *Tom Rice*
Sch ...... *Kelly Vander Ploeg* **Press** .... *Taryn Fritz*
Bio: b. 1/2/54 San Antonio, TX; Baptist; BJ Univ. of TX, 1976; Broadcast Executive; sep.
Comm.: Appropriations
Dist. Offices: San Antonio, 210-697-9055; Laredo, 956-726-4682; Alpine, 915-837-1313; Del Rio, 830-774-6547

Jo Bonner (R-1st/AL)   202-225-4931
315 CHOB   2nd Term/63%   Fax: 202-225-0562
Website: bonner.house.gov
CoS .... *Alan Spencer* **LD** .... *Kelle Strickland*
Appt .... *Marcy Pack* **Press** .... *Matt Rhodes*
Bio: b. 11/19/59 Selma, AL; Episcopal; BA Univ. of AL, 1982; Congressional Aide; m. Janee
Comm.: Agriculture; Budget; Science
Dist. Offices: Mobile, 251-690-2811; Foley, 251-943-2073

Mary Bono (R-45th/CA)   202-225-5330
405 CHOB   5th Term/66%   Fax: 202-225-2961
Website: www.house.gov/bono
CoS .... *Frank Cullen, Jr.* **LD** .... *Linda Valter*
Appt .... *Katie Angliss* **CD** .... *Kimberly Pencille*
Bio: b. 10/24/61 Cleveland, OH; Protestant; BFA USC, 1984; Small Business Owner; m. Glenn Baxley
Comm.: Energy & Commerce
Dist. Offices: Palm Springs, 760-320-1076; Hemet, 909-658-2312

REPRESENTATIVES

John Boozman (R-3rd/AR)   202-225-4301
1519 LHOB   3rd Term/59%   Fax: 202-225-5713
Website: boozman.house.gov
CoS .... Matt Sagely   **LD** .... Vivian Moeglein
Sch .... Jennifer Brady   **CD** .... Patrick Creamer
Bio: b. 12/10/50 Shreveport, LA; Baptist; OD Southern Col. of Optometry, 1977; Optometrist; m. Cathy
Comm.: International Relations; Transportation & Infrastructure; Veterans' Affairs
Dist. Offices: Ft. Smith, 479-782-7787; Fayetteville, 479-442-5258; Harrison, 870-741-6900

Madeleine Z. Bordallo (D/GU)   202-225-1188
427 CHOB   2nd Term/Unc.   Fax: 202-226-0341
Website: www.house.gov/bordallo
CoS .... John Whitt   **LD** .... John Whitt
Sch .... Rosanne Meno   **Press** .... Neil Weare
Bio: b. 5/31/33 Graceville, MN; Catholic; AA St. Katherine's Col., 1953; Public Official; widowed
Comm.: Armed Services; Resources; Small Business
Dist. Office: Hagatna, 671-477-4272

Dan Boren (D-2nd/OK)   202-225-2701
216 CHOB   1st Term/66%   Fax: 202-225-3038
Website: www.house.gov/boren
CoS .... Pete Regan   **LD** .... Karen Kuhlman
Appt .... Beth Barefoot   **Press** .... Michael Allen
Bio: b. 8/2/73 Shawnee, OK; Methodist; MBA Univ. of OK, 2000; Education Administrator; eng.
Comm.: Armed Services; Resources
Dist. Offices: Muskogee, 918-687-2533; Claremore, 918-341-9336; McAlester, 918-423-5951

Leonard L. Boswell (D-3rd/IA)   202-225-3806
1427 LHOB   5th Term/55%   Fax: 202-225-5608
E-mail: rep.boswell.ia03@mail.house.gov
Website: www.house.gov/boswell
CoS .... Ned Michalek   **LD** .... Eric Witte
Sch .... Sandy Carter   **CD** .... Eric Witte
Bio: b. 1/10/34 Harrison Co., MO; Community of Christ; BA Graceland Col., 1969; USA, 1956-76; Farmer; m. Dody
Comm.: Agriculture; Transportation & Infrastructure; Select Intelligence
Dist. Office: Des Moines, 515-282-1909

Rick Boucher (D-9th/VA)   202-225-3861
2187 RHOB   12th Term/59%   Fax: 202-225-0442
E-mail: ninthnet@mail.house.gov
Website: www.house.gov/boucher
CoS .... Becky Coleman   **LD** .... Laura Vaught
Appt .... Melissa Bruns   **Press** .... Amanda Potter
Bio: b. 8/1/46 Abingdon, VA; Methodist; JD Univ. of VA, 1971; Attorney; single
Comm.: Energy & Commerce; Judiciary
Dist. Offices: Abingdon, 276-628-1145; Pulaski, 540-980-4310; Big Stone Gap, 276-523-5450

Charles W. Boustany, Jr. (R-7th/LA)   202-225-2031
1117 LHOB   1st Term/55%   Fax: 202-225-5724
Website: www.house.gov/boustany
CoS .... Jeff Dobrozsi   **LD** .... Anne Bradbury
Sch .... Michelle Wizov   **Press** .... Amy Jones
Bio: b. 2/21/56 New Orleans, LA; Episcopal; MD LA St. Univ., 1982; Surgeon; m. Bridget
Comm.: Agriculture; Education & the Workforce; Transportation & Infrastructure
Dist. Office: Lafayette, 337-235-6322

REPRESENTATIVES

F. Allen Boyd, Jr. (D-2nd/FL)   202-225-5235
1227 LHOB   5th Term/62%   Fax: 202-225-5615
Website: www.house.gov/boyd
AA .... *Libby Greer* **LD** .... *Jason Quaranto*
Sch .... *Robin Nichols* **Press** .... *Melanie Morris*
Bio: b. 6/6/45 Valdosta, GA; Methodist; BS FL St. Univ., 1969; USA, 1969-71; Farmer; m. Cissy
Comm.: Appropriations
Dist. Offices: Tallahassee, 850-561-3979; Panama City, 850-785-0812

Jeb Bradley (R-1st/NH)   202-225-5456
1218 LHOB   2nd Term/63%   Fax: 202-225-5822
Website: www.house.gov/bradley
CoS .... *Debra Vanderbeek* **LD** .... *Michael Liles*
Appt .... *Soraya Vanderbeek* **Press** .... *Stephanie DuBois*
Bio: b. 10/20/52 Rumford, ME; Protestant; BA Tufts Univ., 1974; Small Business Owner; m. Barbara
Comm.: Armed Services; Budget; Small Business; Veterans' Affairs
Dist. Offices: Manchester, 603-641-9536; Dover, 603-743-4813

Kevin P. Brady (R-8th/TX)   202-225-4901
428 CHOB   5th Term/69%   Fax: 202-225-5524
E-mail: rep.brady@mail.house.gov
Website: www.house.gov/brady
CoS .... *Doug Centilli* **LD** .... *David Malech*
Appt .... *Joel Noyes* **Press** .... *Sarah Stephens*
Bio: b. 4/11/55 Vermillion, SD; Catholic; BS Univ. of SD, 1990; Chamber of Commerce Executive; m. Cathy
Comm.: Ways & Means; Joint Economic
Dist. Office: Conroe, 936-441-5700

Robert A. Brady (D-1st/PA)   202-225-4731
206 CHOB   5th Term/86%   Fax: 202-225-0088
Website: www.house.gov/robertbrady
CoS .... *Stan White* **LD** .... *Teri Morgan*
Sch .... *Kristie Muchnok* **Press** .... *Karen Warrington*
Bio: b. 4/7/45 Philadelphia, PA; Catholic; HS Diploma; Carpenter, Union Official; m. Debra
Comm.: Armed Services; House Administration; Joint Printing
Dist. Offices: Philadelphia, 215-389-4627; Chester, 610-874-7094

Corrine Brown (D-3rd/FL)   202-225-0123
2444 RHOB   7th Term/Unc.   Fax: 202-225-2256
Website: www.house.gov/corrinebrown
CoS .... *Ronnie Simmons* **LD** .... *Nick Martinelli*
Sch .... *Darla Smallwood* **Press** .... *David Simon*
Bio: b. 11/11/46 Jacksonville, FL; Baptist; EdS Univ. of FL, 1974; Educator; single
Comm.: Transportation & Infrastructure; Veterans' Affairs
Dist. Offices: Jacksonville, 904-354-1652; Orlando, 407-872-0656

Henry E. Brown, Jr. (R-1st/SC)   202-225-3176
1124 LHOB   3rd Term/88%   Fax: 202-225-3407
Website: www.house.gov/henrybrown
CoS .... *Delores DaCosta* **LD** .... *Chris Berardini*
Sch .... *Renee Brockinton* **Press** .... *Sharon Axson*
Bio: b. 12/20/35 Bishopville, SC; Southern Baptist; Attended Charleston Southern Univ. & The Citadel; SCNG, 1953-62; Businessman; m. Billye
Comm.: Resources; Transportation & Infrastructure; Veterans' Affairs
Dist. Offices: North Charleston, 843-747-4175; Myrtle Beach, 843-445-6459

REPRESENTATIVES

Sherrod Brown (D-13th/OH)   202-225-3401
2332 RHOB   7th Term/67%   Fax: 202-225-2266
E-mail: sherrod@mail.house.gov
Website: www.house.gov/sherrodbrown
CoS .... *Jack Dover* **LD** .... *Ellie Dehoney*
Sch .... *Dan Flave-Novak* **Press** .... *Joanna Kuebler*
Bio: b. 11/9/52 Mansfield, OH; Lutheran; MPA OH St. Univ., 1981; Teacher; m. Connie Schultz
Comm.: Energy & Commerce; International Relations
Dist. Offices: Lorain, 440-245-5350; Akron, 330-865-8450

Ginny Brown-Waite (R-5th/FL)   202-225-1002
414 CHOB   2nd Term/66%   Fax: 202-226-6559
Website: www.house.gov/brown-waite
CoS .... *Pete Meachum* **LD** .... *Amie Woeber*
Sch .... *Jennifer Fay* **CD** .... *Charlie Keller*
Bio: b. 10/5/43 Albany, NY; Catholic; MS Russell Sage Col., 1984; Consultant, College Professor; m. Harvey
Comm.: Financial Services; Government Reform; Veterans' Affairs
Dist. Offices: Dade City, 352-567-6707; Brooksville, 352-799-8354

Michael C. Burgess (R-26th/TX)   202-225-7772
1721 LHOB   2nd Term/66%   Fax: 202-225-2919
Website: burgess.house.gov
CoS .... *Barry Brown* **LD** .... *Josh Martin*
Sch .... *Brenna Head* **CD** .... *Michelle Stein*
Bio: b. 12/23/50 Rochester, MN; Episcopal; MD Univ. of TX, 1977; Obstetrician; m. Laura
Comm.: Energy & Commerce
Dist. Office: Lewisville, 972-434-9700

Dan Burton (R-5th/IN)   202-225-2276
2185 RHOB   12th Term/72%   Fax: 202-225-0016
Website: www.house.gov/burton
CoS .... *Mark Walker* **LD** .... *Brian Fauls*
Sch .... *Diane Menorca* **Press** .... *Nick Mutton*
Bio: b. 6/21/38 Indianapolis, IN; Protestant; Attended IN Univ.; USA, 1956-57; USAR, 1957-62; Insurance, Real Estate Agent; widowed
Comm.: Government Reform; International Relations; Veterans' Affairs
Dist. Offices: Indianapolis, 317-848-0201; Marion, 765-662-6770

G.K. Butterfield (D-1st/NC)   202-225-3101
413 CHOB   2nd Term/64%   Fax: 202-225-3354
Website: www.house.gov/butterfield
CoS .... *Corliss James* **LD** .... *Alexander Silbey*
Appt .... *Darnise Pearson* **Press** .... *Ken Willis*
Bio: b. 4/27/47 Wilson, NC; Baptist; JD NC Central Univ., 1974; USA, 1968-70; Judge, Attorney; div.
Comm.: Agriculture; Armed Services
Dist. Offices: Williamston, 252-789-4939; Wilson, 252-237-9816; Tarboro, 252-823-0236; Weldon, 252-538-4123

Steve Buyer (R-4th/IN)   202-225-5037
2230 RHOB   7th Term/70%   Fax: 202-225-2267
Website: www.house.gov/buyer
CoS .... *Myrna Dugan* **LD** .... *Myrna Dugan*
Sch .... *Sarah Milligan* **Press** .... *Laura Zuckerman*
Bio: b. 11/26/58 Rensselaer, IN; Methodist; JD Valparaiso Univ., 1984; USA, 1984-87; USAR, 1980-84, 1987-present; Attorney; m. Joni
Comm.: Energy & Commerce; Veterans' Affairs (Chair)
Dist. Offices: Plainfield, 317-838-0404; Monticello, 574-583-9819; Bedford, 812-277-9590

REPRESENTATIVES

Ken Calvert (R-44th/CA)   **202-225-1986**
2201 RHOB   7th Term/62%   Fax: 202-225-2004
Website: www.house.gov/calvert
CoS .... *Dave Ramey* **LD** .... *Maria Bowie*
Sch .... *Linda Ulrich* **CD** .... *Bob Carretta*
Bio: b. 6/8/53 Corona, CA; Protestant; BA San Diego St. Univ., 1975; Small Business Owner; div.
Comm.: Armed Services; Resources; Science
Dist. Offices: Riverside, 951-784-4300; San Clemente, 949-496-2343

Dave Camp (R-4th/MI)   **202-225-3561**
137 CHOB   8th Term/64%   Fax: 202-225-9679
Website: www.house.gov/camp
CoS .... *Jim Brandell* **LD** .... *Joanna Foust*
Appt .... *Sarah Ahlgren* **CD** .... *Sage Eastman*
Bio: b. 7/9/53 Midland, MI; Catholic; JD Univ. of San Diego, 1978; Attorney; m. Nancy
Comm.: Ways & Means
Dist. Offices: Midland, 989-631-2552; Traverse City, 231-929-4711

Chris Cannon (R-3rd/UT)   **202-225-7751**
2436 RHOB   5th Term/61%   Fax: 202-225-5629
E-mail: cannon.ut03@mail.house.gov
Website: chriscannon.house.gov
CoS .... *Joe Hunter* **LD** .... *Todd Thorpe*
Appt .... *Jenny Davis* **Press** .... *Charles Isom*
Bio: b. 10/20/50 Salt Lake City, UT; Mormon; JD Brigham Young Univ., 1980; Attorney; m. Claudia Ann
Comm.: Government Reform; Judiciary; Resources
Dist. Offices: Provo, 801-851-2500; West Valley City, 801-955-3631

Eric I. Cantor (R-7th/VA)   **202-225-2815**
329 CHOB   3rd Term/76%   Fax: 202-225-0011
Website: cantor.house.gov
CoS .... *Rob Collins* **LD** .... *Colleen Maloney*
Sch .... *Kristin Young* **Press** .... *Geoff Embler*
Bio: b. 6/6/63 Richmond, VA; Jewish; MS Columbia Univ., 1989; Attorney; m. Diana Fine
Comm.: Ways & Means
Dist. Offices: Glen Allen, 804-747-4073; Culpeper, 540-825-8960

Shelley Moore Capito (R-2nd/WV)   **202-225-2711**
1431 LHOB   3rd Term/58%   Fax: 202-225-7856
Website: capito.house.gov
CoS .... *Martin Baker* **LD** .... *Rob Steptoe*
Sch .... *Alison Bibbee* **Press** .... *R.C. Hammond*
Bio: b. 11/26/53 Glen Dale, WV; Presbyterian; MEd Univ. of VA, 1976; Career Counselor; m. Charles
Comm.: Rules
Dist. Offices: Charleston, 304-925-5964; Martinsburg, 304-264-8810

Lois Capps (D-23rd/CA)   **202-225-3601**
1707 LHOB   5th Term/64%   Fax: 202-225-5632
Website: www.house.gov/capps
CoS .... *Jeremy Rabinovitz* **LD** .... *Randolph Harrison*
Appt .... *Erin Shaughnessy* **Press** ..... *Shannon Lohrmann*
Bio: b. 1/10/38 Ladysmith, WI; Lutheran; MA Univ. of CA - Santa Barbara, 1990; Nurse, Teacher; widowed
Comm.: Budget; Energy & Commerce
Dist. Offices: Santa Barbara, 805-730-1710; San Luis Obispo, 805-546-8348; Oxnard, 805-385-3440

REPRESENTATIVES

Michael Capuano (D-8th/MA)   **202-225-5111**
1530 LHOB   4th Term/Unc.   Fax: 202-225-9322
Website: www.house.gov/capuano
CoS .... *Robert Primus* **LD** .... *Jon Skarin*
Sch .... *Mary Doherty* **Press** .... *Alison Mills*
Bio: b. 1/9/52 Somerville, MA; Catholic; JD Boston Col., 1977; Attorney, Public Official; m. Barbara
Comm.: Financial Services; Transportation & Infrastructure
Dist. Offices: Cambridge, 617-621-6208; Roxbury, 617-621-6208

Benjamin L. Cardin (D-3rd/MD)   **202-225-4016**
2207 RHOB   10th Term/63%   Fax: 202-225-9219
E-mail: rep.cardin@mail.house.gov
Website: www.cardin.house.gov
CoS .... *Christopher Lynch* **LD** .... *Priscilla Ross*
Appt .... *Debbie Yamada* **Press** .... *Susan Sullam*
Bio: b. 10/5/43 Baltimore, MD; Jewish; LLB/JD Univ. of MD, 1967; Attorney; m. Myrna
Comm.: Ways & Means
Dist. Office: Baltimore, 410-433-8886

Dennis Cardoza (D-18th/CA)   **202-225-6131**
435 CHOB   2nd Term/68%   Fax: 202-225-0819
Website: www.house.gov/cardoza
CoS .... *Mark Garrett* **LD** .... *Gary Palmquist*
Appt .... *Beth Elliott* **Press** .... *Bret Ladine*
Bio: b. 3/31/59 Merced, CA; Catholic; BA Univ. of MD, 1982; Businessman; m. Kathleen McLoughlin
Comm.: Agriculture; International Relations; Resources
Dist. Offices: Merced, 209-383-4455; Modesto, 209-527-1914; Stockton, 209-946-0361

Russ Carnahan (D-3rd/MO)   **202-225-2671**
1232 LHOB   1st Term/53%   Fax: 202-225-7452
Website: www.house.gov/carnahan
CoS .... *Todd Patterson* **LD** .... *Cary Gibson*
Sch .... *Paul Schmid* **Press** ... *Heather Lasher Todd*
Bio: b. 7/10/58 Columbia, MO; Methodist; JD Univ. of MO - Columbia, 1983; Attorney; m. Debra
Comm.: Science; Transportation & Infrastructure
Dist. Office: St. Louis, 314-962-1523

Julia M. Carson (D-7th/IN)   **202-225-4011**
1535 LHOB   5th Term/54%   Fax: 202-225-5633
Website: juliacarson.house.gov
CoS .... *Sarge Visher* **LD** .... *Marti Thomas*
Sch .... *Aarti Nayak* **CD** .... *Adairius Gardner*
Bio: b. 7/8/38 Louisville, KY; Baptist; Attended IN Univ.-Purdue Univ.; Human Resources Director, Public Official; div.
Comm.: Financial Services; Transportation & Infrastructure
Dist. Office: Indianapolis, 317-283-6516

John R. Carter (R-31st/TX)   **202-225-3864**
408 CHOB   2nd Term/65%   Fax: 202-225-5886
Website: www.house.gov/carter
CoS .... *Ryan Henry* **LD** .... *Vacant*
Appt ..... *Brooke McWhirter* **Press** .... *Gretchen Hamel*
Bio: b. 11/6/41 Houston, TX; Christian; JD Univ. of TX, 1969; Judge; m. Erika
Comm.: Appropriations
Dist. Offices: Round Rock, 512-246-1600; Belton, 254-933-1392

REPRESENTATIVES

Ed Case (D-2nd/HI)   202-225-4906
115 CHOB   2nd Term/61%   Fax: 202-225-4987
E-mail: ed.case@mail.house.gov
Website: www.house.gov/case
CoS .... *Esther Kia'aina*   **LD** .... *Anne Stewart*
Appt .... *Pamela Okimoto*   **Press** .... *Randy Obata*
Bio: b. 9/27/52 Hilo, HI; Protestant; JD Univ. of CA, 1981; Attorney; m. Audrey
Comm.: Agriculture; Budget; Small Business
Dist. Office: Honolulu, 808-541-1986

Michael Castle (R-At Large/DE)   202-225-4165
1233 LHOB   7th Term/69%   Fax: 202-225-2291
Website: www.house.gov/castle
CoS .... *Mike Quaranta*   **LD** .... *Kate Dickens*
Sch .... *Amy Greenan*   **CD** .... *Elizabeth Wenk*
Bio: b. 7/2/39 Wilmington, DE; Catholic; JD Georgetown Univ., 1964; Attorney; m. Jane
Comm.: Education & the Workforce; Financial Services
Dist. Offices: Wilmington, 302-428-1902; Dover, 302-736-1666

Steve Chabot (R-1st/OH)   202-225-2216
129 CHOB   6th Term/60%   Fax: 202-225-3012
Website: www.house.gov/chabot
CoS .... *Gary Lindgren*   **LD** .... *Kevin Fitzpatrick*
Sch .... *Angela Oswald*   **CD** .... *Todd Lindgren*
Bio: b. 1/22/53 Cincinnati, OH; Catholic; JD Northern KY Univ., 1978; Attorney; m. Donna
Comm.: International Relations; Judiciary; Small Business
Dist. Office: Cincinnati, 513-684-2723

Ben Chandler (D-6th/KY)   202-225-4706
1504 LHOB   2nd Term/59%   Fax: 202-225-2122
Website: chandler.house.gov
CoS .... *Denis Fleming*   **LD** .... *Clinton Dockery*
Sch .... *Keri Kohler*   **CD** .... *Lillian Pace*
Bio: b. 9/12/59 Versailles, KY; Presbyterian; JD Univ. of KY, 1986; Attorney; m. Jennifer
Comm.: Agriculture; International Relations; Transportation & Infrastructure
Dist. Office: Lexington, 859-219-1366

Chris Chocola (R-2nd/IN)   202-225-3915
510 CHOB   2nd Term/54%   Fax: 202-225-6798
Website: chocola.house.gov
CoS .... *Brooks Kochvar*   **LD** .... *Rob Vernon*
Sch .... *Katie Pike*   **Press** .... *Vacant*
Bio: b. 2/24/62 Jackson, MI; Presbyterian; JD Thomas Cooley Law School, 1988; Businessman; m. Sarah
Comm.: Ways & Means
Dist. Offices: South Bend, 574-251-0596; Logansport, 574-753-4700

Donna M. Christensen (D/VI)   202-225-1790
1510 LHOB   5th Term/66%   Fax: 202-225-5517
Website: www.house.gov/christian-christensen
CoS .... *Monique*   **LD** .... *Brian Modeste*
             Clendinen Watson
Sch .... *Shelley Thomas*   **CD** .... *Monique*
                                                    Clendinen Watson
Bio: b. 9/19/45 Teaneck, NJ; Moravian; MD George Washington Univ., 1970; Physician; m. Chris
Comm.: Homeland Security; Resources; Small Business
Dist. Offices: St. Thomas, 340-774-4408; St. Croix, 340-778-5900; St. John, 340-776-1212

REPRESENTATIVES

Wm. Lacy Clay (D-1st/MO)   202-225-2406
131 CHOB   3rd Term/75%   Fax: 202-225-1725
Website: www.house.gov/clay
CoS .... *Darryl Piggee* **LD** .... *Michele Bogdanovich*
Appt .... *Karyn Long* **Press** .... *Ishmael-Lateef Ahmad*
Bio: b. 7/27/56 St. Louis, MO; Catholic; BS Univ. of MD, 1983; Public Official; m. Ivie Lewellen
Comm.: Financial Services; Government Reform
Dist. Offices: St. Louis, 314-890-0349; St. Louis, 314-367-1970

Emanuel Cleaver (D-5th/MO)   202-225-4535
1641 LHOB   1st Term/55%   Fax: 202-225-4403
E-mail: emanuel.cleaver@mail.house.gov
Website: www.house.gov/cleaver
CoS .... *Susan McAvoy* **LD** .... *Sudafi Henry*
Sch .... *Joyce Elkins* **Press** .... *Amber Moon*
Bio: b. 10/26/44 Waxahachie, TX; Methodist; MDiv St. Paul School of Theology, 1974; Pastor, Public Official; m. Dianne
Comm.: Financial Services
Dist. Office: Kansas City, 816-842-4545

James Clyburn (D-6th/SC)   202-225-3315
2135 RHOB   7th Term/67%   Fax: 202-225-2313
E-mail: jclyburn@mail.house.gov
Website: www.house.gov/clyburn
CoS .... *Yelberton Watkins* **LD** .... *Danny Cromer*
Sch .... *Jennie Chaplin* **CD** .... *Lindy Birch*
Bio: b. 7/21/40 Sumter, SC; African Methodist Episcopal; BS SC St. Col., 1962; Educator; m. Emily
Comm.: Appropriations
Dist. Offices: Columbia, 803-799-1100; Florence, 843-662-1212; Santee, 803-854-4700

Howard Coble (R-6th/NC)   202-225-3065
2468 RHOB   11th Term/73%   Fax: 202-225-8611
E-mail: howard.coble@mail.house.gov
Website: coble.house.gov
CoS .... *Edward McDonald* **LD** .... *Anna Sagely*
EA .. *Mary Elizabeth Tillman* **Press** ...... *Edward McDonald*
Bio: b. 3/18/31 Greensboro, NC; Presbyterian; JD UNC, 1962; USCG, 1952-56; USCGR, 1960-82; Attorney; single
Comm.: Judiciary; Transportation & Infrastructure
Dist. Offices: Greensboro, 336-333-5005; Asheboro, 336-626-3060; High Point, 336-886-5106; Salisbury, 704-645-8082; Graham, 336-229-0159

Tom Cole (R-4th/OK)   202-225-6165
236 CHOB   2nd Term/78%   Fax: 202-225-3512
Website: www.house.gov/cole
CoS .... *Pete Kirkham* **LD** .... *Chris Caron*
Appt .... *Jennings Palmer* **Press** .... *Julie Bley*
Bio: b. 4/28/49 Shreveport, LA; Methodist; PhD Univ. of OK, 1984; Professor, Public Official; m. Ellen
Comm.: Rules; Standards of Official Conduct
Dist. Offices: Norman, 405-329-6500; Lawton, 580-357-2131; Ada, 580-436-5375

Mike Conaway (R-11th/TX)   202-225-3605
511 CHOB   1st Term/77%   Fax: 202-225-1783
Website: www.house.gov/conaway
CoS .... *Jeff Burton* **LD** .... *Michael Beckerman*
Sch ...... *Cassandra Harrison* **Press** .... *Ken Spain*
Bio: b. 6/11/48 Borger, TX; Baptist; BBA Texas A&M Univ., 1970; USA, 1970-72; Accountant; m. Suzanne
Comm.: Agriculture; Armed Services; Budget
Dist. Offices: Midland, 432-687-2390; San Angelo, 325-659-4010

REPRESENTATIVES

John Conyers, Jr. (D-14th/MI)   **202-225-5126**
2426 RHOB   21st Term/84%   Fax: 202-225-0072
E-mail: john.conyers@mail.house.gov
Website: www.house.gov/conyers
CoS .... *None*   **LD** .... *Cynthia Martin*
Sch .... *Rinia Shelby*   **Press** .... *Dena Graziano*
Bio: b. 5/16/29 Detroit, MI; Baptist; LLB Wayne St. Univ., 1958; USARNG, 1950-54; USAR, 1954-57; Attorney; m. Monica
Comm.: Judiciary (Rnk. Mem.)
Dist. Offices: Detroit, 313-961-5670; Southgate, 734-285-5624

Jim Cooper (D-5th/TN)   **202-225-4311**
1536 LHOB   8th Term/69%   Fax: 202-226-1035
Website: cooper.house.gov
CoS .... *Greg Hinote*   **LD** .... *Anne Kim*
EA .... *Carolyn Waugh*   **CD** .... *Murfy Alexander*
Bio: b. 6/19/54 Nashville, TN; Episcopal; JD Harvard Univ., 1980; Attorney; m. Martha
Comm.: Armed Services; Budget
Dist. Offices: Nashville, 615-736-5295; Mt. Juliet, 615-773-2305

Jim Costa (D-20th/CA)   **202-225-3341**
1004 LHOB   1st Term/54%   Fax: 202-225-9308
E-mail: congressmanjimcosta@mail.house.gov
Website: www.house.gov/costa
CoS .... *Scott Nishioki*   **LD** .... *Scott Nishioki*
Sch .... *Kerri Hatfield*   **Press** .... *Tracy Sherman*
Bio: b. 4/13/52 Fresno, CA; Catholic; BA CA St. Univ.-Fresno, 1974; Public Official; single
Comm.: Agriculture; Resources; Science
Dist. Office: Fresno, 559-495-1620

Jerry F. Costello (D-12th/IL)   **202-225-5661**
2269 RHOB   10th Term/70%   Fax: 202-225-0285
Website: www.house.gov/costello
CoS .... *David Gillies*   **LD** .... *Christa Fornarotto*
Sch .... *Karl Britton*   **Press** .... *David Gillies*
Bio: b. 9/25/49 East St. Louis, IL; Catholic; BA Maryville Col., 1973; Law Enforcement Official; m. Georgia
Comm.: Science; Transportation & Infrastructure
Dist. Offices: Belleville, 618-233-8026; Granite City, 618-451-7065; Carbondale, 618-529-3791; East St. Louis, 618-397-8833; Chester, 618-826-3043; West Frankfort, 618-937-6402

Christopher Cox (R-48th/CA)   **202-225-5611**
2402 RHOB   9th Term/65%   Fax: 202-225-9177
Website: cox.house.gov
CoS .... *Peter Uhlmann*   **LD** .... *James Freeman*
Appt .... *Mary Christ*   **Press** .... *Marilyn Cosenza*
Bio: b. 10/16/52 St. Paul, MN; Catholic; JD/MBA Harvard Univ., 1977; Attorney; m. Rebecca
Comm.: Homeland Security (Chair)
Dist. Office: Newport Beach, 949-756-2244

Robert E. "Bud" Cramer, Jr.
(D-5th/AL)   **202-225-4801**
2368 RHOB   8th Term/73%   Fax: 202-225-4392
E-mail: budmail@mail.house.gov
Website: cramer.house.gov
CoS .... *Carter Wells*   **LD** .... *Jenny DiJames*
Sch .... *Alex Igou*   **Press** .... *Adam Muhlendorf*
Bio: b. 8/22/47 Huntsville, AL; Methodist; JD Univ. of AL, 1972; USA, 1976-78; USAR, 1976-78; Attorney; widowed
Comm.: Appropriations; Select Intelligence
Dist. Offices: Huntsville, 256-551-0190; Tuscumbia, 256-381-3450; Decatur, 256-355-9400

REPRESENTATIVES

Ander Crenshaw (R-4th/FL)   202-225-2501
127 CHOB   3rd Term/Unc.   Fax: 202-225-2504
Website: crenshaw.house.gov
CoS .... *John Ariale* **LD** .... *Erica Striebel*
Sch .... *Lynn Miller* **CD** .... *Ken Lundberg*
Bio: b. 9/1/44 Jacksonville, FL; Episcopal; JD Univ. of FL, 1969; Investment Banker; m. Kitty
Comm.: Appropriations; Budget
Dist. Offices: Jacksonville, 904-598-0481; Lake City, 386-365-3316

Joseph Crowley (D-7th/NY)   202-225-3965
312 CHOB   4th Term/80%   Fax: 202-225-1909
Website: crowley.house.gov
CoS .... *Chris McCannell* **LD** .... *Kevin Casey*
Sch .... *Shawn Hodjati* **Press** .... *Jennifer Psaki*
Bio: b. 3/16/62 New York, NY; Catholic; BA Queens Col., 1985; Public Official; m. Kasey
Comm.: Financial Services; International Relations
Dist. Offices: Jackson Heights, 718-779-1400; Bronx, 718-931-1400; Bronx, 718-320-2314

Barbara Cubin (R-At Large/WY)   202-225-2311
1114 LHOB   6th Term/55%   Fax: 202-225-3057
Website: www.house.gov/cubin
CoS .... *Tom Wiblemo* **LD** .... *Rick Axthelm*
Sch .... *Brandi Schmick* **Press** .... *Joe Milczewski*
Bio: b. 11/30/46 Salinas, CA; Episcopal; BS Creighton Univ., 1969; Teacher, Chemist; m. Frederick
Comm.: Energy & Commerce; Resources (Vice Chair)
Dist. Offices: Casper, 307-261-6595; Rock Springs, 307-362-4095; Cheyenne, 307-772-2595

Henry Cuellar (D-28th/TX)   202-225-1640
1404 LHOB   1st Term/59%   Fax: 202-225-1641
Website: www.house.gov/cuellar
CoS .... *Colin Strother* **LD** .... *Billy Peche*
Sch .... *Jennifer Milek* **Press** .... *Sandra Abrevay*
Bio: b. 9/19/55 Laredo, TX; Catholic; PhD Univ. of TX, 1998; Attorney, Customs Broker; m. Imelda
Comm.: Agriculture; Budget
Dist. Offices: San Antonio, 210-271-2851; San Marcos, 512-392-2364; Laredo, 956-725-0639

John A. Culberson (R-7th/TX)   202-225-2571
1728 LHOB   3rd Term/64%   Fax: 202-225-4381
Website: www.culberson.house.gov
CoS .... *Bill Crow* **LD** .... *Ellie Essalih*
Sch .... *Jamie Gahun* **Press** .... *Sarah Goldston*
Bio: b. 8/24/56 Houston, TX; Methodist; JD S. TX Col. of Law, 1988; Civil Defense Attorney; m. Belinda
Comm.: Appropriations
Dist. Office: Houston, 713-682-8828

Elijah Cummings (D-7th/MD)   202-225-4741
2235 RHOB   6th Term/74%   Fax: 202-225-3178
Website: www.house.gov/cummings
CoS .... *Vernon Simms* **LD** .... *Kimberly Ross*
Sch .... *Deborah Perry* **Press** .... *Devika Koppikar*
Bio: b. 1/18/51 Baltimore, MD; Baptist; JD Univ. of MD, 1976; Attorney; single
Comm.: Government Reform; Transportation & Infrastructure; Joint Economic
Dist. Offices: Baltimore, 410-685-9199; Catonsville, 410-719-8777

REPRESENTATIVES

Randy "Duke" Cunningham (R-50th/CA)   202-225-5452
2350 RHOB   8th Term/58%   Fax: 202-225-2558
Website: www.house.gov/cunningham
CoS .... *Harmony Allen* **LD** .... *Nancy Lifset*
Sch .... *Becky Kuhn* **Press** .... *Mark Olson*
Bio: b. 12/8/41 Los Angeles, CA; Christian; MBA National Univ., 1985; USN, 1966-87; Navy Pilot, Businessman; m. Nancy
Comm.: Appropriations; Select Intelligence
Dist. Office: Escondido, 760-737-8438

Artur Davis (D-7th/AL)   202-225-2665
208 CHOB   2nd Term/75%   Fax: 202-226-9567
Website: www.house.gov/arturdavis
CoS .... *Dana Gresham* **LD** .... *Amy Chevalier Efantis*
EA .... *Kiona Daniels* **Press** .... *Corey Ealons*
Bio: b. 10/9/67 Montgomery, AL; Baptist; JD Harvard Univ., 1993; Attorney; single
Comm.: Budget; Financial Services
Dist. Offices: Birmingham, 205-254-1960; Tuscaloosa, 205-752-5380; Selma, 334-877-4414; Livingston, 205-652-5834; Demopolis, 334-287-0860

Danny K. Davis (D-7th/IL)   202-225-5006
1526 LHOB   5th Term/86%   Fax: 202-225-5641
Website: www.house.gov/davis
CoS .... *Richard Boykin* **LD** .... *Caleb Gilchrist*
Sch .... *Kimberly Stevens* **CD** .... *Ira Cohen*
Bio: b. 9/6/41 Parkdale, AR; Baptist; PhD Union Inst., 1977; Educator, Health Care Planner; m. Vera
Comm.: Education & the Workforce; Government Reform; Small Business
Dist. Offices: Chicago, 773-533-7520; Broadview, 708-345-6857

Geoff Davis (R-4th/KY)   202-225-3465
1541 LHOB   1st Term/55%   Fax: 202-225-0003
Website: www.house.gov/geoffdavis
CoS .... *Justin Brasell* **LD** .... *Vacant*
Sch .... *Roberta Quis* **CD** .... *Jessica Towhey*
Bio: b. 10/26/58 New Castle, PA; Christian; BS United States Military Academy, 1981; USA, 1976-87; Manufacturing Consultant; m. Pat
Comm.: Armed Services; Financial Services
Dist. Offices: Fort Mitchell, 859-426-0080; Ashland, 606-324-9898

Jim Davis (D-11th/FL)   202-225-3376
409 CHOB   5th Term/86%   Fax: 202-225-5652
Website: www.house.gov/jimdavis
CoS .... *Karl Koch* **Dep CoS** ... *Tricia Barrentine*
Sch .. *Joan Rodriguez-Vogel* **Press** ... *Diane Pratt-Heavner*
Bio: b. 10/11/57 Tampa, FL; Episcopal; JD Univ. of FL, 1982; Attorney; m. Peggy
Comm.: Energy & Commerce
Dist. Offices: Tampa, 813-354-9217; St. Petersburg, 727-867-5301

Jo Ann S. Davis (R-1st/VA)   202-225-4261
1123 LHOB   3rd Term/80%   Fax: 202-225-4382
Website: joanndavis.house.gov
CoS .... *Chris Connelly* **LD** .... *Mary Springer*
Appt .... *Jenny Stein* **CD** .... *Chris Connelly*
Bio: b. 6/29/50 Rowan Co., NC; Assembly of God; Attended Hampton Roads Business Col.; Real Estate Broker, Small Businesswoman; m. Charles
Comm.: Armed Services; International Relations; Select Intelligence
Dist. Offices: Yorktown, 757-874-6687; Fredericksburg, 540-548-1086; Tappahannock, 804-443-0668

REPRESENTATIVES

Lincoln Davis (D-4th/TN)   202-225-6831
410 CHOB   2nd Term/55%   Fax: 202-226-5172
Website: www.house.gov/lincolndavis
CoS .... Beecher Frasier   **LD** .... Brandi McBride
Appt .... Emily Buttrey   **Press** .... Tom Hayden
Bio: b. 9/13/43 Pall Mall, TN; Southern Baptist; BS TN Tech. Univ., 1966; Public Official; m. Lynda
Comm.: Agriculture; Science; Transportation & Infrastructure
Dist. Offices: Jamestown, 931-879-2361; Rockwood, 865-354-3323; Columbia, 931-490-8699; McMinnville, 931-473-7251

Susan A. Davis (D-53rd/CA)   202-225-2040
1224 LHOB   3rd Term/67%   Fax: 202-225-2948
Website: www.house.gov/susandavis
CoS .... Lisa Sherman   **LD** .... Todd Houchins
Appt .... Cynthia Patton   **Press** .... Aaron Hunter
Bio: b. 4/13/44 Cambridge, MA; Jewish; MA UNC, 1968; Social Worker; m. Steve
Comm.: Armed Services; Education & the Workforce
Dist. Office: San Diego, 619-280-5353

Thomas M. Davis III (R-11th/VA)   202-225-1492
2348 RHOB   6th Term/60%   Fax: 202-225-3071
E-mail: tom.davis@mail.house.gov
Website: tomdavis.house.gov
CoS .... David Thomas   **LD** .... Bill Womack
Sch .... Gabriele Forsyth   **CD** .... David Marin
Bio: b. 1/5/49 Minot, ND; Christian Science; JD Univ. of VA, 1975; USA, 1971-72; USAR, 1972-79; Attorney; m. Jeannemarie
Comm.: Government Reform (Chair); Homeland Security
Dist. Offices: Annandale, 703-916-9610; Woodbridge, 703-590-4599

Nathan Deal (R-10th/GA)   202-225-5211
2133 RHOB   7th Term/Unc.   Fax: 202-225-8272
E-mail: congressmandeal@mail.house.gov
Website: www.house.gov/deal
CoS .... Chris Riley   **LD** .... Todd Smith
Sch .... Laura Holland   **Press** .... Chris Riley
Bio: b. 8/25/42 Millen, GA; Baptist; JD Mercer Univ., 1966; USA, 1966-68; Attorney, Judge; m. Sandra
Comm.: Energy & Commerce
Dist. Offices: Gainesville, 770-535-2592; LaFayette, 706-638-7042; Dalton, 706-226-5320

Peter A. DeFazio (D-4th/OR)   202-225-6416
2134 RHOB   10th Term/61%   Fax: 202-225-0032
Website: www.house.gov/defazio
CoS .... Penny Dodge   **LD** .... Tom Vinson
Sch .... Jamie Harrell   **Press** .... Kristie Greco
Bio: b. 5/27/47 Needham, MA; Catholic; MS Univ. of OR, 1977; USAF, 1967-71; Gerontologist, Congressional Aide; m. Myrnie Daut
Comm.: Homeland Security; Resources; Transportation & Infrastructure
Dist. Offices: Eugene, 541-465-6732; Coos Bay, 541-269-2609; Roseburg, 541-440-3523

Diana L. DeGette (D-1st/CO)   202-225-4431
1527 LHOB   5th Term/73%   Fax: 202-225-5657
Website: www.house.gov/degette
CoS .... Lisa Cohen   **LD** .... Shannon Good
Appt .... Michael Carey   **CD** .... Josh Freed
Bio: b. 7/29/57 Tachikawa AFB, Japan; Presbyterian; JD NYU, 1982; Attorney; m. Lino Lipinsky
Comm.: Energy & Commerce
Dist. Office: Denver, 303-844-4988 1100

REPRESENTATIVES

William Delahunt (D-10th/MA)   202-225-3111
2454 RHOB   5th Term/66%   Fax: 202-225-5658
E-mail: william.delahunt@mail.house.gov
Website: www.house.gov/delahunt
CoS .... *Steven Schwadron* **LD** .... *Steven Schwadron*
Sch .... *Steven Broderick* **Press** .... *Steven Schwadron*
Bio: b. 7/18/41 Quincy, MA; Catholic; JD Boston Col., 1967; USCGR, 1963-71; Attorney; div.
Comm.: International Relations; Judiciary
Dist. Offices: Quincy, 617-770-3700; Hyannis, 508-771-0666

Rosa DeLauro (D-3rd/CT)   202-225-3661
2262 RHOB   8th Term/72%   Fax: 202-225-4890
Website: www.house.gov/delauro
CoS .... *Ashley Turton* **LD** .... *Rebecca Salay*
Sch .... *Nancy Mulry* **Press** .... *Kate Cyrul*
Bio: b. 3/2/43 New Haven, CT; Catholic; MA Columbia Univ., 1966; Political Advisor; m. Stanley Greenberg
Comm.: Appropriations; Budget
Dist. Office: New Haven, 203-562-3718

Tom DeLay (R-22nd/TX)   202-225-5951
242 CHOB   11th Term/55%   Fax: 202-225-5241
Website: tomdelay.house.gov
CoS .... *Tim Berry* **LD** .... *David James*
Appt .... *Dawn Loffredo* **CD** .... *Dan Allen*
Bio: b. 4/8/47 Laredo, TX; Baptist; BS Univ. of Houston, 1970; Businessman; m. Christine
Comm.: Majority Leader
Dist. Office: Stafford, 281-240-3700

Charles W. Dent (R-15th/PA)   202-225-6411
502 CHOB   1st Term/59%   Fax: 202-226-0778
Website: www.house.gov/dent
CoS .... *George McElwee* **LD** .... *Pete Richards*
Sch .... *Heather Smith* **Press** .... *Gregg Bortz*
Bio: b. 5/24/60 Allentown, PA; Protestant; MPA Lehigh Univ., 1993; Public Official; m. Pamela Jane Serfass
Comm.: Government Reform; Homeland Security; Transportation & Infrastructure
Dist. Office: Bethlehem, 610-861-9734

Lincoln Diaz-Balart (R-21st/FL)   202-225-4211
2244 RHOB   7th Term/72%   Fax: 202-225-8576
Website: diaz-balart.house.gov
CoS .... *Ana Carbonell* **LD** .... *Towner French*
Sch .... *Bettina Inclan* **Press** .... *Danielle Holland*
Bio: b. 8/13/54 Havana, Cuba; Catholic; JD Case Western Reserve Univ., 1979; Attorney; m. Cristina
Comm.: Rules
Dist. Office: Miami, 305-470-8555

Mario Diaz-Balart (R-25th/FL)   202-225-2778
313 CHOB   2nd Term/Unc.   Fax: 202-226-0346
Website: www.house.gov/mariodiaz-balart
CoS .... *Omar Franco* **LD** .... *Charles Cooper*
Sch .... *January Igot* **Press** .... *Thomas Bean*
Bio: b. 9/25/61 Ft. Lauderdale, FL; Catholic; Attended Univ. of S. FL; Public Official; single
Comm.: Budget; Transportation & Infrastructure
Dist. Offices: Miami, 305-225-6866; Naples, 239-348-1620

REPRESENTATIVES

Norman D. Dicks (D-6th/WA)   202-225-5916
2467 RHOB   15th Term/69%   Fax: 202-226-1176
Website: www.house.gov/dicks
CoS .... *George Behan* **LD** .... *Pete Modaff*
Appt .... *Alyson Daly* **Press** .... *George Behan*
Bio: b. 12/16/40 Bremerton, WA; Lutheran; JD Univ. of WA, 1968; Attorney; m. Suzie
Comm.: Appropriations; Homeland Security
Dist. Offices: Tacoma, 253-593-6536; Bremerton, 360-479-4011; Port Angeles, 360-452-3370

John D. Dingell (D-15th/MI)   202-225-4071
2328 RHOB   26th Term/71%   Fax: 202-226-0371
Website: www.house.gov/dingell
CoS .... *Rick Kessler* **LD** .... *Joshua Tzuker*
Appt .... *Beth Siniawsky* **Press** .... *Adam Benson*
Bio: b. 7/8/26 Colorado Springs, CO; Catholic; JD Georgetown Univ., 1952; USA, 1944-46; Attorney, Park Ranger; m. Deborah
Comm.: Energy & Commerce (Rnk. Mem.)
Dist. Offices: Dearborn, 313-278-2936; Monroe, 734-243-1849; Ypsilanti, 734-481-1100

Lloyd Doggett (D-25th/TX)   202-225-4865
201 CHOB   6th Term/68%   Fax: 202-225-2947
Website: www.house.gov/doggett
CoS .... *Michael Mucchetti* **LD** .... *Michael Mucchetti*
Sch .... *Diana Ramirez* **Press** .... *Jess Fassler*
Bio: b. 10/6/46 Austin, TX; Methodist; JD Univ. of TX, 1970; Attorney; m. Libby
Comm.: Ways & Means
Dist. Office: Austin, 512-916-5921

John T. Doolittle (R-4th/CA)   202-225-2511
2410 RHOB   8th Term/65%   Fax: 202-225-5444
Website: www.house.gov/doolittle
CoS .... *Richard Robinson* **LD** .... *Jason Larrabee*
Sch .... *Alisha Perkins* **CD** .... *Laura Blackann*
Bio: b. 10/30/50 Glendale, CA; Mormon; JD Univ. of the Pacific, 1978; Attorney; m. Julia
Comm.: Appropriations; House Administration; Joint Printing
Dist. Office: Granite Bay, 916-786-5560

Mike Doyle (D-14th/PA)   202-225-2135
401 CHOB   6th Term/Unc.   Fax: 202-225-3084
E-mail: rep.doyle@mail.house.gov
Website: www.house.gov/doyle
CoS .... *David Lucas* **LD** .... *Pat Cavanagh*
Sch .... *Ellen Young* **Press** .... *Matt Dinkel*
Bio: b. 8/5/53 Pittsburgh, PA; Catholic; BS Penn St. Univ., 1975; Businessman; m. Susan
Comm.: Energy & Commerce; Standards of Official Conduct
Dist. Offices: Penn Hills, 412-241-6055; McKeesport, 412-664-4049; Pittsburgh, 412-261-5091

Thelma D. Drake (R-2nd/VA)   202-225-4215
1208 LHOB   1st Term/55%   Fax: 202-225-4218
Website: www.house.gov/drake
CoS .... *Tom Gordy* **LD** .... *Sarah Hamlett*
Sch .... *Jennifer Lawrence* **Press** .... *Jim Jeffries*
Bio: b. 11/20/49 Elyria, OH; United Church of Christ; HS Diploma; Realtor; m. Ted
Comm.: Armed Services; Education & the Workforce; Resources
Dist. Offices: Virginia Beach, 757-497-6859; Accomac, 757-787-7836

REPRESENTATIVES

David Dreier (R-26th/CA)   202-225-2305
233 CHOB   13th Term/54%   Fax: 202-225-7018
Website: dreier.house.gov
CoS .... *Brad Smith* **LD** .... *Alisa Do*
Sch .... *Ryan Maxson* **Press** .... *Jo Maney*
Bio: b. 7/5/52 Kansas City, MO; Christian Science; MA Claremont McKenna Col., 1976; Real Estate Developer; single
Comm.: Rules (Chair)
Dist. Office: Glendora, 626-852-2626

John J. Duncan, Jr. (R-2nd/TN)   202-225-5435
2267 RHOB   10th Term/79%   Fax: 202-225-6440
Website: www.house.gov/duncan
CoS .... *Bob Griffitts* **LD** .... *Don Walker*
Sch .... *Victoria Jansma* **CD** .... *Matt Lehigh*
Bio: b. 7/21/47 Lebanon, TN; Presbyterian; JD George Washington Univ., 1973; USARNG, 1970-87; Attorney, Judge; m. Lynn
Comm.: Government Reform; Resources; Transportation & Infrastructure
Dist. Offices: Knoxville, 865-523-3772; Maryville, 865-984-5464; Athens, 423-745-4671

Chet Edwards (D-17th/TX)   202-225-6105
2264 RHOB   8th Term/51%   Fax: 202-225-2234
Website: edwards.house.gov
CoS .... *Chris Chwastyk* **LD** .... *John Conger*
Sch .... *Sara Bamford* **Press** .... *Josh Taylor*
Bio: b. 11/24/51 Corpus Christi, TX; Methodist; MBA Harvard Univ., 1981; Radio Station Owner; m. Lea Ann Wood
Comm.: Appropriations; Budget
Dist. Offices: Waco, 254-752-9600; College Station, 979-691-8797; Cleburne, 817-645-4743

Vernon Ehlers (R-3rd/MI)   202-225-3831
1714 LHOB   7th Term/67%   Fax: 202-225-5144
Website: www.house.gov/ehlers
CoS .... *Bill McBride* **LD** .... *Matt Reiffer*
Appt .... *Loraine Kehl* **Press** .... *Jon Brandt*
Bio: b. 2/6/34 Pipestone, MN; Christian Reformed; PhD Univ. of CA - Berkeley, 1960; Professor; m. Johanna
Comm.: Education & the Workforce; House Administration; Science; Transportation & Infrastructure; Joint Library
Dist. Office: Grand Rapids, 616-451-8383

Rahm Emanuel (D-5th/IL)   202-225-4061
1319 LHOB   2nd Term/76%   Fax: 202-225-5603
Website: www.house.gov/emanuel
CoS ... *Elizabeth Sears Smith* **LD** .... *Pete Spiro*
Sch .... *Koren Bell* **Press** .... *Kathleen Connery*
Bio: b. 11/29/59 Chicago, IL; Jewish; MS Northwestern Univ., 1985; Businessman; m. Amy
Comm.: Ways & Means
Dist. Office: Chicago, 773-267-5926

Jo Ann H. Emerson (R-8th/MO)   202-225-4404
2440 RHOB   5th Term/72%   Fax: 202-226-0326
Website: www.house.gov/emerson
CoS .... *Lloyd Smith* **LD** .... *Grant Erdel*
Sch .... *Atalie Ebersole* **CD** .... *Jeffrey Connor*
Bio: b. 9/16/50 Bethesda, MD; Presbyterian; BA OH Wesleyan Univ., 1972; Association Executive; m. Ron Gladney
Comm.: Appropriations
Dist. Offices: Cape Girardeau, 573-335-0101; Rolla, 573-364-2455; Farmington, 573-756-9755

REPRESENTATIVES

Eliot Engel (D-17th/NY)   202-225-2464
2161 RHOB   9th Term/76%   Fax: 202-225-5513
Website: www.house.gov/engel
CoS .... *Jason Steinbaum* **LD** .... *Pete Leon*
Appt ...... *Michelle Shwimer* **Press** .... *Gary Meltz*
Bio: b. 2/18/47 Bronx, NY; Jewish; JD NY Law School, 1987; Teacher; m. Patricia
Comm.: Energy & Commerce; International Relations
Dist. Offices: Bronx, 718-796-9700; West Nyack, 845-735-1000; Mt. Vernon, 914-699-4100

Philip S. English (R-3rd/PA)   202-225-5406
1410 LHOB   6th Term/60%   Fax: 202-225-3103
Website: www.house.gov/english
AA .... *Bob Holste* **LD** .... *David Stewart*
Sch .... *Annette Carr* **Press** .... *Idil Oyman*
Bio: b. 6/20/56 Erie, PA; Catholic; BA Univ. of PA, 1979; Legislative Aide; m. Chris
Comm.: Ways & Means; Joint Economic
Dist. Offices: Erie, 814-456-2038; Butler, 724-285-7005; Hermitage, 724-342-6132; Meadville, 814-724-8414; Warren, 814-723-7282

Anna Eshoo (D-14th/CA)   202-225-8104
205 CHOB   7th Term/70%   Fax: 202-225-8890
Website: eshoo.house.gov
CoS .... *Jason Mahler* **LD** .... *Steven Keenan*
Sch .... *Dana Sandman* **Press** .... *Jason Mahler*
Bio: b. 12/13/42 New Britain, CT; Catholic; AA Canada Col., 1975; Public Official; div.
Comm.: Energy & Commerce; Select Intelligence
Dist. Office: Palo Alto, 650-323-2984

Bob Etheridge (D-2nd/NC)   202-225-4531
1533 LHOB   5th Term/63%   Fax: 202-225-5662
Website: www.house.gov/etheridge
CoS .... *Julie Dwyer* **LD** .... *Patrick Devlin*
Appt .... *Leigh Ann Smith* **Press** ...... *Sara Yawn Lang*
Bio: b. 8/7/41 Sampson Co., NC; Presbyterian; BS Campbell Univ., 1965; USA, 1965-67; Small Businessman; m. Faye
Comm.: Agriculture; Homeland Security
Dist. Offices: Raleigh, 919-829-9122; Lillington, 910-814-0335

Lane Evans (D-17th/IL)   202-225-5905
2211 RHOB   12th Term/61%   Fax: 202-225-5396
E-mail: lane.evans@mail.house.gov
Website: www.house.gov/evans
CoS .... *Dennis King* **LD** .... *Kevin Gash*
Sch .... *Eda Robinson* **Press** .... *Steve Vetzner*
Bio: b. 8/4/51 Rock Island, IL; Catholic; JD Georgetown Univ., 1978; USMC, 1969-71; Attorney; single
Comm.: Armed Services; Veterans' Affairs (Rnk. Mem.)
Dist. Offices: Moline, 309-793-5760; Galesburg, 309-342-4411; Decatur, 217-422-9150

Terry Everett (R-2nd/AL)   202-225-2901
2312 RHOB   7th Term/71%   Fax: 202-225-8913
Website: www.house.gov/everett
CoS .... *Wade Heck* **LD** .... *Forrest Allen*
Sch .... *Susan Swift* **Press** .... *Mike Lewis*
Bio: b. 2/15/37 Dothan, AL; Baptist; Attended Enterprise St. Jr. Col.; USAF, 1955-59; Newspaper Publisher; m. Barbara
Comm.: Agriculture; Armed Services; Veterans' Affairs; Select Intelligence
Dist. Offices: Dothan, 334-794-9680; Montgomery, 334-277-9113; Opp, 334-493-9253

REPRESENTATIVES

Eni F.H. Faleomavaega (D/AS)   202-225-8577
2422 RHOB   9th Term/53%   Fax: 202-225-8757
E-mail: faleomavaega@mail.house.gov
Website: www.house.gov/faleomavaega
CoS .... Alex Godinet **LD** .... Lisa Williams
Sch .... Vili Le'i **Press** .... Lisa Williams
Bio: b. 8/15/43 Vailoatai Village, AS; Mormon; LLM Univ. of CA - Berkeley, 1973; USA, 1966-69; Attorney; m. Hinanui Bambridge Cave
Comm.: International Relations; Resources; Small Business
Dist. Office: Pago Pago, 684-633-1372

Sam Farr (D-17th/CA)   202-225-2861
1221 LHOB   7th Term/67%   Fax: 202-225-6791
Website: www.farr.house.gov
CoS .... Rochelle Dornatt **LD** .... Debbie Merrill
Appt .... Tom Tucker **Press** .... Jessica Schafer
Bio: b. 7/4/41 San Francisco, CA; Episcopal; BS Willamette Univ., 1963; Budget Analyst; m. Shary
Comm.: Appropriations
Dist. Offices: Salinas, 831-424-2229; Santa Cruz, 831-429-1976

Chaka Fattah (D-2nd/PA)   202-225-4001
2301 RHOB   6th Term/88%   Fax: 202-225-5392
Website: www.house.gov/fattah
CoS .... Michelle **LD** .... Jerome Murray
               Anderson-Lee
Sch .... Debra Anderson **CD** .... Debra Anderson
Bio: b. 11/21/56 Philadelphia, PA; Baptist; MA Univ. of PA, 1986; Public Official; m. Renee
Comm.: Appropriations
Dist. Offices: Philadelphia, 215-387-6404; Philadelphia, 215-848-9386

Tom Feeney (R-24th/FL)   202-225-2706
323 CHOB   2nd Term/Unc.   Fax: 202-226-6299
Website: www.house.gov/feeney
CoS .... Jason Roe **LD** .... Ryan Visco
Appt .... Audra Ozols **Press** .... Shannon Conklin
Bio: b. 5/21/58 Abington, PA; Presbyterian; JD Univ. of Pittsburgh, 1983; Attorney; m. Ellen Stewart
Comm.: Financial Services; Judiciary; Science
Dist. Offices: Orlando, 407-208-1106; Port Orange, 386-756-9798; Titusville, 321-264-6113

Michael A. Ferguson (R-7th/NJ)   202-225-5361
214 CHOB   3rd Term/57%   Fax: 202-225-9460
Website: www.house.gov/ferguson
CoS .... Chris Jones **LD** .... Greg Orlando
Sch .... Erin Connolly **Press** .... Abby Bird
Bio: b. 7/22/70 Ridgewood, NJ; Catholic; MPP Georgetown Univ., 1995; Educator, Small Businessman; m. Maureen
Comm.: Energy & Commerce
Dist. Office: Warren, 908-757-7835

Bob Filner (D-51st/CA)   202-225-8045
2428 RHOB   7th Term/62%   Fax: 202-225-9073
Website: www.house.gov/filner
CoS .... Tony Buckles **LD** .... Thaddeus Hoffmeister
Sch .... Kim Messineo **Press** .... Marielena
                                           Castellanos
Bio: b. 9/4/42 Pittsburgh, PA; Jewish; PhD Cornell Univ., 1973; Professor; m. Jane
Comm.: Transportation & Infrastructure; Veterans' Affairs
Dist. Offices: Chula Vista, 619-422-5963; Imperial, 760-355-8800

REPRESENTATIVES

Mike Fitzpatrick (R-8th/PA)   202-225-4276
1516 LHOB   1st Term/55%   Fax: 202-225-9511
E-mail: michael.fitzpatrick@mail.house.gov
Website: www.house.gov/fitzpatrick
CoS .... *Mike Conallen* **LD** .... *Mike Conallen*
Sch .... *Faith Leichliter* **CD** .... *Mike Conallen*
Bio: b. 6/28/63 Philadelphia, PA; Catholic; JD Dickinson School of Law, 1988; Attorney; m. Kathleen
Comm.: Financial Services; Small Business
Dist. Offices: Langhorne, 215-752-7711; Doylestown, 215-348-7511

Jeff Flake (R-6th/AZ)   202-225-2635
424 CHOB   3rd Term/79%   Fax: 202-226-4386
Website: www.house.gov/flake
CoS .... *Margaret Klessig* **LD** .... *Brian Clifford*
Appt .. *Noelle LeCheminant* **Press** .... *Matthew Specht*
Bio: b. 12/31/62 Snowflake, AZ; Mormon; MA Brigham Young Univ., 1987; Businessman; m. Cheryl
Comm.: International Relations; Judiciary; Resources
Dist. Office: Mesa, 480-833-0092

Mark Foley (R-16th/FL)   202-225-5792
104 CHOB   6th Term/68%   Fax: 202-225-3132
Website: www.house.gov/foley
CoS .... *Don Kiselewski* **LD** .... *Bradley Schreiber*
OpD .... *Dean Lester* **CD** .... *Jason Kello*
Bio: b. 9/8/54 Newton, MA; Catholic; Attended Palm Beach Comm. Col.; Real Estate Broker; single
Comm.: Ways & Means
Dist. Offices: Palm Beach Gardens, 561-627-6192; Port St. Lucie, 772-878-3181; Port Charlotte, 941-627-9100

Randy Forbes (R-4th/VA)   202-225-6365
307 CHOB   3rd Term/65%   Fax: 202-226-1170
Website: www.house.gov/forbes
CoS .... *Dee Gilmore* **LD** .... *Andrew Halataei*
Sch .... *Bonnie Benn* **CD** .... *Christy Boardman*
Bio: b. 2/17/52 Chesapeake, VA; Baptist; JD Univ. of VA, 1977; Attorney; m. Shirley Lee Hendricks
Comm.: Armed Services; Judiciary; Science
Dist. Offices: Chesapeake, 757-382-0080; Emporia, 434-634-5575; Colonial Heights, 804-526-4969

Harold E. Ford, Jr. (D-9th/TN)   202-225-3265
325 CHOB   5th Term/82%   Fax: 202-225-5663
E-mail: rep.harold.ford.jr@mail.house.gov
Website: www.house.gov/ford
CoS .... *Mark Schuermann* **LD** .... *Scott Keefer*
Appt ...... *Amy Mollenkamp* **Press** .... *Zac Wright*
Bio: b. 5/11/70 Memphis, TN; Baptist; JD Univ. of MI, 1996; Law Clerk; single
Comm.: Budget; Financial Services
Dist. Office: Memphis, 901-544-4131

Jeff Fortenberry (R-1st/NE)   202-225-4806
1517 LHOB   1st Term/54%   Fax: 202-225-5686
E-mail: jeff.fortenberry@mail.house.gov
Website: www.house.gov/fortenberry
CoS .... *Ben Sasse* **LD** .... *Ginger Langemeier*
Sch .... *Tyler Grassmeyer* **Press** .... *Brian Lee*
Bio: b. 12/27/60 Baton Rouge, LA; Catholic; MA Franciscan Univ. 1996; Publishing Executive; m. Celeste Gregory
Comm.: Agriculture; International Relations; Small Business
Dist. Office: Lincoln, 402-438-1598; Fremont, 402-727-0888

REPRESENTATIVES

Luis Fortuño (R/PR)   202-225-2615
126 CHOB   1st Term/49%   Fax: 202-225-2154
Website: www.house.gov/fortuno
CoS .... Luis E. Baco   LD .... Luis E. Baco
Sch .... Mary Taronji   Press ...... Nicole Guillemard
Bio: b. 10/31/60 San Juan, PR; Catholic; JD Univ. of VA; Attorney; m. Luce
Comm.: Education & the Workforce; Resources; Transportation & Infrastructure
Dist. Office: Old San Juan, 787-723-6333

Vito Fossella (R-13th/NY)   202-225-3371
1239 LHOB   5th Term/59%   Fax: 202-226-1272
E-mail: vito.fossella@mail.house.gov
Website: www.house.gov/fossella
CoS .... Tom Quaadman   LD .... Brendon Weiss
Sch .... Vicki Hook   Press .... Craig Donner
Bio: b. 3/9/65 Staten Island, NY; Catholic; JD Fordham Univ., 1993; Public Official; m. Mary Pat
Comm.: Energy & Commerce; Financial Services
Dist. Offices: Staten Island, 718-356-8400; Brooklyn, 718-630-5277

Virginia Foxx (R-5th/NC)   202-225-2071
503 CHOB   1st Term/59%   Fax: 202-225-2995
Website: www.house.gov/foxx
CoS .... Richard Hudson   PD .... Deana Funderburk
EA .... Eliza Baker   CD .... Amy Auth
Bio: b. 6/29/43 New York, NY; Catholic; EdD UNC - Greensboro, 1985; Business Owner; m. Thomas
Comm.: Agriculture; Education & the Workforce; Government Reform
Dist. Office: Clemmons, 336-778-0173

Barney Frank (D-4th/MA)   202-225-5931
2252 RHOB   13th Term/78%   Fax: 202-225-0182
Website: www.house.gov/frank
CoS .... Peter Kovar   LD .... Peter Kovar
Appt .... Maria Giesta   Press .... Peter Kovar
Bio: b. 3/31/40 Bayonne, NJ; Jewish; JD Harvard Univ., 1977; Attorney; single
Comm.: Financial Services (Rnk. Mem.)
Dist. Offices: Newton, 617-332-3920; Taunton, 508-822-4796; New Bedford, 508-999-6462

Trent Franks (R-2nd/AZ)   202-225-4576
1237 LHOB   2nd Term/59%   Fax: 202-225-6328
Website: www.house.gov/franks
CoS .... Tom Stallings   LD .... Doyle Scott
Appt .... Lisa Teschler   Press .... Vacant
Bio: b. 6/19/57 Uravan, CO; Baptist; Attended Ottawa Univ.; Business Owner, Commentator; m. Josephine
Comm.: Armed Services; Judiciary
Dist. Office: Glendale, 623-776-7911

Rodney Frelinghuysen (R-11th/NJ)   202-225-5034
2442 RHOB   6th Term/68%   Fax: 202-225-3186
Website: frelinghuysen.house.gov
CoS .... Nancy Fox   LD .... Steve Wilson
Sch .... Meredith Kenny   Press .... Steve O'Halloran
Bio: b. 4/29/46 New York, NY; Episcopal; BA Hobart Col., 1969; USA, 1969-71; Public Official; m. Virginia
Comm.: Appropriations
Dist. Office: Morristown, 973-984-0711

REPRESENTATIVES

Elton Gallegly (R-24th/CA) — 202-225-5811
2427 RHOB   10th Term/62%   Fax: 202-225-1100
Website: www.house.gov/gallegly
CoS .... *Patrick Murphy* **LD** .... *Kevin Studer*
Sch .... *Pamela Roller* **Press** .... *Tom Pfeifer*
Bio: b. 3/7/44 Huntington Park, CA; Protestant; Attended CA St. Univ. - Los Angeles; Real Estate Broker; m. Janice Shrader
Comm.: International Relations; Judiciary; Resources; Select Intelligence
Dist. Offices: Thousand Oaks, 805-497-2224; Solvang, 805-686-2525

Scott Garrett (R-5th/NJ) — 202-225-4465
1318 LHOB   2nd Term/58%   Fax: 202-225-9048
Website: www.house.gov/garrett
CoS .... *Evan Kozlow* **LD** .... *Jay Fahrer*
Sch .... *Laurel Edmondson* **Press** .... *Phillip Brown*
Bio: b. 7/9/59 Englewood, NJ; Protestant; JD Rutgers Univ., 1984; Public Official, Attorney; m. Mary Ellen Cosmas
Comm.: Budget; Financial Services
Dist. Offices: Paramus, 201-712-0330; Newton, 973-300-2000

Jim Gerlach (R-6th/PA) — 202-225-4315
308 CHOB   2nd Term/51%   Fax: 202-225-8440
Website: www.house.gov/gerlach
CoS .... *Linda Pedigo* **LD** .... *Bill Tighe*
Sch .... *Michael Robinson* **CD** .... *John Gentzel*
Bio: b. 2/25/55 Ellwood City, PA; Protestant; JD Dickinson School of Law, 1980; Public Official; m. Karen
Comm.: Financial Services; Transportation & Infrastructure
Dist. Offices: Exton, 610-594-1415; Wyomissing, 610-376-7630; Trappe, 610-409-2780

James A. Gibbons (R-2nd/NV) — 202-225-6155
100 CHOB   5th Term/67%   Fax: 202-225-5679
Website: www.house.gov/gibbons
CoS .... *Amy Spanbauer* **LD** .... *Corry Kennedy*
Sch .... *Pia Pyle* **CD** .... *Amy Spanbauer*
Bio: b. 12/16/44 Sparks, NV; Church of Jesus Christ of Latter-day Saints; JD Southwestern Univ., 1979; USAF, 1967-71; USANG, 1975-96; Attorney, Airline Pilot; m. Dawn
Comm.: Armed Services; Homeland Security; Resources
Dist. Offices: Reno, 775-686-5760; Elko, 775-777-7920; Las Vegas, 702-255-1651

Wayne Gilchrest (R-1st/MD) — 202-225-5311
2245 RHOB   8th Term/76%   Fax: 202-225-0254
Website: gilchrest.house.gov
CoS .... *Tony Caligiuri* **LD** .... *Dave Solan*
Sch .... *Kathy Hicks* **CD** .... *Cathy Bassett*
Bio: b. 4/15/46 Rahway, NJ; Methodist; BA DE St. Univ., 1973; USMC, 1964-68; Educator; m. Barbara
Comm.: Resources; Science; Transportation & Infrastructure
Dist. Offices: Chestertown, 410-778-9407; Salisbury, 410-749-3184; Bel Air, 410-838-2517

Paul E. Gillmor (R-5th/OH) — 202-225-6405
1203 LHOB   9th Term/67%   Fax: 202-225-1985
Website: gillmor.house.gov
CoS .... *Mark Wellman* **LD** .... *Erin Mincemoyer*
Sch .... *Kelley Kurtz* **Press** .... *Brad Mascho*
Bio: b. 2/1/39 Tiffin, OH; Methodist; JD Univ. of MI, 1964; USAF, 1965-66; Attorney; m. Karen
Comm.: Energy & Commerce; Financial Services
Dist. Offices: Tiffin, 419-448-9016; Defiance, 419-782-1996; Norwalk, 419-668-0206

REPRESENTATIVES

Phil Gingrey (R-11th/GA)   202-225-2931
119 CHOB   2nd Term/57%   Fax: 202-225-2944
E-mail: gingrey.ga@mail.house.gov
Website: www.house.gov/gingrey
CoS .... Mitch Hunter **LD** .... Rob Herriott
Sch .... Catherine Gabrysh **Press** .... Becky Ruby
Bio: b. 7/10/42 Augusta, GA; Catholic; MD Medical Col. of GA, 1969; Obstetrician, Gynecologist; m. Billie
Comm.: Rules
Dist. Offices: Marietta, 770-429-1776; Rome, 706-290-1776; Carrollton, 770-836-8130

Louie Gohmert (R-1st/TX)   202-225-3035
508 CHOB   1st Term/62%   Fax: 202-225-5866
Website: www.house.gov/gohmert
CoS .... Samantha Jordan **LD** .... Michael Tomberlin
Sch .... Lauren Huly **Press** .... Amos Snead
Bio: b. 8/18/53 Pittsburg, TX; Baptist; JD Baylor Univ., 1977; USA, 1977-82; Judge, Attorney; m. Kathy
Comm.: Judiciary; Resources; Small Business
Dist. Offices: Tyler, 903-561-6349; Longview, 903-236-8597

Charles A. Gonzalez (D-20th/TX)   202-225-3236
327 CHOB   4th Term/66%   Fax: 202-225-1915
Website: www.house.gov/gonzalez
CoS .... Kevin Kimble **LD** .... Tony Zaffirini
Sch .. Rose Ann Maldonado **Press** .... Adrian Saenz
Bio: b. 5/5/45 San Antonio, TX; Catholic; JD St. Mary's Univ., 1972; TXANG, 1969-75; Judge; div.
Comm.: Energy & Commerce
Dist. Office: San Antonio, 210-472-6195

Virgil H. Goode, Jr. (R-5th/VA)   202-225-4711
1520 LHOB   5th Term/64%   Fax: 202-225-5681
Website: www.house.gov/goode
CoS .... Jerr Rosenbaum **LD** .... David Jennings
Sch .... Judy Mattox **Press** .... Linwood Duncan
Bio: b. 10/17/46 Richmond, VA; Baptist; JD Univ. of VA, 1973; VANG, 1969-75; Attorney; m. Lucy
Comm.: Appropriations
Dist. Offices: Charlottesville, 434-295-6372; Danville, 434-792-1280; Farmville, 434-392-8331; Rocky Mount, 540-484-1254

Bob Goodlatte (R-6th/VA)   202-225-5431
2240 RHOB   7th Term/Unc.   Fax: 202-225-9681
Website: www.house.gov/goodlatte
CoS .... Shelley Husband **LC** .... Carrie Meadows
Appt .... Suzanne Michel **Press** .... Kathryn Rexrode
Bio: b. 9/22/52 Holyoke, MA; Christian Science; JD Washington & Lee Univ., 1977; Attorney; m. Maryellen
Comm.: Agriculture (Chair); Judiciary
Dist. Offices: Roanoke, 540-857-2672; Staunton, 540-885-3861; Harrisonburg, 540-432-2391; Lynchburg, 434-845-8306

Bart Gordon (D-6th/TN)   202-225-4231
2304 RHOB   11th Term/64%   Fax: 202-225-6887
Website: gordon.house.gov
CoS .... Chuck Atkins **LD** .... David Plunkett
Sch .... Julie Eubank **Press** .... Keith Talley
Bio: b. 1/24/49 Murfreesboro, TN; Methodist; JD Univ. of TN, 1973; USAR, 1971-72; Attorney; m. Leslie
Comm.: Energy & Commerce; Science (Rnk. Mem.)
Dist. Offices: Murfreesboro, 615-896-1986; Cookeville, 931-528-5907; Gallatin, 615-451-5174

REPRESENTATIVES

Kay Granger (R-12th/TX)   202-225-5071
440 CHOB   5th Term/72%   Fax: 202-225-5683
Website: kaygranger.house.gov
CoS .... *Vacant*   **LD** .... *Robert Head*
Sch .... *Stacey Kounelias*   **Press** .... *Caitlin Carroll*
Bio: b. 1/18/43 Greenville, TX; Methodist; BS TX Wesleyan Univ., 1965; Teacher, Insurance Agent; div.
Comm.: Appropriations
Dist. Office: Ft. Worth, 817-338-0909

Sam Graves (R-6th/MO)   202-225-7041
1513 LHOB   3rd Term/64%   Fax: 202-225-8221
E-mail: sam.graves@mail.house.gov
Website: www.house.gov/graves
CoS .... *Jeff Roe*   **Dep CoS** .... *Mike Falencki*
Sch .... *Nancy Potter*   **Press** .... *Jason Klindt*
Bio: b. 11/7/63 Tarkio, MO; Baptist; BS Univ. of MO - Columbia, 1986; Farmer; m. Lesley
Comm.: Agriculture; Small Business; Transportation & Infrastructure
Dist. Offices: Liberty, 816-792-3976; St. Joseph, 816-233-9818

Al Green (D-9th/TX)   202-225-7508
1529 LHOB   1st Term/72%   Fax: 202-225-2947
E-mail: al.green@mail.house.gov
Website: www.house.gov/algreen
CoS .... *Jacqueline Ellis*   **LD** .... *Oscar Ramirez*
Sch .... *Brett Merfish*   **CD** .... *Ashley Etienne*
Bio: b. 9/1/47 New Orleans, LA; Baptist; JD TX Southern Univ., 1974; Attorney; single
Comm.: Financial Services; Science
Dist. Office: Houston, 713-383-9234

Gene Green (D-29th/TX)   202-225-1688
2335 RHOB   7th Term/Unc.   Fax: 202-225-9903
Website: www.house.gov/green
CoS .... *Rhonda Jackson*   **LD** .... *Andrew Wallace*
Appt .... *Abigail Pinkele*   **CD** .... *Celinda Gonzalez*
Bio: b. 10/17/47 Houston, TX; Methodist; BA Univ. of Houston, 1971; Attorney; m. Helen
Comm.: Energy & Commerce; Standards of Official Conduct
Dist. Offices: Houston, 281-999-5879; Houston, 713-330-0761

Mark Green (R-8th/WI)   202-225-5665
1314 LHOB   4th Term/70%   Fax: 202-225-5729
E-mail: mark.green@mail.house.gov
Website: www.house.gov/markgreen
CoS .... *Chris Tuttle*   **PD** .... *Dan Roehl*
OpD .... *Nicole Vernon*   **Press** ..... *Luke Punzenberger*
Bio: b. 6/1/60 Boston, MA; Catholic; JD Univ. of WI - Madison, 1987; Attorney; m. Sue
Comm.: International Relations; Judiciary
Dist. Offices: Green Bay, 920-437-1954; Appleton, 920-380-0061

Raúl M. Grijalva (D-7th/AZ)   202-225-2435
1440 LHOB   2nd Term/61%   Fax: 202-226-6846
Website: www.house.gov/grijalva
CoS .... *Glenn Miller*   **LD** .... *Chris Kaumo*
Appt .... *Amy Emerick*   **Press** .... *Natalie Luna*
Bio: b. 2/19/48 Tucson, AZ; Catholic; BA Univ. of AZ, 1986; Public Official; m. Ramona
Comm.: Education & the Workforce; Resources; Small Business
Dist. Offices: Tucson, 520-622-6788; Yuma, 928-343-7933

REPRESENTATIVES

Luis V. Gutierrez (D-4th/IL)   202-225-8203
2367 RHOB   7th Term/84%   Fax: 202-225-7810
Website: luisgutierrez.house.gov
CoS .... *Jennice Fuentes* **LD** .... *Susan Collins*
Sch .... *Joan Kato* **CD** .... *Scott Frotman*
Bio: b. 12/10/53 Chicago, IL; Catholic; BA Northeastern IL Univ., 1974; Educator; m. Soraida Arocho
Comm.: Financial Services; Veterans' Affairs
Dist. Offices: Chicago, 773-384-1655; Chicago, 312-666-3882

Gil Gutknecht (R-1st/MN)   202-225-2472
425 CHOB   6th Term/60%   Fax: 202-225-3246
Website: www.gil.house.gov
CoS .... *Stephanie Brand* **LD** .... *Ryan McLaughlin*
Sch .... *April Dabney* **Press** .... *Bryan Anderson*
Bio: b. 3/20/51 Cedar Falls, IA; Catholic; BA Univ. of Northern IA, 1973; Real Estate Auctioneer; m. Mary
Comm.: Agriculture; Government Reform; Science
Dist. Offices: Rochester, 507-252-9841; Fairmont, 507-238-2835

Ralph M. Hall (R-4th/TX)   202-225-6673
2405 RHOB   13th Term/68%   Fax: 202-225-3332
Website: www.house.gov/ralphhall
CoS .. *Janet Perry Poppleton* **LD** .... *Grace Warren*
Appt .... *Katie Comer* **CD** .... *Leslee Gilbert*
Bio: b. 5/3/23 Fate, TX; Methodist; LLB Southern Methodist Univ., 1951; USN, 1942-45; Attorney; m. Mary Ellen
Comm.: Energy & Commerce; Science
Dist. Offices: Rockwall, 972-771-9118; Sherman, 903-892-1112

Jane Harman (D-36th/CA)   202-225-8220
2400 RHOB   6th Term/62%   Fax: 202-226-7290
Website: www.house.gov/harman
CoS .... *John Hess* **LD** .... *Eric Edwards*
Sch .... *Sharon Liggett* **CD** .... *Tom Reynolds*
Bio: b. 6/28/45 New York, NY; Jewish; JD Harvard Univ., 1969; College Professor, Businesswoman; m. Sidney
Comm.: Homeland Security; Select Intelligence (Rnk. Mem.)
Dist. Offices: El Segundo, 310-643-3636; Wilmington, 310-549-8282

Katherine Harris (R-13th/FL)   202-225-5015
116 CHOB   2nd Term/55%   Fax: 202-226-0828
E-mail: katherine.harris@mail.house.gov
Website: harris.house.gov
CoS .... *Chris Battle* **LD** .... *Jennifer Platt*
Sch .... *Mona Tate Yost* **Press** .... *Garrison Courtney*
Bio: b. 4/5/57 Key West, FL; Presbyterian; MA Harvard Univ., 1996; Commercial Real Estate Broker; m. Anders Ebbeson
Comm.: Financial Services; Homeland Security; International Relations
Dist. Offices: Sarasota, 941-951-6643; Bradenton, 941-747-9081

Melissa A. Hart (R-4th/PA)   202-225-2565
1024 LHOB   3rd Term/63%   Fax: 202-226-2274
Website: hart.house.gov
CoS .... *Bill Ries* **LD** .... *William Rys*
Sch .... *Emilee Brasell* **Press** .... *Lee Cohen*
Bio: b. 4/4/62 Pittsburgh, PA; Catholic; JD Univ. of Pittsburgh, 1987; Attorney; single
Comm.: Standards of Official Conduct; Ways & Means
Dist. Offices: Allison Park, 412-492-0161; Ellwood City, 724-752-0490

REPRESENTATIVES

J. Dennis Hastert (R-14th/IL)   202-225-2976
235 CHOB   10th Term/69%   Fax: 202-225-0697
Website: www.house.gov/hastert
CoS .... *Scott Palmer* **LD** .... *Anthony Reed*
Appt .... *Helen Morrell* **Press** .... *Ron Bonjean*
Bio: b. 1/2/42 Aurora, IL; Protestant; MS Northern IL Univ., 1967; Educator; m. Jean
Comm.: Speaker
Dist. Offices: Batavia, 630-406-1114; Dixon, 815-288-0680

Alcee L. Hastings (D-23rd/FL)   202-225-1313
2353 RHOB   7th Term/Unc.   Fax: 202-225-1171
Website: www.alceehastings.house.gov
CoS .... *Fred Turner* **LD** .... *David Goldenberg*
Sch .... *Barbara Harper* **Press** .... *Fred Turner*
Bio: b. 9/5/36 Altamonte Springs, FL; African Methodist Episcopal; JD FL A&M Univ., 1963; Attorney; single
Comm.: Rules; Select Intelligence
Dist. Offices: Ft. Lauderdale, 954-733-2800; West Palm Beach, 561-684-0565

Doc Hastings (R-4th/WA)   202-225-5816
1323 LHOB   6th Term/63%   Fax: 202-225-3251
Website: www.house.gov/hastings
CoS .... *Ed Cassidy* **LD** .... *Todd Young*
Sch .... *Ilene Clauson* **Press** .... *Jessica Gleason*
Bio: b. 2/7/41 Spokane, WA; Not Stated; Attended Central WA Univ.; USAR, 1963-69; Businessman; m. Claire
Comm.: Rules; Standards of Official Conduct (Chair)
Dist. Offices: Pasco, 509-543-9396; Yakima, 509-452-3243

Robin Hayes (R-8th/NC)   202-225-3715
130 CHOB   4th Term/56%   Fax: 202-225-4036
Website: hayes.house.gov
CoS .... *Andrew Duke* **LD** .... *Jennifer Thompson*
Sch .... *Casey Talley* **Press** .... *Carolyn Hern*
Bio: b. 8/14/45 Concord, NC; Presbyterian; BA Duke Univ., 1967; Textile Mill Owner; m. Barbara
Comm.: Agriculture; Armed Services; Transportation & Infrastructure
Dist. Offices: Concord, 704-786-1612; Rockingham, 910-997-2070

J.D. Hayworth (R-5th/AZ)   202-225-2190
2434 RHOB   6th Term/60%   Fax: 202-225-3263
Website: hayworth.house.gov
CoS .... *Joe Eule* **LD** .... *Katharine Mottley*
EA .... *Tricia Evans* **Press** .... *Larry VanHoose*
Bio: b. 7/12/58 High Point, NC; Baptist; BA NC St. Univ., 1980; Businessman, Media Commentator; m. Mary
Comm.: Resources; Ways & Means
Dist. Office: Scottsdale, 480-926-4151

Joel Hefley (R-5th/CO)   202-225-4422
2372 RHOB   10th Term/71%   Fax: 202-225-1942
Website: www.house.gov/hefley
CoS .... *Loren Whittemore* **LD** .... *Larry Hojo*
Sch .... *Rebecca Ross* **Press** .... *Kim Sears*
Bio: b. 4/18/35 Ardmore, OK; Presbyterian; MS OK St. Univ., 1962; Non-Profit Executive; m. Lynn
Comm.: Armed Services
Dist. Office: Colorado Springs, 719-520-0055

REPRESENTATIVES

Jeb Hensarling (R-5th/TX)   **202-225-3484**
132 CHOB   2nd Term/65%   Fax: 202-226-4888
Website: www.house.gov/hensarling
CoS .... *Dee Buchanan* **LD** .... *Gerry O'Shea*
Appt .... *Andi Small* **Press** .... *Mike Walz*
Bio: b. 5/29/57 Stephenville, TX; Episcopal; JD Univ. of TX, 1982; Businessman; m. Melissa
Comm.: Budget; Financial Services
Dist. Offices: Dallas, 214-349-9996; Athens, 903-675-8288

Wally Herger (R-2nd/CA)   **202-225-3076**
2268 RHOB   10th Term/67%   Fax: 202-226-0852
Website: www.house.gov/herger
CoS .... *John Magill* **LD** .... *Derek Harley*
Appt .... *Laura Cannon* **Press** .... *Daniel MacLean*
Bio: b. 5/20/45 Yuba City, CA; Mormon; AA American River Comm. Col., 1967; Rancher; m. Pamela
Comm.: Ways & Means
Dist. Offices: Chico, 530-893-8363; Redding, 530-223-5898

Stephanie Herseth (D-At Large/SD) **202-225-2801**
331 CHOB   2nd Term/53%   Fax: 202-225-5823
E-mail: stephanie.herseth@mail.house.gov
Website: www.house.gov/herseth
CoS .... *Jeff Navin* **LD** .... *Ryan Stroschein*
Sch ...... *McLean Thompson* **Press** .... *Russ Levsen*
Bio: b. 12/3/70 Aberdeen, SD; Not Stated; JD Georgetown Univ., 1997; Attorney; single
Comm.: Agriculture; Resources; Veterans' Affairs
Dist. Offices: Sioux Falls, 605-367-8371; Rapid City, 605-394-5280; Aberdeen, 605-626-3440

Brian M. Higgins (D-27th/NY)   **202-225-3306**
431 CHOB   1st Term/51%   Fax: 202-226-0347
Website: www.house.gov/higgins
AA .... *Suzanne Anziska* **LD** .... *Moira Campion*
Sch .... *Caitlin Lenihan* **CD** .... *Suzanne Anziska*
Bio: b. 10/6/59 Buffalo, NY; Catholic; MA Harvard Univ., 1996; Public Official; m. Mary Jane
Comm.: Government Reform; Transportation & Infrastructure
Dist. Offices: Buffalo, 716-852-3501; Jamestown, 716-484-0729

Maurice Hinchey (D-22nd/NY)   **202-225-6335**
2431 RHOB   7th Term/67%   Fax: 202-226-0774
Website: www.house.gov/hinchey
CoS .... *Wendy Darwell* **LD** .... *Mike Iger*
Appt .... *Sara Curtis* **Press** .... *Jeff Lieberson*
Bio: b. 10/27/38 New York, NY; Catholic; MA SUNY - New Paltz, 1970; USN, 1956-59; Public Official; m. Ilene
Comm.: Appropriations; Joint Economic
Dist. Offices: Kingston, 845-331-4466; Binghamton, 607-773-2768; Ithaca, 607-273-1388; Monticello, 845-791-7116; Middletown, 845-344-3211

Rubén E. Hinojosa (D-15th/TX)   **202-225-2531**
2463 RHOB   5th Term/58%   Fax: 202-225-5688
Website: hinojosa.house.gov
CoS .... *Rita Jaramillo* **LD** .... *Connie Humphrey*
Sch .... *Melinda Mills* **Press** .... *Ciaran Clayton*
Bio: b. 8/20/40 Edcouch, TX; Catholic; MBA Univ. of TX - Pan American, 1980; Businessman; m. Marty
Comm.: Education & the Workforce; Financial Services
Dist. Offices: McAllen, 956-682-5545; Beeville, 361-358-8400

REPRESENTATIVES

David Hobson (R-7th/OH)   202-225-4324
2346 RHOB   8th Term/65%   Fax: 202-225-1984
Website: www.house.gov/hobson
CoS .... *Wayne Struble* **LD** .... *Kenny Kraft*
Appt .... *Virginia Gano* **Press** .... *Sara Perkins*
Bio: b. 10/17/36 Cincinnati, OH; Methodist; JD OH St. Univ., 1963; USANG, 1958-63; Businessman; m. Carolyn
Comm.: Appropriations
Dist. Offices: Springfield, 937-325-0474; Lancaster, 740-654-5149

Peter Hoekstra (R-2nd/MI)   202-225-4401
2234 RHOB   7th Term/69%   Fax: 202-226-0779
Website: hoekstra.house.gov
CoS .... *Amy Plaster* **LD** .... *Justin Wormmeester*
Appt .... *Leah Scott* **Press** .... *Dave Yonkman*
Bio: b. 10/30/53 Groningen, Netherlands; Reformed Church of America; MBA Univ. of MI, 1977; Business Executive; m. Diane
Comm.: Transportation & Infrastructure; Select Intelligence (Chair)
Dist. Offices: Holland, 616-395-0030; Muskegon, 231-722-8386; Cadillac, 231-775-0050

Tim Holden (D-17th/PA)   202-225-5546
2417 RHOB   7th Term/59%   Fax: 202-226-0996
Website: www.holden.house.gov
CoS ..... *Trish Reilly-Hudock* **LD** .... *Ari Strauss*
Sch .... *Rebecca Spangler* **Press** .... *Trish Reilly-Hudock*
Bio: b. 3/5/57 St. Clair, PA; Catholic; BA Bloomsburg Univ., 1980; Real Estate, Insurance Agent; m. Gwen
Comm.: Agriculture; Transportation & Infrastructure
Dist. Offices: Harrisburg, 717-234-5904; Pottsville, 570-622-4212; Temple, 610-921-3502; Lebanon, 717-270-1395

Rush Holt (D-12th/NJ)   202-225-5801
1019 LHOB   4th Term/59%   Fax: 202-225-6025
Website: holt.house.gov
CoS .... *Jim Papa* **LD** .... *Bill Goold*
EA .... *Lesley Muldoon* **Press** .... *Patrick Eddington*
Bio: b. 10/15/48 Weston, WV; Protestant; PhD NYU, 1981; Physicist; m. Margaret Lancefield
Comm.: Education & the Workforce; Select Intelligence
Dist. Office: West Windsor, 609-750-9365

Michael M. Honda (D-15th/CA)   202-225-2631
1713 LHOB   3rd Term/72%   Fax: 202-225-2699
E-mail: mike.honda@mail.house.gov
Website: honda.house.gov
CoS .... *Jennifer* **LD** .... *Chris Mitchell*
      Van der Heide Escobar
Appt .... *Barbara Hamlett* **CD** .... *Jay Staunton*
Bio: b. 6/27/41 Walnut Creek, CA; Protestant; MA San Jose St. Univ., 1973; Educator, Public Official; widowed
Comm.: Science; Transportation & Infrastructure
Dist. Office: Campbell, 408-558-8085

Darlene Hooley (D-5th/OR)   202-225-5711
2430 RHOB   5th Term/53%   Fax: 202-225-5699
Website: www.house.gov/hooley
CoS .... *Joan Mooney* **LD** .... *Mark Dedrick*
Appt .... *Anne Marie Feeney* **Press** .... *Joan Mooney*
Bio: b. 4/4/39 Williston, ND; Lutheran; BS OR St. Univ., 1961; Teacher; div.
Comm.: Financial Services; Science; Veterans' Affairs
Dist. Offices: Salem, 503-588-9100; West Linn, 503-557-1324

REPRESENTATIVES

John N. Hostettler (R-8th/IN)   202-225-4636
1214 LHOB   6th Term/53%   Fax: 202-225-3284
E-mail: john.hostettler@mail.house.gov
Website: www.house.gov/hostettler
CoS .... Carl Little   **LD** .... Jim Dolbow
Sch .... Kate Stusrud   **Press** .... Michael Jahr
Bio: b. 7/19/61 Evansville, IN; Baptist; BSME Rose-Hulman Inst. of Tech., 1983; Mechanical Engineer; m. Elizabeth Ann
Comm.: Armed Services; Judiciary
Dist. Offices: Evansville, 812-465-6484; Vincennes, 812-882-0632; Terre Haute, 812-232-0523; Covington, 765-793-2161

Steny H. Hoyer (D-5th/MD)   202-225-4131
1705 LHOB   13th Term/69%   Fax: 202-225-4300
Website: hoyer.house.gov
CoS .... Cory Alexander   **LD** .... Geoff Plague
Appt .... Kathy May   **Press** .... Katie Elbert
Bio: b. 6/14/39 New York, NY; Baptist; JD Georgetown Univ., 1966; Attorney; widowed
Comm.: Appropriations; Minority Whip
Dist. Offices: Greenbelt, 301-474-0119; Waldorf, 301-843-1577

Kenny C. Hulshof (R-9th/MO)   202-225-2956
412 CHOB   5th Term/65%   Fax: 202-225-5712
Website: hulshof.house.gov
CoS .... Manning Feraci   **LD** .... Caroline Moody
Sch .... Eileen Gardner   **Press** .... Scott Baker
Bio: b. 5/22/58 Sikeston, MO; Catholic; JD Univ. of MS, 1983; Attorney, Prosecutor; m. Renee
Comm.: Budget; Ways & Means
Dist. Offices: Columbia, 573-449-5111; Hannibal, 573-221-1200; Washington, 636-239-4001

Duncan Hunter (R-52nd/CA)   202-225-5672
2265 RHOB   13th Term/69%   Fax: 202-225-0235
Website: www.house.gov/hunter
CoS .... Vicki Middleton   **LD** .... Lorissa Bounds
Appt .... Valerie Snesko   **Press** .... Joe Kasper
Bio: b. 5/31/48 Riverside, CA; Baptist; JD Western St. Univ., 1976; USA, 1969-71; Attorney; m. Lynne
Comm.: Armed Services (Chair)
Dist. Office: El Cajon, 619-579-3001

Henry J. Hyde (R-6th/IL)   202-225-4561
2110 RHOB   16th Term/56%   Fax: 202-225-1166
Website: www.house.gov/hyde
CoS .... Judy Wolverton   **LD** .... Blaine Aaron
Appt .... Susan Schiesser   **Press** .... Jennifer Palmer
Bio: b. 4/18/24 Chicago, IL; Catholic; JD Loyola Univ., 1949; USN, 1942-46; USNR, 1946-68; Attorney; widowed
Comm.: International Relations (Chair); Judiciary
Dist. Office: Addison, 630-832-5950

Bob Inglis (R-4th/SC)   202-225-6030
330 CHOB   4th Term/70%   Fax: 202-226-1177
Website: www.house.gov/inglis
CoS .... Wayne Roper   **LD** .... Jason Morris
Sch .... Barbara Grogan   **CD** .... Price Atkinson
Bio: b. 10/11/59 Savannah, GA; Presbyterian; JD Univ. of VA, 1984; Attorney; m. Mary Anne
Comm.: Education & the Workforce; Judiciary; Science
Dist. Offices: Greenville, 864-232-1141; Spartanburg, 582-232-6422; Union, 864-427-2205

REPRESENTATIVES

Jay Inslee (D-1st/WA) 202-225-6311
403 CHOB 5th Term/62% Fax: 202-226-1606
E-mail: jay.inslee@mail.house.gov
Website: www.house.gov/inslee
CoS .... *Joby Shimomura* **LD** .... *Brian Bonlender*
EA .... *Kate Kriner* **CD** .... *Sara O'Connell*
Bio: b. 2/9/51 Seattle, WA; Christian; JD Willamette School of Law, 1976; Attorney; m. Trudi
Comm.: Energy & Commerce; Resources
Dist. Offices: Mountlake Terrace, 425-640-0233; Poulsbo, 360-598-2342

Steve J. Israel (D-2nd/NY) 202-225-3335
432 CHOB 3rd Term/67% Fax: 202-225-4669
Website: www.house.gov/israel
CoS .... *Jack Pratt* **LD** .... *Heather McHugh*
Sch .... *Meghan Dubyak* **Press** .... *Ryan Rudominer*
Bio: b. 5/30/58 Brooklyn, NY; Jewish; BA George Washington Univ., 1982; Congressional Aide, Public Relations Executive; m. Marlene Budd
Comm.: Armed Services; Financial Services
Dist. Office: Hauppauge, 631-951-2210

Darrell Issa (R-49th/CA) 202-225-3906
211 CHOB 3rd Term/63% Fax: 202-225-3303
Website: www.issa.house.gov
CoS .... *Dale Neugebauer* **LD** .... *Paige Anderson*
Sch .... *Suzy Augustyn* **Press** .... *Frederick Hill*
Bio: b. 11/1/53 Cleveland, OH; Christian; BA Siena Heights Col., 1976; USA, 1970-72, 1976-80; USAR, 1980-90; Businessman; m. Katharine
Comm.: Government Reform; International Relations; Judiciary
Dist. Office: Vista, 760-599-5000

Ernest Istook, Jr. (R-5th/OK) 202-225-2132
2404 RHOB 7th Term/66% Fax: 202-226-1463
Website: www.house.gov/istook
CoS .... *John Albaugh* **LD** .... *Kurt Conrad*
Sch .... *Kim Rubin* **Press** .... *Micah Leydorf*
Bio: b. 2/11/50 Ft. Worth, TX; Mormon; JD Oklahoma City Univ., 1976; Attorney; m. Judy
Comm.: Appropriations
Dist. Offices: Oklahoma City, 405-234-9900; Shawnee, 405-273-6202; Seminole, 405-303-2868

Jesse Jackson, Jr. (D-2nd/IL) 202-225-0773
2419 RHOB 6th Term/88% Fax: 202-225-0899
Website: www.house.gov/jackson
CoS .... *Kenneth Edmonds* **LD** .... *Charles Dujon*
Sch .... *Deborah Posey* **Press** .... *Frank Watkins*
Bio: b. 3/11/65 Greenville, SC; Baptist; JD Univ. of IL, 1993; Community Activist; m. Sandi
Comm.: Appropriations
Dist. Offices: Homewood, 708-798-6000; Chicago, 773-241-6500

Sheila Jackson Lee (D-18th/TX) 202-225-3816
2435 RHOB 6th Term/89% Fax: 202-225-3317
Website: www.jacksonlee.house.gov
CoS .... *Leon Buck* **Dep CoS** .... *Dana Thompson*
Sch .... *Jeanette Lenoir* **Press** .... *Rebecca Gale*
Bio: b. 1/12/50 Jamaica, NY; Seventh-day Adventist; JD Univ. of VA, 1975; Attorney; m. Elwyn
Comm.: Homeland Security; Judiciary; Science
Dist. Offices: Houston, 713-655-0050; Houston, 713-691-4882; Houston, 713-861-4070

REPRESENTATIVES

William J. Jefferson (D-2nd/LA)   202-225-6636
2113 RHOB   8th Term/79%   Fax: 202-225-1988
E-mail: jeffersonmc@mail.house.gov
Website: www.house.gov/jefferson
CoS .... *Nicole Venable* **LD** .... *None*
Appt .... *Roberta Hopkins* **CD** .... *Melanie Roussell*
Bio: b. 3/14/47 Lake Providence, LA; Baptist; LLM Georgetown Univ., 1995; USA, 1975; Attorney; m. Andrea
Comm.: Budget; Ways & Means
Dist. Offices: New Orleans, 504-589-2274; Gretna, 504-369-7019

William L. Jenkins (R-1st/TN)   202-225-6356
1207 LHOB   5th Term/74%   Fax: 202-225-5714
Website: www.house.gov/jenkins
CoS .... *Brenda Otterson* **LD** .... *Richard Vaughn*
Sch .... *Dennis LeNard* **Press** .... *Paul Mays*
Bio: b. 11/29/36 Detroit, MI; Baptist; JD Univ. of TN, 1961; USA, 1959-60; USAR, 1960-69; Attorney, Farmer; m. Mary Kathryn
Comm.: Agriculture; Judiciary
Dist. Office: Kingsport, 423-247-8161

Bobby Jindal (R-1st/LA)   202-225-3015
1205 LHOB   1st Term/78%   Fax: 202-226-0386
E-mail: bobby.jindal@mail.house.gov
Website: www.house.gov/jindal
CoS .... *Timmy Teepell* **LD** .... *Sapna Delacourt*
Sch .... *Allee Bautsch* **Press** .... *Chris Paolino*
Bio: b. 6/10/71 Baton Rouge, LA; Catholic; MA Oxford Univ., 1994; Public Official; m. Supriya Jolly
Comm.: Education & the Workforce; Homeland Security; Resources
Dist. Office: Metairie, 504-837-1259

Eddie Bernice Johnson (D-30th/TX) 202-225-8885
1511 LHOB   7th Term/Unc.   Fax: 202-226-1477
Website: www.house.gov/ebjohnson
CoS .... *Murat Gokcigdem* **LD** .... *Murat Gokcigdem*
Sch .... *Julie Reistrup* **CD** .... *Lisa Hanna*
Bio: b. 12/3/35 Waco, TX; Baptist; MPA Southern Methodist Univ., 1976; Businesswoman, Nurse; div.
Comm.: Science; Transportation & Infrastructure
Dist. Offices: Dallas, 214-922-8885; Dallas, 214-324-0080

Nancy L. Johnson (R-5th/CT)   202-225-4476
2409 RHOB   12th Term/60%   Fax: 202-225-4488
Website: www.house.gov/nancyjohnson
CoS .... *Dave Karvelas* **LD** .... *Doug Lathrop*
Appt .... *Katie Godburn* **Press** .... *Brian Schubert*
Bio: b. 1/5/35 Chicago, IL; Unitarian; BA Radcliffe Col., 1957; Public Official; m. Theodore
Comm.: Ways & Means; Joint Taxation
Dist. Offices: New Britain, 860-223-8412; Waterbury, 203-573-1418; Danbury, 203-790-6856; Meriden, 203-630-1903

Sam Johnson (R-3rd/TX)   202-225-4201
1211 LHOB   8th Term/86%   Fax: 202-225-1485
Website: www.samjohnson.house.gov
CoS .... *Cody Lusk* **LD** .... *Layton Skelly*
Appt ..... *Ellie Mae Harrison* **CD** .... *McCall Cameron*
Bio: b. 10/11/30 San Antonio, TX; Methodist; MSIA George Washington Univ., 1974; USAF, 1951-79; Home Builder; m. Shirley
Comm.: Education & the Workforce; Ways & Means
Dist. Office: Richardson, 972-470-0892

REPRESENTATIVES

Timothy V. Johnson (R-15th/IL)   202-225-2371
1229 LHOB   3rd Term/61%   Fax: 202-226-0791
Website: www.house.gov/timjohnson
CoS .... *Stephen Borg*   LD .... *Stephen Borg*
Sch .... *Alison Myers*   Press .... *Matt Bisbee*
Bio: b. 7/23/46 Champaign, IL; Christian; JD Univ. of IL, 1972; Attorney; div.
Comm.: Agriculture; Science; Transportation & Infrastructure
Dist. Offices: Champaign, 217-403-4690; Bloomington, 309-663-7049; Charleston, 217-348-6759; Mt. Carmel, 618-262-8719

Walter Jones, Jr. (R-3rd/NC)   202-225-3415
422 CHOB   6th Term/71%   Fax: 202-225-3286
Website: jones.house.gov
CoS .... *Glen Downs*   LD .... *Josh Bowlen*
Sch .... *Emily Chapman*   Press .... *Kristen Quigley*
Bio: b. 2/10/43 Farmville, NC; Catholic; BA Atlantic Christian Col., 1966; USARNG, 1967-71; Businessman; m. Joe Anne
Comm.: Armed Services; Financial Services; Resources
Dist. Office: Greenville, 252-931-1003

Paul E. Kanjorski (D-11th/PA)   202-225-6511
2188 RHOB   11th Term/Unc.   Fax: 202-225-0764
Website: kanjorski.house.gov
CoS .... *Karen Feather*   LD .... *Todd Harper*
Appt .... *Donna Giobbi*   Press .... *Gretchen Wintermantel*
Bio: b. 4/2/37 Nanticoke, PA; Catholic; Attended Dickinson School of Law; USA, 1960-61; Attorney; m. Nancy
Comm.: Financial Services; Government Reform
Dist. Offices: Wilkes-Barre, 570-825-2200; Scranton, 570-496-1011; Mount Pocono, 570-895-4176

Marcy Kaptur (D-9th/OH)   202-225-4146
2366 RHOB   12th Term/68%   Fax: 202-225-7711
E-mail: rep.kaptur@mail.house.gov
Website: www.house.gov/kaptur
CoS .... *Roger Szemraj*   LD .... *Steve Fought*
Sch .... *Norma Olsen*   Press .... *Elizabeth Ferranti*
Bio: b. 6/17/46 Toledo, OH; Catholic; MA Univ. of MI, 1974; Urban Planner; single
Comm.: Appropriations
Dist. Office: Toledo, 419-259-7500

Ric Keller (R-8th/FL)   202-225-2176
419 CHOB   3rd Term/61%   Fax: 202-225-0999
Website: keller.house.gov
CoS .... *Bryan Malenius*   LD .... *Mike Shutley*
Sch .... *Stefanie Higgins*   Press .... *Bryan Malenius*
Bio: b. 9/5/64 Johnson City, TN; Methodist; JD Vanderbilt Univ., 1992; Attorney; div.
Comm.: Education & the Workforce; Judiciary; Small Business
Dist. Offices: Orlando, 407-872-1962; Eustis, 888-642-1211; Ocala, 888-642-1211

Sue W. Kelly (R-19th/NY)   202-225-5441
2182 RHOB   6th Term/67%   Fax: 202-225-3289
Website: suekelly.house.gov
CoS .... *Mike Giuliani*   Dep CoS .... *Nick Curran*
Sch .... *Sally Collins*   Press .... *Kevin Callahan*
Bio: b. 9/26/36 Lima, OH; Presbyterian; MA Sarah Lawrence Col., 1985; Small Business Owner; m. Edward
Comm.: Financial Services (Vice Chair); Small Business; Transportation & Infrastructure
Dist. Offices: Fishkill, 845-897-5200; Goshen, 845-291-4100; Yorktown Heights, 914-962-0761

REPRESENTATIVES

Mark R. Kennedy (R-6th/MN)   **202-225-2331**
1415 LHOB   3rd Term/54%   Fax: 202-225-6475
E-mail: mark.kennedy@mail.house.gov
Website: www.markkennedy.house.gov
CoS .... *Pat Shortridge* **LD** .... *Edward Skala*
Sch .... *Kate Schmucker* **Press** .... *Anne Mason*
Bio: b. 4/11/57 Benson, MN; Catholic; MBA Univ. of MI, 1983; Businessman; m. Debbie
Comm.: Financial Services; Transportation & Infrastructure
Dist. Offices: Buffalo, 763-684-1600; St. Cloud, 320-259-0099; Hugo, 651-653-5933

Patrick J. Kennedy (D-1st/RI)   **202-225-4911**
407 CHOB   6th Term/64%   Fax: 202-225-3290
Website: www.house.gov/patrickkennedy
CoS .... *Sean Richardson* **LD** .... *Kimber Colton*
EA .... *Terri Alford* **Press** .... *Ernesto Anguilla*
Bio: b. 7/14/67 Brighton, MA; Catholic; BA Providence Col., 1991; Public Official; single
Comm.: Appropriations
Dist. Office: Pawtucket, 401-729-5600

Dale E. Kildee (D-5th/MI)   **202-225-3611**
2107 RHOB   15th Term/67%   Fax: 202-225-6393
Website: www.house.gov/kildee
CoS ... *Christopher Mansour* **LD** .... *Callie Coffman*
Appt .... *Greta Moore* **Press** .... *Peter Karafotas*
Bio: b. 9/16/29 Flint, MI; Catholic; MA Univ. of MI, 1961; Educator; m. Gayle
Comm.: Education & the Workforce; Resources
Dist. Offices: Flint, 810-239-1437; Saginaw, 989-755-8904; Bay City, 989-891-0990

Carolyn C. Kilpatrick (D-13th/MI)   **202-225-2261**
1610 LHOB   5th Term/78%   Fax: 202-225-5730
Website: www.house.gov/kilpatrick
CoS .... *Kimberly Rudolph* **LD** .... *Gene Fisher*
EA .... *Gerri Houston* **Press** .... *Denise Mixon*
Bio: b. 6/25/45 Detroit, MI; African Methodist Episcopal; MS Univ. of MI, 1977; High School Teacher; div.
Comm.: Appropriations
Dist. Office: Detroit, 313-965-9004

Ron J. Kind (D-3rd/WI)   **202-225-5506**
1406 LHOB   5th Term/57%   Fax: 202-225-5739
Website: www.house.gov/kind
CoS .... *Cindy Brown* **Sr PA** .... *Darin Schroeder*
Sch .... *Dan Guilbeault* **Press** .... *Stephanie Lundberg*
Bio: b. 3/16/63 La Crosse, WI; Lutheran; JD Univ. of MN, 1990; District Attorney; m. Tawni
Comm.: Budget; Education & the Workforce; Resources
Dist. Offices: LaCrosse, 608-782-2558; Eau Claire, 715-831-9214

Peter King (R-3rd/NY)   **202-225-7896**
436 CHOB   7th Term/63%   Fax: 202-226-2279
Website: www.house.gov/king
CoS .... *Robert O'Connor* **LD** .... *Kevin Fogarty*
Sch .... *Ryan Travis* **Press** .... *Kevin Fogarty*
Bio: b. 4/5/44 Manhattan, NY; Catholic; JD Notre Dame Univ., 1968; USARNG, 1968-73; Attorney; m. Rosemary
Comm.: Financial Services; Homeland Security; International Relations
Dist. Office: Massapequa Park, 516-541-4225

REPRESENTATIVES

Steve King (R-5th/IA)   202-225-4426
1432 LHOB   2nd Term/63%   Fax: 202-225-3193
Website: www.house.gov/steveking
CoS .... *Chuck Laudner* **LD** .... *Paula Steiner*
Appt ... *Melissa Obermoller* **Press** .... *Summer Stitz*
Bio: b. 5/28/49 Storm Lake, IA; Roman Catholic; Attended NW MO St. Univ.; Earthmoving Contractor; m. Marilyn
Comm.: Agriculture; Judiciary; Small Business
Dist. Offices: Storm Lake, 712-732-4197; Sioux City, 712-224-4692; Council Bluffs, 712-325-1404

Jack Kingston (R-1st/GA)   202-225-5831
2242 RHOB   7th Term/Unc.   Fax: 202-226-2269
E-mail: jack.kingston@mail.house.gov
Website: www.house.gov/kingston
CoS .... *Bill Johnson* **LD** .... *Heather McNatt*
Sch .... *Meg Gilley* **CD** .... *Jennifer Hing*
Bio: b. 4/24/55 Bryan, TX; Episcopal; BA Univ. of GA, 1978; Insurance Executive; m. Libby
Comm.: Appropriations
Dist. Offices: Savannah, 912-352-0101; Brunswick, 912-265-9010; Baxley, 912-367-7403; Warner Robins, 478-923-8987

Mark S. Kirk (R-10th/IL)   202-225-4835
1717 LHOB   3rd Term/64%   Fax: 202-225-0837
Website: www.house.gov/kirk
CoS .... *Liesl Hickey* **LD** .... *Jeannette Windon*
Appt .... *Kim Brisky* **Press** .... *Matt Towson*
Bio: b. 9/15/59 Champaign, IL; Congregationalist; JD Georgetown Univ., 1992; USNR, 1989-present; Attorney; m. Kimberly
Comm.: Appropriations
Dist. Offices: Deerfield, 847-940-0202; Waukegan, 847-662-0101

John Kline (R-2nd/MN)   202-225-2271
1429 LHOB   2nd Term/56%   Fax: 202-225-2595
Website: www.house.gov/kline
CoS .... *Steven Sutton* **LD** .... *Jean Hinz*
Sch .... *Brooke Dorobiala* **Press** .... *Angelyn Shapiro*
Bio: b. 9/6/47 Allentown, PA; Methodist; MPA Shippensburg Univ., 1988; USMC, 1969-94; Consultant, Farmer; m. Vicky
Comm.: Armed Services; Education & the Workforce
Dist. Office: Burnsville, 952-808-1213

Joseph Knollenberg (R-9th/MI)   202-225-5802
2349 RHOB   7th Term/59%   Fax: 202-226-2356
Website: www.house.gov/knollenberg
CoS .... *Jeff Onizuk* **LD** .... *Craig Albright*
Sch .... *Sue Geibel* **CD** .... *Chris Close*
Bio: b. 11/28/33 Mattoon, IL; Catholic; BS Eastern IL Univ., 1955; USA, 1955-57; Insurance Agent; m. Sandie
Comm.: Appropriations
Dist. Offices: Farmington Hills, 248-851-1366; Troy, 248-619-0531

Jim Kolbe (R-8th/AZ)   202-225-2542
237 CHOB   11th Term/60%   Fax: 202-225-0378
Website: www.house.gov/kolbe
CoS .... *Kevin Messner* **LD** .... *Mark Morehouse*
Sch .... *Patrick Baugh* **Press** .... *Kristen Hellmer*
Bio: b. 6/28/42 Evanston, IL; Methodist; MBA Stanford Univ., 1967; USN, 1968-69; Business Consultant; div.
Comm.: Appropriations
Dist. Offices: Tucson, 520-881-3588; Sierra Vista, 520-459-3115

REPRESENTATIVES

Dennis J. Kucinich (D-10th/OH)   202-225-5871
1730 LHOB   5th Term/60%   Fax: 202-225-5745
Website: www.house.gov/kucinich
AD .... *Doug Gordon* **LD** .... *Jaron Bourke*
Appt .... *Catherine Veith* **Press** .... *Doug Gordon*
Bio: b. 10/8/46 Cleveland, OH; Catholic; MA Case Western Reserve Univ., 1973; College Professor; div.
Comm.: Education & the Workforce; Government Reform
Dist. Offices: Lakewood, 216-228-8850; Parma, 440-845-2707

Randy Kuhl (R-29th/NY)   202-225-3161
1505 LHOB   1st Term/51%   Fax: 202-226-6599
Website: www.house.gov/kuhl
CoS .... *Brian Fitzpatrick* **LD** .... *Bob Van Wicklin*
Appt .... *Sarah Bitting* **Press** .... *Bob Van Wicklin*
Bio: b. 4/19/43 Bath, NY; Episcopal; JD Syracuse Univ., 1969; Attorney, Public Official; div.
Comm.: Agriculture; Education & the Workforce; Transportation & Infrastructure
Dist. Office: Corning, 607-937-3333

Ray H. LaHood (R-18th/IL)   202-225-6201
1424 LHOB   6th Term/70%   Fax: 202-225-9249
Website: www.house.gov/lahood
CoS .... *Diane Liesman* **LD** .... *Diane Liesman*
Appt .... *Joan De Boer* **Press** .... *Joan De Boer*
Bio: b. 12/6/45 Peoria, IL; Catholic; BS Bradley Univ., 1971; Educator; m. Kathy
Comm.: Appropriations; Select Intelligence
Dist. Offices: Peoria, 309-671-7027; Jacksonville, 217-245-1431; Springfield, 217-793-0808

James R. Langevin (D-2nd/RI)   202-225-2735
109 CHOB   3rd Term/75%   Fax: 202-225-5976
Website: www.house.gov/langevin
CoS .... *Kristin Nicholson* **LD** .... *Brian Daniels*
Sch .... *Stu Rose* **CD** ...... *Michael K. Guilfoyle*
Bio: b. 4/22/64 Providence, RI; Catholic; MA Harvard Univ., 1994; Public Official; single
Comm.: Armed Services; Homeland Security
Dist. Office: Warwick, 401-732-9400

Tom Lantos (D-12th/CA)   202-225-3531
2413 RHOB   13th Term/68%   Fax: 202-226-4183
Website: lantos.house.gov
CoS .... *Robert King* **LD** .... *Ron Grimes*
Sch .... *Guido Zucconi* **Press** .... *Lynne Weil*
Bio: b. 2/1/28 Budapest, Hungary; Jewish; PhD Univ. of CA - Berkeley, 1953; Economist; m. Annette
Comm.: Government Reform; International Relations (Rnk. Mem.)
Dist. Office: San Mateo, 650-342-0300

Rick Larsen (D-2nd/WA)   202-225-2605
107 CHOB   3rd Term/64%   Fax: 202-225-4420
E-mail: rick.larsen@mail.house.gov
Website: www.house.gov/larsen
CoS .... *Jeff Bjornstad* **LD** .... *Evan Schatz*
Sch .... *Kimberly Johnston* **CD** .... *Abbey Blake*
Bio: b. 6/17/65 Arlington, WA; Methodist; MA Univ. of MN, 1990; Public Official; m. Tiia Karlen
Comm.: Agriculture; Armed Services; Transportation & Infrastructure
Dist. Offices: Everett, 425-252-3188; Bellingham, 360-733-4500

REPRESENTATIVES

John B. Larson (D-1st/CT)   202-225-2265
1005 LHOB   4th Term/73%   Fax: 202-225-1031
Website: www.house.gov/larson
CoS .... *Elliot Ginsberg* **LD** .... *Jonathan Renfrew*
Sch .... *Evelene Corrigan* **Press** .... *Michael Kirk*
Bio: b. 7/22/48 Hartford, CT; Catholic; BS Central CT St. Univ., 1971; Public Official, Businessman; m. Leslie
Comm.: Ways & Means
Dist. Office: Hartford, 860-278-8888

Tom Latham (R-4th/IA)   202-225-5476
2447 RHOB   6th Term/61%   Fax: 202-225-3301
E-mail: tom.latham@mail.house.gov
Website: www.house.gov/latham
CoS .... *Michael Gruber* **LD** .... *Kevin Berents*
Sch .... *Jennifer Crall* **Press** .... *James Carstensen*
Bio: b. 7/14/48 Hampton, IA; Lutheran; Attended IA St. Univ.; Businessman; m. Kathy
Comm.: Appropriations
Dist. Offices: Ames, 515-232-2885; Ft. Dodge, 515-573-2738; Clear Lake, 641-357-5225

Steven C. LaTourette (R-14th/OH)   202-225-5731
2453 RHOB   6th Term/63%   Fax: 202-225-3307
Website: www.house.gov/latourette
CoS .... *Matt Wallen* **LD** .... *Jason Kratovil*
Sch .... *Kathy Kato* **CD** .... *Deborah Setliff*
Bio: b. 7/22/54 Cleveland, OH; Methodist; JD Cleveland St. Univ., 1979; Attorney; m. Jennifer Laptook
Comm.: Financial Services; Government Reform; Transportation & Infrastructure
Dist. Office: Painesville, 440-352-3939

Jim Leach (R-2nd/IA)   202-225-6576
2186 RHOB   15th Term/60%   Fax: 202-226-1278
Website: www.house.gov/leach
CoS ..... *Gregory Wierzynski* **LD** .... *Mary Andrus*
Appt .... *Jackie Abba* **Press** .... *Gregory Wierzynski*
Bio: b. 10/15/42 Davenport, IA; Episcopal; MA Johns Hopkins Univ., 1966; Foreign Service Officer; m. Deba
Comm.: Financial Services; International Relations
Dist. Offices: Cedar Rapids, 319-363-4773; Iowa City, 319-351-0789; Burlington, 319-754-1106; Ottumwa, 641-684-4024

Barbara Lee (D-9th/CA)   202-225-2661
1724 LHOB   5th Term/84%   Fax: 202-225-9817
Website: www.house.gov/lee
CoS .... *Julie Nickson* **LD** .... *Ven Neralla*
Sch .... *Tatyana Kalinga* **Press** .... *Nathan Britton*
Bio: b. 7/16/46 El Paso, TX; Not Stated; MSW Univ. of CA - Berkeley, 1975; Congressional Aide, Social Worker; single
Comm.: Financial Services; International Relations
Dist. Office: Oakland, 510-763-0370

Sander M. Levin (D-12th/MI)   202-225-4961
2300 RHOB   12th Term/69%   Fax: 202-226-1033
Website: www.house.gov/levin
CoS .... *Hilarie Chambers* **LD** .... *Dan Jourdan*
Sch .... *Monica Chrzaszcz* **Press** .... *Matthew Beck*
Bio: b. 9/6/31 Detroit, MI; Jewish; LLB Harvard Univ., 1957; Attorney; m. Victoria
Comm.: Ways & Means
Dist. Office: Roseville, 586-498-7122

REPRESENTATIVES

Jerry Lewis (R-41st/CA)   202-225-5861
2112 RHOB   14th Term/83%   Fax: 202-225-6498
Website: www.house.gov/jerrylewis
CoS .... *Arlene Willis*   **LD** .... *Jim Specht*
Appt ....*Julie Hooks*   **Press** .... *Jim Specht*
Bio: b. 10/21/34 Seattle, WA; Presbyterian; BA UCLA, 1956; Insurance Executive; m. Arlene
Comm.: Appropriations (Chair)
Dist. Office: Redlands, 909-862-6030

John Lewis (D-5th/GA)   202-225-3801
343 CHOB   10th Term/Unc.   Fax: 202-225-0351
Website: www.house.gov/johnlewis
CoS .... *Michael Collins*   **LD** .... *Michaeleen Crowell*
Sch .... *Jacob Gillison*   **CD** .... *Brenda Jones*
Bio: b. 2/21/40 Troy, AL; Baptist; BA Fisk Univ., 1963; Consultant; m. Lillian
Comm.: Ways & Means
Dist. Office: Atlanta, 404-659-0116

Ron Lewis (R-2nd/KY)   202-225-3501
2418 RHOB   7th Term/68%   Fax: 202-226-2019
Website: www.house.gov/ronlewis
CoS .... *Daniel London*   **LD** .... *Eric Bergren*
Sch .... *Lindy Salem*   **Press** .... *Michael Dodge*
Bio: b. 9/14/46 South Shore, KY; Baptist; MA Morehead St. Univ., 1981; USN, 1972; Small Business Owner, College Professor; m. Kayi
Comm.: Ways & Means
Dist. Offices: Elizabethtown, 270-765-4360; Bowling Green, 270-842-9896; Owensboro, 270-688-8858

John Linder (R-7th/GA)   202-225-4272
1026 LHOB   7th Term/Unc.   Fax: 202-225-4696
Website: linder.house.gov
CoS .... *Rob Woodall*   **LD** .... *Don Green*
Sch .... *Joy Burch*   **Press** ...... *Gretchen Learman*
Bio: b. 9/9/42 Deer River, MN; Presbyterian; DDS Univ. of MN, 1967; USAF, 1967-69; Dentist, Small Businessman; m. Lynne
Comm.: Homeland Security; Ways & Means
Dist. Offices: Duluth, 770-232-3005; Canton, 770-479-1888

Dan Lipinski (D-3rd/IL)   202-225-5701
1217 LHOB   1st Term/74%   Fax: 202-225-1012
Website: www.house.gov/lipinski
CoS .... *Jennifer Sypolt*   **LD** .... *John Rattliff*
Appt .... *Jennifer Sypolt*   **CD** .... *Chris Ganschow*
Bio: b. 7/15/66 Chicago, IL; Not Stated; PhD Duke Univ., 1998; Professor; m. Judy
Comm.: Science; Small Business
Dist. Offices: Chicago, 312-886-0481; La Grange, 708-352-0524

Frank A. LoBiondo (R-2nd/NJ)   202-225-6572
225 CHOB   6th Term/65%   Fax: 202-225-3318
Website: www.house.gov/lobiondo
CoS ...... *Mary Annie Harper*   **LD** .... *Geoffrey Gosselin*
EA .... *Heather Fallon*   **Press** .... *Joe Brenckle*
Bio: b. 5/12/46 Bridgeton, NJ; Catholic; BA St. Joseph's Univ., 1968; Businessman; m. Tina
Comm.: Armed Services; Transportation & Infrastructure
Dist. Office: Mays Landing, 609-625-5008

REPRESENTATIVES

Zoe Lofgren (D-16th/CA)   **202-225-3072**
102 CHOB   6th Term/71%   Fax: 202-225-3336
E-mail: zoe.lofgren@mail.house.gov
Website: zoelofgren.house.gov
CoS .... *David Thomas*   **Sr PA** .... *David Carreiro*
Sch .... *Bridget Fallon*   **Press** .... *Heather Wong*
Bio: b. 12/21/47 San Mateo, CA; Lutheran; JD Univ. of Santa Clara, 1975; Attorney; m. John Marshall Collins
Comm.: Homeland Security; House Administration; Judiciary; Joint Library
Dist. Office: San Jose, 408-271-8700

Nita M. Lowey (D-18th/NY)   **202-225-6506**
2329 RHOB   9th Term/69%   Fax: 202-225-0546
Website: www.house.gov/lowey
CoS .... *Clare Coleman*   **LD** .... *Mark Carrato*
EA .... *Katie Papa*   **Press** .... *Julie Edwards*
Bio: b. 7/5/37 Bronx, NY; Jewish; BA Mt. Holyoke Col., 1959; Public Official; m. Stephen
Comm.: Appropriations; Homeland Security
Dist. Offices: White Plains, 914-428-1707; New City, 845-639-3485

Frank D. Lucas (R-3rd/OK)   **202-225-5565**
2342 RHOB   7th Term/82%   Fax: 202-225-8698
Website: www.house.gov/lucas
CoS .... *Stacey Glasscock*   **LD** .... *Nicole Scott*
Sch .... *Jessica Reinsch*   **Press** .... *Jim Luetkemeyer*
Bio: b. 1/6/60 Cheyenne, OK; Baptist; BS OK St. Univ., 1982; Farmer, Rancher; m. Lynda
Comm.: Agriculture; Financial Services; Science
Dist. Offices: Yukon, 405-373-1958; Woodward, 580-256-5752; Stillwater, 405-624-6407

Dan Lungren (R-3rd/CA)   **202-225-5716**
2448 RHOB   6th Term/62%   Fax: 202-226-1298
Website: www.house.gov/lungren
CoS .... *Victor Arnold-Bik*   **LD** .... *Kevin Holsclaw*
Sch .... *Caley White*   **Press** .... *Brian Seitchik*
Bio: b. 9/22/46 Long Beach, CA; Catholic; JD Georgetown Univ., 1971; Attorney; m. Bobbi
Comm.: Budget; Homeland Security; Judiciary
Dist. Office: Gold River, 916-859-9906

Stephen F. Lynch (D-9th/MA)   **202-225-8273**
319 CHOB   3rd Term/Unc.   Fax: 202-225-3984
E-mail: stephen.lynch@mail.house.gov
Website: www.house.gov/lynch
CoS .... *Kevin Ryan*   **LD** .... *Caroline Powers*
Sch .... *Greta Hebert*   **Press** .... *Matt Ferraguto*
Bio: b. 3/31/55 Boston, MA; Catholic; JD Boston Col., 1991; Attorney; m. Margaret Shaughnessy
Comm.: Financial Services; Government Reform
Dist. Offices: Boston, 617-428-2000; Brockton, 508-586-5555

Connie Mack (R-14th/FL)   **202-225-2536**
317 CHOB   1st Term/68%   Fax: 202-226-0439
Website: www.house.gov/mack
CoS .... *Jeff Cohen*   **LD** .... *Francis Gibbs*
Sch .... *Betsy Kampas*   **Press** .... *Jeff Cohen*
Bio: b. 8/12/67 Ft. Myers, FL; Catholic; BS Univ. of FL, 1990; Marketing Executive; m. Ann
Comm.: Budget; International Relations; Transportation & Infrastructure
Dist. Office: Fort Myers, 239-322-4677; Naples, 239-774-8035

REPRESENTATIVES

Carolyn Maloney (D-14th/NY)   202-225-7944
2331 RHOB   7th Term/81%   Fax: 202-225-4709
Website: www.house.gov/maloney
CoS .... *Ben Chevat* **LD** .... *Orly Isaacson*
Appt .... *Sarah Lawrence* **Press** .... *Afshin Mohamadi*
Bio: b. 2/19/48 Greensboro, NC; Presbyterian; BA Greensboro Col., 1968; Educator; m. Clifton
Comm.: Financial Services; Government Reform; Joint Economic
Dist. Offices: New York, 212-860-0606; Astoria, 718-932-1804

Donald A. Manzullo (R-16th/IL)   202-225-5676
2228 RHOB   7th Term/69%   Fax: 202-225-5284
Website: manzullo.house.gov
CoS .... *Adam Magary* **LD** .... *John Westmoreland*
Sch .... *Mary Ellen Brown* **CD** .... *Rich Carter*
Bio: b. 3/24/44 Rockford, IL; Christian; JD Marquette Univ., 1970; Attorney; m. Freda
Comm.: Financial Services; Small Business (Chair)
Dist. Offices: Rockford, 815-394-1231; Crystal Lake, 815-356-9800

Kenny Marchant (R-24th/TX)   202-225-6605
501 CHOB   1st Term/64%   Fax: 202-225-0074
Website: www.marchant.house.gov
CoS .... *Brian Thomas* **LD** .... *Vacant*
Appt .... *Sarah Phipps* **Press** .... *Annie Christian*
Bio: b. 2/23/51 Bonham, TX; Church of the Nazarene; BVA South Nazarene Univ., 1974; Public Official, Homebuilder; m. Donna
Comm.: Education & the Workforce; Government Reform; Transportation & Infrastructure
Dist. Office: Irving, 972-556-0162

Edward J. Markey (D-7th/MA)   202-225-2836
2108 RHOB   15th Term/74%   Fax: 202-226-0092
Website: www.house.gov/markey
CoS .... *David Moulton* **LD** .... *Jeff Duncan*
Sch .... *Nancy Morrissey* **Press** .... *Tara McGuinness*
Bio: b. 7/11/46 Malden, MA; Catholic; JD Boston Col., 1972; USAR, 1968-73; Attorney; m. Susan Blumenthal
Comm.: Energy & Commerce; Homeland Security; Resources
Dist. Offices: Medford, 781-396-2900; Framingham, 508-875-2900

Jim Marshall (D-3rd/GA)   202-225-6531
515 CHOB   2nd Term/63%   Fax: 202-225-3013
Website: www.house.gov/marshall
CoS .... *John Kirincich* **LD** .... *Bradley Edgell*
Sch .... *Toby Watkins* **CD** .... *Douglas Moore*
Bio: b. 3/31/48 Ithaca, NY; Catholic; JD Boston Univ., 1977; USA, 1968-70; Law Professor; m. Camille
Comm.: Agriculture; Armed Services
Dist. Offices: Macon, 478-464-0255; Dublin, 478-296-2101

Jim Matheson (D-2nd/UT)   202-225-3011
1222 LHOB   3rd Term/56%   Fax: 202-225-5638
Website: www.house.gov/matheson
CoS .... *Stacey Alexander* **LD** .... *Julie Slocum*
Sch .... *Wendy Ware* **Press** .... *Alyson Heyrend*
Bio: b. 3/21/60 Salt Lake City, UT; Mormon; MBA UCLA, 1987; Energy Consultant; m. Amy
Comm.: Financial Services; Science; Transportation & Infrastructure
Dist. Offices: South Salt Lake, 801-486-1236; St. George, 435-627-0880

REPRESENTATIVES

Doris Matsui (D-5th/CA)   202-225-7163
2310 RHOB   1st Term/69%   Fax: 202-225-0566
Website: www.house.gov/matsui
CoS .... *Joe Trahern* **LD** .... *Shari Davenport*
Sch .... *Shirley Queja* **Press** .... *Rob Leonard*
Bio: b. 9/25/44 Dinuba, CA; BA Univ. of CA - Berkeley; Policy Advisor; widowed
Comm.: Rules
Dist. Office: Sacramento, 916-498-5600

Carolyn McCarthy (D-4th/NY)   202-225-5516
106 CHOB   5th Term/63%   Fax: 202-225-5758
Website: carolynmccarthy.house.gov
CoS .... *Jim Hart* **LD** .... *Bob Dobek*
Sch .... *Jennifer Oh* **CD** .... *Rob Recklaus*
Bio: b. 1/5/44 Brooklyn, NY; Catholic; LPN Glen Cove Nursing School, 1964; Nurse; widowed
Comm.: Education & the Workforce; Financial Services
Dist. Office: Garden City, 516-739-3008

Michael McCaul (R-10th/TX)   202-225-2401
415 CHOB   1st Term/84%   Fax: 202-225-5955
Website: www.house.gov/mccaul
CoS .... *Matt Miller* **LD** .... *Gene Irisari*
Sch .... *Kelly Richardson* **Press** .... *Jack Hirschfield*
Bio: b. 1/14/62 Dallas, TX; Catholic; JD St. Mary's Univ., 1987; Attorney, Federal Prosecutor; m. Linda
Comm.: Homeland Security; International Relations; Science
Dist. Offices: Austin, 512-473-2357; Tomball, 281-733-0999

Betty McCollum (D-4th/MN)   202-225-6631
1029 LHOB   3rd Term/58%   Fax: 202-225-1968
Website: www.mccollum.house.gov
CoS .... *Bill Harper* **LD** .... *Emily Lawrence*
Sch .... *Shelly Schafer* **CD** .... *Josh Straka*
Bio: b. 7/12/54 Minneapolis, MN; Catholic; BS Col. of St. Catherine, 1987; Teacher, Retail Sales; div.
Comm.: Education & the Workforce; International Relations
Dist. Office: St. Paul, 651-224-9191

Thaddeus G. McCotter (R-11th/MI)   202-225-8171
1632 LHOB   2nd Term/57%   Fax: 202-225-2667
Website: mccotter.house.gov
CoS .... *Martin* **LD** .... *Patrick Rothwell*
Van Valkenburg
Sch .... *Megan Moore* **Press** .... *Bob Jackson*
Bio: b. 8/22/65 Detroit, MI; Roman Catholic; JD Univ. of Detroit, 1990; Attorney; m. Rita
Comm.: Budget; International Relations; Small Business; Joint Economic
Dist. Office: Livonia, 734-632-0314

Jim McCrery (R-4th/LA)   202-225-2777
2104 RHOB   10th Term/Unc.   Fax: 202-225-8039
Website: mccrery.house.gov
CoS .... *Bob Brooks* **LD** .... *None*
Sch .... *Mimi Roberts* **CD** .... *Brooke Alexander*
Bio: b. 9/18/49 Shreveport, LA; Methodist; JD LA St. Univ., 1975; Attorney; m. Johnette
Comm.: Ways & Means
Dist. Offices: Shreveport, 318-798-2254; Leesville, 337-238-0778

REPRESENTATIVES

Jim McDermott (D-7th/WA)   202-225-3106
1035 LHOB   9th Term/80%   Fax: 202-225-6197
Website: www.house.gov/mcdermott
CoS .... *Jan Shinpoch*   **Sr LA** .... *Jayme White*
EA .... *Beverly Swain*   **CD** .... *Mike DeCesare*
Bio: b. 12/28/36 Chicago, IL; Episcopal; MD Univ. of IL, 1963; USN, 1968-70; Psychiatrist; m. Therese Hansen
Comm.: Ways & Means
Dist. Office: Seattle, 206-553-7170

James P. McGovern (D-3rd/MA)   202-225-6101
430 CHOB   5th Term/71%   Fax: 202-225-5759
Website: www.house.gov/mcgovern
CoS ...... *Christopher Philbin*   **LD** .... *Cindy Buhl*
Sch .... *Daniel Holt*   **Press** .... *Michael Mershon*
Bio: b. 11/20/59 Worcester, MA; Catholic; MPA American Univ., 1984; Congressional Aide; m. Lisa
Comm.: Rules
Dist. Offices: Worcester, 508-831-7356; Fall River, 508-677-0140; Attleboro, 508-431-8025; Marlborough, 508-460-9292

Patrick McHenry (R-10th/NC)   202-225-2576
224 CHOB   1st Term/64%   Fax: 202-225-0316
Website: www.house.gov/mchenry
CoS .... *Dee Stewart*   **LD** .... *Jon Causey*
Sch .... *Cendy Gonzalez*   **Press** .... *Jonathan Collegio*
Bio: b. 10/22/75 Mecklenburg Co., NC; Catholic; BA Belmont Abbey Col., 2000; Realtor, Small Business Owner; single
Comm.: Budget; Financial Services; Government Reform
Dist. Office: Hickory, 828-327-6100

John McHugh (R-23rd/NY)   202-225-4611
2333 RHOB   7th Term/71%   Fax: 202-226-0621
Website: mchugh.house.gov
CoS .... *Robert Taub*   **LD** .... *Judith Brewer*
Sch .... *Donna Bell*   **Press** .... *Brynn Barnett*
Bio: b. 9/29/48 Watertown, NY; Catholic; MPA SUNY - Albany, 1977; Public Official; div.
Comm.: Armed Services; Government Reform; Select Intelligence
Dist. Offices: Watertown, 315-782-3150; Plattsburgh, 518-563-1406; Mayfield, 518-661-6486; Canastota, 315-697-2063

Mike McIntyre (D-7th/NC)   202-225-2731
2437 RHOB   5th Term/72%   Fax: 202-225-5773
Website: www.house.gov/mcintyre
CoS .... *Dean Mitchell*   **LD** .... *Jeff Hogg*
Sch .... *Audrey Lesesne*   **Press** .... *Dean Mitchell*
Bio: b. 8/6/56 Lumberton, NC; Presbyterian; JD UNC, 1981; Attorney; m. Dee
Comm.: Agriculture; Armed Services
Dist. Offices: Fayetteville, 910-323-0260; Wilmington, 910-815-4959; Lumberton, 910-671-6223

Howard "Buck" McKeon (R-25th/CA)   202-225-1956
2351 RHOB   7th Term/65%   Fax: 202-226-0683
Website: mckeon.house.gov
CoS .... *Bob Cochran*   **LD** .... *Brandi Ballou*
Sch .... *Michelle Baker*   **Press** .... *Vartan Djihanian*
Bio: b. 9/9/38 Tujunga, CA; Mormon; BS Brigham Young Univ., 1985; Businessman; m. Patricia Kunz
Comm.: Armed Services; Education & the Workforce
Dist. Offices: Santa Clarita, 661-254-2111; Palmdale, 661-274-9688

REPRESENTATIVES

Cynthia McKinney (D-4th/GA)   202-225-1605
320 CHOB   6th Term/64%   Fax: 202-226-0691
Website: www.house.gov/mckinney
CoS .... *Afra Yehwalashet* **LD** .... *None*
Appt .... *Afra Yehwalashet* **CD** .... *Hugh Esco*
Bio: b. 3/17/55 Atlanta, GA; Catholic; BA USC, 1978; Educator; div.
Comm.: Armed Services; Budget
Dist. Offices: Decatur, 404-633-0927; Atlanta, 404-320-2001

Cathy McMorris (R-5th/WA)   202-225-2006
1708 LHOB   1st Term/60%   Fax: 202-225-3392
E-mail: cathy.mcmorris@mail.house.gov
Website: www.mcmorris.house.gov
CoS .... *Connie Correll* **LD** .... *Jack Silzel Partoyan*
Appt .... *Julie Blackorby* **Press** .... *Jill Strait*
Bio: b. 5/22/69 Salem, OR; Christian; MBA Univ. of WA, 2002; Orchardist; single
Comm.: Armed Services; Education & the Workforce; Resources
Dist. Offices: Spokane, 509-353-2374; Colville, 509-684-3481; Walla Walla, 509-529-9358

Michael R. McNulty (D-21st/NY)   202-225-5076
2210 RHOB   9th Term/70%   Fax: 202-225-5077
E-mail: mike.mcnulty@mail.house.gov
Website: www.house.gov/mcnulty
CoS .... *David Torian* **LD** .... *Jim Glenn*
Appt ... *Christopher Raymond* **Press** .... *Michael Wojnar*
Bio: b. 9/16/47 Troy, NY; Catholic; BA Holy Cross Col., 1969; Insurance Broker; m. Nancy
Comm.: Ways & Means
Dist. Offices: Albany, 518-465-0700; Amsterdam, 518-843-3400; Schenectady, 518-374-4547; Troy, 518-271-0822; Johnstown, 518-762-3568

Marty Meehan (D-5th/MA)   202-225-3411
2229 RHOB   7th Term/67%   Fax: 202-226-0771
Website: www.house.gov/meehan
CoS .... *Lori Loureiro* **LD** .... *Ron Carlton*
Appt .... *Shilpa Phadke* **Press** .... *Matt Vogel*
Bio: b. 12/30/56 Lowell, MA; Catholic; JD Suffolk Univ., 1986; Attorney; m. Ellen Murphy
Comm.: Armed Services; Judiciary
Dist. Offices: Lowell, 978-459-0101; Lawrence, 978-681-6200; Haverhill, 978-521-1845

Kendrick B. Meek (D-17th/FL)   202-225-4506
1039 LHOB   2nd Term/Unc.   Fax: 202-226-0777
Website: kendrickmeek.house.gov
CoS .... *John Schelble* **LD** .... *Clarence Williams*
Sch .... *Lisa Kohnke* **Press** .... *Drew Hammill*
Bio: b. 9/6/66 Miami, FL; Baptist; BS FL A&M Univ., 1989; Public Official; m. Leslie Dixon
Comm.: Armed Services; Homeland Security
Dist. Offices: Miami, 305-690-5905; Pembroke Pines, 954-450-6767

Gregory W. Meeks (D-6th/NY)   202-225-3461
1710 LHOB   5th Term/Unc.   Fax: 202-226-4169
E-mail: congmeeks@mail.house.gov
Website: www.house.gov/meeks
CoS .. *Jameel Aalim-Johnson* **LD** .... *Sophia King*
Appt .... *Pat Fisher* **Press** .... *Candace Sandy*
Bio: b. 9/25/53 East Harlem, NY; Baptist; JD Howard Univ., 1978; Public Official; m. Simone-Marie
Comm.: Financial Services; International Relations
Dist. Offices: St. Albans, 718-949-5600; Far Rockaway, 718-327-9791

REPRESENTATIVES

Charlie Melancon (D-3rd/LA)   **202-225-4031**
404 CHOB   1st Term/50%   Fax: 202-226-3944
Website: www.house.gov/melancon
CoS .... *Casey O'Shea*   **LD** .... *Jacob Roche*
Sch .... *Jody Comeaux*   **Press** .... *Ellery Gould*
Bio: b. 10/3/47 Napoleanville, LA; Catholic; BS Univ. of Southwestern LA, 1971; Businessman; m. Alida
Comm.: Agriculture; Resources; Science
Dist. Offices: Gonzales, 225-621-8490; Houma, 985-876-3033; New Iberia, 337-367-8231; Chalmette, 504-271-1707

Robert Menendez (D-13th/NJ)   **202-225-7919**
2238 RHOB   7th Term/76%   Fax: 202-226-0792
E-mail: menendez@mail.house.gov
Website: menendez.house.gov
CoS .... *E. Ivan Zapien*   **LD** .... *Chris Schloesser*
Sch .... *Judi Wolford*   **CD** .... *Andrew Kauders*
Bio: b. 1/1/54 New York, NY; Catholic; JD Rutgers Univ., 1979; Attorney; sep.
Comm.: International Relations; Transportation & Infrastructure
Dist. Offices: Jersey City, 201-222-2828; Bayonne, 201-823-2900; Perth Amboy, 732-324-6212; Union City, 201-558-0800

John Mica (R-7th/FL)   **202-225-4035**
2313 RHOB   7th Term/Unc.   Fax: 202-226-0821
Website: www.house.gov/mica
CoS .... *Russell L. Roberts*   **LD** .... *Gary Burns*
Appt .... *Lawrence Lyman*   **Press** .... *Gary Burns*
Bio: b. 1/27/43 Binghamton, NY; Episcopal; BA Univ. of FL, 1967; Businessman; m. Pat
Comm.: Government Reform; House Administration; Transportation & Infrastructure
Dist. Offices: Maitland, 407-657-8080; Deltona, 386-860-1499; Ormond Beach, 386-676-7750; St. Augustine, 904-810-5048; Palatka, 386-328-1622; Palm Coast, 386-246-6042

Michael H. Michaud (D-2nd/ME)   **202-225-6306**
437 CHOB   2nd Term/58%   Fax: 202-225-2943
Website: michaud.house.gov
CoS .... *Peter Chandler*   **LD** .... *Matt Robison*
Sch .... *Diane Smith*   **Press** ..... *Monica Castellanos*
Bio: b. 1/18/55 Millinocket, ME; Catholic; HS Diploma; Mill Worker; single
Comm.: Small Business; Transportation & Infrastructure; Veterans' Affairs
Dist. Offices: Bangor, 207-942-6935; Lewiston, 207-782-3704; Presque Isle, 207-764-1036

Juanita Millender-McDonald
(D-37th/CA)   **202-225-7924**
2445 RHOB   6th Term/75%   Fax: 202-225-7926
Website: www.house.gov/millender-mcdonald
CoS .... *Shirley Cooks*   **LD** .... *John Young*
Appt .... *Angela Smith*   **Press** .... *Craig Rasmussen*
Bio: b. 9/7/38 Birmingham, AL; Baptist; MEd CA St. - Los Angeles, 1987; Educator; m. James
Comm.: House Administration (Rnk. Mem.); Small Business; Transportation & Infrastructure; Joint Library; Joint Printing
Dist. Office: Torrance, 310-538-1190

Brad Miller (D-13th/NC)   **202-225-3032**
1722 LHOB   2nd Term/59%   Fax: 202-225-0181
Website: www.house.gov/bradmiller
CoS .... *Mark Harkins*   **LD** .... *Tom Koonce*
EA .... *Eleanor Blaine*   **Press** .... *Joe Bonfiglio*
Bio: b. 5/19/53 Fayetteville, NC; Episcopal; JD Columbia Univ., 1979; Attorney; m. Esther Hall
Comm.: Financial Services; Science
Dist. Offices: Raleigh, 919-836-1313; Greensboro, 336-574-2909

REPRESENTATIVES

Candice Miller (R-10th/MI)   202-225-2106
228 CHOB   2nd Term/69%   Fax: 202-226-1169
Website: candicemiller.house.gov
CoS .... *Jamie Roe*   LD .... *Sean Moran*
Sch .... *Adam Stachecki*   Press .... *Jamie Roe*
Bio: b. 5/7/54 St. Clair Shores, MI; Presbyterian; Attended Northwood Univ.; Public Official; m. Donald
Comm.: Armed Services; Government Reform; House Administration; Joint Library
Dist. Office: Shelby Township, 586-997-5010

Gary G. Miller (R-42nd/CA)   202-225-3201
1037 LHOB   4th Term/68%   Fax: 202-226-6962
E-mail: gary.miller@mail.house.gov
Website: www.house.gov/garymiller
CoS .... *John Rothrock*   LD .. *Lesli McCollum Gooch*
Sch .... *Kevin McKee*   Press .... *Kevin McKee*
Bio: b. 10/16/48 Huntsville, AR; Christian; Attended Mt. San Antonio Col.; USA, 1967-68; Home Builder; m. Cathy
Comm.: Financial Services; Transportation & Infrastructure
Dist. Offices: Brea, 714-257-1142; Mission Viejo, 949-470-8484

George Miller (D-7th/CA)   202-225-2095
2205 RHOB   16th Term/76%   Fax: 202-225-5609
E-mail: george.miller@mail.house.gov
Website: www.house.gov/georgemiller
CoS .... *Daniel Weiss*   LD .... *Justin Hamilton*
Appt .... *Sylvia Arthur*   Press .... *Thomas Kiley*
Bio: b. 5/17/45 Richmond, CA; Catholic; JD Univ. of CA - Davis, 1972; Attorney; m. Cynthia
Comm.: Education & the Workforce (Rnk. Mem.); Resources
Dist. Offices: Concord, 925-602-1880; Richmond, 510-262-6500; Vallejo, 707-645-1888

Jeff Miller (R-1st/FL)   202-225-4136
324 CHOB   3rd Term/77%   Fax: 202-225-3414
Website: jeffmiller.house.gov
CoS .... *Dan McFaul*   LD .... *Helen Walker*
Sch .... *Kelly Adamson*   Press .... *Dan McFaul*
Bio: b. 6/27/59 St. Petersburg, FL; Methodist; BA Univ. of FL, 1984; Real Estate Broker; m. Vicki
Comm.: Armed Services; Veterans' Affairs
Dist. Offices: Pensacola, 850-479-1183; Ft. Walton Beach, 850-664-1266

Alan B. Mollohan (D-1st/WV)   202-225-4172
2302 RHOB   12th Term/68%   Fax: 202-225-7564
Website: www.house.gov/mollohan
CoS .... *Colleen McCarty*   LD .... *Angela Ohm*
Sch .... *Jill Butash*   Press .... *Ron Hudok*
Bio: b. 5/14/43 Fairmont, WV; Baptist; JD WV Univ., 1970; USAR, 1970-83; Attorney; m. Barbara
Comm.: Appropriations; Standards of Official Conduct (Rnk. Mem.)
Dist. Offices: Morgantown, 304-292-3019; Parkersburg, 304-428-0493; Wheeling, 304-232-5390; Clarksburg, 304-623-4422

Dennis Moore (D-3rd/KS)   202-225-2865
1727 LHOB   4th Term/55%   Fax: 202-225-2807
Website: www.house.gov/moore
CoS .... *Howard Bauleke*   LD .... *Andy Lewin*
Sch .... *Andrew Shaw*   CD .... *Christie Appelhanz*
Bio: b. 11/8/45 Anthony, KS; Protestant; JD Washburn Univ., 1970; USA, 1970; USAR, 1970-73; Attorney; m. Stephene
Comm.: Budget; Financial Services
Dist. Offices: Overland Park, 913-383-2013; Lawrence, 785-842-9313; Kansas City, 913-621-0832

REPRESENTATIVES

Gwen S. Moore (D-4th/WI)   202-225-4572
1408 LHOB   1st Term/70%   Fax: 202-225-8135
Website: www.house.gov/gwenmoore
CoS .... *Shirley Ellis* **LD** .... *Win Boerckel*
Sch .... *Kendra Murray* **Press** .... *Vacant*
Bio: b. 4/18/51 Racine, WI; Baptist; BA Marquette Univ., 1978; Public Official, Civic Activist; single
Comm.: Financial Services; Small Business
Dist. Office: Milwaukee, 414-297-1140

James P. Moran (D-8th/VA)   202-225-4376
2239 RHOB   8th Term/60%   Fax: 202-225-0017
Website: moran.house.gov
CoS .... *Melissa Koloszar* **LD** .... *Tim Aiken*
Sch .... *Amanda Ruff* **Press** .... *Austin Durrer*
Bio: b. 5/16/45 Buffalo, NY; Catholic; MPA Univ. of Pittsburgh, 1970; Stockbroker; m. LuAnn Bennett
Comm.: Appropriations
Dist. Offices: Alexandria, 703-971-4700; Reston, 703-481-4339

Jerry Moran (R-1st/KS)   202-225-2715
2443 RHOB   5th Term/91%   Fax: 202-225-5124
Website: www.house.gov/moranks01
CoS .... *Travis Murphy* **LD** .... *Jennie Guttery*
Appt .... *Crystal Emel* **Press** .... *Ryan Wright*
Bio: b. 5/29/54 Great Bend, KS; Methodist; JD Univ. of KS, 1981; Attorney, Bank Officer; m. Robba
Comm.: Agriculture; Transportation & Infrastructure; Veterans' Affairs
Dist. Offices: Hutchinson, 620-665-6138; Hays, 785-628-6401

Timothy F. Murphy (R-18th/PA)   202-225-2301
322 CHOB   2nd Term/63%   Fax: 202-225-1844
Website: murphy.house.gov
CoS .... *Susan Mosychuk* **LD** .... *Kelly Gosselin*
Sch .... *Pat Koch* **Press** .... *Mark Carpenter*
Bio: b. 9/11/52 Cleveland, OH; Catholic; PhD Univ. of Pittsburgh, 1979; Psychologist; m. Nanette
Comm.: Energy & Commerce
Dist. Offices: Pittsburgh, 412-344-5583; Greensburg, 724-850-7312

John P. Murtha (D-12th/PA)   202-225-2065
2423 RHOB   17th Term/Unc.   Fax: 202-225-5709
Website: www.house.gov/murtha
CoS .... *John Hugya* **LD** .... *Debra Tekavec*
Sch .... *Jane Phipps* **CD** .... *Cindy Abram*
Bio: b. 6/17/32 New Martinsville, WV; Catholic; BA Univ. of Pittsburgh, 1962; USMC, 1952-55, 1966-67; USMCR, 1955-66, 1967-90; Small Business Owner; m. Joyce
Comm.: Appropriations
Dist. Office: Johnstown, 814-535-2642

Marilyn Musgrave (R-4th/CO)   202-225-4676
1507 LHOB   2nd Term/52%   Fax: 202-225-5870
Website: www.house.gov/musgrave
CoS .... *Guy Short* **Sr LA** .... *Nina Schmidgall*
Sch .... *Michele Rager* **CD** .... *Aaron Johnson*
Bio: b. 1/27/49 Greeley, CO; Assembly of God; BA CO St. Univ., 1972; Businesswoman, Teacher; m. Steven
Comm.: Agriculture; Education & the Workforce; Resources; Small Business
Dist. Offices: Loveland, 970-663-3536; Sterling, 970-522-1788; Las Animas, 719-456-0925; Greeley, 970-352-4037; Longmont, 720-494-4336

REPRESENTATIVES

Sue Myrick (R-9th/NC)   202-225-1976
230 CHOB   6th Term/70%   Fax: 202-225-3389
E-mail: myrick@mail.house.gov
Website: myrick.house.gov
AA .... *Ashley Hoy*   **LD** .... *Matt Priest*
Sch .... *Hollie Arnold*   **Press** .... *Andy Polk*
Bio: b. 8/1/41 Tiffin, OH; Methodist; Attended Heidelberg Col.; Businesswoman; m. Ed
Comm.: Energy & Commerce
Dist. Offices: Charlotte, 704-362-1060; Gastonia, 704-861-1976

Jerrold Nadler (D-8th/NY)   202-225-5635
2334 RHOB   7th Term/80%   Fax: 202-225-6923
Website: www.house.gov/nadler
CoS .... *Amy Rutkin*   **LD** .... *Lisette Morton*
Appt .... *Janice Siegel*   **CD** .... *Reid Cherlin*
Bio: b. 6/13/47 Brooklyn, NY; Jewish; JD Fordham Univ., 1978; Attorney; m. Joyce Miller
Comm.: Judiciary; Transportation & Infrastructure
Dist. Offices: New York, 212-367-7350; Brooklyn, 718-373-3198

Grace F. Napolitano (D-38th/CA)   202-225-5256
1609 LHOB   4th Term/Unc.   Fax: 202-225-0027
Website: www.napolitano.house.gov
CoS .... *Kate Krause*   **LD** .... *Daniel Chao*
Sch .... *Jen Silva*   **Press** .... *Joel Eskovitz*
Bio: b. 12/4/36 Brownsville, TX; Catholic; HS Diploma; Public Official; m. Frank
Comm.: International Relations; Resources
Dist. Office: Santa Fe Springs, 562-801-2134

Richard E. Neal (D-2nd/MA)   202-225-5601
2266 RHOB   9th Term/Unc.   Fax: 202-225-8112
Website: www.house.gov/neal
CoS .... *Ann Jablon*   **LD** .... *Peg McGlinch*
Appt .... *Sarah Bontempo*   **Press** ...... *William Tranghese*
Bio: b. 2/14/49 Springfield, MA; Catholic; MPA Univ. of Hartford, 1976; Educator; m. Maureen
Comm.: Budget; Ways & Means
Dist. Offices: Springfield, 413-785-0325; Milford, 508-634-8198

Randy Neugebauer (R-19th/TX)   202-225-4005
429 CHOB   2nd Term/58%   Fax: 202-225-9615
Website: www.randy.house.gov
CoS .... *Gayland Barksdale*   **LD** .... *Jodi Detwiler*
Sch .... *Pamela Mattox*   **CD** .... *Josh Noland*
Bio: b. 12/24/49 Lubbock, TX; Baptist; BBA TX Tech Univ., 1972; Land Developer; m. Dana
Comm.: Agriculture; Financial Services
Dist. Offices: Lubbock, 806-763-1611; Abilene, 325-675-9779; Big Spring, 432-264-7592

Bob Ney (R-18th/OH)   202-225-6265
2438 RHOB   6th Term/66%   Fax: 202-225-3394
E-mail: bobney@mail.house.gov
Website: ney.house.gov
CoS .... *Will Heaton*   **LD** .... *Chris Otillio*
Sch .... *Jennie Vollor*   **CD** .... *Brian Walsh*
Bio: b. 7/5/54 Wheeling, WV; Catholic; BS OH St. Univ., 1976; Public Official; m. Elizabeth
Comm.: Financial Services; House Administration (Chair); Transportation & Infrastructure; Joint Library (Chair); Joint Printing (Vice Chair)
Dist. Offices: St. Clairsville, 740-699-2704; Zanesville, 740-452-7023; New Philadelphia, 330-364-6380; Jackson, 740-288-1430; Chillicothe, 740-779-1634

REPRESENTATIVES

Anne M. Northup (R-3rd/KY)   202-225-5401
2459 RHOB   5th Term/60%   Fax: 202-225-5776
Website: northup.house.gov
CoS .... *Terry Carmack* **LD** .... *Clinton Blair*
Sch .... *Beth Strategier* **Press** .... *Annie Reed*
Bio: b. 1/22/48 Louisville, KY; Catholic; BA St. Mary's Col., 1970; Teacher; m. Robert
Comm.: Appropriations
Dist. Office: Louisville, 502-582-5129

Eleanor Holmes Norton (D/DC)   202-225-8050
2136 RHOB   8th Term/Unc.   Fax: 202-225-3002
Website: www.norton.house.gov
CoS .... *Julia Hudson* **LD** .... *Rosalind Parker*
Sch .... *Raven Roddey* **CD** .... *Doxie McCoy*
Bio: b. 6/13/37 Washington, DC; Episcopal; LLB Yale Univ., 1964; Attorney; div.
Comm.: Government Reform; Homeland Security; Transportation & Infrastructure
Dist. Offices: Washington, 202-783-5065; Washington, 202-678-8900

Charles Norwood (R-9th/GA)   202-225-4101
2452 RHOB   6th Term/74%   Fax: 202-226-0776
Website: www.house.gov/norwood
CoS .... *John Walker* **LD** .... *Jennie Derge*
Sch .... *Kathleen Smoak* **CD** .... *John Stone*
Bio: b. 7/27/41 Valdosta, GA; Methodist; DDS Georgetown Univ., 1967; USA, 1967-69; Dentist; m. Gloria
Comm.: Education & the Workforce; Energy & Commerce
Dist. Offices: Augusta, 706-733-7066; Toccoa, 706-886-2776

Devin Nunes (R-21st/CA)   202-225-2523
1017 LHOB   2nd Term/73%   Fax: 202-225-3404
Website: www.nunes.house.gov
CoS .... *Johnny Amaral* **LD** .... *Damon Nelson*
Appt .... *Jennifer Buckley* **Press** .... *Justin Stoner*
Bio: b. 10/1/73 Tulare Co., CA; Catholic; MS CA Polytechnic Univ., 1996; Dairy Farmer; m. Elizabeth
Comm.: Agriculture; Resources; Veterans' Affairs
Dist. Offices: Visalia, 559-733-3861; Clovis, 559-323-5235

Jim Nussle (R-1st/IA)   202-225-2911
303 CHOB   8th Term/55%   Fax: 202-225-9129
Website: nussle.house.gov
CoS .... *Tom Wolfe* **LD** .... *Christopher Bliley*
AA .... *Barbra Snitker* **Press** .... *Kim Deti*
Bio: b. 6/27/60 Des Moines, IA; Lutheran; JD Drake Univ., 1985; Attorney; m. Karen
Comm.: Budget (Chair); Ways & Means
Dist. Offices: Manchester, 563-927-5141; Dubuque, 563-557-7740; Waterloo, 319-235-1109; Davenport, 563-326-1841

James L. Oberstar (D-8th/MN)   202-225-6211
2365 RHOB   16th Term/65%   Fax: 202-225-0699
Website: oberstar.house.gov
CoS .... *Bill Richard* **LD** .... *Chip Gardiner*
Sch .... *Jeri Sparling* **Press** .... *Mary Kerr*
Bio: b. 9/10/34 Chisholm, MN; Catholic; MA Col. of Europe (Belgium), 1957; Congressional Aide; m. Jean
Comm.: Transportation & Infrastructure (Rnk. Mem.)
Dist. Offices: Duluth, 218-727-7474; Chisholm, 218-254-5761; Brainerd, 218-828-4400; North Branch, 651-277-1234

REPRESENTATIVES

David R. Obey (D-7th/WI)   202-225-3365
2314 RHOB   19th Term/86%   Fax: 715-842-4488
Website: www.house.gov/obey
CoS .... *Will Stone*   **LD** .... *Paul Carver*
Appt .... *Carly Burns*   **Press** .... *Ellis Brachman*
Bio: b. 10/3/38 Okmulgee, OK; Catholic; MA Univ. of WI, 1962; Realtor; m. Joan
Comm.: Appropriations (Rnk. Mem.)
Dist. Offices: Wausau, 715-842-5606; Superior, 715-398-4426

John W. Olver (D-1st/MA)   202-225-5335
1111 LHOB   8th Term/Unc.   Fax: 202-226-1224
Website: www.house.gov/olver
CoS .... *Hunter Ridgway*   **LD** .... *Abbie Meador*
Sch .... *Nicole Letourneau*   **Press** ...... *Nicole Letourneau*
Bio: b. 9/3/36 Honesdale, PA; Not Stated; PhD MIT, 1961; Professor; m. Rose
Comm.: Appropriations
Dist. Offices: Pittsfield, 413-442-0946; Holyoke, 413-532-7010; Fitchburg, 978-342-8722

Solomon P. Ortiz (D-27th/TX)   202-225-7742
2470 RHOB   12th Term/63%   Fax: 202-226-1134
Website: www.house.gov/ortiz
CoS .... *Florencio Rendon*   **LD** .... *Fernando Gomez*
Sch .... *Rhiannon Burruss*   **Press** .... *Cathy Travis*
Bio: b. 6/3/37 Robstown, TX; Methodist; Attended Del Mar Col.; USA, 1960-62; Law Enforcement Official; div.
Comm.: Armed Services; Resources
Dist. Offices: Corpus Christi, 361-883-5868; Brownsville, 956-541-1242

Tom Osborne (R-3rd/NE)   202-225-6435
507 CHOB   3rd Term/88%   Fax: 202-226-1385
Website: www.house.gov/osborne
CoS .... *Bruce Rieker*   **LD** .... *Erin Duncan*
Appt .... *Daffnei O'Bryan*   **Press** .... *Erin Hegge*
Bio: b. 2/23/37 Hastings, NE; Methodist; PhD Univ. of NE, 1965; USANG, 1960-66; Educator, College Football Coach; m. Nancy
Comm.: Agriculture; Education & the Workforce; Transportation & Infrastructure
Dist. Offices: Grand Island, 308-381-5555; Scottsbluff, 308-632-3333; Kearney, 308-236-1330; McCook, 308-345-3328

C.L. "Butch" Otter (R-1st/ID)   202-225-6611
1711 LHOB   3rd Term/70%   Fax: 202-225-3029
Website: www.house.gov/otter
CoS .... *Jeff Malmen*   **LD** .... *Jani L. Revier*
Appt .... *Solara Linehan*   **CD** .... *Mark Warbis*
Bio: b. 5/3/42 Caldwell, ID; Catholic; BA Col. of ID, 1967; IDNG, 1968-73; Businessman; single
Comm.: Energy & Commerce
Dist. Offices: Boise, 208-336-9831; Coeur d'Alene, 208-667-0127; Lewiston, 208-298-0030; Nampa, 208-466-4503

Major R. Owens (D-11th/NY)   202-225-6231
2309 RHOB   12th Term/Unc.   Fax: 202-226-0112
Website: www.house.gov/owens
CoS .... *Theda Zawaiza*   **LD** .... *Norman A. Meyer*
Appt ...... *Lauren Thompson*   **CD** .... *Theda Zawaiza*
Bio: b. 6/28/36 Memphis, TN; Baptist; MS Atlanta Univ., 1957; Librarian; m. Maria
Comm.: Education & the Workforce; Government Reform
Dist. Offices: Brooklyn, 718-773-3100; Brooklyn, 718-940-3213

REPRESENTATIVES

Michael G. Oxley (R-4th/OH)   202-225-2676
2308 RHOB   13th Term/59%   Fax: 202-226-0577
Website: oxley.house.gov
CoS .... *Jim Conzelman*   LD .... *Tim Johnson*
Sch .... *Debra Deimling*   Press .... *Tim Johnson*
Bio: b. 2/11/44 Findlay, OH; Lutheran; JD OH St. Univ., 1969; Attorney; m. Patricia
Comm.: Financial Services (Chair)
Dist. Offices: Findlay, 419-423-3210; Lima, 419-999-6455; Mansfield, 419-522-5757

Frank Pallone, Jr. (D-6th/NJ)   202-225-4671
420 CHOB   9th Term/67%   Fax: 202-225-9665
Website: www.house.gov/pallone
CoS .... *Jeff Carroll*   LD .... *Kathy Kulkarni*
Sch .... *Angineh Babooian*   Press .... *Andrew Souvall*
Bio: b. 10/30/51 Long Branch, NJ; Catholic; JD Rutgers Univ., 1978; Attorney; m. Sarah
Comm.: Energy & Commerce; Resources
Dist. Offices: Long Branch, 732-571-1140; New Brunswick, 732-249-8892; Hazlet, 732-264-9104

Bill Pascrell, Jr. (D-8th/NJ)   202-225-5751
2464 RHOB   5th Term/69%   Fax: 202-225-5782
Website: pascrell.house.gov
CoS .... *Ed Farmer*   LD .... *Ben Rich*
Sch .... *Selvin White*   Press .... *Sabrina Glavan*
Bio: b. 1/25/37 Paterson, NJ; Catholic; MA Fordham Univ., 1961; USA, 1961-62; USAR, 1962-67; Teacher; m. Elsie
Comm.: Homeland Security; Transportation & Infrastructure
Dist. Offices: Paterson, 973-523-5152; Passaic, 973-472-4510; Bloomfield, 973-680-1361

Ed Pastor (D-4th/AZ)   202-225-4065
2465 RHOB   8th Term/70%   Fax: 202-225-1655
Website: www.house.gov/pastor
CoS .... *None*   LD .... *Eve Young*
Sch .... *Laura Campos*   Press .... *Maura Saavedra*
Bio: b. 6/28/43 Claypool, AZ; Catholic; JD AZ St. Univ., 1974; Educator; m. Verma
Comm.: Appropriations
Dist. Office: Phoenix, 602-256-0551

Ron E. Paul (R-14th/TX)   202-225-2831
203 CHOB   9th Term/Unc.   Fax: 202-226-6288
Website: www.house.gov/paul
CoS .... *Tom Lizardo*   LD .... *Norman Singleton*
Sch .... *Jennifer Roell*   Press .... *Jeff Deist*
Bio: b. 8/20/35 Pittsburgh, PA; Christian; MD Duke Univ., 1961; USAF, 1963-65; USANG, 1965-68; Physician; m. Carol
Comm.: Financial Services; International Relations; Joint Economic
Dist. Offices: Victoria, 361-576-1231; Freeport, 979-230-0000

Donald M. Payne (D-10th/NJ)   202-225-3436
2209 RHOB   9th Term/Unc.   Fax: 202-225-4160
Website: www.house.gov/payne
CoS .... *Kerry McKenney*   LD .... *Kerry McKenney*
Sch .... *Darlene Murray*   Press .... *Kerry McKenney*
Bio: b. 7/16/34 Newark, NJ; Baptist; BA Seton Hall Univ., 1957; Businessman; widowed
Comm.: Education & the Workforce; International Relations
Dist. Offices: Newark, 973-645-3213; Elizabeth, 908-629-0222; Jersey City, 201-369-0392

REPRESENTATIVES

Steve Pearce (R-2nd/NM)   202-225-2365
1607 LHOB   2nd Term/60%   Fax: 202-225-9599
Website: pearce.house.gov
CoS .... *Vacant* **LD** .... *Matt Meagher*
Appt .... *Peggy Mallow* **Press** .... *Jim Burns*
Bio: b. 8/24/47 Lamesa, TX; Baptist; MBA Eastern NM Univ., 1991; USAF, 1970-76; Business Owner; m. Cynthia
Comm.: Financial Services; Homeland Security; Resources
Dist. Offices: Las Cruces, 505-522-2219; Roswell, 505-622-0055; Hobbs, 505-392-8325; Socorro, 505-838-7516

Nancy Pelosi (D-8th/CA)   202-225-4965
2371 RHOB   10th Term/85%   Fax: 202-225-8259
E-mail: sf.nancy@mail.house.gov
Website: www.house.gov/pelosi
CoS .... *George Crawford* **LD** .... *Vacant*
Sch .... *Cortney Bright* **Press** .... *Brendan Daly*
Bio: b. 3/26/40 Baltimore, MD; Catholic; BA Trinity Col. (DC), 1962; Public Relations Consultant; m. Paul
Comm.: Minority Leader
Dist. Office: San Francisco, 415-556-4862

Mike Pence (R-6th/IN)   202-225-3021
426 CHOB   3rd Term/67%   Fax: 202-225-3382
Website: mikepence.house.gov
CoS .... *Bill Smith* **LD** .... *Ryan Fisher*
Sch .... *Jennifer Marsh* **CD** .... *Matt Lloyd*
Bio: b. 6/7/59 Columbus, IN; Christian; JD IN Univ., 1986; Radio Talk Show Host; m. Karen
Comm.: Agriculture; International Relations; Judiciary
Dist. Office: Anderson, 765-640-2919

Collin Peterson (D-7th/MN)   202-225-2165
2159 RHOB   8th Term/66%   Fax: 202-225-1593
Website: collinpeterson.house.gov
CoS .... *Mark Brownell* **LD** .... *Robin Goracke*
Sch .... *Cherie Slayton* **Press** .... *Allison Myhre*
Bio: b. 6/29/44 Fargo, ND; Lutheran; BA Moorhead St. Univ., 1966; NDARNG, 1963-69; Accountant; div.
Comm.: Agriculture (Rnk. Mem.)
Dist. Offices: Detroit Lakes, 218-847-5056; Red Lake Falls, 218-253-4356; Willmar, 320-235-1061; Marshall, 507-537-2299; Montevideo, 320-269-8888; Redwood Falls, 507-637-2270

John E. Peterson (R-5th/PA)   202-225-5121
123 CHOB   5th Term/88%   Fax: 202-225-5796
Website: www.house.gov/johnpeterson
CoS .... *Jordan Clark* **LD** .... *Jeff Vorberger*
Sch .... *Regina Tallman* **CD** .... *Paul Feenstra*
Bio: b. 12/25/38 Titusville, PA; Methodist; Attended Penn St. Univ.; USA, 1957-63; Grocery Store Owner; m. Saundra
Comm.: Appropriations; Resources
Dist. Offices: State College, 814-238-1776; Titusville, 814-827-3985

Thomas E. Petri (R-6th/WI)   202-225-2476
2462 RHOB   14th Term/67%   Fax: 202-225-2356
Website: www.house.gov/petri
CoS .... *Debbie Gebhardt* **LD** .... *Debbie Gebhardt*
Sch .... *Lindsay Bowers* **Press** .... *Niel Wright*
Bio: b. 5/28/40 Marinette, WI; Lutheran; JD Harvard Univ., 1965; Attorney; m. Anne
Comm.: Education & the Workforce (Vice Chair); Transportation & Infrastructure
Dist. Offices: Fond du Lac, 920-922-1180; Oshkosh, 920-231-6333

REPRESENTATIVES

Charles "Chip" Pickering, Jr. (R-3rd/MS)   202-225-5031
229 CHOB   5th Term/81%   Fax: 202-225-5797
Website: www.house.gov/pickering
CoS .... Susan Butler   **LD** .... Mike Hurst
Sch .... Marcy Scoggins   **CD** .... Brian Perry
Bio: b. 8/10/63 Laurel, MS; Baptist; MBA Baylor Univ., 1989; Congressional Aide; m. Leisha
Comm.: Energy & Commerce (Vice Chair)
Dist. Offices: Pearl, 601-932-2410; Meridian, 601-693-6681; Starkville, 662-324-0007; Brookhaven, 601-823-3400; Natchez, 601-442-2515

Joseph R. Pitts (R-16th/PA)   202-225-2411
221 CHOB   5th Term/64%   Fax: 202-225-2013
Website: www.house.gov/pitts
CoS .... Gabe Neville   **LD** .... Ken Miller
Sch .... Mary O'Connor   **CD** .... Derek Karchner
Bio: b. 10/10/39 Lexington, KY; Protestant; MEd West Chester Univ., 1972; USAF, 1963-69; Teacher; m. Virginia
Comm.: Energy & Commerce
Dist. Offices: Lancaster, 717-393-0667; Unionville, 610-444-4581

Todd R. Platts (R-19th/PA)   202-225-5836
1032 LHOB   3rd Term/Unc.   Fax: 202-226-1000
Website: www.house.gov/platts
CoS .... Scott Miller   **LD** .... Joe Thomas
Sch .... Carol Wiest   **Press** .... Robert Reilly
Bio: b. 3/5/62 York, PA; Episcopal; JD Pepperdine Univ., 1991; Attorney; m. Leslie
Comm.: Education & the Workforce; Government Reform; Transportation & Infrastructure
Dist. Offices: York, 717-600-1919; Carlisle, 717-249-0190; Gettysburg, 717-338-1919

Ted Poe (R-2nd/TX)   202-225-6565
1605 LHOB   1st Term/56%   Fax: 202-225-5547
Website: www.house.gov/poe
CoS .... Heather Ramsey   **LD** .... Alan Knapp
Sch .... Rebecca Baca   **Press** .... Anouck McCall
Bio: b. 10/13/48 Temple, TX; Church of Christ; JD Univ. of Houston, 1973; USAFR, 1970-76; Judge; m. Carol
Comm.: International Relations; Small Business; Transportation & Infrastructure
Dist. Offices: Humble, 281-446-0242; Beaumont, 409-212-1997

Richard Pombo (R-11th/CA)   202-225-1947
2411 RHOB   7th Term/61%   Fax: 202-226-0861
Website: www.house.gov/pombo
CoS .... Jessica Carter   **LD** .... Marla Sousa
Sch .... Jon Haubert   **Press** ... Nicole Taylor Philbin
Bio: b. 1/8/61 Tracy, CA; Catholic; Attended CA St. Univ. - Pomona; Rancher; m. Annette
Comm.: Agriculture; Resources (Chair)
Dist. Offices: Stockton, 209-951-3091; San Ramon, 925-866-7040

Earl Pomeroy (D-At Large/ND)   202-225-2611
1501 LHOB   7th Term/60%   Fax: 202-226-0893
Website: www.pomeroy.house.gov
CoS .... Bob Siggins   **LD** .... Aleta Botts
Sch .... Stacy Austad   **Press** .... Mac Schneider
Bio: b. 9/2/52 Valley City, ND; Presbyterian; JD Univ. of ND, 1979; Attorney; single
Comm.: Agriculture; Ways & Means
Dist. Offices: Bismarck, 701-224-0355; Fargo, 701-235-9760

REPRESENTATIVES

Jon C. Porter (R-3rd/NV)   202-225-3252
218 CHOB   2nd Term/55%   Fax: 202-225-2185
Website: www.house.gov/porter
CoS .... *Windsor Freemyer* **LD** .... *Trevor Kolego*
AA .... *Stacey Parker* **CD** .... *Adam Mayberry*
Bio: b. 5/16/55 Ft. Dodge, IA; Catholic; Attended Briar Cliff Col.; Public Official, Insurance Executive; m. Laurie
Comm.: Education & the Workforce; Government Reform; Transportation & Infrastructure
Dist. Office: Henderson, 702-387-4941

Rob J. Portman (R-2nd/OH)   202-225-3164
238 CHOB   7th Term/72%   Fax: 202-225-1992
E-mail: portmail@mail.house.gov
Website: portman.house.gov
CoS .... *Rob Lehman* **LD** .... *Barbara Pate*
Sch .... *Lise Sackett* **CD** .... *Kyle Downey*
Bio: b. 12/19/55 Cincinnati, OH; Methodist; JD Univ. of MI, 1984; Attorney; m. Jane
Comm.: Budget (Vice Chair); Ways & Means
Dist. Offices: Cincinnati, 513-791-0381; Portsmouth, 740-354-1440
(Rep. Portman was nominated to be US Trade Representative.)

David E. Price (D-4th/NC)   202-225-1784
2162 RHOB   9th Term/64%   Fax: 202-225-2014
Website: price.house.gov
CoS .... *Jean-Louise Beard* **LD** .... *Darek Newby*
Sch .... *Elizabeth Gottschalk* **Press** .... *Bridget Lowell*
Bio: b. 8/17/40 Erwin, TN; Baptist; PhD Yale Univ., 1969; Professor; m. Lisa
Comm.: Appropriations
Dist. Offices: Raleigh, 919-859-5999; Chapel Hill, 919-967-7924; Durham, 919-688-3004

Tom Price (R-6th/GA)   202-225-4501
506 CHOB   1st Term/Unc.   Fax: 202-225-4656
Website: www.house.gov/tomprice
CoS .... *Matt McGinley* **LD** .... *Tim Robison*
Sch .... *Claire Benson* **Press** .... *Jim Billimoria*
Bio: b. 10/8/54 Roswell, GA; Presbyterian; MD Univ. of MI, 1979; Physician; m. Elizabeth
Comm.: Education & the Workforce; Financial Services
Dist. Office: Marietta, 770-565-4990

Deborah Pryce (R-15th/OH)   202-225-2015
204 CHOB   7th Term/62%   Fax: 202-225-3529
Website: www.house.gov/pryce
CoS .... *Lori Salley* **LD** .... *Shiloh Roehl*
Sch .... *Sara Rogers* **Press** .... *John McClelland*
Bio: b. 7/29/51 Warren, OH; Presbyterian; JD Capital Univ., 1976; Attorney; single
Comm.: Financial Services
Dist. Office: Columbus, 614-469-5614

Adam Putnam (R-12th/FL)   202-225-1252
1213 LHOB   3rd Term/65%   Fax: 202-226-0585
Website: www.house.gov/putnam
CoS .... *John Hambel* **LD** .... *Karen Williams*
Appt .... *Chanel Dedes* **CD** .... *Shawn Dhar*
Bio: b. 7/31/74 Bartow, FL; Episcopal; BS Univ. of FL - Gainesville, 1995; Farmer, Rancher; m. Melissa
Comm.: Budget; Rules
Dist. Office: Bartow, 863-534-3530

REPRESENTATIVES

George P. Radanovich (R-19th/CA) 202-225-4540
438 CHOB   6th Term/66%   Fax: 202-225-3402
Website: radanovich.house.gov
CoS .... *Ted Maness* **LD** .... *Tricia Geringer*
EA .... *Connie Dwyer* **Press** .... *Heather Davis*
Bio: b. 6/20/55 Mariposa, CA; Catholic; BS CA Polytechnic St. Univ., 1978; Winery Owner; m. Ethie Weaver
Comm.: Energy & Commerce; Resources
Dist. Offices: Fresno, 559-449-2490; Turlock, 209-656-8660

Nick J. Rahall II (D-3rd/WV) 202-225-3452
2307 RHOB   15th Term/65%   Fax: 202-225-9061
E-mail: nrahall@mail.house.gov
Website: www.rahall.house.gov
CoS .... *Kent Keyser* **LD** .... *Stefan Bailey*
Appt .... *Vickie Bandy* **Press** .... *Kevin Baker*
Bio: b. 5/20/49 Beckley, WV; Presbyterian; BA Duke Univ., 1971; Broadcast Executive; m. Melinda Ross
Comm.: Resources (Rnk. Mem.); Transportation & Infrastructure
Dist. Offices: Beckley, 304-252-5000; Bluefield, 304-325-6222; Huntington, 304-522-6425; Logan, 304-752-4934

Jim Ramstad (R-3rd/MN) 202-225-2871
103 CHOB   8th Term/65%   Fax: 202-225-6351
E-mail: mn03@mail.house.gov
Website: www.house.gov/ramstad
CoS .... *Dean Peterson* **LD** .... *Karin Hope*
Sch .... *Valerie Nelson* **Press** .... *Dean Peterson*
Bio: b. 5/6/46 Jamestown, ND; Protestant; JD George Washington Univ., 1973; USAR, 1968-74; Attorney, Legislative Aide; single
Comm.: Ways & Means
Dist. Office: Minnetonka, 952-738-8200

Charles B. Rangel (D-15th/NY) 202-225-4365
2354 RHOB   18th Term/90%   Fax: 202-225-0816
Website: rangel.house.gov
CoS .... *George Dalley* **LD** .... *Emile Milne*
Appt .... *Brenda Swygert* **Press** .... *Emile Milne*
Bio: b. 6/11/30 Harlem, NY; Catholic; LLB St. John's Univ., 1960; USA, 1948-52; Attorney; m. Alma
Comm.: Ways & Means (Rnk. Mem.); Joint Taxation
Dist. Office: New York, 212-663-3900

Ralph Regula (R-16th/OH) 202-225-3876
2306 RHOB   17th Term/67%   Fax: 202-225-3059
Website: www.house.gov/regula
CoS .... *Lori Rowley* **LD** .... *Lori Rowley*
Sch .... *Sylvia Snyder* **Press** .... *Lori Rowley*
Bio: b. 12/3/24 Beach City, OH; Episcopal; LLB William McKinley School of Law, 1952; USN, 1944-46; Attorney; m. Mary
Comm.: Appropriations (Vice Chair)
Dist. Offices: Canton, 330-489-4414; Medina, 330-722-3793

Dennis Rehberg (R-At Large/MT) 202-225-3211
516 CHOB   3rd Term/64%   Fax: 202-225-5687
Website: www.house.gov/rehberg
CoS .... *Erik Iverson* **LD** .... *Julia Gustafson*
Sch .... *Katie Brackin* **CD** .... *Brad Keena*
Bio: b. 10/5/55 Billings, MT; Episcopal; BA WA St. Univ., 1977; Rancher, Public Official; m. Jan
Comm.: Appropriations
Dist. Offices: Billings, 406-256-1019; Helena, 406-443-7878; Great Falls, 406-454-1066; Missoula, 406-543-9550

REPRESENTATIVES

Dave Reichert (R-8th/WA) — 202-225-7761
1223 LHOB 1st Term/52% Fax: 202-225-4282
E-mail: representative.reichert@mail.house.gov
Website: www.house.gov/reichert
CoS .... *Mike Shields* **LD** .... *Chris Miller*
Sch .... *Nicole Robison* **Press** .... *Vacant*
Bio: b. 8/29/50 Detroit Lakes, MN; Lutheran; AA Concordia Lutheran College, 1970; Law Enforcement Official; m. Julie
Comm.: Homeland Security; Science; Transportation & Infrastructure
Dist. Office: Mercer Island, 206-275-3438

Rick Renzi (R-1st/AZ) — 202-225-2315
418 CHOB 2nd Term/59% Fax: 202-226-9739
Website: www.house.gov/renzi
CoS .... *Karen Lynch* **LD** .... *Alix Crockett*
Appt .... *Teri Grier* **Press** .... *Matthew Ash*
Bio: b. 6/11/58 Sierra Vista, AZ; Catholic; JD Catholic Univ., 2002; Businessman; m. Roberta
Comm.: Financial Services; Resources; Select Intelligence
Dist. Offices: Show Low, 928-537-2800; Flagstaff, 928-213-3434; Casa Grande, 520-876-0929; Prescott, 928-708-9120; Window Rock, 928-853-3750; Safford, 928-587-3417; San Carlos, 928-475-3733; Whiteriver, 928-521-2810

Silvestre Reyes (D-16th/TX) — 202-225-4831
2433 RHOB 5th Term/68% Fax: 202-225-2016
Website: www.house.gov/reyes
CoS ...... *Perry Finney Brody* **LD** .... *Alison Rosso*
Sch .... *Liza Lynch* **Press** .... *Kira Maas*
Bio: b. 11/10/44 Canutillo, TX; Catholic; AA El Paso Comm. Col., 1977; USA, 1966-68; Border Patrol Agent; m. Carolina
Comm.: Armed Services; Veterans' Affairs; Select Intelligence
Dist. Office: El Paso, 915-534-4400

Thomas Reynolds (R-26th/NY) — 202-225-5265
332 CHOB 4th Term/56% Fax: 202-225-5910
Website: www.house.gov/reynolds
CoS .... *Michael Brady* **LD** .... *Tina Mufford*
EA .... *Karen Kaumeier* **Press** .... *Chad Scarborough*
Bio: b. 9/3/50 Bellefonte, PA; Protestant; Attended Kent St. Univ.; NYANG, 1970-76; Public Official; m. Donna
Comm.: House Administration; Ways & Means; Joint Printing
Dist. Offices: Williamsville, 716-634-2324; Rochester, 585-663-5570

Harold Rogers (R-5th/KY) — 202-225-4601
2406 RHOB 13th Term/Unc. Fax: 202-225-0940
E-mail: talk2hal@mail.house.gov
Website: www.house.gov/rogers
CoS .... *Will Smith* **LD** .... *Mike Robinson*
Appt .... *Angela Hope* **Press** .... *Leslie Cupp*
Bio: b. 12/31/37 Barrier, KY; Baptist; LLB Univ. of KY, 1964; USARNG, 1957-64; Attorney; m. Cynthia Doyle
Comm.: Appropriations
Dist. Offices: Somerset, 606-679-8346; Hazard, 606-439-0794; Prestonburg, 606-886-0844

Michael D. Rogers (R-3rd/AL) — 202-225-3261
514 CHOB 2nd Term/61% Fax: 202-226-8485
Website: www.house.gov/mike-rogers
CoS .... *Rob Jesmer* **LD** .... *Chris Brinson*
Sch .... *Shea Snider* **CD** .... *Marshall Macomber*
Bio: b. 7/16/58 Hammond, IN; Baptist; JD Birmingham School of Law, 1991; Attorney; m. Beth
Comm.: Agriculture; Armed Services; Homeland Security
Dist. Offices: Anniston, 256-236-5655; Opelika, 334-745-6221; Montgomery, 334-277-4210

REPRESENTATIVES

Michael J. Rogers (R-8th/MI)　　**202-225-4872**
133 CHOB　　3rd Term/61%　　Fax: 202-225-5820
Website: mikerogers.house.gov
CoS .... Matt Strawn　**LD** .... Heather Keiser
Appt .... Amy Cook　**Press** .... Sylvia Warner
Bio: b. 6/2/63 Livingston Co., MI; Methodist; BS Adrian Col., 1985; USA, 1985-88; Business Owner; m. Diane
Comm.: Energy & Commerce; Select Intelligence
Dist. Office: Lansing, 517-702-8000

Dana Rohrabacher (R-46th/CA)　　**202-225-2415**
2338 RHOB　　9th Term/62%　　Fax: 202-225-0145
E-mail: dana@mail.house.gov
Website: rohrabacher.house.gov
CoS ...... Richard T. Dykema　**LD** .... Richard T. Dykema
Sch .... Krissy Rodriguez　**Press** .... Rebecca Rudman
Bio: b. 6/21/47 Coronado, CA; Christian; MA USC, 1975; Journalist, Speech Writer; m. Rhonda
Comm.: International Relations; Science
Dist. Office: Huntington Beach, 714-960-6483

Ileana Ros-Lehtinen (R-18th/FL)　　**202-225-3931**
2160 RHOB　　9th Term/65%　　Fax: 202-225-5620
Website: www.house.gov/ros-lehtinen
CoS .... Art Estopinan　**LD** .... Fred Ratliff
Sch ... Christine Del Portillo　**Press** .... Alex Cruz
Bio: b. 7/15/52 Havana, Cuba; Episcopal; MS FL International Univ., 1987; Educator; m. Dexter
Comm.: Budget; Government Reform; International Relations
Dist. Office: Miami, 305-275-1800

Mike Ross (D-4th/AR)　　**202-225-3772**
314 CHOB　　3rd Term/Unc.　　Fax: 202-225-1314
Website: www.house.gov/ross
CoS .... Cori Smith　**LD** .... Monique Frazier
Appt .... Rachel Kleinman　**CD** .... Adrienne Elrod
Bio: b. 9/1/61 Texarkana, AR; Methodist; BA Univ. of AR - Little Rock, 1987; Small Business Owner; m. Holly
Comm.: Energy & Commerce
Dist. Offices: Pine Bluff, 870-536-3376; Prescott, 870-887-6787; El Dorado, 870-881-0681; Hot Springs, 501-520-5892

Steven R. Rothman (D-9th/NJ)　　**202-225-5061**
2303 RHOB　　5th Term/67%　　Fax: 202-225-5851
Website: rothman.house.gov
CoS .... Bob Decheine　**LD** .... Kelly Dougherty
Appt .... Mary K. Flanagan　**Press** .... Bob Decheine
Bio: b. 10/14/52 Englewood, NJ; Jewish; JD Washington Univ., 1977; Attorney; div.
Comm.: Appropriations
Dist. Offices: Hackensack, 201-646-0808; Jersey City, 201-798-1366

Lucille Roybal-Allard (D-34th/CA)　　**202-225-1766**
2330 RHOB　　7th Term/75%　　Fax: 202-226-0350
Website: www.house.gov/roybal-allard
CoS .... Ellen Riddleberger　**LD** .... Don DeArmon
EA .... Lisa Pablo　**CD** .... Helen Machado
Bio: b. 6/12/41 Los Angeles, CA; Catholic; BA CA St. Univ. - Los Angeles, 1965; Public Relations Executive; m. Edward Allard III
Comm.: Appropriations; Standards of Official Conduct
Dist. Office: Los Angeles, 213-628-9230

REPRESENTATIVES

Ed Royce (R-40th/CA)   202-225-4111
2202 RHOB   7th Term/68%   Fax: 202-226-0335
Website: www.royce.house.gov
CoS .... *Amy Porter* **LD** .... *Amy Porter*
Appt .... *Sacha Bice* **CD** .... *Julianne Smith*
Bio: b. 10/12/51 Los Angeles, CA; Catholic; BA CA St. Univ. - Fullerton, 1977; Small Businessman, Corporate Tax Manager; m. Marie Porter
Comm.: Financial Services; International Relations
Dist. Office: Fullerton, 714-992-8081

C.A. "Dutch" Ruppersberger (D-2nd/MD)   202-225-3061
1630 LHOB   2nd Term/67%   Fax: 202-225-3094
Website: dutch.house.gov
CoS .... *Heather Molino* **LD** .... *Walter Gonzales*
Appt .... *Brenda Connolly* **Press** .... *Heather Molino*
Bio: b. 1/31/46 Baltimore, MD; Christian; JD Univ. of Baltimore, 1970; Public Official; m. Kay
Comm.: Government Reform; Select Intelligence
Dist. Office: Timonium, 410-628-2701

Bobby Rush (D-1st/IL)   202-225-4372
2416 RHOB   7th Term/85%   Fax: 202-226-0333
Website: www.house.gov/rush
CoS .... *Kimberly Parker* **Dep CoS** .... *Yardly Pollas*
Appt .... *N. Lenette Myers* **CD** .... *Tasha Harris*
Bio: b. 11/23/46 Albany, GA; Baptist; MA McCormick Seminary, 1998; USA, 1963-68; Activist; m. Carolyn
Comm.: Energy & Commerce
Dist. Offices: Chicago, 773-224-6500; Midlothian, 708-385-9550

Paul D. Ryan (R-1st/WI)   202-225-3031
1113 LHOB   4th Term/65%   Fax: 202-225-3393
Website: www.house.gov/ryan
CoS .... *Andrew Speth* **LD** .... *Peter Fotos*
Sch .... *Maureen Mitchell* **Press** .... *Kate Matus*
Bio: b. 1/29/70 Janesville, WI; Catholic; BA Miami Univ. of OH, 1992; Marketing Consultant, Congressional Aide; m. Janna
Comm.: Budget; Ways & Means; Joint Economic
Dist. Offices: Janesville, 608-752-4050; Kenosha, 262-654-1901; Racine, 262-637-0510

Tim Ryan (D-17th/OH)   202-225-5261
222 CHOB   2nd Term/77%   Fax: 202-225-3719
Website: timryan.house.gov
CoS .... *Mary Anne Walsh* **LD** .... *John Stephan*
Appt .... *Erin Isenberg* **CD** .... *Ryan Keating*
Bio: b. 7/16/73 Niles, OH; Catholic; JD Franklin Pierce Law Center, 2000; Public Official; m. Julie
Comm.: Armed Services; Education & the Workforce
Dist. Offices: Youngstown, 330-740-0193; Warren, 330-373-0074; Akron, 330-630-7311

Jim R. Ryun (R-2nd/KS)   202-225-6601
1110 LHOB   5th Term/56%   Fax: 202-225-7986
Website: ryun.house.gov
CoS .... *Mark Kelly* **Dep CoS** .... *Jay Rinehart*
Sch .... *Laura Niver* **CD** .... *Nick Reid*
Bio: b. 4/29/47 Wichita, KS; Evangelical Presbyterian; BA Univ. of KS, 1970; Businessman, Athlete; m. Anne
Comm.: Armed Services; Budget; Financial Services
Dist. Offices: Topeka, 785-232-4500; Pittsburg, 620-232-6100

REPRESENTATIVES

Martin Olav Sabo (D-5th/MN)   202-225-4755
2336 RHOB   14th Term/70%   Fax: 202-225-4886
Website: sabo.house.gov
CoS .... *Michael Erlandson* **LD** .... *Marjorie Duske*
Appt .... *Bonnie Gottwald* **Press** ...... *Jenifer McCormick*
Bio: b. 2/28/38 Crosby, ND; Lutheran; BA Augsburg Col., 1959; Public Official; m. Sylvia
Comm.: Appropriations
Dist. Office: Minneapolis, 612-664-8000

John T. Salazar (D-3rd/CO)   202-225-4761
1531 LHOB   1st Term/51%   Fax: 202-226-9669
E-mail: john.salazar@mail.house.gov
Website: www.house.gov/salazar
CoS .... *Ronnie Carleton* **LD** .... *Laura Marquez*
Sch .... *Brian Ross* **Press** .... *Nayyera Haq*
Bio: b. 7/21/53 Alamosa, CO; Catholic; BS Adams St. Col., 1981; USA, 1973-76; Farmer, Rancher, Small Business Owner; m. Mary Lou
Comm.: Agriculture; Transportation & Infrastructure
Dist. Offices: Pueblo, 719-543-8200; Grand Junction, 970-245-7107

Linda T. Sánchez (D-39th/CA)   202-225-6676
1007 LHOB   2nd Term/61%   Fax: 202-226-1012
Website: www.lindasanchez.house.gov
CoS .... *Janice Morris* **LD** .... *Virginia Mosqueda*
Sch .... *Ruth Carnegie* **CD** .... *Betsy Arnold*
Bio: b. 1/28/69 Orange, CA; Catholic; JD UCLA, 1995; Attorney; m. Mark
Comm.: Government Reform; Judiciary; Small Business
Dist. Office: Lakewood, 562-429-8499

Loretta Sanchez (D-47th/CA)   202-225-2965
1230 LHOB   5th Term/60%   Fax: 202-225-5859
E-mail: loretta@mail.house.gov
Website: www.lorettasanchez.house.gov
CoS .... *Lee Godown* **LD** .... *Edward Steiner*
Appt .... *Caroline Valdez* **CD** .... *Carrie Brooks*
Bio: b. 1/7/60 Lynwood, CA; Catholic; MBA American Univ., 1984; Investment Banker; div.
Comm.: Armed Services; Homeland Security; Joint Economic
Dist. Office: Garden Grove, 714-621-0102

Bernard Sanders (I-At Large/VT)   202-225-4115
2233 RHOB   8th Term/68%   Fax: 202-225-6790
Website: bernie.house.gov
CoS .... *Jeff Weaver* **LD** .... *Warren Gunnels*
Sch .... *Roxanne Scott* **Press** .... *Joel Barkin*
Bio: b. 9/8/41 Brooklyn, NY; Jewish; BA Univ. of Chicago, 1964; Educator; m. Jane
Comm.: Financial Services; Government Reform
Dist. Offices: Burlington, 802-862-0697; Brattleboro, 802-254-8732

Jim Saxton (R-3rd/NJ)   202-225-4765
2217 RHOB   11th Term/63%   Fax: 202-225-0778
Website: www.house.gov/saxton
CoS .... *Elise Kenderian* **LD** .... *Elise Kenderian*
              Aronson   *Aronson*
Appt .... *Derek Walker* **Press** .... *Jeff Sagnip*
Bio: b. 1/22/43 Nicholson, PA; Methodist; BA East Stroudsburg St. Col., 1965; Educator, Realtor; div.
Comm.: Armed Services; Resources; Joint Economic (Chair)
Dist. Offices: Mt. Holly, 609-261-5800; Cherry Hill, 856-428-0520; Toms River, 732-914-2020

REPRESENTATIVES

Janice D. Schakowsky (D-9th/IL)   **202-225-2111**
1027 LHOB   4th Term/76%   Fax: 202-226-6890
Website: www.house.gov/schakowsky
CoS .... *Cathy Hurwit*   **LD** .... *Jon Samuels*
Appt .... *Kim Muzeroll*   **Press** .... *Nadeam Elshami*
Bio: b. 5/26/44 Chicago, IL; Jewish; BS Univ. of IL, 1965; Public Official; m. Robert Creamer
Comm.: Energy & Commerce
Dist. Offices: Chicago, 773-506-7100; Evanston, 847-328-3399; Park Ridge, 847-298-2128

Adam Schiff (D-29th/CA)   **202-225-4176**
326 CHOB   3rd Term/65%   Fax: 202-225-5828
Website: www.house.gov/schiff
CoS .... *Gail Ravnitzky*   **LD** .... *Tim Bergreen*
Appt ..... *Christopher Hoven*   **Press** .... *Rebecca Kutler*
Bio: b. 6/22/60 Framingham, MA; Jewish; JD Harvard Univ., 1985; Attorney, Educator; m. Eve Sanderson
Comm.: International Relations; Judiciary
Dist. Office: Pasadena, 626-304-2727

Allyson Y. Schwartz (D-13th/PA)   **202-225-6111**
423 CHOB   1st Term/56%   Fax: 202-226-0611
Website: www.house.gov/schwartz
CoS .... *Daniel McElhatton*   **LD** .... *Kate Winkler*
Sch .... *Vanessa Menaged*   **CD** .... *Rachel Leed*
Bio: b. 10/3/48 New York, NY; Jewish; MSS Bryn Mawr Col., 1972; Health Care Administrator; m. David
Comm.: Budget; Transportation & Infrastructure
Dist. Offices: Philadelphia, 215-335-3355; Jenkintown, 215-517-6572

Joe Schwarz (R-7th/MI)   **202-225-6276**
128 CHOB   1st Term/58%   Fax: 202-225-6281
Website: www.house.gov/schwarz
CoS .... *Matt Marsden*   **LD** .... *Charles Yessaian*
Appt .... *Faye Armstrong*   **Press** .... *Matt Marsden*
Bio: b. 11/15/37 Battle Creek, MI; Catholic; MD Wayne State Univ., 1964; USN, 1965-67; Physician; widowed
Comm.: Agriculture; Armed Services; Science
Dist. Offices: Lansing, 517-323-6600; Jackson, 517-783-4486; Battle Creek, 269-965-9066

Bobby Scott (D-3rd/VA)   **202-225-8351**
1201 LHOB   7th Term/70%   Fax: 202-225-8354
E-mail: bobby.scott@mail.house.gov
Website: www.house.gov/scott
CoS .... *Joni Ivey*   **LD** .... *Vacant*
Sch .... *Larry Dillard*   **Press** .... *Larry Dillard*
Bio: b. 4/30/47 Washington, DC; Episcopal; JD Boston Col., 1973; USAR, 1970-74; MARNG, 1974-76; Attorney; div.
Comm.: Education & the Workforce; Judiciary
Dist. Offices: Newport News, 757-380-1000; Richmond, 804-644-4845

David Scott (D-13th/GA)   **202-225-2939**
417 CHOB   2nd Term/Unc.   Fax: 202-225-4628
Website: davidscott.house.gov
CoS .... *Rob Griner*   **LD** .... *Donni Turner*
EA .... *Angie Borja*   **Press** .... *Rob Griner*
Bio: b. 6/27/46 Aynor, SC; Baptist; MBA University of Pennsylvania, 1969; Advertising Executive; m. Alfreda
Comm.: Agriculture; Financial Services
Dist. Office: Jonesboro, 770-210-5073

REPRESENTATIVES

F. James Sensenbrenner, Jr. (R-5th/WI)   202-225-5101
2449 RHOB   14th Term/67%   Fax: 202-225-3190
E-mail: sensenbrenner@mail.house.gov
Website: www.house.gov/sensenbrenner
CoS .... *Tom Schreibel* **LD** .... *Mike Lenn*
Sch .... *Emily Sanders* **Press** .... *Rajesh Bharwani*
Bio: b. 6/14/43 Chicago, IL; Episcopal; JD Univ. of WI, 1968; Attorney; m. Cheryl
Comm.: Judiciary (Chair)
Dist. Office: Brookfield, 262-784-1111

José E. Serrano (D-16th/NY)   202-225-4361
2227 RHOB   9th Term/95%   Fax: 202-225-6001
E-mail: jserrano@mail.house.gov
Website: www.house.gov/serrano
CoS .... *Paul Lipson* **LD** .... *Nadine Berg*
Appt .... *Elisa Howie* **Press** .... *Ben Allen*
Bio: b. 10/24/43 Mayaguez, PR; Catholic; Attended City Univ. of NY - Lehman Col.; USA, 1964-66; Public Official; m. Mary
Comm.: Appropriations
Dist. Office: Bronx, 718-620-0084

Pete Sessions (R-32nd/TX)   202-225-2231
1514 LHOB   5th Term/54%   Fax: 202-225-5878
E-mail: petes@mail.house.gov
Website: sessions.house.gov
CoS .... *Guy Harrison* **LD** .... *Tucker Anderson*
Sch .... *Meagan Brown* **CD** .... *Gina Vaughn*
Bio: b. 3/22/55 Waco, TX; Methodist; BS Southwestern Univ., 1978; Phone Company Executive; m. Juanita
Comm.: Budget; Rules
Dist. Office: Dallas, 972-392-0505

John B. Shadegg (R-3rd/AZ)   202-225-3361
306 CHOB   6th Term/80%   Fax: 202-225-3462
Website: johnshadegg.house.gov
CoS .... *Elise Finley* **LD** .... *Eric Schlecht*
EA .... *Kristin Nelthorpe* **Press** .... *Michael Steel*
Bio: b. 10/22/49 Phoenix, AZ; Episcopal; JD Univ. of AZ, 1975; USANG, 1969-75; Attorney; m. Shirley
Comm.: Energy & Commerce
Dist. Office: Phoenix, 602-263-5300

E. Clay Shaw, Jr. (R-22nd/FL)   202-225-3026
1236 LHOB   13th Term/63%   Fax: 202-225-8398
Website: shaw.house.gov
CoS .... *Eric Eikenberg* **LD** .... *Christine Pollack*
Sch .... *Julie Donovan* **Press** .... *Gail Gitcho*
Bio: b. 4/19/39 Miami, FL; Catholic; JD Stetson Univ., 1966; Attorney; m. Emilie
Comm.: Ways & Means; Joint Taxation
Dist. Offices: Ft. Lauderdale, 954-522-1800; West Palm Beach, 561-832-3007

Christopher Shays (R-4th/CT)   202-225-5541
1126 LHOB   10th Term/52%   Fax: 202-225-9629
Website: www.house.gov/shays
CoS .... *Betsy Hawkings* **LD** .... *Matt Meyer*
Appt .... *Diana White* **Press** .... *Sarah Moore*
Bio: b. 10/18/45 Darien, CT; Christian Science; MPA NYU, 1978; Public Official; m. Betsi
Comm.: Financial Services; Government Reform (Vice Chair); Homeland Security
Dist. Offices: Bridgeport, 203-579-5870; Stamford, 203-357-8277

REPRESENTATIVES

Brad Sherman (D-27th/CA)   202-225-5911
1030 LHOB   5th Term/62%   Fax: 202-225-5879
Website: www.house.gov/sherman
CoS .... *Andrew Wright* **LD** .... *Ryan Donovan*
Appt .... *Kerri Wood* **Press** .... *Sharon Singh*
Bio: b. 10/24/54 Los Angeles, CA; Jewish; JD Harvard Univ., 1979; Attorney, Accountant; single
Comm.: Financial Services; International Relations; Science
Dist. Office: Sherman Oaks, 818-501-9200

Don Sherwood (R-10th/PA)   202-225-3731
1131 LHOB   4th Term/Unc.   Fax: 202-225-9594
Website: www.house.gov/sherwood
CoS .... *John Enright* **LD** .... *John Enright*
Sch .... *Matt Allen* **Press** .... *Jake O'Donnell*
Bio: b. 3/5/41 Nicholson, PA; Methodist; BA Dartmouth Col., 1963; USA, 1963-65; Car Dealership Owner; m. Carol
Comm.: Appropriations
Dist. Offices: Clarks Summit, 570-585-8190; Williamsport, 570-327-8161; Sunbury, 570-286-1723

John M. Shimkus (R-19th/IL)   202-225-5271
513 CHOB   5th Term/69%   Fax: 202-225-5880
Website: www.house.gov/shimkus
CoS .... *Craig Roberts* **LD** .... *Ray Fitzgerald*
Appt .... *Carren Crossley* **Press** ..... *Steve Tomaszewski*
Bio: b. 2/21/58 Collinsville, IL; Lutheran; MBA Southern IL Univ., 1997; USA, 1980-86; USAR, 1986-present; Teacher; m. Karen
Comm.: Energy & Commerce
Dist. Offices: Springfield, 217-492-5090; Collinsville, 618-344-3065; Centralia, 618-532-9676; Olney, 618-392-7737; Harrisburg, 618-252-8271

Bill Shuster (R-9th/PA)   202-225-2431
1108 LHOB   3rd Term/70%   Fax: 202-225-2486
Website: www.house.gov/shuster
CoS .... *Alex Mistri* **LD** .... *Joel Brubaker*
Sch .... *Robbe Diehl* **CD** .... *Tory Mazzola*
Bio: b. 1/10/61 McKeesport, PA; Lutheran; MBA American Univ., 1987; Car Dealership Owner; m. Becky
Comm.: Armed Services; Small Business; Transportation & Infrastructure
Dist. Offices: Hollidaysburg, 814-696-6318; Chambersburg, 717-264-8308; Indiana, 724-463-0516; Somerset, 814-443-3918

Robert R. Simmons (R-2nd/CT)   202-225-2076
215 CHOB   3rd Term/54%   Fax: 202-225-4977
Website: www.house.gov/simmons
CoS .... *Todd Mitchell* **LD** .... *Lise Lynam*
Sch .... *Shauna Hewes* **Press** .... *Todd Mitchell*
Bio: b. 2/11/43 New York, NY; Episcopal; MPA Harvard Univ., 1979; USA, 1965-69; USAR, 1970-2000; Congressional Aide, Public Official; m. Heidi
Comm.: Armed Services; Homeland Security; Transportation & Infrastructure
Dist. Offices: Norwich, 860-886-0139; Enfield, 860-741-4053

Mike Simpson (R-2nd/ID)   202-225-5531
1339 LHOB   4th Term/71%   Fax: 202-225-8216
Website: www.house.gov/simpson
CoS .... *Lindsay Slater* **LD** .... *John Revier*
Sch .... *Megan Milam* **CD** .... *Nikki Watts*
Bio: b. 9/8/50 Burley, ID; Mormon; DDS Washington Univ. - St. Louis, 1977; Dentist; m. Kathy
Comm.: Appropriations; Budget
Dist. Offices: Boise, 208-334-1953; Idaho Falls, 208-523-6701; Twin Falls, 208-734-7219; Pocatello, 208-478-4160

REPRESENTATIVES

Ike Skelton (D-4th/MO)   202-225-2876
2206 RHOB   15th Term/66%   Fax: 202-225-2695
Website: www.house.gov/skelton
CoS .... *Bob Hagedorn* **LD** .... *Dana O'Brien*
Appt .... *Kyle Wilkens* **Press** .... *Lara Battles*
Bio: b. 12/20/31 Lexington, MO; Disciples of Christ; LLB Univ. of MO, 1956; Attorney; m. Susan
Comm.: Armed Services (Rnk. Mem.)
Dist. Offices: Blue Springs, 816-228-4242; Lebanon, 417-532-7964; Jefferson City, 573-635-3499; Sedalia, 660-826-2675

Louise McIntosh Slaughter (D-28th/NY)   202-225-3615
2469 RHOB   10th Term/72%   Fax: 202-225-7822
Website: www.louise.house.gov
CoS .... *Sally Schaeffer* **LD** .... *Rosaline Cohen*
Sch .... *Danielle Sullivan* **CD** .... *Eric Burns*
Bio: b. 8/14/29 Harlan Co., KY; Episcopal; MS Univ. of KY, 1953; Bacteriologist; m. Robert
Comm.: Rules (Rnk. Mem.)
Dist. Offices: Rochester, 585-232-4850; Buffalo, 716-853-5813; Niagara Falls, 716-282-1274

Adam Smith (D-9th/WA)   202-225-8901
227 CHOB   5th Term/63%   Fax: 202-225-5893
Website: www.house.gov/adamsmith
CoS .... *John Mulligan* **LD** .... *Shana Chandler*
Sch .... *Katie Kuciemba* **CD** .... *Lars Anderson*
Bio: b. 6/15/65 Washington, DC; Christian; JD Univ. of WA, 1990; Prosecutor; m. Sara
Comm.: Armed Services; International Relations; Judiciary
Dist. Office: Tacoma, 253-593-6600

Christopher H. Smith (R-4th/NJ)   202-225-3765
2373 RHOB   13th Term/67%   Fax: 202-225-7768
Website: www.house.gov/chrissmith
CoS .... *Mary Noonan* **LD** .... *Andy Napoli*
Sch .... *Katie Doherty* **Press** .... *Dave Kush*
Bio: b. 3/4/53 Rahway, NJ; Catholic; BA Trenton St. Col., 1975; Sporting Goods Wholesaler; m. Marie
Comm.: International Relations (Vice Chair)
Dist. Offices: Hamilton, 609-585-7878; Whiting, 732-350-2300

Lamar S. Smith (R-21st/TX)   202-225-4236
2184 RHOB   10th Term/62%   Fax: 202-225-8628
Website: lamarsmith.house.gov
CoS .... *Joseph Gibson* **Sr LA** ...... *Cameron Gilreath*
AA .... *Jennifer Brown* **Press** .... *Blair Jones*
Bio: b. 11/19/47 San Antonio, TX; Christian Science; JD Southern Methodist Univ., 1975; Attorney; m. Beth
Comm.: Homeland Security; Judiciary; Science; Standards of Official Conduct
Dist. Offices: San Antonio, 210-821-5024; Austin, 512-402-9743

Vic Snyder (D-2nd/AR)   202-225-2506
1330 LHOB   5th Term/58%   Fax: 202-225-5903
Website: www.house.gov/snyder
CoS .... *Ed Fry* **LD** .... *Mike Casey*
Sch .... *Linsley Matteson* **Press** .... *Jennifer Oglesby*
Bio: b. 9/27/47 Medford, OR; Presbyterian; JD Univ. of AR - Little Rock, 1988; USMC, 1967-69; Physician; m. Betsy Singleton
Comm.: Armed Services; Veterans' Affairs
Dist. Office: Little Rock, 501-324-5941

REPRESENTATIVES

Mike Sodrel (R-9th/IN)   202-225-5315
1508 LHOB   1st Term/49%   Fax: 202-226-6866
Website: www.house.gov/sodrel
CoS .... *Tom Washburne*   **LD** .... *Tom Washburne*
Sch .... *Kristen Sabella*   **Press** .... *Cam Savage*
Bio: b. 12/17/45 New Albany, IN; Christian; Attended IN Univ. Southeast; INNG, 1966-73; Business Owner; m. Marquita
Comm.: Science; Small Business; Transportation & Infrastructure
Dist. Office: Jeffersonville, 812-288-3999

Hilda L. Solis (D-32nd/CA)   202-225-5464
1725 LHOB   3rd Term/85%   Fax: 202-225-5467
Website: solis.house.gov
CoS .... *Don Lyster*   **LD** .... *Jennifer Grodsky*
Sch .... *Juan Lopez*   **CD** .... *Edith Robles*
Bio: b. 10/20/57 Los Angeles, CA; Not Stated; MS USC, 1981; Public Official; m. Sam H. Sayyad
Comm.: Energy & Commerce
Dist. Offices: El Monte, 626-448-1271; East Los Angeles, 323-307-9904

Mark Souder (R-3rd/IN)   202-225-4436
2231 RHOB   6th Term/69%   Fax: 202-225-3479
E-mail: souder@mail.house.gov
Website: souder.house.gov
CoS .... *Renee Howell*   **LD** .... *Erika Heikkila*
Appt .... *Dawn Gerson*   **Press** .... *Martin Green*
Bio: b. 7/18/50 Ft. Wayne, IN; Evangelical; MBA Univ. of Notre Dame, 1974; Congressional Aide, Businessman; m. Diane
Comm.: Education & the Workforce; Government Reform; Homeland Security
Dist. Offices: Ft. Wayne, 260-424-3041; Goshen, 574-533-5802; Winona Lake, 574-269-1940

John M. Spratt, Jr. (D-5th/SC)   202-225-5501
1401 LHOB   12th Term/63%   Fax: 202-225-0464
Website: www.house.gov/spratt
CoS .... *Ellen Buchanan*   **LD** .... *Dawn Myers*
Appt .... *Tish Mills*   **Press** .... *Chuck Fant*
Bio: b. 11/1/42 Charlotte, NC; Presbyterian; LLB Yale Univ., 1969; USA, 1969-71; Attorney; m. Jane
Comm.: Armed Services; Budget (Rnk. Mem.)
Dist. Offices: Rock Hill, 803-327-1114; Sumter, 803-773-3362; Darlington, 843-393-3998

Fortney H. "Pete" Stark (D-13th/CA)   202-225-5065
239 CHOB   17th Term/71%   Fax: 202-226-3805
Website: www.house.gov/stark
CoS .... *Debbie Curtis*   **LD** .... *Debbie Curtis*
Sch .... *Deborah Chusmir*   **Press** .... *Lindsey Capps*
Bio: b. 11/11/31 Milwaukee, WI; Unitarian; MBA Univ. of CA - Berkeley, 1960; USAF, 1955-57; Banker; m. Deborah
Comm.: Ways & Means; Joint Taxation
Dist. Office: Fremont, 510-494-1388

Cliff Stearns (R-6th/FL)   202-225-5744
2370 RHOB   9th Term/64%   Fax: 202-225-3973
Website: www.house.gov/stearns
CoS .... *Jack Seum*   **LD** .... *Lauren Semeniuk*
Sch .... *Joan Smutko*   **Press** .... *Paul Flusche*
Bio: b. 4/16/41 Washington, DC; Presbyterian; BS George Washington Univ., 1963; USAF, 1963-67; Small Business Owner; m. Joan
Comm.: Energy & Commerce; Veterans' Affairs
Dist. Offices: Ocala, 352-351-8777; Orange Park, 904-269-3203; Gainesville, 352-337-0003

REPRESENTATIVES

Ted Strickland (D-6th/OH)   202-225-5705
336 CHOB   6th Term/Unc.   Fax: 202-225-5907
Website: www.house.gov/strickland
CoS .... *John Haseley* **LD** .... *Michelle Dallafior*
Sch .... *Joan Gregory* **Press** .... *Chad Tanner*
Bio: b. 8/4/41 Lucasville, OH; Methodist; PhD Univ. of KY, 1980; Professor; m. Frances
Comm.: Energy & Commerce; Veterans' Affairs
Dist. Offices: Marietta, 740-376-0868; Wheelersburg, 740-574-2676; Boardman, 330-965-4220; Martins Ferry, 740-633-2275

Bart Stupak (D-1st/MI)   202-225-4735
2352 RHOB   7th Term/66%   Fax: 202-225-4744
Website: www.house.gov/stupak
CoS .... *Scott Schloegel* **LD** .... *Amy Fuerstenau*
Sch .... *Anne Stanski* **Press** .... *Adrianne Marsh*
Bio: b. 2/29/52 Milwaukee, WI; Catholic; JD Thomas M. Cooley Law School, 1981; Attorney; m. Laurie
Comm.: Energy & Commerce
Dist. Offices: Petoskey, 231-348-0657; Marquette, 906-228-3700; Alpena, 989-356-0690; Escanaba, 906-786-4504; Houghton, 906-482-1371; Crystal Falls, 906-875-3751; West Branch, 989-345-2258

John Sullivan (R-1st/OK)   202-225-2211
114 CHOB   3rd Term/60%   Fax: 202-225-9187
Website: sullivan.house.gov
CoS .... *Elizabeth Bartheld* **LD** .... *Wendy Der*
Sch .... *Brooke Stegall* **CD** .... *Shane Saunder*
Bio: b. 1/1/65 Tulsa, OK; Catholic; BBA Northeastern St. Univ., 1992; Real Estate Broker; m. Judith
Comm.: Energy & Commerce
Dist. Office: Tulsa, 918-749-0014

John E. Sweeney (R-20th/NY)   202-225-5614
416 CHOB   4th Term/66%   Fax: 202-225-6234
Website: www.house.gov/sweeney
CoS .... *Chris Fish* **LD** .... *Jennifer Taylor*
Sch .... *Amanda Cernik* **CD** ...... *Demetrios Karoutsos*
Bio: b. 8/9/55 Troy, NY; Catholic; JD Western New England School of Law, 1990; Attorney; eng.
Comm.: Appropriations
Dist. Offices: Clifton Park, 518-371-8839; Redhook, 845-758-1222; Glens Falls, 518-792-3031; Delhi, 607-746-9700

Thomas G. Tancredo (R-6th/CO)   202-225-7882
1130 LHOB   4th Term/60%   Fax: 202-226-4623
Website: www.house.gov/tancredo
CoS .... *Jacque Ponder* **LD** .... *Mac Zimmerman*
Appt .... *Rachel Hayes* **Press** .... *Carlos Espinosa*
Bio: b. 12/20/45 North Denver, CO; Christian; BA Univ. of Northern CO, 1968; Non-Profit Executive; m. Jackie
Comm.: International Relations; Resources
Dist. Office: Centennial, 720-283-9772

John S. Tanner (D-8th/TN)   202-225-4714
1226 LHOB   9th Term/74%   Fax: 202-225-1765
Website: www.house.gov/tanner
CoS .... *Vickie Walling* **LD** .... *Doug Thompson*
Appt .... *Kathy Becker* **Press** .... *Randy Ford*
Bio: b. 9/22/44 Halls, TN; Disciples of Christ; JD Univ. of TN, 1968; USN, 1968-72; USARNG, 1974-present; Attorney; m. Betty Ann
Comm.: Ways & Means
Dist. Offices: Union City, 731-885-7070; Jackson, 731-423-4848; Millington, 901-873-5690

REPRESENTATIVES

Ellen O. Tauscher (D-10th/CA) 202-225-1880
1034 LHOB   5th Term/66%   Fax: 202-225-5914
Website: www.house.gov/tauscher
CoS .... *Peter Muller* **LD** .... *Simon Limage*
EA .... *Kevin Graham* **Press** .... *Hayley Rumback*
Bio: b. 11/15/51 Newark, NJ; Catholic; BS Seton Hall Univ., 1974; Investment Banker; div.
Comm.: Armed Services; Transportation & Infrastructure
Dist. Offices: Walnut Creek, 925-932-8899; Antioch, 925-757-7187; Fairfield, 707-428-7792

Charles H. Taylor (R-11th/NC) 202-225-6401
339 CHOB   8th Term/55%   Fax: 202-226-6422
Website: www.house.gov/charlestaylor
CoS .... *Sean Dalton* **LD** .... *Adam Shepherd*
Sch .... *Michael Calvo* **Press** .... *Deborah Potter*
Bio: b. 1/23/41 Brevard, NC; Baptist; JD Wake Forest Univ., 1966; Tree Farmer; m. Elizabeth
Comm.: Appropriations
Dist. Offices: Asheville, 828-251-1988; Murphy, 828-837-3249; Waynesville, 828-456-7559; Rutherfordton, 828-286-8750; Hendersonville, 828-697-8539

Gene Taylor (D-4th/MS) 202-225-5772
2311 RHOB   9th Term/64%   Fax: 202-225-7074
Website: www.house.gov/genetaylor
CoS .... *Stephen Peranich* **LD** .... *Stacy Ballow*
Sch .... *Courtney Littig* **Press** .... *Courtney Littig*
Bio: b. 9/17/53 New Orleans, LA; Catholic; BA Tulane Univ., 1974; USCGR, 1971-84; Salesman; m. Margaret
Comm.: Armed Services; Transportation & Infrastructure
Dist. Offices: Gulfport, 228-864-7670; Hattiesburg, 601-582-3246; Ocean Springs, 228-872-7950; Laurel, 601-425-3905

Lee Terry (R-2nd/NE) 202-225-4155
1524 LHOB   4th Term/62%   Fax: 202-226-5452
Website: leeterry.house.gov
CoS .... *Eric Hultman* **LD** .... *Jamie Karl*
Sch .... *Lindsey Witt* **CD** .... *Jenn Hein*
Bio: b. 1/29/62 Omaha, NE; Methodist; JD Creighton Univ., 1987; Attorney; m. Robyn
Comm.: Energy & Commerce
Dist. Office: Omaha, 402-397-9944

William M. Thomas (R-22nd/CA) 202-225-2915
2208 RHOB   14th Term/Unc.   Fax: 202-225-8798
Website: billthomas.house.gov
CoS .... *James Min* **LD** .... *Mike Holland*
Sch .... *Renee Edelen* **Press** .... *Tim Wood*
Bio: b. 12/6/41 Wallace, ID; Baptist; MA San Francisco St. Univ., 1965; Professor; m. Sharon
Comm.: Ways & Means (Chair); Joint Taxation (Chair)
Dist. Offices: Bakersfield, 661-327-3611; Atascadero, 805-461-1034

Bennie G. Thompson (D-2nd/MS) 202-225-5876
2432 RHOB   7th Term/58%   Fax: 202-225-5898
E-mail: thompsonms2nd@mail.house.gov
Website: benniethompson.house.gov
CoS .... *I. Lanier Avant* **Sr LA** .... *Karis Gutter*
Sch .... *Jennifer Tolliver* **CD** .... *I. Lanier Avant*
Bio: b. 1/28/48 Bolton, MS; Methodist; MS Jackson St. Univ., 1972; Educator; m. London
Comm.: Homeland Security (Rnk. Mem.)
Dist. Offices: Bolton, 601-866-9003; Marks, 662-326-9003; Greenwood, 662-455-9003; Greenville, 662-335-9003; Mound Bayou, 662-741-9003

REPRESENTATIVES

Mike Thompson (D-1st/CA)   202-225-3311
231 CHOB   4th Term/67%   Fax: 202-225-4335
Website: mikethompson.house.gov
CoS .... *Ed Matovcik* **LD** .... *Jonathan Birdsong*
Sch .... *Laura Knapp* **Press** .... *Matt Gerien*
Bio: b. 1/24/51 St. Helena, CA; Catholic; MA Univ. of CA - Chico, 1996; USA, 1969-72; Public Official; m. Janet
Comm.: Ways & Means
Dist. Offices: Napa, 707-226-9898; Ft. Bragg, 707-962-0933; Eureka, 707-269-9595; Woodland, 530-662-5272

William "Mac" Thornberry (R-13th/TX)   202-225-3706
2457 RHOB   6th Term/Unc.   Fax: 202-225-3486
Website: www.house.gov/thornberry
CoS .... *Bill Harris* **LD** .... *Trey Bahm*
Sch .... *Aimee Kindig* **CD** .... *James Hunt*
Bio: b. 7/15/58 Clarendon, TX; Presbyterian; JD Univ. of TX, 1983; Rancher, Attorney; m. Sally
Comm.: Armed Services; Select Intelligence
Dist. Offices: Amarillo, 806-371-8844; Wichita Falls, 940-692-1700

Todd Tiahrt (R-4th/KS)   202-225-6216
2441 RHOB   6th Term/66%   Fax: 202-225-3489
Website: www.house.gov/tiahrt
CoS .... *Jeff Kahrs* **LD** .... *AmyClaire Brusch*
Appt .... *Melissa James* **CD** .... *Chuck Knapp*
Bio: b. 6/15/51 Vermillion, SD; Christian; MBA SW MO St. Univ., 1989; Aerospace Executive; m. Vicki
Comm.: Appropriations; Select Intelligence
Dist. Office: Wichita, 316-262-8992

Patrick J. Tiberi (R-12th/OH)   202-225-5355
113 CHOB   3rd Term/66%   Fax: 202-226-4523
Website: www.house.gov/tiberi
CoS .... *Chris Zeigler* **LD** .... *Adam Francis*
Appt .... *Nancy Kolb* **Press** ...... *Bruce Cuthbertson*
Bio: b. 10/21/62 Columbus, OH; Catholic; BA OH St. Univ., 1985; Public Official, Real Estate Agent; m. Denice
Comm.: Education & the Workforce; Financial Services
Dist. Office: Columbus, 614-523-2555

John F. Tierney (D-6th/MA)   202-225-8020
120 CHOB   5th Term/70%   Fax: 202-225-5915
Website: www.house.gov/tierney
CoS .... *Christine Pelosi* **LD** .... *Kevin McDermott*
Appt .... *Bambi Yingst* **CD** .... *Patrick McKiernan*
Bio: b. 9/18/51 Salem, MA; Not Stated; JD Suffolk Univ., 1976; Attorney; m. Patrice
Comm.: Education & the Workforce; Select Intelligence
Dist. Offices: Peabody, 978-531-1669; Lynn, 781-595-7375

Edolphus Towns (D-10th/NY)   202-225-5936
2232 RHOB   12th Term/91%   Fax: 202-225-1018
Website: www.house.gov/towns
CoS .... *Brenda Pillors* **Sr LA** .... *Alex Beckles*
Appt .... *Gerri Taylor* **Press** .... *Andrew Delia*
Bio: b. 7/21/34 Chadbourn, NC; Baptist; MSW Adelphi Univ., 1973; USA, 1956-58; Social Worker; m. Gwen
Comm.: Energy & Commerce; Government Reform
Dist. Offices: Brooklyn, 718-855-8018; Brooklyn, 718-272-1175; Brooklyn, 718-774-5682; Brooklyn, 718-434-7931

REPRESENTATIVES

Stephanie Tubbs Jones (D-11th/OH) 202-225-7032
1009 LHOB 4th Term/Unc. Fax: 202-225-1339
Website: www.house.gov/tubbsjones
CoS ...... Patrice Willoughby **LD** .... Melvina Gueye
Sch ...... Hannah B. Ramsey **CD** .... Nicole Williams
Bio: b. 9/10/49 Cleveland, OH; Baptist; JD Case Western Reserve Univ., 1974; Attorney; widowed
Comm.: Standards of Official Conduct; Ways & Means
Dist. Office: Shaker Heights, 216-522-4900

Michael Turner (R-3rd/OH) 202-225-6465
1740 LHOB 2nd Term/62% Fax: 202-225-6754
Website: www.house.gov/miketurner
CoS ..... Stacy Palmer-Barton **LD** .... Neil Siefring
Sch ..... Matthew McDowell **CD** .... Andy Bloom
Bio: b. 1/11/60 Dayton, OH; Protestant; MBA Univ. of Dayton, 1992; Attorney, Public Official; m. Lori
Comm.: Armed Services; Government Reform; Veterans' Affairs
Dist. Offices: Dayton, 937-225-2843; Wilmington, 937-383-8931

Mark Udall (D-2nd/CO) 202-225-2161
240 CHOB 4th Term/67% Fax: 202-226-7840
Website: markudall.house.gov
CoS .... Alan Salazar **LD** .... Stan Sloss
Sch .... Lisa Carpenter **Press** ...... Lawrence Pacheco
Bio: b. 7/18/50 Tucson, AZ; Not Affiliated; BA Williams Col., 1972; Public Official; m. Margaret
Comm.: Armed Services; Resources; Science
Dist. Offices: Westminster, 303-650-7820; Minturn, 970-827-4154

Tom Udall (D-3rd/NM) 202-225-6190
1414 LHOB 4th Term/69% Fax: 202-226-1331
Website: tomudall.house.gov
CoS .... Tom Nagle **LD** .... Mike Collins
Sch .... Donda Morgan **Press** .... Glen Loveland
Bio: b. 5/18/48 Tucson, AZ; Mormon; JD Univ. of NM, 1977; Public Official; m. Jill Cooper
Comm.: Resources; Small Business; Veterans' Affairs
Dist. Offices: Santa Fe, 505-984-8950; Rio Rancho, 505-994-0499; Clovis, 505-763-7616; Gallup, 505-863-0582; Farmington, 505-324-1005; Las Vegas, 505-454-4080

Fred Upton (R-6th/MI) 202-225-3761
2183 RHOB 10th Term/65% Fax: 202-225-4986
Website: www.house.gov/upton
CoS .... Joan Hillebrands **LD** .... Debra Marshall
Sch .... Ryan Hollowell **CD** .... Sean Bonyun
Bio: b. 4/23/53 St. Joseph, MI; Protestant; BA Univ. of MI, 1975; Congressional Aide; m. Amey
Comm.: Energy & Commerce
Dist. Offices: Kalamazoo, 269-385-0039; St. Joseph, 269-982-1986

Chris Van Hollen, Jr. (D-8th/MD) 202-225-5341
1419 LHOB 2nd Term/75% Fax: 202-225-0375
Website: www.house.gov/vanhollen
CoS .... Kay Casstevens **LD** .... Phil Alperson
Appt .... Johanna Berkson **Press** .... Marilyn Campbell
Bio: b. 1/10/59 Karachi, Pakistan; Not Stated; JD Georgetown Univ., 1990; Attorney; m. Katherine
Comm.: Education & the Workforce; Government Reform; Judiciary
Dist. Offices: Rockville, 301-424-3501; Mt. Rainier, 301-927-5223

REPRESENTATIVES

Nydia M. Velázquez (D-12th/NY)   202-225-2361
2241 RHOB   7th Term/85%   Fax: 202-226-0327
Website: www.house.gov/velazquez
CoS .... *Michael Day*   **LD** .... *Julie Carr*
Appt ...... *Clarinda Landeros*   **Press** .... *Kate Davis*
Bio: b. 3/28/53 Yabucoa, PR; Catholic; MA NYU, 1976; Columnist; m. Paul Bader
Comm.: Financial Services; Small Business (Rnk. Mem.)
Dist. Offices: Brooklyn, 718-599-3658; New York, 212-673-3997; Brooklyn, 718-222-5819

Peter J. Visclosky (D-1st/IN)   202-225-2461
2256 RHOB   11th Term/68%   Fax: 202-225-2493
Website: www.house.gov/visclosky
CoS .... *Chuck Brimmer*   **LD** .... *Tom Quinn*
Sch .... *Korry Baack*   **Press** .... *Justin Kitsch*
Bio: b. 8/13/49 Gary, IN; Catholic; LLM Georgetown Univ., 1982; Attorney; div.
Comm.: Appropriations
Dist. Office: Merrillville, 219-795-1844

Greg Walden (R-2nd/OR)   202-225-6730
1210 LHOB   4th Term/72%   Fax: 202-225-5774
Website: walden.house.gov
CoS .... *Brian MacDonald*   **LD** .... *Brian Hard*
Sch .... *Jill Wyman*   **Press** .... *Angela Wilhelms*
Bio: b. 1/10/57 The Dalles, OR; Episcopal; BS Univ. of OR, 1981; Business Owner; m. Mylene
Comm.: Energy & Commerce; Resources
Dist. Offices: Medford, 541-776-4646; Bend, 541-389-4408

James T. Walsh (R-25th/NY)   202-225-3701
2369 RHOB   9th Term/91%   Fax: 202-225-4042
E-mail: rep.james.walsh@mail.house.gov
Website: www.house.gov/walsh
CoS .... *Art Jutton*   **LD** .... *Art Jutton*
EA .... *Kristin Calabrese*   **Press** .... *Dan Gage*
Bio: b. 6/19/47 Syracuse, NY; Catholic; BA St. Bonaventure Univ., 1970; Businessman; m. DeDe
Comm.: Appropriations
Dist. Offices: Syracuse, 315-423-5657; Palmyra, 315-597-6138

Zach Wamp (R-3rd/TN)   202-225-3271
1436 LHOB   6th Term/65%   Fax: 202-225-3494
E-mail: tn03@legslators.com
Website: www.house.gov/wamp
CoS .... *Helen Hardin*   **Dep CoS** .... *Rob Hobart*
Sch .... *Lindsey Meyer*   **Press** .... *Rachel Carter*
Bio: b. 10/28/57 Ft. Benning, GA; Baptist; Attended UNC & Univ. of TN; Real Estate Broker; m. Kim
Comm.: Appropriations
Dist. Offices: Chattanooga, 423-756-2342; Oak Ridge, 865-576-1976

Debbie Wasserman Schultz
(D-20th/FL)   202-225-7931
118 CHOB   1st Term/70%   Fax: 202-225-8456
Website: www.house.gov/wasserman-schultz
CoS .... *Steve Paikowsky*   **LD** .... *Marcus Jadotte*
Sch .... *Evonne Marche*   **CD** .... *Jonathan Beeton*
Bio: b. 9/27/66 Forest Hills, NY; Jewish; MA Univ. of FL, 1990; Public Official; m. Steve
Comm.: Financial Services
Dist. Office: Pembroke Pines, 954-437-3936

REPRESENTATIVES

Maxine Waters (D-35th/CA)   202-225-2201
2344 RHOB   8th Term/80%   Fax: 202-225-7854
Website: www.house.gov/waters
CoS .... *Vacant* **LD** .... *Gary Goldberg*
Appt .... *Joyce Freeland* **Press** .... *Mikael Moore*
Bio: b. 8/15/38 St. Louis, MO; Christian; BA CA St. Univ. - Los Angeles, 1970; Public Official; m. Sidney Willliams
Comm.: Financial Services; Judiciary
Dist. Office: Los Angeles, 323-757-8900

Diane Watson (D-33rd/CA)   202-225-7084
125 CHOB   3rd Term/89%   Fax: 202-225-2422
Website: www.house.gov/watson
CoS .... *Jim Clarke* **LD** .... *Gregory Adams*
Sch .... *Jim Clarke* **CD** .... *Bert Hammond*
Bio: b. 11/12/33 Los Angeles, CA; Catholic; PhD Claremont Graduate Univ., 1987; Public Official, School Psychologist; single
Comm.: Government Reform; International Relations
Dist. Office: Los Angeles, 323-965-1422

Melvin L. Watt (D-12th/NC)   202-225-1510
2236 RHOB   7th Term/67%   Fax: 202-225-1512
Website: www.house.gov/watt
CoS .... *Joyce Brayboy* **LD** .... *None*
Sch ...... *Melissa Williamson* **Press** ..... *Melissa Williamson*
Bio: b. 8/26/45 Charlotte, NC; Presbyterian; JD Yale Univ., 1970; Attorney; m. Eulada
Comm.: Financial Services; Judiciary
Dist. Offices: Charlotte, 704-344-9950; Greensboro, 336-275-9950

Henry A. Waxman (D-30th/CA)   202-225-3976
2204 RHOB   16th Term/71%   Fax: 202-225-4099
Website: www.house.gov/waxman
AA .... *Patricia Delgado* **LD** .... *Patricia Delgado*
Sch .... *Amanda Molson* **Press** .... *Karen Lightfoot*
Bio: b. 9/12/39 Los Angeles, CA; Jewish; JD UCLA, 1964; Attorney; m. Janet
Comm.: Energy & Commerce; Government Reform (Rnk. Mem.)
Dist. Office: Los Angeles, 323-651-1040

Anthony D. Weiner (D-9th/NY)   202-225-6616
1122 LHOB   4th Term/70%   Fax: 202-226-7253
E-mail: weiner@mail.house.gov
Website: www.house.gov/weiner
CoS .... *Marc Dunkelman* **LD** .... *Marc Dunkelman*
Sch .... *Michael Marcy* **Press** .... *Kathryn Prael*
Bio: b. 9/4/64 Brooklyn, NY; Jewish; BA SUNY - Plattsburgh, 1985; Public Official; single
Comm.: Judiciary; Transportation & Infrastructure
Dist. Offices: Kew Gardens, 718-520-9001; Rockaway, 718-318-9255; Brooklyn, 718-743-0441

Curt Weldon (R-7th/PA)   202-225-2011
2466 RHOB   10th Term/59%   Fax: 202-225-8137
E-mail: curtpa07@mail.house.gov
Website: www.house.gov/curtweldon
CoS .... *Russ Caso* **LD** ..... *Xenia Horczakiwskyj*
Sch .. *Margaret Lemmerman* **Press** .... *Angela Sowa*
Bio: b. 7/22/47 Marcus Hook, PA; Protestant; BA West Chester Univ., 1969; Educator; m. Mary
Comm.: Armed Services; Homeland Security; Science
Dist. Offices: Upper Darby, 610-259-0700; Bridgeport, 610-270-1486

REPRESENTATIVES

Dave Weldon (R-15th/FL)   202-225-3671
2347 RHOB   6th Term/65%   Fax: 202-225-3516
Website: www.house.gov/weldon
CoS .... *Dana Gartzke*   **LD** .... *Paul Webster*
Sch .... *Cathy Graham*   **Press** .... *Jaillene Hunter*
Bio: b. 8/31/53 Amityville, NY; Christian Non-Denominational; MD SUNY - Buffalo, 1981; USA, 1981-87; USAR, 1987-92; Physician; m. Nancy
Comm.: Appropriations
Dist. Office: Melbourne, 321-632-1776

Jerry Weller (R-11th/IL)   202-225-3635
108 CHOB   6th Term/59%   Fax: 202-225-3521
Website: weller.house.gov
CoS .... *Jeanette Whitener*   **LD** .... *Alan Tennille*
Appt .... *Erinn Lockner*   **Press** .... *Telly Lovelace*
Bio: b. 7/7/57 Streator, IL; Christian; BS Univ. of IL, 1979; Public Official; m. Zury Rios Sosa
Comm.: International Relations; Ways & Means
Dist. Office: Joliet, 815-740-2028

Lynn A. Westmoreland (R-8th/GA)   202-225-5901
1118 LHOB   1st Term/76%   Fax: 202-225-2515
Website: www.house.gov/westmoreland
CoS .... *Chip Lake*   **LD** .... *Joe Lillis*
Sch .... *Alice James*   **Press** .... *Brian Robinson*
Bio: b. 4/2/50 Atlanta, GA; Baptist; Attended Georgia State University; Builder; m. Joan
Comm.: Government Reform; Small Business; Transportation & Infrastructure
Dist. Office: Newnan, 770-683-2033

Robert I. Wexler (D-19th/FL)   202-225-3001
213 CHOB   5th Term/Unc.   Fax: 202-225-5974
Website: www.house.gov/wexler
CoS .... *Eric Johnson*   **LD** .... *Jonathan Katz*
Sch .... *Lisa White*   **Press** .... *Lale Mamaux*
Bio: b. 1/2/61 Queens, NY; Jewish; JD George Washington Univ., 1985; Attorney; m. Laurie
Comm.: International Relations; Judiciary
Dist. Offices: Boca Raton, 561-988-6302; Margate, 954-972-6454

Edward Whitfield (R-1st/KY)   202-225-3115
301 CHOB   6th Term/67%   Fax: 202-225-3547
Website: www.house.gov/whitfield
CoS .... *Karen Long*   **LD** .... *John Halliwell*
Sch .... *Emily Chandler*   **Press** .... *Jeff Miles*
Bio: b. 5/25/43 Hopkinsville, KY; Methodist; JD Univ. of KY, 1969; USAR, 1967-73; Attorney; m. Constance
Comm.: Energy & Commerce
Dist. Offices: Hopkinsville, 270-885-8079; Tompkinsville, 270-487-9509; Henderson, 270-826-4180; Paducah, 270-442-6901

Roger Wicker (R-1st/MS)   202-225-4306
2455 RHOB   6th Term/80%   Fax: 202-225-3549
Website: www.house.gov/wicker
CoS .... *John Keast*   **LD** .... *Aubert Kimbrell*
Appt .... *Michelle Barlow*   **Press** .... *Kyle Steward*
Bio: b. 7/5/51 Pontotoc, MS; Baptist; JD Univ. of MS, 1975; USAF, 1976-80; USAFR, 1980-present; Attorney; m. Gayle
Comm.: Appropriations; Budget
Dist. Offices: Tupelo, 662-844-5437; Southaven, 662-342-3942; Grenada, 662-294-1321; Columbus, 662-327-0748

REPRESENTATIVES

Heather A. Wilson (R-1st/NM)   202-225-6316
318 CHOB   5th Term/55%   Fax: 202-225-4975
Website: wilson.house.gov
CoS .... *Bryce Dustman* **LD** .... *Erik Einertson*
EA .... *Barbara Cohen* **Press** .... *Joel Hannahs*
Bio: b. 12/30/60 Keene, NH; Methodist; PhD Oxford Univ., 1985; USAF, 1982-89; Public Official, Businesswoman; m. Jay Hone
Comm.: Energy & Commerce; Select Intelligence
Dist. Office: Albuquerque, 505-346-6781

Joe Wilson (R-2nd/SC)   202-225-2452
212 CHOB   3rd Term/65%   Fax: 202-225-2455
E-mail: joe.wilson@mail.house.gov
Website: joewilson.house.gov
CoS .... *Eric Dell* **LD** .... *Laurin Groover*
Sch .... *Jessica Eggimann* **Press** .... *Emily Lawrimore*
Bio: b. 7/31/47 Charleston, SC; Presbyterian; JD Univ. of SC, 1972; USAR, 1972-75; SCANG, 1975-present; Attorney; m. Roxanne
Comm.: Armed Services; Education & the Workforce; International Relations
Dist. Offices: Beaufort, 843-521-2530; West Columbia, 803-939-0041

Frank R. Wolf (R-10th/VA)   202-225-5136
241 CHOB   13th Term/64%   Fax: 202-225-0437
Website: www.house.gov/wolf
CoS .... *Dan Scandling* **LD** .... *Janet Shaffron*
Sch .... *Kristin Erb* **Press** .... *Dan Scandling*
Bio: b. 1/30/39 Philadelphia, PA; Presbyterian; LLB Georgetown Univ., 1965; USA, 1962-63; USAR, 1963-67; Attorney; m. Carolyn
Comm.: Appropriations
Dist. Offices: Herndon, 703-709-5800; Winchester, 540-667-0990

Lynn Woolsey (D-6th/CA)   202-225-5161
2263 RHOB   7th Term/72%   Fax: 202-225-5163
Website: woolsey.house.gov
CoS .... *Nora Matus* **LD** .... *Maggie Gumbinner*
Sch .... *Deanne Samuels* **Press** ... *Susannah Cernojevich*
Bio: b. 11/3/37 Seattle, WA; Presbyterian; BS Univ. of San Francisco, 1981; Businesswoman; div.
Comm.: Education & the Workforce; Science
Dist. Offices: Santa Rosa, 707-542-7182; San Rafael, 415-507-9554

David Wu (D-1st/OR)   202-225-0855
1023 LHOB   4th Term/58%   Fax: 202-225-9497
Website: www.house.gov/wu
CoS .... *Julie Tippens* **LD** .... *Brian Branton*
Sch .... *Ajah Maloney* **CD** .... *Patrick Morris*
Bio: b. 4/8/55 Taiwan; Presbyterian; JD Yale Univ., 1982; Attorney; m. Michelle
Comm.: Education & the Workforce; Science
Dist. Office: Portland, 503-326-2901

Albert Wynn (D-4th/MD)   202-225-8699
434 CHOB   7th Term/75%   Fax: 202-225-8714
Website: www.wynn.house.gov
CoS .... *Curt Clifton* **LD** .... *Alon Kupferman*
Sch .... *Norma Collins* **CD** .... *Amaya Smith*
Bio: b. 9/10/51 Philadelphia, PA; Baptist; JD Georgetown Univ., 1977; Attorney; m. Gaines
Comm.: Energy & Commerce
Dist. Offices: Largo, 301-773-4094; Olney, 301-929-3462

REPRESENTATIVES

C.W. Bill Young (R-10th/FL)   **202-225-5961**
2407 RHOB   18th Term/69%   Fax: 202-225-9764
E-mail: bill.young@mail.house.gov
Website: www.house.gov/young
CoS .... *Harry Glenn* **LD** .... *Brad Stine*
Sch .... *Vacant* **Press** .... *Harry Glenn*
Bio: b. 12/16/30 Harmarville, PA; Methodist; HS Diploma; USARNG, 1948-57; Insurance Executive; m. Beverly
Comm.: Appropriations
Dist. Offices: St. Petersburg, 727-893-3191; Largo, 727-581-0980

Don Young (R-At Large/AK)   **202-225-5765**
2111 RHOB   17th Term/72%   Fax: 202-225-0425
Website: www.house.gov/donyoung
CoS .... *Mike Anderson* **LD** .... *Chuck Cogar*
Sch .... *Sara Parsons* **CD** .... *Grant Thompson*
Bio: b. 6/9/33 Meridian, CA; Episcopal; BA Chico St. Col., 1958; USA, 1955-57; Educator, Trapper; m. Lula
Comm.: Homeland Security; Resources; Transportation & Infrastructure (Chair)
Dist. Offices: Anchorage, 907-271-5978; Kenai, 907-283-5808; Ketchikan, 907-225-6880; Juneau, 907-586-7400; Fairbanks, 907-456-0210; Wasilla, 907-376-7665; Bethel, 907-543-1639

Selected Congressional Caucus Information

21ST CENTURY HEALTH CARE CAUCUS
- Timothy F. Murphy (R-18th/PA) 202-225-2301
- Patrick J. Kennedy (D-1st/RI) 202-225-4911

9/11 COMMISSION CAUCUS
www.house.gov/maloney/911caucus
- Carolyn Maloney (D-14th/NY) 202-225-7944
- Christopher Shays (R-4th/CT) 202-225-5541

BIPARTISAN DISABILITIES CAUCUS
www.house.gov/ramstad/caucus/Disbility/disadv.htm
- James R. Langevin (D-2nd/RI) 202-225-2735
- Jim Ramstad (R-3rd/MN) 202-225-2871
- Major R. Owens (D-11th/NY) 202-225-6231
- Nancy L. Johnson (R-5th/CT) 202-225-4476

BLUE DOG COALITION
democraticleader.house.gov/bluedogs/bluedogs.htm
- Jim Matheson (D-2nd/UT) 202-225-3011
- Jim Cooper (D-5th/TN) 202-225-4311
- Dennis Cardoza (D-18th/CA) 202-225-6131
- Mike Ross (D-4th/AR) 202-225-3772

COALITION ON AUTISM RESEARCH AND EDUCATION
www.house.gov/doyle/autism.shtml
- Christopher H. Smith (R-4th/NJ) 202-225-3765
- Mike Doyle (D-14th/PA) 202-225-2135

CONGRESSIONAL ARTS CAUCUS
- Louise McIntosh Slaughter (D-28th/NY) 202-225-3615
- Christopher Shays (R-4th/CT) 202-225-5541

CONGRESSIONAL AUTOMOTIVE CAUCUS
www.house.gov/kildee/auto_caucus.shtml
- Dale E. Kildee (D-5th/MI) 202-225-3611
- Fred Upton (R-6th/MI) 202-225-3761

CONGRESSIONAL BIOTECHNOLOGY CAUCUS
- Bobby Rush (D-1st/IL) 202-225-4372
- Bob Goodlatte (R-6th/VA) 202-225-5431
- John M. Shimkus (R-19th/IL) 202-225-5271

CONGRESSIONAL BLACK CAUCUS
www.house.gov/cummings/cbc/cbchome.htm
- Melvin L. Watt (D-12th/NC) 202-225-1510

CONGRESSIONAL BOATING CAUCUS
- E. Clay Shaw, Jr. (R-22nd/FL) 202-225-3026
- Gene Taylor (D-4th/MS) 202-225-5772

CONGRESSIONAL BORDER CAUCUS
- Solomon P. Ortiz (D-27th/TX) 202-225-7742
- Henry Bonilla (R-23rd/TX) 202-225-4511

Selected Congressional Caucus Information

CONGRESSIONAL CAUCUS FOR WOMEN'S ISSUES
Ginny Brown-Waite (R-5th/FL) 202-225-1002
Hilda L. Solis (D-32nd/CA) 202-225-5464
Lois Capps (D-23rd/CA) 202-225-3601
Ileana Ros-Lehtinen (R-18th/FL) 202-225-3931

CONGRESSIONAL CAUCUS ON THE JUDICIAL BRANCH
Adam Smith (D-9th/WA) 202-225-8901
Judy Biggert (R-13th/IL) 202-225-3515

CONGRESSIONAL CHILDRENíS CAUCUS
Sheila Jackson Lee (D-18th/TX) 202-225-3816

CONGRESSIONAL COALITION ON ADOPTION
James L. Oberstar (D-8th/MN) 202-225-6211
Dave Camp (R-4th/MI) 202-225-3561
Larry E. Craig (R-ID) 202-224-2752
Mary Landrieu (D-LA) 202-224-5824

CONGRESSIONAL FITNESS CAUCUS
Zach Wamp (R-3rd/TN) 202-225-3271
Mark Udall (D-2nd/CO) 202-225-2161

CONGRESSIONAL GAMING CAUCUS
James A. Gibbons (R-2nd/NV) 202-225-6155
Shelley Berkley (D-1st/NV) 202-225-5965

CONGRESSIONAL HISPANIC CAUCUS
www.napolitano.house.gov/chc
Grace F. Napolitano (D-38th/CA) 202-225-5256
Joe Baca (D-43rd/CA) 202-225-6161
Raúl M. Grijalva (D-7th/AZ) 202-225-2435
Lucille Roybal-Allard (D-34th/CA) 202-225-1766

CONGRESSIONAL HISPANIC CONFERENCE
Ileana Ros-Lehtinen (R-18th/FL) 202-225-3931
Luis Fortuño (R/PR) 202-225-2615

CONGRESSIONAL HUMAN RIGHTS CAUCUS
lantos.house.gov/HoR/CA12/Human+Rights+Caucus
Tom Lantos (D-12th/CA) 202-225-3531
Frank R. Wolf (R-10th/VA) 202-225-5136

CONGRESSIONAL HUMANITIES CAUCUS
Jim Leach (R-2nd/IA) 202-225-6576
David E. Price (D-4th/NC) 202-225-1784

CONGRESSIONAL INTERNATIONAL ANTI-PIRACY CAUCUS
Adam Smith (D-9th/WA) 202-225-8901
Bob Goodlatte (R-6th/VA) 202-225-5431

CONGRESSIONAL IRAQI WOMEN'S CAUCUS
Tom Osborne (R-3rd/NE) 202-225-6435
Kay Granger (R-12th/TX) 202-225-5071
Ellen O. Tauscher (D-10th/CA) 202-225-1880

Selected Congressional Caucus Information

CONGRESSIONAL MANUFACTURING CAUCUS
- Donald A. Manzullo (R-16th/IL) 202-225-5676
- Tim Ryan (D-17th/OH) 202-225-5261

CONGRESSIONAL MANUFACTURING TASK FORCE
- Marty Meehan (D-5th/MA) 202-225-3411
- Sherwood L. Boehlert (R-24th/NY) 202-225-3665
- Mike Doyle (D-14th/PA) 202-225-2135
- Steven C. LaTourette (R-14th/OH) 202-225-5731

CONGRESSIONAL MENTAL HEALTH CAUCUS
- Grace F. Napolitano (D-38th/CA) 202-225-5256
- Timothy F. Murphy (R-18th/PA) 202-225-2301

CONGRESSIONAL MENTORING CAUCUS
- Tom Osborne (R-3rd/NE) 202-225-6435
- Betty McCollum (D-4th/MN) 202-225-6631
- Ric Keller (R-8th/FL) 202-225-2176
- Susan A. Davis (D-53rd/CA) 202-225-2040

CONGRESSIONAL PRO-CHOICE CAUCUS
- Diana L. DeGette (D-1st/CO) 202-225-4431
- Louise McIntosh Slaughter (D-28th/NY) 202-225-3615

CONGRESSIONAL PROGRESSIVE CAUCUS
bernie.house.gov/pc
- Dennis J. Kucinich (D-10th/OH) 202-225-5871
- Barbara Lee (D-9th/CA) 202-225-2661

HOUSE PRO-LIFE CAUCUS
- Christopher H. Smith (R-4th/NJ) 202-225-3765
- James L. Oberstar (D-8th/MN) 202-225-6211

CONGRESSIONAL SAVINGS AND OWNERSHIP CAUCUS
- Philip S. English (R-3rd/PA) 202-225-5406
- Jim Cooper (D-5th/TN) 202-225-4311
- Chris Chocola (R-2nd/IN) 202-225-3915
- Harold E. Ford, Jr. (D-9th/TN) 202-225-3265

CONGRESSIONAL SECOND AMENDMENT CAUCUS
- Marilyn Musgrave (R-4th/CO) 202-225-4676
- Virgil H. Goode, Jr. (R-5th/VA) 202-225-4711

CONGRESSIONAL SKI AND SNOWBOARD CAUCUS
- John E. Sweeney (R-20th/NY) 202-225-5614
- Mark Udall (D-2nd/CO) 202-225-2161

CONGRESSIONAL STEEL CAUCUS
- Philip S. English (R-3rd/PA) 202-225-5406
- Peter J. Visclosky (D-1st/IN) 202-225-2461

CONGRESSIONAL VICTIM'S RIGHTS CAUCUS
- Ted Poe (R-2nd/TX) 202-225-6565
- Katherine Harris (R-13th/FL) 202-225-5015

Selected Congressional Caucus Information

CONGRESSIONAL WESTERN CAUCUS
www.house.gov/cannon/wc.htm
- Chris Cannon (R-3rd/UT) 202-225-7751
- Jeff Flake (R-6th/AZ) 202-225-2635

HISTORIC PRESERVATION CAUCUS
- Brad Miller (D-13th/NC) 202-225-3032
- Michael Turner (R-3rd/OH) 202-225-6465

HOUSE BEEF CAUCUS
- Bob Beauprez (R-7th/CO) 202-225-2645
- Dennis Cardoza (D-18th/CA) 202-225-6131

HOUSE OCEANS CAUCUS
- Thomas H. Allen (D-1st/ME) 202-225-6116
- Sam Farr (D-17th/CA) 202-225-2861
- Jim Saxton (R-3rd/NJ) 202-225-4765
- Curt Weldon (R-7th/PA) 202-225-2011
- Wayne Gilchrest (R-1st/MD) 202-225-5311
- Jay Inslee (D-1st/WA) 202-225-6311

MILITARY VETERANS CAUCUS
- Michael Bilirakis (R-9th/FL) 202-225-5755
- Charles Norwood (R-9th/GA) 202-225-4101
- Collin Peterson (D-7th/MN) 202-225-2165
- Mike Thompson (D-1st/CA) 202-225-3311

MINOR LEAGUE BASEBALL CAUCUS
- Sherwood L. Boehlert (R-24th/NY) 202-225-3665
- John E. Sweeney (R-20th/NY) 202-225-5614

PUBLIC BROADCASTING CAUCUS
- Earl Blumenauer (D-3rd/OR) 202-225-4811
- Paul E. Gillmor (R-5th/OH) 202-225-6405

REPUBLICAN STUDY COMMITTEE
johnshadegg.house.gov/rsc
- Mike Pence (R-6th/IN) 202-225-3021
- Sue Myrick (R-9th/NC) 202-225-1976
- John B. Shadegg (R-3rd/AZ) 202-225-3361
- Dan Burton (R-5th/IN) 202-225-2276
- John T. Doolittle (R-4th/CA) 202-225-2511
- Ernest Istook, Jr. (R-5th/OK) 202-225-2132
- Sam Johnson (R-3rd/TX) 202-225-4201

SEX AND VIOLENCE IN THE MEDIA CAUCUS
- Joe Baca (D-43rd/CA) 202-225-6161
- Tom Osborne (R-3rd/NE) 202-225-6435

House Committees and Subcommittees

AGRICULTURE

Phone: (202) 225-2171—Room: 1301 LHOB—Fax: 225-0917
http://agriculture.house.gov

Republicans (25)
Bob Goodlatte, 6th-VA, *Chair**
John A. Boehner, 8th-OH, *Vice Chair*
Richard Pombo, 11th-CA
Terry Everett, 2nd-AL
Frank D. Lucas, 3rd-OK
Jerry Moran, 1st-KS
William L. Jenkins, 1st-TN
Gil Gutknecht, 1st-MN
Robin Hayes, 8th-NC
Timothy V. Johnson, 15th-IL
Tom Osborne, 3rd-NE
Mike Pence, 6th-IN
Sam Graves, 6th-MO
Jo Bonner, 1st-AL
Michael D. Rogers, 3rd-AL
Steve King, 5th-IA
Marilyn Musgrave, 4th-CO
Devin Nunes, 21st-CA
Randy Neugebauer, 19th-TX
Charles W. Boustany, Jr., 7th-LA
Joe Schwarz, 7th-MI
Randy Kuhl, 29th-NY
Virginia Foxx, 5th-NC
Mike Conaway, 11th-TX
Jeff Fortenberry, 1st-NE

Democrats (21)
Collin Peterson, 7th-MN, *Rnk. Mem.**
Tim Holden, 17th-PA
Mike McIntyre, 7th-NC
Bob Etheridge, 2nd-NC
Joe Baca, 43rd-CA
Ed Case, 2nd-HI
Dennis Cardoza, 18th-CA
David Scott, 13th-GA
Jim Marshall, 3rd-GA
Stephanie Herseth, At Large-SD
G.K. Butterfield, 1st-NC
Henry Cuellar, 28th-TX
Charlie Melancon, 3rd-LA
Jim Costa, 20th-CA
John T. Salazar, 3rd-CO
John Barrow, 12th-GA
Earl Pomeroy, At Large-ND
Leonard L. Boswell, 3rd-IA
Rick Larsen, 2nd-WA
Lincoln Davis, 4th-TN
Ben Chandler, 6th-KY

Maj. Staff Dir.:
William O'Conner
225-2171, 1301 LHOB

Min. Staff Dir.:
Rob Larew
225-0317, 1305 LHOB

*Ex officio members on all subcommittees.

Agriculture Subcommittees

Conservation, Credit, Rural Development and Research
225-2171/1301 LHOB/Fax: 225-0917

Rep: Lucas, *Chair;* Moran; Osborne, *Vice Chair;* Graves; Rogers; King; Boustany; Schwarz; Fortenberry
Dem: Holden, *Rnk. Mem.;* Cuellar; McIntyre; Etheridge; Case; Davis; Herseth; Butterfield
Maj. Staff Dir.: Ryan Weston, 225-2171, 1301 LHOB
Min. Consultant: Anne Simmons, 225-0317, 1305 LHOB

Department Operations, Oversight, Dairy, Nutrition and Forestry
225-2171/1301 LHOB/Fax: 225-0917

Rep: Gutknecht, *Chair;* Pombo; Moran; Bonner, *Vice Chair;* Nunes; Foxx; Fortenberry
Dem: Baca, *Rnk. Mem.;* Cardoza; Butterfield; Holden; Cuellar; Costa
Maj. Staff Dir.: Ben Anderson, 225-2171, 1301 LHOB
Min. Consultant: Tony Jackson, 225-0317, 1305 LHOB

General Farm Commodities and Risk Management
225-2171/1301 LHOB/Fax: 225-0917

Rep: Moran, *Chair;* Boehner; Everett; Lucas; Jenkins; Johnson, *Vice Chair;* Pence; Graves; Bonner; King; Musgrave; Neugebauer; Boustany; Conaway; Fortenberry
Dem: Etheridge, *Rnk. Mem.;* Salazar; Marshall; Herseth; Butterfield; Melancon; Barrow; Pomeroy; Boswell; Larsen; Chandler; Scott; Costa
Maj. Staff Dir.: Tyler Wegmeyer, 225-2171, 1301 LHOB
Min. Consultant: John Riley, 225-0317, 1305 LHOB

Livestock and Horticulture
225-2171/1301 LHOB/Fax: 225-0917

Rep: Hayes, *Chair;* Boehner; Pombo; Osborne; Pence, *Vice Chair;* Rogers; King; Nunes; Neugebauer; Kuhl; Foxx; Conaway
Dem: Case, *Rnk. Mem.;* Scott; Herseth; Costa; Cardoza; Salazar; Boswell; Larsen; Pomeroy; Barrow
Maj. Staff Dir.: Pam Scott, 225-2171, 1301 LHOB
Min. Consultant: Chandler Goule, 225-0317, 1305 LHOB

Agriculture Subcommittees

Specialty Crops and Foreign Agriculture Programs
225-2171/1301 LHOB/Fax: 225-0917

Rep: Jenkins, *Chair;* Everett, *Vice Chair;* Gutknecht; Hayes; Rogers; Neugebauer; Schwarz; Foxx
Dem: McIntyre, *Rnk. Mem.;* Marshall; Melancon; Barrow; Scott; Chandler; Cuellar
Maj. Staff Dir.: Pelham Straughn, 225-2171, 1301 LHOB
Min. Consultant: Russell Middleton, 225-0317, 1305 LHOB

APPROPRIATIONS

Phone: (202) 225-2771—Room: H-218 Capitol
http://www.house.gov/appropriations

Republicans (37)
Jerry Lewis, 41st-CA, **Chair***
C.W. Bill Young, 10th-FL
Ralph Regula, 16th-OH, **Vice Chair**
Harold Rogers, 5th-KY
Frank R. Wolf, 10th-VA
Jim Kolbe, 8th-AZ
James T. Walsh, 25th-NY
Charles H. Taylor, 11th-NC
David Hobson, 7th-OH
Ernest Istook, Jr., 5th-OK
Henry Bonilla, 23rd-TX
Joseph Knollenberg, 9th-MI
Jack Kingston, 1st-GA
Rodney Frelinghuysen, 11th-NJ
Roger Wicker, 1st-MS
Randy Cunningham, 50th-CA
Todd Tiahrt, 4th-KS
Zach Wamp, 3rd-TN
Tom Latham, 4th-IA
Anne M. Northup, 3rd-KY
Robert B. Aderholt, 4th-AL
Jo Ann H. Emerson, 8th-MO
Kay Granger, 12th-TX
John E. Peterson, 5th-PA
Virgil H. Goode, Jr., 5th-VA
John T. Doolittle, 4th-CA
Ray H. LaHood, 18th-IL
John E. Sweeney, 20th-NY
Don Sherwood, 10th-PA
Dave Weldon, 15th-FL
Mike Simpson, 2nd-ID
John A. Culberson, 7th-TX
Mark S. Kirk, 10th-IL
Ander Crenshaw, 4th-FL
Dennis Rehberg, At Large-MT
John R. Carter, 31st-TX
Rodney Alexander, 5th-LA

Democrats (29)
David R. Obey, 7th-WI, **Rnk. Mem.***
John P. Murtha, 12th-PA
Norman D. Dicks, 6th-WA
Martin Olav Sabo, 5th-MN
Steny H. Hoyer, 5th-MD
Alan B. Mollohan, 1st-WV
Marcy Kaptur, 9th-OH
Peter J. Visclosky, 1st-IN
Nita M. Lowey, 18th-NY
José E. Serrano, 16th-NY
Rosa DeLauro, 3rd-CT
James P. Moran, 8th-VA
John W. Olver, 1st-MA
Ed Pastor, 4th-AZ
David E. Price, 4th-NC
Chet Edwards, 17th-TX
Robert E. Cramer, Jr., 5th-AL
Patrick J. Kennedy, 1st-RI
James Clyburn, 6th-SC
Maurice Hinchey, 22nd-NY
Lucille Roybal-Allard, 34th-CA
Sam Farr, 17th-CA
Jesse Jackson, Jr., 2nd-IL
Carolyn C. Kilpatrick, 13th-MI
F. Allen Boyd, Jr., 2nd-FL
Chaka Fattah, 2nd-PA
Steven R. Rothman, 9th-NJ
Sanford Bishop, Jr., 2nd-GA
Marion Berry, 1st-AR

Maj. Staff Dir.:
Frank Cushing
225-2771, H-218 Capitol

Min. Staff Dir.:
Rob Nabors
225-3481, 1016 LHOB

*Ex officio members on all subcommittees.

Appropriations Subcommittees

Agriculture, Rural Development, Food and Drug Administration and Related Agencies
225-2638/2362A RHOB/Fax: 225-2535

Rep: Bonilla, *Chair;* Kingston; Latham; Emerson; Goode; LaHood, *Vice Chair;* Doolittle; Alexander
Dem: DeLauro, *Rnk. Mem.;* Hinchey; Farr; Boyd; Kaptur
Maj. Clerk: Martin Delgado, 225-2638, 2362A RHOB
Min. Prof. Staff Mem.: Martha Foley, 225-3481, 1016 LHOB

Appropriations Subcommittees

Defense
225-2847/H-149 Capitol/Fax: 225-2822

Rep: Young, *Chair;* Hobson; Bonilla; Cunningham; Frelinghuysen, *Vice Chair;* Tiahrt; Wicker; Kingston; Granger
Dem: Murtha, *Rnk. Mem.;* Dicks; Sabo; Visclosky; Moran; Kaptur
Maj. Clerk: John Shank, 225-3351, H-149 Capitol
Min. Prof. Staff Mem.: David Morrison, 225-3481, 1016 LHOB

Energy and Water Development and Related Agencies
225-3421/2362B RHOB/Fax: 225-1566

Rep: Hobson, *Chair;* Frelinghuysen; Latham; Wamp; Emerson; Doolittle, *Vice Chair;* Simpson; Rehberg
Dem: Visclosky, *Rnk. Mem.;* Edwards; Pastor; Clyburn; Berry
Maj. Prof. Staff Mem.: Kevin Cook, 225-3421, 2362B RHOB
Min. Prof. Staff Mem.: Dixon Butler, 225-3481, 1016 LHOB

Foreign Operations, Export Financing and Related Programs
225-2041/HB-26 Capitol/Fax: 226-7922

Rep: Kolbe, *Chair;* Knollenberg; Kirk; Crenshaw; Sherwood, *Vice Chair;* Sweeney; Rehberg; Carter
Dem: Lowey, *Rnk. Mem.;* Jackson; Kilpatrick; Rothman; Fattah
Maj. Clerk: Betsy Phillips, 225-2041, HB-26 Capitol
Min. Prof. Staff Mem.: Mark Murray, 225-3481, 1016 LHOB

Homeland Security
225-5834/B-307 RHOB/Fax: 225-5895

Rep: Rogers, *Chair;* Wamp; Latham; Emerson; Sweeney; Kolbe; Istook, *Vice Chair;* LaHood; Crenshaw; Carter
Dem: Sabo, *Rnk. Mem.;* Price; Serrano; Roybal-Allard; Bishop; Berry; Edwards
Maj. Clerk: Michelle Mrdeza, 225-5834, B-307 RHOB
Min. Prof. Staff Mem.: Beverly Pheto, 225-3481, 1016 LHOB

Interior, Environment and Related Agencies
225-3081/B-308 RHOB/Fax: 225-9069

Rep: Taylor, *Chair;* Wamp; Peterson; Sherwood; Istook; Aderholt; Doolittle; Simpson, *Vice Chair*
Dem: Dicks, *Rnk. Mem.;* Moran; Hinchey; Olver; Mollohan
Maj. Clerk: Debbie Weatherly, 225-3081, B-308 RHOB
Min. Prof. Staff Mem.: Michael Stephens, 225-3481, 1016 LHOB

Labor, Health and Human Services, Education and Related Agencies
225-3508/2358 RHOB/Fax: 225-3509

Rep: Regula, *Chair;* Istook; Wicker; Northup, *Vice Chair;* Cunningham; Granger; Peterson; Sherwood; Weldon; Walsh
Dem: Obey, *Rnk. Mem.;* Hoyer; Lowey; DeLauro; Jackson; Kennedy; Roybal-Allard
Maj. Clerk: Craig Higgins, 225-3508, 2358 RHOB
Min. Prof. Staff Mems.: David Reich, Cheryl Smith, 225-3481, 1016 LHOB

Military Quality of Life and Veterans Affairs and Related Agencies
225-3047/H-143 Capitol/Fax: 225-3099

Rep: Walsh, *Chair;* Aderholt, *Vice Chair;* Northup; Simpson; Crenshaw; Young; Kirk; Rehberg; Carter
Dem: Edwards, *Rnk. Mem.;* Farr; Boyd; Bishop; Price; Cramer
Maj. Clerk: Carol Murphy, 225-3047, H-143 Capitol
Min. Prof. Staff Mem.: Tom Forhan, 225-3481, 1016 LHOB

Science, State, Justice and Commerce and Related Agencies
225-3351/H-309 Capitol

Rep: Wolf, *Chair;* Taylor; Kirk; Weldon, *Vice Chair;* Goode; LaHood; Culberson; Alexander
Dem: Mollohan, *Rnk. Mem.;* Serrano; Cramer; Kennedy; Fattah
Maj. Clerk: Mike Ringler, 225-3351, H-309 Capitol
Min. Prof. Staff Mems.: Michelle Burkett, David Pomerantz, 225-3481, 1016 LHOB

Transportation, Treasury and Housing and Urban Development, the Judiciary, District of Columbia
225-2141/2358 RHOB/Fax: 225-0900

Rep: Knollenberg, *Chair;* Wolf; Rogers; Tiahrt; Northup; Aderholt; Sweeney, *Vice Chair;* Culberson; Regula
Dem: Olver, *Rnk. Mem.;* Hoyer; Pastor; Kilpatrick; Clyburn; Rothman
Maj. Clerk: Dena Baron, 225-2141, 2358 RHOB
Min. Prof. Staff Mem.: Mike Malone, 225-3481, 1016 LHOB

ARMED SERVICES

Phone: (202) 225-4151—Room: 2120 RHOB—Fax: 225-9077
http://www.house.gov/hasc

Republicans (34)
Duncan Hunter, 52nd-CA, *Chair**
Curt Weldon, 7th-PA
Joel Hefley, 5th-CO
Jim Saxton, 3rd-NJ
John McHugh, 23rd-NY
Terry Everett, 2nd-AL
Roscoe Bartlett, 6th-MD
Howard McKeon, 25th-CA
William Thornberry, 13th-TX
John N. Hostettler, 8th-IN
Walter Jones, Jr., 3rd-NC
Jim R. Ryun, 2nd-KS
James A. Gibbons, 2nd-NV
Robin Hayes, 8th-NC
Ken Calvert, 44th-CA
Robert R. Simmons, 2nd-CT
Jo Ann S. Davis, 1st-VA
Todd Akin, 2nd-MO
Randy Forbes, 4th-VA
Jeff Miller, 1st-FL
Joe Wilson, 2nd-SC
Frank A. LoBiondo, 2nd-NJ
Jeb Bradley, 1st-NH
Michael Turner, 3rd-OH
John Kline, 2nd-MN
Candice Miller, 10th-MI
Michael D. Rogers, 3rd-AL
Trent Franks, 2nd-AZ
Bill Shuster, 9th-PA
Thelma D. Drake, 2nd-VA
Joe Schwarz, 7th-MI
Cathy McMorris, 5th-WA
Mike Conaway, 11th-TX
Geoff Davis, 4th-KY

Democrats (28)
Ike Skelton, 4th-MO, **Rnk. Mem.***
John M. Spratt, Jr., 5th-SC
Solomon P. Ortiz, 27th-TX
Lane Evans, 17th-IL
Gene Taylor, 4th-MS
Neil Abercrombie, 1st-HI
Marty Meehan, 5th-MA
Silvestre Reyes, 16th-TX
Vic Snyder, 2nd-AR
Adam Smith, 9th-WA
Loretta Sanchez, 47th-CA
Mike McIntyre, 7th-NC
Ellen O. Tauscher, 10th-CA
Robert A. Brady, 1st-PA
Robert E. Andrews, 1st-NJ
Susan A. Davis, 53rd-CA
James R. Langevin, 2nd-RI
Steve J. Israel, 2nd-NY
Rick Larsen, 2nd-WA
Jim Cooper, 5th-TN
Jim Marshall, 3rd-GA
Kendrick B. Meek, 17th-FL
Madeleine Z. Bordallo, GU
Tim Ryan, 17th-OH
Mark Udall, 2nd-CO
G.K. Butterfield, 1st-NC
Cynthia McKinney, 4th-GA
Dan Boren, 2nd-OK

Maj. Staff Dir.:
Robert Rangel
225-4151, 2120 RHOB

Min. Staff Dir. & Counsel:
Jim Schweiter
225-4158, 2340 RHOB

*Ex officio members on all subcommittees of which they are not regular members.

Armed Services Subcommittees

Military Personnel
225-4151/2340 RHOB/Fax: 226-0789
Rep: McHugh, *Chair;* Davis (VA); Kline; Drake; Conaway; Saxton; Jones; Ryun; Hayes
Dem: Snyder, *Rnk. Mem.;* Meehan; Sanchez; Andrews; Davis; Udall; McKinney
Maj. Prof. Staff Mem.: John Chapla, 225-7560, 2120 RHOB
Min. Prof. Staff Mem.: Debra Wada, 226-5662, 2340 RHOB

Projection Forces
225-4151/2120 RHOB/Fax: 225-9077
Rep: Bartlett, *Chair;* Simmons; Davis (VA); Miller (FL); Drake; Weldon; Saxton; Hostettler; Calvert
Dem: Taylor, *Rnk. Mem.;* Tauscher; Langevin; Israel; Marshall; Bordallo; Boren
Maj. Prof. Staff Mem.: Bob Lautrup, 225-0883, 2120 RHOB
Min. Prof. Staff Mem.: Bill Natter, 226-2336, 2340 RHOB

Armed Services Subcommittees

Readiness
225-4151/2120 RHOB/Fax: 225-9077

Rep: Hefley, *Chair;* Hostettler; Jones; Ryun; Forbes; Miller (FL); Rogers; Schwarz; McMorris; McHugh; McKeon; Hayes; Simmons; Bradley; Miller (MI); Franks

Dem: Ortiz, *Rnk. Mem.;* Evans; Taylor; Abercrombie; Reyes; Snyder; Brady; Davis; Marshall; Meek; Bordallo; Ryan; Udall; Butterfield

Maj. Prof. Staff Mem.: Mary Ellen Fraser, 225-0641, 2120 RHOB
Min. Prof. Staff Mem.: Paul Arcangeli, 226-9007, 2340 RHOB

Strategic Forces
225-4151/2120 RHOB/Fax: 225-9077

Rep: Everett, *Chair;* Thornberry; Franks; Turner; Rogers; Schwarz; McMorris; Davis (KY)

Dem: Reyes, *Rnk. Mem.;* Spratt; Sanchez; Tauscher; Larsen; Cooper

Maj. Prof. Staff Mem.: Bill Ostendorff, 225-0532, 2120 RHOB
Min. Prof. Staff Mem.: Hugh Brady, 225-2191, 2340 RHOB

Tactical Air and Land Forces
225-4151/2120 RHOB/Fax: 225-9077

Rep: Weldon, *Chair;* McKeon; Gibbons; Calvert; LoBiondo; Bradley; Turner; Conaway; Everett; Bartlett; Jones; Ryun; Akin; Forbes; Wilson; Shuster

Dem: Abercrombie, *Rnk. Mem.;* Skelton; Spratt; Ortiz; Evans; Smith; McIntyre; Brady; Israel; Cooper; Meek; Ryan; Butterfield; Boren

Maj. Prof. Staff Mem.: Doug Roach, 225-4440, 2120 RHOB
Min. Prof. Staff Mem.: Andrew Hunter, 225-6703, 2340 RHOB

Terrorism, Unconventional Threats and Capabilities
225-4151/2120 RHOB/Fax: 225-9077

Rep: Saxton, *Chair;* Hayes; Akin; Wilson; Kline; Shuster; Davis (KY); Hefley; Thornberry; Gibbons; Miller (FL); LoBiondo

Dem: Meehan, *Rnk. Mem.;* Smith; McIntyre; Tauscher; Andrews; Langevin; Larsen; Cooper; Marshall; McKinney

Maj. Prof. Staff Mem.: Thomas Hawley, 225-7120, 2120 RHOB
Min. Prof. Staff Mem.: Bill Natter, 226-2336, 2340 RHOB

BUDGET

Phone: (202) 226-7270—Room: 309 CHOB—Fax: 226-7174
http://www.house.gov/budget

Republicans (22)
Jim Nussle, 1st-IA, *Chair*
Rob J. Portman, 2nd-OH, *Vice Chair*
Jim R. Ryun, 2nd-KS
Ander Crenshaw, 4th-FL
Adam Putnam, 12th-FL
Roger Wicker, 1st-MS
Kenny C. Hulshof, 9th-MO
Jo Bonner, 1st-AL
Scott Garrett, 5th-NJ
J. Gresham Barrett, 3rd-SC
Thaddeus G. McCotter, 11th-MI
Mario Diaz-Balart, 25th-FL
Jeb Hensarling, 5th-TX
Ileana Ros-Lehtinen, 18th-FL
Dan Lungren, 3rd-CA
Pete Sessions, 32nd-TX
Paul D. Ryan, 1st-WI
Mike Simpson, 2nd-ID
Jeb Bradley, 1st-NH
Patrick McHenry, 10th-NC
Connie Mack, 14th-FL
Mike Conaway, 11th-TX

Democrats (17)
John M. Spratt, Jr., 5th-SC, *Rnk. Mem.*
Dennis Moore, 3rd-KS
Richard E. Neal, 2nd-MA
Rosa DeLauro, 3rd-CT
Chet Edwards, 17th-TX
Harold E. Ford, Jr., 9th-TN
Lois Capps, 23rd-CA
Brian Baird, 3rd-WA
Jim Cooper, 5th-TN
Artur Davis, 7th-AL
William J. Jefferson, 2nd-LA
Thomas H. Allen, 1st-ME
Ed Case, 2nd-HI
Cynthia McKinney, 4th-GA
Henry Cuellar, 28th-TX
Allyson Y. Schwartz, 13th-PA
Ron J. Kind, 3rd-WI

Maj. Chief of Staff:
James Bates
226-7270, 309 CHOB

Min. Staff Dir. & Chief Counsel:
Thomas S. Kahn
226-7200, B-71 CHOB

NO SUBCOMMITTEES

EDUCATION AND THE WORKFORCE

Phone: (202) 225-4527—Room: 2181 RHOB—Fax: 225-9571
http://edworkforce.house.gov

Republicans (27)
John A. Boehner, 8th-OH, *Chair**
Thomas E. Petri, 6th-WI, *Vice Chair*
Howard McKeon, 25th-CA
Michael Castle, At Large-DE
Sam Johnson, 3rd-TX
Mark Souder, 3rd-IN
Charles Norwood, 9th-GA
Vernon Ehlers, 3rd-MI
Judy Biggert, 13th-IL
Todd R. Platts, 19th-PA
Patrick J. Tiberi, 12th-OH
Ric Keller, 8th-FL
Tom Osborne, 3rd-NE
Joe Wilson, 2nd-SC
Jon C. Porter, 3rd-NV
John Kline, 2nd-MN
Marilyn Musgrave, 4th-CO
Bob Inglis, 4th-SC
Cathy McMorris, 5th-WA
Kenny Marchant, 24th-TX
Tom Price, 6th-GA
Luis Fortuño, PR
Bobby Jindal, 1st-LA
Charles W. Boustany, Jr., 7th-LA
Virginia Foxx, 5th-NC
Thelma D. Drake, 2nd-VA
Randy Kuhl, 29th-NY

Democrats (22)
George Miller, 7th-CA, *Rnk. Mem.**
Dale E. Kildee, 5th-MI
Major R. Owens, 11th-NY
Donald M. Payne, 10th-NJ
Robert E. Andrews, 1st-NJ
Bobby Scott, 3rd-VA
Lynn Woolsey, 6th-CA
Rubén E. Hinojosa, 15th-TX
Carolyn McCarthy, 4th-NY
John F. Tierney, 6th-MA
Ron J. Kind, 3rd-WI
Dennis J. Kucinich, 10th-OH
David Wu, 1st-OR
Rush Holt, 12th-NJ
Susan A. Davis, 53rd-CA
Betty McCollum, 4th-MN
Danny K. Davis, 7th-IL
Raúl M. Grijalva, 7th-AZ
Chris Van Hollen, Jr., 8th-MD
Tim Ryan, 17th-OH
Tim Bishop, 1st-NY
John Barrow, 12th-GA

Maj. Staff Dir.:
Paula Nowakowski
225-4527, 2181 RHOB

Min. Staff Dir.:
John Lawrence
225-3725, 2101 RHOB

*Ex officio members on all subcommittees of which they are not regular members.

Education and the Workforce Subcommittees

21st Century Competitiveness
225-6558/230 FHOB/Fax: 226-1010
Rep: McKeon, *Chair;* Porter, *Vice Chair;* Boehner; Petri; Castle; Johnson; Ehlers; Tiberi; Keller; Osborne; Inglis; McMorris; Price; Fortuño; Boustany; Foxx; Drake; Kuhl
Dem: Kildee, *Rnk. Mem.;* Payne; McCarthy; Tierney; Kind; Wu; Holt; McCollum; Van Hollen; Ryan; Scott; Davis (CA); Bishop; Barrow; Owens
Maj. Staff Dir.: Paula Nowakowski, 225-4527, 2181 RHOB
Min. Staff Dir.: John Lawrence, 225-3725, 2101 RHOB

Education Reform
225-6558/230 FHOB/Fax: 226-1010
Rep: Castle, *Chair;* Osborne, *Vice Chair;* Souder; Ehlers; Biggert; Platts; Keller; Wilson; Musgrave; Jindal; Kuhl
Dem: Woolsey, *Rnk. Mem.;* Davis (IL); Grijalva; Andrews; Scott; Hinojosa; Kind; Kucinich; Davis (CA)
Maj. Staff Dir.: Paula Nowakowski, 225-4527, 2181 RHOB
Min. Staff Dir.: John Lawrence, 225-3725, 2101 RHOB

Employer-Employee Relations
225-7101/2181 RHOB/Fax: 225-9571
Rep: Johnson, *Chair;* Kline, *Vice Chair;* Boehner; McKeon; Platts; Tiberi; Wilson; Musgrave; Marchant; Jindal; Boustany; Foxx
Dem: Andrews, *Rnk. Mem.;* Kildee; Payne; McCarthy; Tierney; Wu; Holt; McCollum; Grijalva
Maj. Staff Dir.: Paula Nowakowski, 225-4527, 2181 RHOB
Min. Staff Dir.: John Lawrence, 225-3725, 2101 RHOB

Education and the Workforce Subcommittees

Select Education
225-6558/230 FHOB/Fax: 226-1010
Rep: Tiberi, *Chair;* McMorris, *Vice Chair;* Souder; Porter; Inglis; Fortuño
Dem: Hinojosa, *Rnk. Mem.;* Davis (IL); Van Hollen; Ryan
Maj. Staff Dir.: Paula Nowakowski, 225-4527, 2181 RHOB
Min. Staff Dir.: John Lawrence, 225-3725, 2101 RHOB

Workforce Protections
225-7101/2181 RHOB/Fax: 225-9571
Rep: Norwood, *Chair;* Biggert, *Vice Chair;* Keller; Kline; Marchant; Price; Drake
Dem: Owens, *Rnk. Mem.;* Kucinich; Woolsey; Bishop; Barrow
Maj. Staff Dir.: Paula Nowakowski, 225-4527, 2181 RHOB
Min. Staff Dir.: John Lawrence, 225-3725, 2101 RHOB

ENERGY AND COMMERCE

Phone: (202) 225-2927—Room: 2125 RHOB—Fax: 225-1919
http://energycommerce.house.gov

Republicans (31)
Joe Barton, 6th-TX, *Chair**
Ralph M. Hall, 4th-TX
Michael Bilirakis, 9th-FL, *Vice Chair*
Fred Upton, 6th-MI
Cliff Stearns, 6th-FL
Paul E. Gillmor, 5th-OH
Nathan Deal, 10th-GA
Edward Whitfield, 1st-KY
Charles Norwood, 9th-GA
Barbara Cubin, At Large-WY
John M. Shimkus, 19th-IL
Heather A. Wilson, 1st-NM
John B. Shadegg, 3rd-AZ
Charles Pickering, Jr., 3rd-MS, *Vice Chair*
Vito Fossella, 13th-NY
Roy Blunt, 7th-MO
Steve Buyer, 4th-IN
George P. Radanovich, 19th-CA
Charles Bass, 2nd-NH
Joseph R. Pitts, 16th-PA
Mary Bono, 45th-CA
Greg Walden, 2nd-OR
Lee Terry, 2nd-NE
Michael A. Ferguson, 7th-NJ
Michael J. Rogers, 8th-MI
C.L. Otter, 1st-ID
Sue Myrick, 9th-NC
John Sullivan, 1st-OK
Timothy F. Murphy, 18th-PA
Michael C. Burgess, 26th-TX
Marsha Blackburn, 7th-TN

Democrats (26)
John D. Dingell, 15th-MI, *Rnk. Mem.**
Henry A. Waxman, 30th-CA
Edward J. Markey, 7th-MA
Rick Boucher, 9th-VA
Edolphus Towns, 10th-NY
Frank Pallone, Jr., 6th-NJ
Sherrod Brown, 13th-OH
Bart Gordon, 6th-TN
Bobby Rush, 1st-IL
Anna Eshoo, 14th-CA
Bart Stupak, 1st-MI
Eliot Engel, 17th-NY
Albert Wynn, 4th-MD
Gene Green, 29th-TX
Ted Strickland, 6th-OH
Diana L. DeGette, 1st-CO
Lois Capps, 23rd-CA
Mike Doyle, 14th-PA
Thomas H. Allen, 1st-ME
Jim Davis, 11th-FL
Janice D. Schakowsky, 9th-IL
Hilda L. Solis, 32nd-CA
Charles A. Gonzalez, 20th-TX
Jay Inslee, 1st-WA
Tammy Baldwin, 2nd-WI
Mike Ross, 4th-AR

Maj. Staff Dir.:
Bud Albright
225-2927, 2125 RHOB

Min. Staff Dir.:
Reid Stuntz
225-3641, 2322 RHOB

*Ex officio members on all subcommittees.

Energy and Commerce Subcommittees

Commerce, Trade and Consumer Protection
225-2927/2125 RHOB/Fax: 225-1919
Rep: Stearns, *Chair;* Upton; Deal; Cubin; Radanovich; Bass; Pitts; Bono; Terry; Ferguson; Rogers; Otter; Myrick; Murphy; Blackburn
Dem: Schakowsky, *Rnk. Mem.;* Ross; Markey; Towns; Brown; Rush; Green; Strickland; DeGette; Davis; Gonzalez; Baldwin
Maj. Policy Coor.: David Cavicke, 225-2927, 2125 RHOB
Min. Counsel: Jon Cordone, 226-3400, 564 FHOB

Energy and Commerce Subcommittees

Energy and Air Quality
225-2927/2125 RHOB/Fax: 225-1919

Rep: Hall, *Chair;* Bilirakis; Whitfield; Norwood; Shimkus; Wilson; Shadegg; Pickering; Fossella; Radanovich; Bono; Walden; Rogers; Otter; Sullivan; Murphy; Burgess
Dem: Boucher, *Rnk. Mem.;* Ross; Waxman; Markey; Engel; Wynn; Green; Strickland; Capps; Doyle; Allen; Davis; Solis; Gonzalez
Maj. Policy Coor.: Elizabeth Stack, 225-2927, 2125 RHOB
Min. Prof. Staff Mems.: Sue Sheridan, Bruce Harris, 226-3400, 564 FHOB

Environment and Hazardous Materials
225-2927/2125 RHOB/Fax: 225-1919

Rep: Gillmor, *Chair;* Hall; Deal; Wilson; Shadegg; Fossella; Bass; Pitts; Bono; Terry; Rogers; Otter; Myrick; Sullivan; Murphy
Dem: Solis, *Rnk. Mem.;* Pallone; Stupak; Wynn; Capps; Doyle; Allen; Schakowsky; Inslee; Green; Gonzalez; Baldwin
Maj. Policy Coor.: Jerry Couri, 225-2927, 2125 RHOB
Min. Sr. Counsel: Dick Frandsen, 225-3641, 2322 RHOB

Health
225-2927/2125 RHOB/Fax: 225-1919

Rep: Deal, *Chair;* Hall; Bilirakis; Upton; Gillmor; Norwood; Cubin; Shimkus; Shadegg; Pickering; Buyer; Pitts; Bono; Ferguson; Rogers; Myrick; Burgess
Dem: Brown, *Rnk. Mem.;* Waxman; Towns; Pallone; Gordon; Rush; Eshoo; Green; Strickland; DeGette; Capps; Allen; Davis; Baldwin
Maj. Policy Coor.: Vacant, 225-2927, 2125 RHOB
Min. Counsels: John Ford, Amy Hall, Bridgett Taylor, 226-3400, 564 FHOB

Oversight and Investigations
225-2927/2125 RHOB/Fax: 225-1919

Rep: Whitfield, *Chair;* Stearns; Pickering; Bass; Walden; Ferguson; Burgess; Blackburn
Dem: Stupak, *Rnk. Mem.;* DeGette; Schakowsky; Inslee; Baldwin; Waxman
Maj. Policy Coor.: Mark Paoletta, 225-2927, 2125 RHOB
Min. Counsel: Edith Holleman, 226-3400, 564 FHOB

Telecommunications and the Internet
225-2927/2125 RHOB/Fax: 225-1919

Rep: Upton, *Chair;* Bilirakis; Stearns; Gillmor; Whitfield; Cubin; Shimkus; Wilson; Pickering; Fossella; Radanovich; Bass; Walden; Terry; Ferguson; Sullivan; Blackburn
Dem: Markey, *Rnk. Mem.;* Engel; Wynn; Doyle; Gonzalez; Inslee; Boucher; Towns; Pallone; Brown; Gordon; Rush; Eshoo; Stupak
Maj. Policy Coor.: Will Nordwind, 225-2927, 2125 RHOB
Min. Counsels: Peter Filon, Johanna Shelton, 226-3400, 564 FHOB

FINANCIAL SERVICES

Phone: (202) 225-7502—Room: 2129 RHOB—Fax: 226-0682
http://financialservices.house.gov

Republicans (37)
Michael G. Oxley, 4th-OH, *Chair**
Jim Leach, 2nd-IA
Richard H. Baker, 6th-LA
Deborah Pryce, 15th-OH
Spencer Bachus, 6th-AL
Michael Castle, At Large-DE
Peter King, 3rd-NY
Ed Royce, 40th-CA
Frank D. Lucas, 3rd-OK
Bob Ney, 18th-OH
Sue W. Kelly, 19th-NY, *Vice Chair*
Ron E. Paul, 14th-TX
Paul E. Gillmor, 5th-OH
Jim R. Ryun, 2nd-KS
Steven C. LaTourette, 14th-OH
Donald A. Manzullo, 16th-IL
Walter Jones, Jr., 3rd-NC
Judy Biggert, 13th-IL
Christopher Shays, 4th-CT
Vito Fossella, 13th-NY
Gary G. Miller, 42nd-CA
Patrick J. Tiberi, 12th-OH
Mark R. Kennedy, 6th-MN
Tom Feeney, 24th-FL
Jeb Hensarling, 5th-TX
Scott Garrett, 5th-NJ
Ginny Brown-Waite, 5th-FL
J. Gresham Barrett, 3rd-SC
Katherine Harris, 13th-FL
Rick Renzi, 1st-AZ
Jim Gerlach, 6th-PA
Steve Pearce, 2nd-NM
Randy Neugebauer, 19th-TX
Tom Price, 6th-GA
Mike Fitzpatrick, 8th-PA
Geoff Davis, 4th-KY
Patrick McHenry, 10th-NC

Democrats (32)
Barney Frank, 4th-MA, *Rnk. Mem.**
Paul E. Kanjorski, 11th-PA
Maxine Waters, 35th-CA
Carolyn Maloney, 14th-NY
Luis V. Gutierrez, 4th-IL
Nydia M. Velázquez, 12th-NY
Melvin L. Watt, 12th-NC
Gary L. Ackerman, 5th-NY
Darlene Hooley, 5th-OR
Julia M. Carson, 7th-IN
Brad Sherman, 27th-CA
Gregory W. Meeks, 6th-NY
Barbara Lee, 9th-CA
Dennis Moore, 3rd-KS
Michael Capuano, 8th-MA
Harold E. Ford, Jr., 9th-TN
Rubén E. Hinojosa, 15th-TX
Joseph Crowley, 7th-NY
Wm. Lacy Clay, 1st-MO
Steve J. Israel, 2nd-NY
Carolyn McCarthy, 4th-NY
Joe Baca, 43rd-CA
Jim Matheson, 2nd-UT
Stephen F. Lynch, 9th-MA
Brad Miller, 13th-NC
David Scott, 13th-GA
Artur Davis, 7th-AL
Al Green, 9th-TX
Emanuel Cleaver, 5th-MO
Melissa L. Bean, 8th-IL
Debbie Wasserman Schultz, 20th-FL
Gwen S. Moore, 4th-WI

Independent (1)
Bernard Sanders, At Large-VT

Maj. Staff Dir.:
Bob Foster
225-7502, 2129 RHOB

Min. Staff Dir.:
Jeanne Roslanowick
225-4247, B-301C RHOB

*Ex officio members on all subcommittees.

Financial Services Subcommittees

Capital Markets, Insurance, and Government Sponsored Enterprises
225-7502/2129 RHOB/Fax: 225-9040
Rep: Baker, *Chair;* Ryun, *Vice Chair;* Shays; Gillmor; Bachus; Castle; King; Lucas; Manzullo; Royce; Kelly; Ney; Fossella; Biggert; Miller; Kennedy; Tiberi; Barrett; Brown-Waite; Feeney; Gerlach; Harris; Hensarling; Renzi; Davis; Fitzpatrick
Dem: Kanjorski, *Rnk. Mem.;* Ackerman; Hooley; Sherman; Meeks; Moore (KS); Capuano; Ford; Hinojosa; Crowley; Israel; Clay; McCarthy; Baca; Matheson; Lynch; Miller; Scott; Velázquez; Watt; Davis; Bean; Wasserman Schultz
Maj. Sr. Counsel: Vacant, 225-7502, B-303 RHOB
Min. Staff Dir.: Todd Harper, 225-4247, B-301C RHOB

Financial Services Subcommittees

Domestic and International Monetary Policy, Trade, and Technology
225-7502/2129 RHOB/Fax: 225-6635
Rep: Pryce, *Chair;* Biggert, *Vice Chair;* Leach; Castle; Lucas; Paul; LaTourette; Manzullo; Kennedy; Harris; Gerlach; Neugebauer; Price; McHenry
Dem: Maloney, *Rnk. Mem.;* Watt; Waters; Lee; Kanjorski; Sherman; Gutierrez; Bean; Wasserman Schultz; Moore (WI); Crowley
Ind: Sanders
Maj. Sr. Counsel: Vacant, 225-7502, B-303 RHOB
Min. Staff Dir.: Eleni Constantine, 225-4247, B-301C RHOB

Financial Institutions and Consumer Credit
225-7502/2129 RHOB/Fax: 225-3692
Rep: Bachus, *Chair;* Jones, *Vice Chair;* Baker; Castle; Royce; Lucas; Kelly; Paul; Gillmor; Ryun; LaTourette; Biggert; Fossella; Miller; Tiberi; Feeney; Hensarling; Garrett; Brown-Waite; Barrett; Renzi; Pearce; Neugebauer; Price; McHenry
Dem: Maloney; Watt; Ackerman; Sherman; Meeks; Gutierrez; Moore (KS); Kanjorski; Waters; Hooley; Carson; Ford; Hinojosa; Crowley; Israel; McCarthy; Baca; Green; Moore (WI); Clay; Matheson
Ind: Sanders, *Rnk. Mem.*
Maj. Sr. Counsel: Jim Klinger, 225-7502, B-303 RHOB
Min. Staff Dir.: Warren Gunnels, 225-4247, B-301C RHOB

Housing and Community Opportunity
225-7502/B-303 RHOB/Fax: 225-6635
Rep: Ney, *Chair;* Miller, *Vice Chair;* Baker; King; Jones; Shays; Tiberi; Brown-Waite; Harris; Renzi; Pearce; Neugebauer; Fitzpatrick; Davis
Dem: Waters, *Rnk. Mem.;* Velázquez; Carson; Lee; Capuano; Lynch; Miller; Scott; Davis; Cleaver; Green
Ind: Sanders
Maj. Sr. Counsel: Clinton Jones, 225-7502, B-303 RHOB
Min. Staff Dir.: Jeanne Roslanowick, 225-4247, B-301C RHOB

Oversight and Investigations
225-7502/137-9 FHOB/Fax: 225-6635
Rep: Kelly, *Chair;* Paul, *Vice Chair;* Royce; LaTourette; Kennedy; Garrett; Barrett; Price; Fitzpatrick; Davis; McHenry
Dem: Gutierrez, *Rnk. Mem.;* Moore (KS); Maloney; Lynch; Davis; Cleaver; Scott; Wasserman Schultz; Moore (WI)
Maj. Sr. Counsel: Vacant, 225-7502, B-303 RHOB
Min. Staff Dir.: Kellie Larkin, 225-4247, B-301C RHOB

GOVERNMENT REFORM

Phone: (202) 225-5074—Room: 2157 RHOB—Fax: 225-3974
http://reform.house.gov

Republicans (23)
Thomas M. Davis III, 11th-VA, *Chair**
Dan Burton, 5th-IN
Christopher Shays, 4th-CT, *Vice Chair*
Ileana Ros-Lehtinen, 18th-FL
John McHugh, 23rd-NY
John Mica, 7th-FL
Gil Gutknecht, 1st-MN
Mark Souder, 3rd-IN
Steven C. LaTourette, 14th-OH
Todd R. Platts, 19th-PA
Chris Cannon, 3rd-UT
John J. Duncan, Jr., 2nd-TN
Candice Miller, 10th-MI
Michael Turner, 3rd-OH
Darrell Issa, 49th-CA
Ginny Brown-Waite, 5th-FL
Jon C. Porter, 3rd-NV
Kenny Marchant, 24th-TX
Lynn A. Westmoreland, 8th-GA
Patrick McHenry, 10th-NC
Charles W. Dent, 15th-PA
Virginia Foxx, 5th-NC
Vacancy

Democrats (17)
Henry A. Waxman, 30th-CA, *Rnk. Mem.**
Tom Lantos, 12th-CA
Major R. Owens, 11th-NY
Edolphus Towns, 10th-NY
Paul E. Kanjorski, 11th-PA
Carolyn Maloney, 14th-NY
Elijah Cummings, 7th-MD
Dennis J. Kucinich, 10th-OH
Danny K. Davis, 7th-IL
Wm. Lacy Clay, 1st-MO
Diane Watson, 33rd-CA
Stephen F. Lynch, 9th-MA
Chris Van Hollen, Jr., 8th-MD
Linda T. Sánchez, 39th-CA
C.A. Ruppersberger, 2nd-MD
Brian M. Higgins, 27th-NY
Eleanor Holmes Norton, DC

Independent (1)
Bernard Sanders, At Large-VT

Maj. Staff Dir.:
Melissa Wojciak
225-5074, 2157 RHOB

Min. Staff Dir.:
Phil Barnett
225-5051, B-350A RHOB

*Ex officio members on all subcommittees of which they are not regular members.

Government Reform Subcommittees

Criminal Justice, Drug Policy and Human Resources
225-2577/B-377 RHOB/Fax: 225-1154
Rep: Souder, *Chair;* McHenry, *Vice Chair;* Burton; Mica; Gutknecht; LaTourette; Cannon; Miller; Brown-Waite
Dem: Cummings, *Rnk. Mem.;* Davis; Watson; Sánchez; Ruppersberger; Owens; Vacancy
Ind: Sanders
Maj. Staff Dir.: Marc Wheat, 225-2577, B-377 RHOB
Min. Staff Dir.: Phil Barnett, 225-5051, B-350A RHOB

Energy and Resources
225-6427/349C RHOB/Fax: 225-2392
Rep: Issa, *Chair;* Westmoreland, *Vice Chair;* Ros-Lehtinen; McHugh; McHenry; Marchant
Dem: Watson, *Rnk. Mem.;* Higgins; Lantos; Kucinich
Maj. Staff Dir.: Larry Brady, 225-6427, 349C RHOB
Min. Staff Dir.: Phil Barnett, 225-5051, B-350A RHOB

Federal Workforce and Agency Organization
225-5147/B-373A RHOB/Fax: 225-2373
Rep: Porter, *Chair;* Mica, *Vice Chair;* Davis; Issa; Marchant; McHenry; Vacancy
Dem: Davis, *Rnk. Mem.;* Owens; Norton; Cummings; Van Hollen
Maj. Staff Dir.: Ron Martinson, 225-5147, B-373A RHOB
Min. Staff Dir.: Phil Barnett, 225-5051, B-350A RHOB

Federalism and the Census
225-6751/B-349A RHOB/Fax: 225-4960
Rep: Turner, *Chair;* Dent, *Vice Chair;* Shays; Foxx; Vacancy
Dem: Clay, *Rnk. Mem.;* Kanjorski; Maloney
Maj. Staff Dir.: John Buaderes, 225-6751, B-349A RHOB
Min. Staff Dir.: Phil Barnett, 225-5051, B-350A RHOB

Government Reform Subcommittees

Government Management, Finance and Accountability
225-3741/B-371C RHOB/Fax: 225-2544

Rep: Platts, *Chair;* Foxx, *Vice Chair;* Davis; Gutknecht; Duncan; Dent
Dem: Towns, *Rnk. Mem.;* Owens; Kanjorski; Maloney
Maj. Staff Dir.: Mike Hettinger, 225-3741, B-371C RHOB
Min. Staff Dir.: Phil Barnett, 225-5051, B-350A RHOB

National Security, Emerging Threats and International Relations
225-2548/B-372 RHOB/Fax: 225-2382

Rep: Shays, *Chair;* Marchant, *Vice Chair;* Burton; Ros-Lehtinen; McHugh; LaTourette; Platts; Duncan; Porter; Dent
Dem: Kucinich, *Rnk. Mem.;* Lantos; Maloney; Van Hollen; Sánchez; Ruppersberger; Lynch; Higgins
Ind: Sanders
Maj. Staff Dir.: Larry Halloran, 225-2548, B-372 RHOB
Min. Staff Dir.: Phil Barnett, 225-5051, B-350A RHOB

Regulatory Affairs
225-4407/B-373B RHOB/Fax: 225-2441

Rep: Miller, *Chair;* Brown-Waite, *Vice Chair;* Souder; Cannon; Turner; Westmoreland
Dem: Lynch, *Rnk. Mem.;* Clay; Norton; Van Hollen
Maj. Staff Dir.: Ed Schrock, 225-4407, B-373B RHOB
Min. Staff Dir.: Phil Barnett, 225-5051, B-350A RHOB

HOMELAND SECURITY

Phone: (202) 226-8417—Room: 202 ALOC—Fax: 226-3399
http://homeland.house.gov

Republicans (19)
Christopher Cox, 48th-CA, *Chair**
Don Young, At Large-AK
Lamar S. Smith, 21st-TX
Curt Weldon, 7th-PA
Christopher Shays, 4th-CT
Peter King, 3rd-NY
John Linder, 7th-GA
Mark Souder, 3rd-IN
Thomas M. Davis III, 11th-VA
Dan Lungren, 3rd-CA
James A. Gibbons, 2nd-NV
Robert R. Simmons, 2nd-CT
Michael D. Rogers, 3rd-AL
Steve Pearce, 2nd-NM
Katherine Harris, 13th-FL
Bobby Jindal, 1st-LA
Dave Reichert, 8th-WA
Michael McCaul, 10th-TX
Charles W. Dent, 15th-PA

Democrats (15)
Bennie G. Thompson, 2nd-MS, *Rnk. Mem.**
Loretta Sanchez, 47th-CA
Edward J. Markey, 7th-MA
Norman D. Dicks, 6th-WA
Jane Harman, 36th-CA
Peter A. DeFazio, 4th-OR
Nita M. Lowey, 18th-NY
Eleanor Holmes Norton, DC
Zoe Lofgren, 16th-CA
Sheila Jackson Lee, 18th-TX
Bill Pascrell, Jr., 8th-NJ
Donna M. Christensen, VI
Bob Etheridge, 2nd-NC
James R. Langevin, 2nd-RI
Kendrick B. Meek, 17th-FL

Maj. Staff Dir.:
Ben Cohen
226-8417, 202 ALOC

Min. Staff Dir.:
Calvin Humphrey
226-2616, 228 ALOC

*Ex officio members on all subcommittees.

Homeland Security Subcommittees

Economic Security, Infrastructure Protection, and Cybersecurity
226-8417/202 ALOC/Fax: 226-3399

Rep: Lungren, *Chair;* Young; Smith; Linder; Souder; Davis; Rogers; Pearce; Harris; Jindal
Dem: Sanchez, *Rnk. Mem.;* Markey; Dicks; DeFazio; Lofgren; Jackson Lee; Pascrell; Langevin
Maj. Staff Dir.: Ben Cohen, 226-8417, 202 ALOC
Min. Staff Dir.: Calvin Humphrey, 226-2616, 228 ALOC

Homeland Security Subcommittees

Emergency Preparedness, Science, and Technology
226-8417/202 ALOC/Fax: 226-3399

Rep: King, *Chair;* Smith; Weldon; Simmons; Rogers; Pearce; Harris; Reichert; McCaul; Dent
Dem: Pascrell, *Rnk. Mem.;* Sanchez; Dicks; Harman; Lowey; Norton; Christensen; Etheridge
Maj. Staff Dir.: Ben Cohen, 226-8417, 202 ALOC
Min. Staff Dir.: Calvin Humphrey, 226-2616, 228 ALOC

Intelligence, Information Sharing, and Terrorism Risk Assessment
226-8417/202 ALOC/Fax: 226-3399

Rep: Simmons, *Chair;* Weldon; King; Souder; Lungren; Gibbons; Pearce; Jindal; Reichert; Dent
Dem: Lofgren, *Rnk. Mem.;* Sanchez; Harman; Lowey; Jackson Lee; Etheridge; Langevin; Meek
Maj. Staff Dir.: Ben Cohen, 226-8417, 202 ALOC
Min. Staff Dir.: Calvin Humphrey, 226-2616, 228 ALOC

Management, Integration, and Oversight
226-8417/202 ALOC/Fax: 226-3399

Rep: Rogers, *Chair;* Shays; Linder; Davis; Harris; Reichert; McCaul; Dent
Dem: Meek, *Rnk. Mem.;* Markey; Lofgren; Jackson Lee; Pascrell; Christensen
Maj. Staff Dir.: Ben Cohen, 226-8417, 202 ALOC
Min. Staff Dir.: Calvin Humphrey, 226-2616, 228 ALOC

Prevention of Nuclear and Biological Attacks
226-8417/202 ALOC/Fax: 226-3399

Rep: Linder, *Chair;* Young; Shays; Lungren; Gibbons; Simmons; Jindal; McCaul
Dem: Langevin, *Rnk. Mem.;* Markey; Dicks; Harman; Norton; Christensen
Maj. Staff Dir.: Ben Cohen, 226-8417, 202 ALOC
Min. Staff Dir.: Calvin Humphrey, 226-2616, 228 ALOC

HOUSE ADMINISTRATION

Phone: (202) 225-8281—Room: 1309 LHOB—Fax: 225-9957
http://www.house.gov/cha

Republicans (6)
Bob Ney, 18th-OH, ***Chair***
Vernon Ehlers, 3rd-MI
John Mica, 7th-FL
John T. Doolittle, 4th-CA
Thomas Reynolds, 26th-NY
Candice Miller, 10th-MI

Democrats (3)
Juanita Millender-McDonald, 37th-CA, ***Rnk. Mem.***
Robert A. Brady, 1st-PA
Zoe Lofgren, 16th-CA

Maj. Staff Dir.:
Paul Vinovich
225-8281, 1309 LHOB

Min. Staff Dir.:
George Shevlin
225-2061, 1216 LHOB

NO SUBCOMMITTEES

INTERNATIONAL RELATIONS

Phone: (202) 225-5021—Room: 2170 RHOB—Fax: 225-2035
http://www.house.gov/international_relations

Republicans (27)
Henry J. Hyde, 6th-IL, *Chair**
Jim Leach, 2nd-IA
Christopher H. Smith, 4th-NJ, *Vice Chair*
Dan Burton, 5th-IN
Elton Gallegly, 24th-CA
Ileana Ros-Lehtinen, 18th-FL
Dana Rohrabacher, 46th-CA
Ed Royce, 40th-CA
Peter King, 3rd-NY
Steve Chabot, 1st-OH
Thomas G. Tancredo, 6th-CO
Ron E. Paul, 14th-TX
Darrell Issa, 49th-CA
Jeff Flake, 6th-AZ
Jo Ann S. Davis, 1st-VA
Mark Green, 8th-WI
Jerry Weller, 11th-IL
Mike Pence, 6th-IN
Thaddeus G. McCotter, 11th-MI
Katherine Harris, 13th-FL
Joe Wilson, 2nd-SC
John Boozman, 3rd-AR
J. Gresham Barrett, 3rd-SC
Connie Mack, 14th-FL
Jeff Fortenberry, 1st-NE
Michael McCaul, 10th-TX
Ted Poe, 2nd-TX

Democrats (23)
Tom Lantos, 12th-CA, *Rnk. Mem.**
Howard L. Berman, 28th-CA
Gary L. Ackerman, 5th-NY
Eni F.H. Faleomavaega, AS
Donald M. Payne, 10th-NJ
Robert Menendez, 13th-NJ
Sherrod Brown, 13th-OH
Brad Sherman, 27th-CA
Robert I. Wexler, 19th-FL
Eliot Engel, 17th-NY
William Delahunt, 10th-MA
Gregory W. Meeks, 6th-NY
Barbara Lee, 9th-CA
Joseph Crowley, 7th-NY
Earl Blumenauer, 3rd-OR
Shelley Berkley, 1st-NV
Grace F. Napolitano, 38th-CA
Adam Schiff, 29th-CA
Diane Watson, 33rd-CA
Adam Smith, 9th-WA
Betty McCollum, 4th-MN
Ben Chandler, 6th-KY
Dennis Cardoza, 18th-CA

Maj. Staff Dir. & General Counsel:
Tom Mooney
225-5021, 2170 RHOB

Min. Staff Dir.:
Robert King
225-6735, B-360 RHOB

*Ex officio members on all subcommittees.

International Relations Subcommittees

Africa, Global Human Rights and International Operations
226-7812/255 FHOB/Fax: 225-7491
Rep: Smith, *Chair;* Tancredo; Flake; Green; Boozman; Fortenberry; Royce, *Vice Chair*
Dem: Payne, *Rnk. Mem.;* Lee; McCollum; Sherman; Meeks; Watson
Maj. Staff Dir.: Mary Noonan, 226-7812, 255 FHOB
Min. Prof. Staff Mem.: Noelle Lusane, 226-7812, 255 FHOB

Asia and the Pacific
226-7825/B-358 RHOB/Fax: 226-7829
Rep: Leach, *Chair;* Burton, *Vice Chair;* Gallegly; Rohrabacher; Chabot; Paul; Wilson
Dem: Faleomavaega, *Rnk. Mem.;* Brown; Blumenauer; Watson; Smith; Ackerman
Maj. Staff Dir.: James McCormick, 226-7825, B-358 RHOB
Min. Prof. Staff Mem.: Lisa Williams, 225-8577, 2422 RHOB

Europe and Emerging Threats
226-7820/257 FHOB/Fax: 226-2722
Rep: Gallegly, *Chair;* Davis; King, *Vice Chair;* McCotter; Issa; Poe; Barrett
Dem: Wexler, *Rnk. Mem.;* Engel; Berkley; Napolitano; Smith; Chandler
Maj. Staff Dir.: Richard Mereu, 226-7820, 257 FHOB
Min. Prof. Staff Mem.: Jonathan Katz, 226-7820, 257 FHOB

International Relations Subcommittees

International Terrorism and Nonproliferation
226-1500/253 FHOB/Fax: 226-4948

Rep: Royce, *Chair;* King; Tancredo; Issa, *Vice Chair;* McCaul; Poe; Weller; Barrett
Dem: Sherman, *Rnk. Mem.;* Menendez; Wexler; Crowley; McCollum; Cardoza; Watson
Maj. Staff Dir.: Tom Sheehy, 226-1500, 253 FHOB
Min. Staff Dir.: Don McDonald, 226-1500, 253 FHOB

Middle East and Central Asia
225-3345/259A FHOB/Fax: 225-0432

Rep: Ros-Lehtinen, *Chair;* Chabot, *Vice Chair;* McCotter; Boozman; Mack; Fortenberry; Davis; Pence; Harris; Issa
Dem: Ackerman, *Rnk. Mem.;* Berman; Engel; Crowley; Berkley; Schiff; Chandler; Cardoza
Maj. Staff Dir.: Yleem Poblete, 225-3345, 259A FHOB
Min. Prof. Staff Mem.: David Adams, 225-3345, 259A FHOB

Oversight and Investigations
225-5021/2170 RHOB/Fax: 225-2035

Rep: Rohrabacher, *Chair;* Royce; Flake, *Vice Chair;* Green; Pence; Wilson
Dem: Delahunt, *Rnk. Mem.;* Berman; Blumenauer; Schiff
Maj. Staff Dir.: Vacant, 225-5021, 2170 RHOB
Min. Prof. Staff Mem.: Vacant, 225-5021, 2170 RHOB

Western Hemisphere
226-9980/259A FHOB/Fax: 225-7485

Rep: Burton, *Chair;* Paul; Weller, *Vice Chair;* Harris; Leach; Smith; Ros-Lehtinen; Mack; McCaul
Dem: Menendez, *Rnk. Mem.;* Napolitano; Meeks; Faleomavaega; Payne; Delahunt; Lee
Maj. Staff Dir.: Mark Walker, 226-9980, 259A FHOB
Min. Prof. Staff Mem.: Jessica Lewis, 226-9980, 259A FHOB

JUDICIARY

Phone: (202) 225-3951—Room: 2138 RHOB—Fax: 225-7682
http://judiciary.house.gov

Republicans (23)
F. James Sensenbrenner, Jr., 5th-WI, ***Chair*****
Henry J. Hyde, 6th-IL
Howard Coble, 6th-NC
Lamar S. Smith, 21st-TX
Elton Gallegly, 24th-CA
Bob Goodlatte, 6th-VA
Steve Chabot, 1st-OH
Dan Lungren, 3rd-CA
William L. Jenkins, 1st-TN
Chris Cannon, 3rd-UT
Spencer Bachus, 6th-AL
Bob Inglis, 4th-SC
John N. Hostettler, 8th-IN
Mark Green, 8th-WI
Ric Keller, 8th-FL
Darrell Issa, 49th-CA
Jeff Flake, 6th-AZ
Mike Pence, 6th-IN
Randy Forbes, 4th-VA
Steve King, 5th-IA
Tom Feeney, 24th-FL
Trent Franks, 2nd-AZ
Louie Gohmert, 1st-TX

Democrats (17)
John Conyers, Jr., 14th-MI, ***Rnk. Mem.*****
Howard L. Berman, 28th-CA
Rick Boucher, 9th-VA
Jerrold Nadler, 8th-NY
Bobby Scott, 3rd-VA
Melvin L. Watt, 12th-NC
Zoe Lofgren, 16th-CA
Sheila Jackson Lee, 18th-TX
Maxine Waters, 35th-CA
Marty Meehan, 5th-MA
William Delahunt, 10th-MA
Robert I. Wexler, 19th-FL
Anthony D. Weiner, 9th-NY
Adam Schiff, 29th-CA
Linda T. Sánchez, 39th-CA
Adam Smith, 9th-WA
Chris Van Hollen, Jr., 8th-MD

Maj. Chief of Staff & General Counsel:
Philip Kiko
225-3951, 2138 RHOB

Min. Chief of Staff & Counsel:
Perry Apelbaum
225-6504, 2142 RHOB

*Ex officio members on all subcommittees of which they are not regular members.

Judiciary Subcommittees

Commercial and Administrative Law
225-2825/B-353 RHOB/Fax: 225-4299

Rep: Cannon, *Chair;* Coble; Franks; Chabot; Green; Forbes; Gohmert
Dem: Watt, *Rnk. Mem.;* Delahunt; Smith; Van Hollen; Nadler
Maj. Chief Counsel: Raymond Smietanka, 225-2825, B-353 RHOB
Min. Counsel: Stephanie Moore, 225-6906, B-351C RHOB

Constitution
226-7680/362 FHOB/Fax: 225-3746

Rep: Chabot, *Chair;* Franks; Jenkins; Bachus; Hostettler; Green; King; Feeney
Dem: Nadler, *Rnk. Mem.;* Conyers; Scott; Watt; Van Hollen
Maj. Chief Counsel: Paul Taylor, 226-7680, 362 FHOB
Min. Prof. Staff Mem.: David Lachmann, 225-2022, B-336 RHOB

Courts, the Internet and Intellectual Property
225-5741/B-352 RHOB/Fax: 225-3673

Rep: Smith, *Chair;* Hyde; Gallegly; Goodlatte; Jenkins; Bachus; Inglis; Keller; Issa; Cannon; Pence; Forbes
Dem: Berman, *Rnk. Mem.;* Conyers; Boucher; Lofgren; Waters; Meehan; Wexler; Weiner; Schiff; Sánchez
Maj. Chief Counsel: Blaine Merritt, 225-5741, B-352 RHOB
Min. Counsel: Alec French, 225-2022, B-336 RHOB

Crime, Terrorism and Homeland Security
225-3926/207 CHOB/Fax: 225-3737

Rep: Coble, *Chair;* Lungren; Green; Feeney; Chabot; Keller; Flake; Pence; Forbes; Gohmert
Dem: Scott, *Rnk. Mem.;* Jackson Lee; Waters; Meehan; Delahunt; Weiner
Maj. Chief Counsel: Jay Apperson, 225-3926, 207 CHOB
Min. Counsel: Bobby Vassar, 225-2022, B-336 RHOB

Immigration, Border Security and Claims
225-5727/B-370B RHOB/Fax: 225-3672

Rep: Hostettler, *Chair;* King; Gohmert; Smith; Gallegly; Goodlatte; Lungren; Flake; Inglis; Issa
Dem: Jackson Lee, *Rnk. Mem.;* Berman; Lofgren; Sánchez; Waters; Meehan
Maj. Chief Counsel: George Fishman, 225-5727, B-370B RHOB
Min. Counsel: Nolan Rappaport, 225-6906, B-351C RHOB

RESOURCES

Phone: (202) 225-2761—Room: 1324 LHOB—Fax: 225-5929
http://resourcescommittee.house.gov

Republicans (27)
Richard Pombo, 11th-CA, *Chair**
Don Young, At Large-AK
Jim Saxton, 3rd-NJ
Elton Gallegly, 24th-CA
John J. Duncan, Jr., 2nd-TN
Wayne Gilchrest, 1st-MD
Ken Calvert, 44th-CA
Barbara Cubin, At Large-WY, *Vice Chair*
George P. Radanovich, 19th-CA
Walter Jones, Jr., 3rd-NC
Chris Cannon, 3rd-UT
John E. Peterson, 5th-PA
James A. Gibbons, 2nd-NV
Greg Walden, 2nd-OR
Thomas G. Tancredo, 6th-CO
J.D. Hayworth, 5th-AZ
Jeff Flake, 6th-AZ
Rick Renzi, 1st-AZ
Steve Pearce, 2nd-NM
Devin Nunes, 21st-CA
Henry E. Brown, Jr., 1st-SC
Thelma D. Drake, 2nd-VA
Luis Fortuño, PR
Cathy McMorris, 5th-WA
Bobby Jindal, 1st-LA
Louie Gohmert, 1st-TX
Marilyn Musgrave, 4th-CO

Democrats (22)
Nick J. Rahall II, 3rd-WV, *Rnk. Mem.**
Dale E. Kildee, 5th-MI
Eni F.H. Faleomavaega, AS
Neil Abercrombie, 1st-HI
Solomon P. Ortiz, 27th-TX
Frank Pallone, Jr., 6th-NJ
Donna M. Christensen, VI
Ron J. Kind, 3rd-WI
Grace F. Napolitano, 38th-CA
Tom Udall, 3rd-NM
Raúl M. Grijalva, 7th-AZ
Madeleine Z. Bordallo, GU
Jim Costa, 20th-CA
Charlie Melancon, 3rd-LA
Dan Boren, 2nd-OK
George Miller, 7th-CA
Edward J. Markey, 7th-MA
Peter A. DeFazio, 4th-OR
Jay Inslee, 1st-WA
Mark Udall, 2nd-CO
Dennis Cardoza, 18th-CA
Stephanie Herseth, At Large-SD

Maj. Chief of Staff:
Steve Ding
225-2761, 1324 LHOB

Min. Staff Dir.:
Jim Zoia
225-6065, 1329 LHOB

*Ex officio members on all subcommittees.

Resources Subcommittees

Energy and Mineral Resources
225-9297/1626 LHOB/Fax: 225-5255
Rep: Gibbons, *Chair;* Young; Cubin; Cannon; Peterson; Pearce; Drake; Jindal; Gohmert
Dem: Grijalva, *Rnk. Mem.;* Faleomavaega; Ortiz; Costa; Melancon; Boren; Markey
Maj. Staff Dir.: Jay Cranford, 225-9297, 1626 LHOB
Min. Staff Dir.: Deborah Lanzone, 226-2311, 186 FHOB

Fisheries and Oceans
226-0200/188 FHOB/Fax: 225-1542
Rep: Gilchrest, *Chair;* Young; Saxton; Jones; Drake; Fortuño; Jindal; Musgrave
Dem: Pallone, *Rnk. Mem.;* Faleomavaega; Abercrombie; Ortiz; Kind; Bordallo
Maj. Staff Dir.: Harry Burroughs, 226-0200, 188 FHOB
Min. Prof. Staff Mem.: Dave Jansen, 226-2311, 186 FHOB

Forests and Forest Health
225-0691/1337 LHOB/Fax: 225-0521
Rep: Walden, *Chair;* Duncan; Gilchrest; Cannon; Peterson; Tancredo; Hayworth; Flake; Renzi; Brown; McMorris
Dem: Udall (NM), *Rnk. Mem.;* Kildee; Abercrombie; Boren; DeFazio; Inslee; Udall (CO); Cardoza; Herseth
Maj. Staff Dir.: Doug Crandall, 225-0691, 1337 LHOB
Min. Prof. Staff Mems.: Meghan Conklin, Amelia Jenkins, 226-2311, 186 FHOB

Resources Subcommittees

National Parks
226-7736/1333 LHOB/Fax: 226-2301

Rep: Nunes, *Chair;* Saxton; Gallegly; Duncan; Radanovich; Jones; Brown; Fortuño; Musgrave
Dem: Christensen, *Rnk. Mem.;* Kildee; Abercrombie; Kind; Udall (NM); Bordallo; Melancon
Maj. Staff Dir.: Rob Howarth, 226-7736, 1333 LHOB
Min. Prof. Staff Mems.: Rick Healy, David Watkins, 226-2311, 186 FHOB

Water and Power
225-8331/1522 LHOB/Fax: 226-6953

Rep: Radanovich, *Chair;* Calvert; Cubin; Walden; Tancredo; Hayworth; Pearce; Nunes; McMorris; Gohmert
Dem: Napolitano, *Rnk. Mem.;* Grijalva; Costa; Miller; Udall (CO); Cardoza; Vacancy; Vacancy
Maj. Staff Dir.: Kiel Weaver, 225-8331, 1522 LHOB
Min. Prof. Staff Mems.: Steve Lanich, Lori Sonken, 226-2311, 186 FHOB

RULES

Phone: (202) 225-9191—Room: H-312 Capitol—Fax: 225-6763
http://www.house.gov/rules

Republicans (9)
David Dreier, 26th-CA, **Chair**
Lincoln Diaz-Balart, 21st-FL
Doc Hastings, 4th-WA
Pete Sessions, 32nd-TX
Adam Putnam, 12th-FL
Shelley Moore Capito, 2nd-WV
Tom Cole, 4th-OK
Rob Bishop, 1st-UT
Phil Gingrey, 11th-GA

Democrats (4)
Louise McIntosh Slaughter, 28th-NY, **Rnk. Mem.**
James P. McGovern, 3rd-MA
Alcee L. Hastings, 23rd-FL
Doris Matsui, 5th-CA

Maj. Staff Dir.:
Hugh Halpern
225-9191, H-312 Capitol

Min. Staff Dir.:
John Daniel
225-9091, H-152 Capitol

Rules Subcommittees

Legislative and Budget Process
225-9191/H-312 Capitol/Fax: 225-6763

Rep: Diaz-Balart, *Chair;* Sessions, *Vice Chair;* Bishop; Gingrey; Dreier
Dem: Hastings, *Rnk. Mem.;* Slaughter
Maj. Staff Dir.: Hugh Halpern, 225-9191, H-312 Capitol
Min. Staff Dir.: John Daniel, 225-9091, H-152 Capitol

Rules and Organization of the House
225-9191/H-312 Capitol/Fax: 225-6763

Rep: Hastings, *Chair;* Putnam, *Vice Chair;* Capito; Cole; Dreier
Dem: McGovern, *Rnk. Mem.;* Slaughter
Maj. Staff Dir.: Hugh Halpern, 225-9191, H-312 Capitol
Min. Staff Dir.: John Daniel, 225-9091, H-152 Capitol

SCIENCE

Phone: (202) 225-6371—Room: 2320 RHOB—Fax: 226-0113
http://www.house.gov/science

Republicans (24)
Sherwood L. Boehlert,
  24th-NY, *Chair**
Ralph M. Hall, 4th-TX
Lamar S. Smith, 21st-TX
Curt Weldon, 7th-PA
Dana Rohrabacher, 46th-CA
Ken Calvert, 44th-CA
Roscoe Bartlett, 6th-MD
Vernon Ehlers, 3rd-MI
Gil Gutknecht, 1st-MN
Frank D. Lucas, 3rd-OK
Judy Biggert, 13th-IL
Wayne Gilchrest, 1st-MD
Todd Akin, 2nd-MO
Timothy V. Johnson, 15th-IL
Randy Forbes, 4th-VA
Jo Bonner, 1st-AL
Tom Feeney, 24th-FL
Bob Inglis, 4th-SC
Dave Reichert, 8th-WA
Mike Sodrel, 9th-IN
Joe Schwarz, 7th-MI
Michael McCaul, 10th-TX
Vacancy
Vacancy

Democrats (20)
Bart Gordon, 6th-TN,
  Rnk. Mem.*
Jerry F. Costello, 12th-IL
Eddie Bernice Johnson, 30th-TX
Lynn Woolsey, 6th-CA
Darlene Hooley, 5th-OR
Mark Udall, 2nd-CO
David Wu, 1st-OR
Michael M. Honda, 15th-CA
Brad Miller, 13th-NC
Lincoln Davis, 4th-TN
Russ Carnahan, 3rd-MO
Dan Lipinski, 3rd-IL
Sheila Jackson Lee, 18th-TX
Brad Sherman, 27th-CA
Brian Baird, 3rd-WA
Jim Matheson, 2nd-UT
Jim Costa, 20th-CA
Al Green, 9th-TX
Charlie Melancon, 3rd-LA
Vacancy

Maj. Chief of Staff:
David Goldston
225-6371, 2320 RHOB

Min. Staff Dir.:
Chuck Atkins
225-6375, 394 FHOB

*Ex officio members on all subcommittees.

Science Subcommittees

Energy
225-9662/390 FHOB/Fax: 226-6983

Rep: Biggert, *Chair;* Hall; Weldon; Bartlett; Ehlers; Akin; Bonner; Inglis; Reichert; Sodrel; Schwarz
Dem: Honda, *Rnk. Mem.;* Woolsey; Davis; Costello; Johnson; Lipinski; Matheson; Jackson Lee; Sherman; Green
Maj. Staff Dir.: Kevin Carroll, 225-9662, 390 FHOB
Min. Prof. Staff Mem.: Charlie Cook, 225-6375, 394 FHOB

Environment, Technology and Standards
225-8844/2319 RHOB/Fax: 225-4438

Rep: Ehlers, *Chair;* Gutknecht; Biggert; Gilchrest; Johnson; Reichert; Schwarz
Dem: Wu, *Rnk. Mem.;* Miller; Udall; Davis; Baird; Matheson
Maj. Staff Dir.: Eric Webster, 225-8844, 2319 RHOB
Min. Prof. Staff Mem.: Michael Quear, 225-8844, 2319 RHOB

Research
225-7858/B-374 RHOB/Fax: 225-7815

Rep: Inglis, *Chair;* Smith; Weldon; Rohrabacher; Gutknecht; Lucas; Akin; Johnson; Reichert; Sodrel; McCaul
Dem: Hooley, *Rnk. Mem.;* Carnahan; Lipinski; Baird; Melancon; Johnson; Vacancy; Vacancy; Vacancy; Vacancy
Maj. Staff Dir.: Dan Byers, 225-7858, B-374 RHOB
Min. Prof. Staff Mem.: Jim Wilson, 225-7858, B-374 RHOB

Space and Aeronautics
225-7858/B-374 RHOB/Fax: 225-6415

Rep: Calvert, *Chair;* Hall; Smith; Rohrabacher; Bartlett; Lucas; Forbes; Bonner; Feeney; McCaul
Dem: Udall, *Rnk. Mem.;* Wu; Honda; Miller; Jackson Lee; Sherman; Costa; Green; Melancon
Maj. Staff Dir.: Bill Adkins, 225-7858, B-374 RHOB
Min. Prof. Staff Mem.: Richard Obermann, 225-7858, B-374 RHOB

SMALL BUSINESS

Phone: (202) 225-5821—Room: 2361 RHOB—Fax: 225-3587
http://www.house.gov/smbiz

Republicans (18)
Donald A. Manzullo, 16th-IL, *Chair**
Roscoe Bartlett, 6th-MD
Sue W. Kelly, 19th-NY
Steve Chabot, 1st-OH
Sam Graves, 6th-MO
Todd Akin, 2nd-MO
Bill Shuster, 9th-PA
Steve King, 5th-IA
Marilyn Musgrave, 4th-CO
Jeb Bradley, 1st-NH
Thaddeus G. McCotter, 11th-MI
Ric Keller, 8th-FL
Ted Poe, 2nd-TX
Mike Sodrel, 9th-IN
Jeff Fortenberry, 1st-NE
Mike Fitzpatrick, 8th-PA
Lynn A. Westmoreland, 8th-GA
Louie Gohmert, 1st-TX

Democrats (15)
Nydia M. Velázquez, 12th-NY, *Rnk. Mem.**
Juanita Millender-McDonald, 37th-CA
Tom Udall, 3rd-NM
Dan Lipinski, 3rd-IL
Eni F.H. Faleomavaega, AS
Danny K. Davis, 7th-IL
Donna M. Christensen, VI
Ed Case, 2nd-HI
Madeleine Z. Bordallo, GU
Raúl M. Grijalva, 7th-AZ
Michael H. Michaud, 2nd-ME
Linda T. Sánchez, 39th-CA
John Barrow, 12th-GA
Melissa L. Bean, 8th-IL
Gwen S. Moore, 4th-WI

Maj. Chief of Staff & Chief Counsel:
Matthew Szymanski
225-5821, 2361 RHOB

Min. Staff Dir.:
Michael Day
225-4038, B-343C RHOB

*Ex officio members on all subcommittees.

Small Business Subcommittees

Regulatory Reform and Oversight
225-5821/2361 RHOB/Fax: 225-3587

Rep: Akin, *Chair;* Sodrel; Westmoreland; Gohmert; Kelly; King; Poe
Dem: Bordallo, *Rnk. Mem.;* Faleomavaega; Christensen; Case
Maj. Staff Dir.: Joe Hartz, 225-5821, 2361 RHOB
Min. Staff Dir.: Michael Day, 225-4038, B-343C RHOB

Rural Enterprises, Agriculture and Technology
225-5821/B-363 RHOB/Fax: 225-3587

Rep: Graves, *Chair;* King; Bartlett; Sodrel; Fortenberry; Fitzpatrick
Dem: Barrow, *Rnk. Mem.;* Udall; Case; Michaud
Maj. Staff Dir.: Piper Largent, 225-5821, 2361 RHOB
Min. Staff Dir.: Michael Day, 225-4038, B-343C RHOB

Tax, Finance and Exports
225-5821/B-363 RHOB/Fax: 225-3587

Rep: Bradley, *Chair;* Kelly; Chabot; Shuster; McCotter; Keller; Poe; Fortenberry
Dem: Millender-McDonald, *Rnk. Mem.;* Lipinski; Faleomavaega; Davis; Case; Michaud; Bean.
Maj. Staff Dir.: Joe Hartz, 225-5821, 2361 RHOB
Min. Staff Dir.: Michael Day, 225-4038, B-343C RHOB

Workforce, Empowerment and Government Programs
225-5821/2361 RHOB/Fax: 225-3587

Rep: Musgrave, *Chair;* Bartlett; Fitzpatrick; Westmoreland; McCotter; Vacancy; Vacancy
Dem: Lipinski, *Rnk. Mem.;* Udall; Davis; Grijalva; Barrow; Bean
Maj. Staff Dir.: Joe Hartz, 225-5821, 2361 RHOB
Min. Staff Dir.: Michael Day, 225-4038, B-343C RHOB

STANDARDS OF OFFICIAL CONDUCT

Phone: (202) 225-7103—Room: HT-2 Capitol—Fax: 225-7392
http://www.house.gov/ethics

Republicans (5)
Doc Hastings, 4th-WA, *Chair*
Judy Biggert, 13th-IL
Lamar S. Smith, 21st-TX
Melissa A. Hart, 4th-PA
Tom Cole, 4th-OK

Democrats (5)
Alan B. Mollohan, 1st-WV, *Rnk. Mem.*
Stephanie Tubbs Jones, 11th-OH
Gene Green, 29th-TX
Lucille Roybal-Allard, 34th-CA
Mike Doyle, 14th-PA

Maj. Counsel:
John Vargo
225-7103, HT-2 Capitol

Min. Counsel:
Colleen McCarty
225-7103, HT-2 Capitol

NO SUBCOMMITTEES

TRANSPORTATION AND INFRASTRUCTURE

Phone: (202) 225-9446—Room: 2165 RHOB—Fax: 225-6782
http://www.house.gov/transportation

Republicans (41)
Don Young, At Large-AK, *Chair**
Thomas E. Petri, 6th-WI
Sherwood L. Boehlert, 24th-NY
Howard Coble, 6th-NC
John J. Duncan, Jr., 2nd-TN
Wayne Gilchrest, 1st-MD
John Mica, 7th-FL
Peter Hoekstra, 2nd-MI
Vernon Ehlers, 3rd-MI
Spencer Bachus, 6th-AL
Steven C. LaTourette, 14th-OH
Sue W. Kelly, 19th-NY
Richard H. Baker, 6th-LA
Bob Ney, 18th-OH
Frank A. LoBiondo, 2nd-NJ
Jerry Moran, 1st-KS
Gary G. Miller, 42nd-CA
Robin Hayes, 8th-NC
Robert R. Simmons, 2nd-CT
Henry E. Brown, Jr., 1st-SC
Timothy V. Johnson, 15th-IL
Todd R. Platts, 19th-PA
Sam Graves, 6th-MO
Mark R. Kennedy, 6th-MN
Bill Shuster, 9th-PA
John Boozman, 3rd-AR
Jim Gerlach, 6th-PA
Mario Diaz-Balart, 25th-FL
Jon C. Porter, 3rd-NV
Tom Osborne, 3rd-NE
Kenny Marchant, 24th-TX
Mike Sodrel, 9th-IN
Charles W. Dent, 15th-PA
Ted Poe, 2nd-TX
Dave Reichert, 8th-WA
Connie Mack, 14th-FL
Randy Kuhl, 29th-NY
Luis Fortuño, PR
Lynn A. Westmoreland, 8th-GA
Charles W. Boustany, Jr., 7th-LA
Vacancy

Democrats (34)
James L. Oberstar, 8th-MN, *Rnk. Mem.**
Nick J. Rahall II, 3rd-WV
Peter A. DeFazio, 4th-OR
Jerry F. Costello, 12th-IL
Eleanor Holmes Norton, DC
Jerrold Nadler, 8th-NY
Robert Menendez, 13th-NJ
Corrine Brown, 3rd-FL
Bob Filner, 51st-CA
Eddie Bernice Johnson, 30th-TX
Gene Taylor, 4th-MS
Juanita Millender-McDonald, 37th-CA
Elijah Cummings, 7th-MD
Earl Blumenauer, 3rd-OR
Ellen O. Tauscher, 10th-CA
Bill Pascrell, Jr., 8th-NJ
Leonard L. Boswell, 3rd-IA
Tim Holden, 17th-PA
Brian Baird, 3rd-WA
Shelley Berkley, 1st-NV
Jim Matheson, 2nd-UT
Michael M. Honda, 15th-CA
Rick Larsen, 2nd-WA
Michael Capuano, 8th-MA
Anthony D. Weiner, 9th-NY
Julia M. Carson, 7th-IN
Tim Bishop, 1st-NY
Michael H. Michaud, 2nd-ME
Lincoln Davis, 4th-TN
Ben Chandler, 6th-KY
Brian H. Higgins, 27th-NY
Russ Carnahan, 3rd-MO
Allyson Y. Schwartz, 13th-PA
John T. Salazar, 3rd-CO

Maj. Chief of Staff:
Lloyd Jones
225-9446, 2165 RHOB

Min. Staff Dir.:
David Heymsfeld
225-4472, 2163 RHOB

*Ex officio members on all subcommittees.

Transportation and Infrastructure Subcommittees

Aviation
226-3220/2251 RHOB/Fax: 225-4629
Rep: Mica, *Chair;* Petri; Coble; Duncan; Ehlers; Bachus; Kelly; Baker; Ney; LoBiondo; Moran; Hayes; Brown; Johnson; Graves; Kennedy; Boozman; Gerlach; Diaz-Balart; Porter; Dent; Poe; Kuhl; Westmoreland; Vacancy
Dem: Costello, *Rnk. Mem.;* Boswell; DeFazio; Norton; Brown; Johnson; Millender-McDonald; Tauscher; Pascrell; Holden; Berkley; Matheson; Honda; Larsen; Capuano; Weiner; Chandler; Carnahan; Salazar; Rahall; Filner
Maj. Staff Dir.: Jim Coon, 226-3220, 2251 RHOB
Min. Staff Dir.: Stacie Soumbeniotis, 225-9161, 2251 RHOB

Coast Guard and Maritime Transportation
226-3552/507 FHOB/Fax: 226-2524
Rep: LoBiondo, *Chair;* Coble; Gilchrest; Hoekstra; Simmons; Diaz-Balart; Reichert; Mack; Fortuño; Boustany
Dem: Filner, *Rnk. Mem.;* Brown; Taylor; Millender-McDonald; Honda; Weiner; Higgins; Baird
Maj. Staff Dir.: John Rayfield, 226-3552, 507 FHOB
Min. Staff Dir.: John Cullather, 226-3587, 585 FHOB

Economic Development, Public Buildings and Emergency Management
225-3014/591 FHOB/Fax: 226-1898
Rep: Shuster, *Chair;* Gerlach; Marchant; Dent; Kuhl
Dem: Norton, *Rnk. Mem.;* Michaud; Davis; Carson
Maj. Staff Dir.: Dan Mathews, 225-3014, 591 FHOB
Min. Staff Dir.: Susan F. Brita, 225-9961, 585 FHOB

Highways, Transit and Pipelines
225-6715/B-370A RHOB/Fax: 225-4623
Rep: Petri, *Chair;* Boehlert; Coble; Duncan; Mica; Hoekstra; Bachus; LaTourette; Kelly; Baker; Ney; LoBiondo; Moran; Miller; Hayes; Simmons; Brown; Johnson; Platts; Graves; Kennedy; Shuster; Boozman; Diaz-Balart; Porter; Osborne; Marchant; Sodrel; Reichert; Vacancy
Dem: DeFazio, *Rnk. Mem.;* Rahall; Nadler; Taylor; Millender-McDonald; Cummings; Blumenauer; Tauscher; Pascrell; Holden; Baird; Berkley; Matheson; Honda; Larsen; Capuano; Weiner; Carson; Bishop; Michaud; Davis; Chandler; Higgins; Carnahan; Schwartz
Maj. Staff Dir.: Graham Hill, 225-6715, B-370A RHOB
Min. Sr. Staff Mem.: Ken House, 225-9989, B-375 RHOB

Railroads
226-0727/589 FHOB/Fax: 226-3475
Rep: LaTourette, *Chair;* Petri; Boehlert; Mica; Bachus; Moran; Miller; Simmons; Platts; Graves; Porter; Osborne; Sodrel; Westmoreland
Dem: Brown, *Rnk. Mem.;* Rahall; Nadler; Menendez; Filner; Cummings; Blumenauer; Boswell; Carson; DeFazio; Costello; Johnson
Maj. Staff Dir.: Glenn Scammel, 226-0727, 589 FHOB
Min. Staff Dir.: Jennifer Esposito, 225-3274, 2251 RHOB

Water Resources and Environment
225-4360/B-376 RHOB/Fax: 226-5435
Rep: Duncan, *Chair;* Boehlert; Gilchrest; Ehlers; LaTourette; Kelly; Baker; Ney; Miller; Brown; Shuster; Boozman; Gerlach; Osborne; Poe; Mack; Fortuño; Boustany; Vacancy
Dem: Johnson, *Rnk. Mem.;* Menendez; Salazar; Costello; Taylor; Baird; Bishop; Higgins; Schwartz; Blumenauer; Tauscher; Pascrell; Carnahan; Rahall; Norton
Maj. Staff Dir.: Susan Bodine, 225-4360, B-376 RHOB
Min. Staff Dir: Ken Kopocis, 225-0060, B-375 RHOB

VETERANS' AFFAIRS

Phone: (202) 225-3527—Room: 335 CHOB—Fax: 225-5486
http://veterans.house.gov

Republicans (16)
Steve Buyer, 4th-IN, *Chair*
Michael Bilirakis, 9th-FL, *Vice Chair*
Terry Everett, 2nd-AL
Cliff Stearns, 6th-FL
Dan Burton, 5th-IN
Jerry Moran, 1st-KS
Richard H. Baker, 6th-LA
Henry E. Brown, Jr., 1st-SC
Jeff Miller, 1st-FL
John Boozman, 3rd-AR
Jeb Bradley, 1st-NH
Ginny Brown-Waite, 5th-FL
Devin Nunes, 21st-CA
Michael Turner, 3rd-OH
Vacancy
Vacancy

Democrats (13)
Lane Evans, 17th-IL, *Rnk. Mem.*
Bob Filner, 51st-CA
Luis V. Gutierrez, 4th-IL
Corrine Brown, 3rd-FL
Vic Snyder, 2nd-AR
Michael H. Michaud, 2nd-ME
Stephanie Herseth, At Large-SD
Ted Strickland, 6th-OH
Darlene Hooley, 5th-OR
Silvestre Reyes, 16th-TX
Shelley Berkley, 1st-NV
Tom Udall, 3rd-NM
Vacancy

Maj. Staff Dir.:
Mike Copher
225-3527, 335 CHOB

Min. Staff Dir.:
James Holley
225-9756, 333 CHOB

Veterans' Affairs Subcommittees

Disability Assistance and Memorial Affairs
225-3527/335 CHOB/Fax: 225-5486

Rep: Miller, *Chair;* Moran, *Vice Chair;* Bradley; Brown-Waite
Dem: Berkley, *Rnk. Mem.;* Udall; Evans
Maj. Staff Dir.: Paige McManus, 225-9164, 337 CHOB
Min. Staff Dir.: Mary Ellen McCarthy, 225-9756, 333 CHOB

Economic Opportunity
225-3527/335 CHOB/Fax: 225-5486

Rep: Boozman, *Chair;* Baker; Brown-Waite, *Vice Chair;* Nunes
Dem: Herseth, *Rnk. Mem.;* Hooley; Evans
Maj. Staff Dir.: Mike Brink, 225-3527, 335 CHOB
Min. Staff Dir.: Geoffrey Collver, 225-9756, 333 CHOB

Health
225-3527/335 CHOB/Fax: 225-5486

Rep: Brown, *Chair;* Stearns, *Vice Chair;* Baker; Moran; Miller; Nunes; Turner
Dem: Michaud, *Rnk. Mem.;* Filner; Gutierrez; Brown; Snyder
Maj. Staff Dir.: Vacant, 225-3527, 335 CHOB
Min. Staff Dir.: Susan Edgerton, 225-9756, 333 CHOB

Oversight and Investigations
225-3527/335 CHOB/Fax: 225-5486

Rep: Bilirakis, *Chair;* Everett, *Vice Chair;* Boozman; Bradley
Dem: Strickland, *Rnk. Mem.;* Reyes; Vacancy
Maj. Staff Dir.: Art Wu, 225-3527, 335 CHOB
Min. Staff Dir.: Len Sistek, 225-9756, 333 CHOB

WAYS AND MEANS

Phone: (202) 225-3625—Room: 1102 LHOB—Fax: 225-2610
http://waysandmeans.house.gov

Republicans (24)
William M. Thomas, 22nd-CA, *Chair**
E. Clay Shaw, Jr., 22nd-FL
Nancy L. Johnson, 5th-CT
Wally Herger, 2nd-CA
Jim McCrery, 4th-LA
Dave Camp, 4th-MI
Jim Ramstad, 3rd-MN
Jim Nussle, 1st-IA
Sam Johnson, 3rd-TX
Rob J. Portman, 2nd-OH
Philip S. English, 3rd-PA
J.D. Hayworth, 5th-AZ
Jerry Weller, 11th-IL
Kenny C. Hulshof, 9th-MO
Ron Lewis, 2nd-KY
Mark Foley, 16th-FL
Kevin P. Brady, 8th-TX
Thomas Reynolds, 26th-NY
Paul D. Ryan, 1st-WI
Eric I. Cantor, 7th-VA
John Linder, 7th-GA
Melissa A. Hart, 4th-PA
Bob Beauprez, 7th-CO
Chris Chocola, 2nd-IN

Democrats (17)
Charles B. Rangel, 15th-NY, *Rnk. Mem.**
Fortney H. Stark, 13th-CA
Sander M. Levin, 12th-MI
Benjamin L. Cardin, 3rd-MD
Jim McDermott, 7th-WA
John Lewis, 5th-GA
Richard E. Neal, 2nd-MA
Michael R. McNulty, 21st-NY
William J. Jefferson, 2nd-LA
John S. Tanner, 8th-TN
Xavier Becerra, 31st-CA
Lloyd Doggett, 25th-TX
Earl Pomeroy, At Large-ND
Stephanie Tubbs Jones, 11th-OH
Mike Thompson, 1st-CA
John B. Larson, 1st-CT
Rahm Emanuel, 5th-IL

Maj. Chief of Staff:
Allison Giles
225-3625, 1102 LHOB

Min. Staff Dir. & Chief Counsel:
Janice Mays
225-4021, 1106 LHOB

*Ex officio members on all subcommittees of which they are not regular members.

Ways and Means Subcommittees

Health
225-3943/1136 LHOB/Fax: 226-1765

Rep: Johnson (CT), *Chair;* McCrery; Johnson (TX); Camp; Ramstad; English; Hayworth; Hulshof
Dem: Stark, *Rnk. Mem.;* Lewis; Doggett; Thompson; Emanuel
Maj. Staff Dir.: Joel White, 225-3943, 1136 LHOB
Min. Prof. Staff Mem.: Cybele Bjorklund, 225-4021, 1106 LHOB

Human Resources
225-1025/B-317 RHOB/Fax: 225-9480

Rep: Herger, *Chair;* Johnson (CT); Beauprez; Hart; Chocola; McCrery; Camp; English
Dem: McDermott, *Rnk. Mem.;* Cardin; Stark; Becerra; Emanuel
Maj. Staff Dir.: Matt Weidinger, 225-1025, B-317 RHOB
Min. Prof. Staff Mem.: Nick Gwyn, 225-4021, 1106 LHOB

Oversight
225-7601/1136 LHOB/Fax: 225-9680

Rep: Ramstad, *Chair;* Cantor; Beauprez; Reynolds; Linder; Shaw; Johnson (TX); Portman
Dem: Lewis, *Rnk. Mem.;* Pomeroy; McNulty; Tanner; Rangel
Maj. Staff Dir.: David Kass, 225-7601, 1136 LHOB
Min. Counsel: Beth Vance, 225-4021, 1106 LHOB

Select Revenue Measures
226-5911/1135 LHOB/Fax: 225-0787

Rep: Camp, *Chair;* Weller; Foley; Reynolds; Cantor; Linder; Hart; Chocola
Dem: McNulty, *Rnk. Mem.;* Doggett; Tubbs Jones; Thompson; Larson
Maj. Staff Dir.: Robert Winters, 226-5911, 1135 LHOB
Min. Staff Dir.: Beth Vance, 225-4021, 1106 LHOB

Ways and Means Subcommittees

Social Security
225-9263/B-316 RHOB/Fax: 225-9480
Rep: McCrery, *Chair;* Shaw; Johnson (TX); Hayworth; Hulshof; Lewis; Brady; Ryan
Dem: Levin, *Rnk. Mem.;* Pomeroy; Becerra; Tubbs Jones; Neal
Maj. Staff Dir.: Kim Hildred, 225-9263, B-316 RHOB
Min. Staff Dir.: Kathryn Olson, 225-4021, 1106 LHOB

Trade
225-6649/1104 LHOB/Fax: 226-0158
Rep: Shaw, *Chair;* Herger; English; Nussle; Portman; Weller; Lewis; Foley; Brady
Dem: Cardin, *Rnk. Mem.;* Levin; Jefferson; Tanner; Larson; McDermott
Maj. Staff Dir.: Angela Ellard, 225-6649, 1104 LHOB
Min. Chief Counsel: Tim Reif, 225-4021, 1106 LHOB

PERMANENT SELECT COMMITTEE ON INTELLIGENCE

Phone: (202) 225-4121—Room: H-405 Capitol—Fax: 225-1991
http://intelligence.house.gov

Republicans (12)
Peter Hoekstra, 2nd-MI, *Chair**
Ray H. LaHood, 18th-IL
Randy Cunningham, 50th-CA
Terry Everett, 2nd-AL
Elton Gallegly, 24th-CA
Heather A. Wilson, 1st-NM
Jo Ann S. Davis, 1st-VA
William Thornberry, 13th-TX
John McHugh, 23rd-NY
Todd Tiahrt, 4th-KS
Michael J. Rogers, 8th-MI
Rick Renzi, 1st-AZ

Democrats (9)
Jane Harman, 36th-CA, *Rnk. Mem.**
Alcee L. Hastings, 23rd-FL
Silvestre Reyes, 16th-TX
Leonard L. Boswell, 3rd-IA
Robert E. Cramer, Jr., 5th-AL
Anna Eshoo, 14th-CA
Rush Holt, 12th-NJ
C.A. Ruppersberger, 2nd-MD
John F. Tierney, 6th-MA

Maj. Staff Dir. & Chief Counsel:
Michael Meermans
225-4121, H-405 Capitol

Min. Staff Dir.:
John Keefe
225-7690, H-405 Capitol

J. Dennis Hastert (R-14th IL) and Nancy Pelosi (D-8th CA) serve as ex officio members.

*Ex officio members on all subcommittees.

Permanent Select Committee on Intelligence Subcommittees

Intelligence Policy
225-4121/H-405 Capitol/Fax: 225-1991
Rep: Davis, *Chair;* Wilson, *Vice Chair;* McHugh; Rogers; Renzi
Dem: Holt, *Rnk. Mem.;* Eshoo; Tierney
Maj. Staff Dir.: Mike Ennis, 225-4121, H-405 Capitol

Oversight
225-4121/H-405 Capitol/Fax: 225-1991
Rep: Thornberry, *Chair;* LaHood, *Vice Chair;* Everett; Wilson; Tiahrt; Rogers; Renzi
Dem: Cramer, *Rnk. Mem.;* Hastings; Reyes; Ruppersberger; Tierney
Maj. Staff Dir.: Riley Perdue, 225-4121, H-405 Capitol

Technical and Tactical Intelligence
225-4121/H-405 Capitol/Fax: 225-1991
Rep: Wilson, *Chair;* Everett, *Vice Chair;* Cunningham; Gallegly; Thornberry; McHugh
Dem: Eshoo, *Rnk. Mem.;* Cramer; Holt; Ruppersberger
Maj. Staff Dir.: John Stopher, 225-4121, H-405 Capitol

Permanent Select Committee on Intelligence Subcommittees

Terrorism, Human Intelligence, Analysis and Counterintelligence
225-4121/H-405 Capitol/Fax: 225-1991
Rep: Cunningham, *Chair;* LaHood, *Vice Chair;* Gallegly; Davis; McHugh; Tiahrt; Renzi
Dem: Boswell, *Rnk. Mem.;* Hastings; Reyes; Ruppersberger
Maj. Staff Dir.: Michele Lang, 225-4121, H-405 Capitol

JOINT ECONOMIC COMMITTEE

Phone: (202) 224-5171—Room: G01 SD—Fax: 224-0240
http://jec.senate.gov

Republicans (12)
Senate
Robert Bennett, UT, *Vice Chair*
Sam Brownback, KS
John E. Sununu, NH
Jim DeMint, SC
Jeff Sessions, AL
John Cornyn, TX

Democrats (8)
Senate
Jack Reed, RI
Edward M. Kennedy, MA
Paul S. Sarbanes, MD
Jeff Bingaman, NM

House
Jim Saxton, 3rd-NJ, *Chair*
Paul D. Ryan, 1st-WI
Philip S. English, 3rd-PA
Ron E. Paul, 14th-TX
Kevin P. Brady, 8th-TX
Thaddeus G. McCotter, 11th-MI

House
Carolyn Maloney, 14th-NY
Maurice Hinchey, 22nd-NY
Loretta Sanchez, 47th-CA
Elijah Cummings, 7th-MD

Maj. Executive Director:
Chris Frenze
224-5171, SD-G01

Min. Staff Dir.:
Wendell Primus
224-0372, SH-804

JOINT COMMITTEE ON THE LIBRARY

Phone: (202) 225-8281—Room: 1309 LHOB

Republicans (6)
Senate
Ted Stevens, AK, *Vice Chair*
Thad Cochran, MS
Trent Lott, MS

Democrats (4)
Senate
Christopher J. Dodd, CT
Charles E. Schumer, NY

House
Bob Ney, 18th-OH, *Chair*
Vernon Ehlers, 3rd-MI
Candice Miller, 10th-MI

House
Juanita Millender-McDonald, 37th-CA
Zoe Lofgren, 16th-CA

JOINT COMMITTEE ON PRINTING

Phone: (202) 225-8281—Room: 1309 LHOB
http://www.house.gov/jcp

Republicans (6)
Senate
Trent Lott, MS, *Chair*
Thad Cochran, MS
Saxby Chambliss, GA

Democrats (4)
Senate
Daniel K. Inouye, HI
Mark Dayton, MN

House
Bob Ney, 18th-OH, *Vice Chair*
John T. Doolittle, 4th-CA
Thomas Reynolds, 26th-NY

House
Juanita Millender-McDonald, 37th-CA
Robert A. Brady, 1st-PA

JOINT COMMITTEE ON TAXATION

Phone: (202) 225-3621—Room: 1015 LHOB—Fax: 225-0832
http://www.house.gov/jct

Republicans (6)
Senate
Charles E. Grassley, IA,
 Vice Chair
Orrin G. Hatch, UT
Trent Lott, MS

House
William M. Thomas, 22nd-CA,
 Chair
E. Clay Shaw, Jr., 22nd-FL
Nancy L. Johnson, 5th-CT

Democrats (4)
Senate
Max Baucus, MT
John D. Rockefeller IV, WV

House
Charles B. Rangel, 15th-NY
Fortney H. Stark, 13th-CA

STATE LEGISLATURE INFORMATION

Alabama Legislature
Phone: 334-242-8000
Website:
 www.legislature.state.al.us
Senate: 25D/10R
House: 62D/41R/2V
Session Dates: February 1,
 2005-May 16, 2005

Alaska Legislature
Phone: 907-465-4648
Website: w3.legis.state.ak.us
Senate: 12R/8D
House: 26R/14D
Session Dates: January 10,
 2005-May 10, 2005

Arizona Legislature
Phone: 602-926-3559
Website: www.azleg.state.az.us
Senate: 18R/12D
House: 38R/22D
Session Dates: January 10,
 2005-TBA

Arkansas General Assembly
Phone: 501-682-3000
Website: www.arkleg.state.ar.us
Senate: 27D/8R
House: 72D/28R
Session Dates: January 10,
 2005-TBA

California Legislature
Phone: 916-319-2856
Website: www.leginfo.ca.gov
Senate: 25D/15R
Assembly: 48D/32R
Session Dates: January 3, 2005-
 September 10, 2005

Colorado General Assembly
Phone: 303-866-5000
Website: www.leg.state.co.us
Senate: 18D/17R
House: 35D/33R
Session Dates: January 12,
 2005-May 11, 2005

Connecticut General Assembly
Phone: 860-240-0400
Website: www.cga.ct.gov
Senate: 24D/12R
House: 99D/52R
Session Dates: January 5, 2005-
 June 4, 2005

Delaware General Assembly
Phone: 302-739-4000
Website: www.legis.state.de.us
Senate: 13D/8R
House: 26R/15D
Session Dates: January 11, 2005-
 June 30, 2005

Florida Legislature
Phone: 850-488-1234
Website: www.leg.state.fl.us
Senate: 26R/14D
House: 84R/36D
Session Dates: March 8, 2005-
 May 6, 2005

Georgia General Assembly
Phone: 404-656-2000
Website: www.legis.state.ga.us
Senate: 34R/22D
House: 99R/80D/1IND
Session Dates: January 10,
 2005-TBA

Hawaii Legislature
Phone: 808-586-2211
Website: www.capitol.hawaii.gov
Senate: 20D/5R
House: 41D/10R
Session Dates: January 19,
 2005-TBA

Idaho Legislature
Phone: 208-332-1000
Website: www.legislature.idaho.gov
Senate: 28R/7D
House: 57R/13D
Session Dates: January 10,
 2005-TBA

Illinois General Assembly
Phone: 217-782-2000
Website: www.ilga.gov
Senate: 31D/27R/1IND
House: 65D/53R
Session Dates: January 12, 2005-
 May 27, 2005

Indiana General Assembly
Phone: 317-232-9856
Website: www.in.gov/legislative
Senate: 33R/17D
House: 52R/48D
Session Dates: January 6, 2005-
 April 29, 2005

State Legislature Information

Iowa General Assembly
Phone: 515-281-5129
Website: www.legis.state.ia.us
Senate: 25R/25D
House: 51R/49D
Session Dates: January 10, 2005-April 29, 2005

Kansas Legislature
Phone: 785-296-0111
Website: www.kslegislature.org
Senate: 30R/10D
House: 82R/42D/1V
Session Dates: January 10, 2005-TBA

Kentucky General Assembly
Phone: 502-564-2500
Website: www.lrc.state.ky.us
Senate: 23R/15D
House: 57D/43R
Session Dates: January 4, 2005-March 22, 2005

Louisiana Legislature
Phone: 225-342-6600
Website: www.legis.state.la.us
Senate: 25D/14R
House: 64D/36R/1IND/1V
Session Dates: April 25, 2005-June 23, 2005

Maine Legislature
Phone: 207-287-1692
Website: janus.state.me.us/legis
Senate: 19D/16R
House: 76D/73R/3IND/1 GREEN
Session Dates: December 1, 2004-June 15, 2005

Maryland General Assembly
Phone: 301-970-5000
Website: www.mlis.state.md.us
Senate: 33D/14R/1V
House: 98D/43R
Session Dates: January 12, 2005-April 11, 2005

General Court of The Commonwealth of Massachusetts
Phone: 617-722-1276
Website: www.state.ma.us/legis
Senate: 34R/6R
House: 138D/21R/1IND
Session Dates: January 5, 2005-November 16, 2005

Michigan Legislature
Phone: 517-373-1837
Website: www.michiganlegislature.org
Senate: 22R/16D
House: 58R/52D
Session Dates: January 12, 2005-December 6, 2005

Minnesota Legislature
Phone: 651-296-3962
Website: www.leg.state.mn.us
Senate: 35DFL/31R/1IND
House: 68R/66DFL
Session dates: January 4, 2005-May 23, 2005

Mississippi Legislature
Phone: 601-359-1000
Website: www.ls.state.ms.us
Senate: 28D/24R
House: 75D/47R
Session Dates: January 4, 2005-April 3, 2005

Missouri General Assembly
Phone: 573-751-2000
Website: www.moga.state.mo.us
Senate: 23R/11D
House: 97R/66D
Session Dates: January 5, 2005-May 13, 2005

Montana Legislature
Phone: 406-444-2511
Website: leg.state.mt.us
Senate: 26D/24R
House: 50D/50R
Session Dates: January 3, 2005-TBA

Nebraska Legislature
Phone: 402-471-2311
Website: www.unicam.state.ne.us
Senate: 49IND
Session Dates: January 5, 2005-TBA

Nevada Legislature
Phone: 775-687-5000
Website: www.leg.state.nv.us
Senate: 12R/9D
House: 26D/16R
Session Dates: February 7, 2005-June 6, 2005

New Hampshire General Court
Phone: 603-271-1110
Website: gencourt.state.nh.us
Senate: 16R/8D
House: 251R/147D
Session Dates: January 5, 2005-TBA

New Jersey Legislature
Phone: 609-292-4840
Website: www.njleg.state.nj.us
Senate: 22D/18R
Assembly: 47D/33R
Session Dates: January 13, 2004-TBA

New Mexico Legislature
Phone: 505-986-4300
Website: legis.state.nm.us
Senate: 24D/18R
House: 42D/28R
Session Dates: January 18, 2005-May 18, 2005

New York Legislature
Phone: 518-474-2121
Website: assembly.state.ny.us
Senate: 35R/27D
Assembly: 104D/46R
Session Dates: January 10, 2005-TBA

North Carolina General Assembly
Phone: 919-733-7928
Website: www.ncga.state.nc.us
Senate: 29D/21R
House: 63D/57R
Session Dates: January 26, 2005-TBA

North Dakota Legislative Assembly
Phone: 701-328-2000
Website: www.state.nd.us/lr
Senate: 32R/15D
House: 67R/27D
Session Dates: January 4, 2005-April 27, 2005

State Legislature Information

Ohio General Assembly
Phone: 614-466-2000
Website:
  www.legislature.state.oh.us
Senate: 22R/11D
House: 60R/39D
Session Dates: January 3, 2005-
  December 31, 2005

Oklahoma Legislature
Phone: 405-521-2011
Website: www.lsb.state.ok.us
Senate: 26D/22R
House: 57R/44D
Session Dates: February 7,
  2005-May 27, 2005

Oregon Legislative Assembly
Phone: 503-986-1388
Website: www.leg.state.or.us
Senate: 18D/12R
House: 32R/27D/1V
Session Dates: January 10,
  2005-TBA

**Pennsylvania General
  Assembly**
Phone: 717-787-2121
Website: www.legis.state.pa.us
Senate: 29R/18D/3V
House: 110R/92D/1V
Session Dates: January 4,
  2005-TBA

**Rhode Island General
  Assembly**
Phone: 401-222-2000
Website: www.rilin.state.ri.us
Senate: 33D/5R
House: 60D/15R
Session Dates: January 4,
  2005-TBA

**South Carolina General
  Assembly**
Phone: 803-896-0000
Website: www.scstatehouse.net
Senate: 26R/20D
House: 74R/51D
Session Dates: January 11,
  2005-June 2, 2005

South Dakota Legislature
Phone: 605-773-3251
Website: legis.state.sd.us
Senate: 25R/10D
House: 51R/19D
Session Dates: January 11,
  2005-March 4, 2005

Tennessee General Assembly
Phone: 615-741-3511
Website:
  www.legislature.state.tn.us
Senate: 17R/15D
House: 53D/46R
Session Dates: January 11,
  2005-TBA

Texas Legislature
Phone: 512-463-4630
Website: www.capitol.state.tx.us
Senate: 19R/12D
House: 86R/63D/1V
Session Dates: January 11, 2005-
  May 30, 2005

Utah Legislature
Phone: 801-538-3000
Website: www.le.state.ut.us
Senate: 21R/8D
House: 56R/19D
Session Dates: January 17, 2005-
  March 2, 2005

Vermont Legislature
Phone: 802-828-2228
Website: www.leg.state.vt.us
Senate: 21D/9R
House: 84D/59R/6PRO/1IND
Session Dates: January 5,
  2005-TBA

Virginia General Assembly
Phone: 804-786-0000
Website: legis.state.va.us
Senate: 24R/16D
House: 60R/37D/2IND/1V
Session Dates: January 12, 2005-
  February 24, 2005

Washington Legislature
Phone: 360-753-5000
Website: www.leg.wa.gov
Senate: 26D/23R
House: 55D/42R
Session Dates: January 10, 2005-
  April 24, 2005

West Virginia Legislature
Phone: 304-347-4800
Website: www.legis.state.wv.us
Senate: 21D/13R
House: 68D/32R
Session Dates: February 11,
  2005-TBA

Wisconsin State Legislature
Phone: 608-266-9960
Website: www.legis.state.wi.us
Senate: 19R/14D
Assembly: 60R/39D
Session Dates: January 3,
  2005-TBA

Wyoming State Legislature
Phone: 307-777-7011
Website: legisweb.state.wy.us
Senate: 23R/7D
House: 46R/14D
Session Dates: January 11, 2005-
  March 9, 2005

LEGISLATIVE GLOSSARY

Act—Legislation that has passed both Houses of Congress and become law.
Adjourn—To close a legislative day.
Amendment—A change in a bill or document by adding, substituting or omitting portions of it.
Appropriations Bill—Legislation that provides funds for authorized programs.
Authorization Bill—Legislation establishing a program and setting funding limits.
Bill—Legislation introduced in either the House or Senate.
By Request—Phrase used when a Member introduces a bill at the request of an executive agency or private organization but does not necessarily endorse the legislation.
Calendar—List and schedule of bills to be considered by a committee.
Caucus—Meeting of Republican or Democratic Members of Congress to determine policy and/or choose leaders.
Chair—Presiding Officer.
Chamber—Place where the entire House or Senate meets to conduct business; also, the House of Representatives or the Senate itself.
Clean Bill—A bill which has been revised in mark-up. Amendments are assembled with unchanged language and the bill is referred to the floor with a new number.
Cloak Rooms—Small rooms off the House and Senate floor where Members can rest and hold informal conferences.
Closed Hearings—Hearings closed to all but Members, staff and witnesses testifying; also called Executive Hearings.
Closed Rule—In the House, a prohibition against amendments not approved by the committee which brought the bill to the floor. The House must either accept or reject the bill as-is.
Cloture—Method of limiting debate or ending a filibuster in the Senate. At least 60 Senators must vote in favor before cloture can be invoked.
Co-sponsor—Member who joins in sponsoring legislation but who is not the principal sponsor or the one who introduced the legislation.
Commit—To refer a bill or matter to a committee.
Committee—A group of Members assigned to give special consideration to certain bills. See Standing Committee, Joint Committee, Special Committee.
Committee of the Whole—A mechanism to expedite business in the House whereby the House itself becomes a committee, allowing for less rigid rules and a quorum of 100 instead of 218.
Companion Bills—Identical bills introduced separately in both the Senate and the House.
Concurrent Resolution—Legislative action used to express the position of the House or Senate. Does not have the force of law.
Conference Committee—Meeting between Representatives and Senators to resolve differences when two versions of a similar bill have been passed by the House and Senate.
Congressional Record—Official transcript of the proceedings in Congress.
Continuing Resolution—A resolution enacted to allow specific Executive Branch agencies to continue operating even though funds have not been appropriated for them for the following fiscal year.
Discharge Petition—A petition for the purpose of removing a bill from the control of a committee. A discharge petition must be signed by a majority of Members in the House or Senate.
Engrossed Bill—Final copy of a bill passed by either the House or Senate with amendments. The bill is then delivered to the other chamber.
Enrolled Bill—Final copy of a bill that has passed both the House and Senate in identical form.
Extension of Remarks—When a Member of Congress inserts material in the Congressional Record which is not directly related to the debate underway.
Filibuster—Tactic used in the Senate whereby a minority intentionally delays a vote.
Final Passage—Adoption of a bill after all amendments have been voted on.
Fiscal Year—Accounting year. For the Federal Government, the fiscal year (FY) is October 1 to September 30 of the following calendar year.
Five-Minute Rule—Rule which allows any House member to propose an amendment and debate it for five minutes. Opponents and supporters of the amendment have five minutes to debate it.
Floor Manager—A Member who attempts to direct a bill through the debate and amendment process to a final vote.
General Consent—A unanimous silent vote. If there is no objection to the matter, it is resolved without a formal vote.
Germane—In the House, all amendments must have some relation to the bill in question.

Legislative Glossary

Hearing—Committee sessions for hearing witnesses.

Holds—A courtesy afforded Senators which allows them to delay legislation for a reasonable period. The Majority Leader can override a hold.

Hopper—Box on the desk of the Clerk of the House where sponsors submit their bills.

Hour Rule—When the House is sitting as the full House, each Member has one hour to debate amendments. In the Committee of the Whole, the five-minute rule is in effect.

Jefferson's Manual—Basic rules of parliamentary procedure adopted by both chambers.

Joint Committee—Committee composed of Members of both the House and Senate.

Joint Resolution—Legislation similar to a bill that has the force of law if passed by both houses and signed by the President, generally used for special circumstances.

Lame Duck—Member of Congress (or the President) who has not been reelected but whose term has not yet expired.

Leader Time—Ten minutes given to the Majority and Minority Leaders at the beginning of each day Congress is in session.

Legislative Day—In the Senate, the period of time between convening until the Senate adjourns, not necessarily a calendar day.

Lobbying—The process of attempting to influence the passage, defeat or content of legislation by individuals or a group other than Members of Congress.

Logrolling—Process whereby Members help each other get particular legislation passed. One Member will help another on one piece of legislation in return for similar help.

Main Motion—Motion that introduces the business or proposal to the assembly for action.

Majority Leader—Chief spokesman and strategist for the majority party, elected by members of the majority party.

Marking Up a Bill—Process, usually in committee, of analyzing a piece of legislation section by section and making changes.

Member—A U.S. Senator or U.S. Representative.

Minority Leader—Chief spokesman and strategist for the minority party, elected by members of the minority party.

Motion—Proposal presented to a legislative body for consideration.

Motion to Table—Proposal to postpone consideration of a matter in the Senate.

Omnibus Bill—Bill regarding a single subject that combines many different aspects of that subject.

One-Day Rule—In the Senate, a requirement that measures reported from committee be held for at least one legislative day before being brought to the floor.

Open Rule—In the House, permission to offer amendments to a particular bill during floor debate.

Override a Veto—When both the House and Senate vote by a two-thirds majority to set aside a Presidential veto of legislation.

Pairing—System whereby two Members jointly agree not to vote on a particular matter.

Petition—Plea by an individual or organization for a chamber to consider particular legislation.

Pocket Veto—When the President does not sign or veto legislation submitted to him by Congress within ten days of adjournment, the bill dies.

Point of Order—An objection that language, an amendment or bill is in violation of a rule. Also used to force a quorum call.

President of the Senate—The Vice President of the United States is designated by the Constitution as the President of the Senate. The President of the Senate casts a vote only in cases of a tie.

Previous Question—In the House, a request to end all debate and force a vote.

Private Bill—Bill designed to benefit a certain individual or business.

President Pro Tempore—Senator who presides over the Senate in the absence of the Vice President of the U.S. The President Pro Tem is usually the longest-serving member of the majority party.

Public Law—Designation used for legislation that has been passed by both chambers and signed by the President.

Quorum—The number of Senators or Representatives who must be present before a legislative body can conduct official business.

Quorum Call—In the Senate, a method of determining whether there is a quorum. Often used to suspend debate without adjourning.

Ranking Members—The members of the majority and minority party on a committee next in seniority after the chairman.

Legislative Glossary

Recess—Temporary halt to proceedings, with a time set for proceedings to resume.

Record Vote—Vote in which Members of Congress indicate their vote orally for listing in the Congressional Record.

Rescission Bill—Legislation that revokes spending authority previously granted by Congress.

Resolution—A measure passed only in one house to express the sentiment of that chamber. A simple resolution does not have the force of law.

Rider—A measure added to another, often unrelated, bill with the purpose of one piece of legislation passing on the strength of another.

Roll Call Vote—In the House, an oral vote for which a record is kept.

Seniority—Length of unbroken service. Often used to determine rank on committees.

Seriatim Consideration—Consideration of a motion line by line.

Sine Die—Final adjournment at the end of a session. Bills under consideration but not enacted must be reintroduced in the next session.

Speaker—The presiding officer of the House, elected by members of the House.

Sponsor—The Representative or Senator who introduces a measure.

Suspend the Rules—Procedural action in the House whereby a two-thirds majority can vote to bring a measure to a vote after forty minutes of debate.

Table a Bill—Motion to kill a bill by cutting off consideration of it. Such motions are not debatable.

Teller Vote—A vote in the House in which Members file past tellers who count the votes. The total vote is recorded, but no record is kept on how each member voted.

Three-Day Rule—In the House, a requirement that measures reported from committee be held for at least three calendar days (not counting weekends and holidays) before being brought to the floor. Similar to the One-Day Rule in the Senate.

Unanimous Consent—A procedure whereby a matter is considered agreed to if no Member on the floor objects. Unanimous Consent motions save time by eliminating the need for a vote.

Unlimited Debate—In the Senate, the right of any Senator to talk as long as desired during floor debates on a bill.

Whip—Assistant leader for each party in each chamber who keeps other members of the party informed of the legislative agenda of the leader. Also tracks sentiment among party members for certain legislation and tries to persuade Members to be present and vote for measures important to the leadership.

Yield—Permission granted by the Member who has the floor to another Member who wishes to make a comment or ask a question.

DISTRICT MAPS

Alabama

- *Hispanic or Latino origin is a category separate from race. People of Hispanic origin will also be included in another racial category.*

2000 Pop.: 4,447,100 **2003 Est.:** 4,500,752
Reg. Voters: 2,356,423 (2002) Party registration not required.
Caucasian: 71% **African-Am.:** 26% **Nat. Am.:** 1% **Asian:** 1% **Other:** 2% **Hisp.:** 2%

Senators
Richard C. Shelby (R)
Jeff Sessions (R)

Representatives
Jo Bonner (R-1st)
Terry Everett (R-2nd)
Michael D. Rogers (R-3rd)
Robert B. Aderholt (R-4th)
Robert E. "Bud" Cramer, Jr. (D-5th)
Spencer Bachus (R-6th)
Artur Davis (D-7th)

Alaska

2000 Pop.: 626,932 **2003 Est.:** 648,818
Reg. Voters: 461,059 **Rep.:** 25% **Dem.:** 15% **Green:** 1% **Other:** 59%
Caucasian: 69% **African-Am.:** 4% **Nat. Am.:** 16% **Asian:** 4% **Other:** 8% **Hisp.:** 4%

Senators
Ted Stevens (R)
Lisa Murkowski (R)

Representative
Don Young (R-At Large)

Due to population, this state has only one district.

I

Arizona

2000 Pop.: 5,130,632 **2003 Est.:** 5,580,811
Reg. Voters: 2,643,331 **Rep.:** 40% **Dem.:** 35% **Other:** 26%
Caucasian: 76% **African-Am.:** 3% **Nat. Am.:** 5% **Asian:** 2% **Other:** 15% **Hisp.:** 25%

Senators
John McCain (R)
Jon L. Kyl (R)

Representatives
Rick Renzi (R-1st)
Trent Franks (R-2nd)
John B. Shadegg (R-3rd)
Ed Pastor (D-4th)
J.D. Hayworth (R-5th)
Jeff Flake (R-6th)
Raúl M. Grijalva (D-7th)
Jim Kolbe (R-8th)

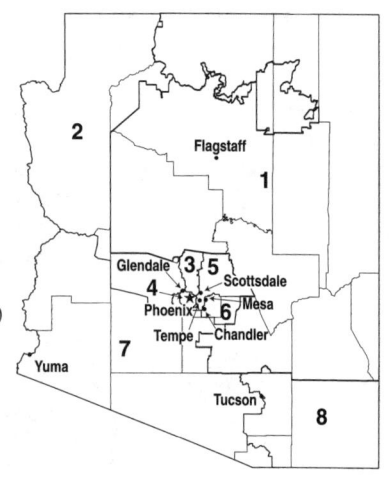

Arkansas

2000 Pop.: 2,673,400 **2003 Est.:** 2,725,714
Reg. Voters: 1,684,684 Party registration not required.
Caucasian: 80% **African-Am.:** 16% **Nat. Am.:** 1% **Asian:** 1% **Other:** 3% **Hisp.:** 3%

Senators
Blanche L. Lincoln (D)
Mark Pryor (D)

Representatives
Marion Berry (D-1st)
Vic Snyder (D-2nd)
John Boozman (R-3rd)
Mike Ross (D-4th)

II

California

2000 Pop.: 33,871,648 **2003 Est.:** 35,484,453
Reg. Voters: 16,557,273 **Rep.:** 35% **Dem.:** 43% **Other:** 22%
Caucasian: 60% **African-Am.:** 7% **Nat. Am.:** 1% **Asian:** 11% **Other:** 22% **Hisp.:** 32%

Senators
Dianne Feinstein (D)
Barbara Boxer (D)

Representatives
Mike Thompson (D-1st)
Wally Herger (R-2nd)
Dan Lungren (R-3rd)
John T. Doolittle (R-4th)
Vacant (5th)
Lynn Woolsey (D-6th)
George Miller (D-7th)
Nancy Pelosi (D-8th)
Barbara Lee (D-9th)
Ellen O. Tauscher (D-10th)
Richard Pombo (R-11th)
Tom Lantos (D-12th)
Fortney H. "Pete" Stark (D-13th)
Anna Eshoo (D-14th)
Michael M. Honda (D-15th)
Zoe Lofgren (D-16th)
Sam Farr (D-17th)
Dennis Cardoza (D-18th)
George P. Radanovich (R-19th)
Jim Costa (D-20th)
Devin Nunes (R-21st)
William M. Thomas (R-22nd)
Lois Capps (D-23rd)
Elton Gallegly (R-24th)
Howard "Buck" McKeon (R-25th)
David Dreier (R-26th)
Brad Sherman (D-27th)
Howard L. Berman (D-28th)
Adam Schiff (D-29th)
Henry A. Waxman (D-30th)
Xavier Becerra (D-31st)
Hilda L. Solis (D-32nd)
Diane Watson (D-33rd)
Lucille Roybal-Allard (D-34th)
Maxine Waters (D-35th)
Jane Harman (D-36th)
Juanita Millender-McDonald (D-37th)
Grace F. Napolitano (D-38th)
Linda T. Sánchez (D-39th)
Ed Royce (R-40th)
Jerry Lewis (R-41st)
Gary G. Miller (R-42nd)
Joe Baca (D-43rd)
Ken Calvert (R-44th)
Mary Bono (R-45th)
Dana Rohrabacher (R-46th)
Loretta Sanchez (D-47th)
Christopher Cox (R-48th)
Darrell Issa (R-49th)
Randy "Duke" Cunningham (R-50th)
Bob Filner (D-51st)
Duncan Hunter (R-52nd)
Susan A. Davis (D-53rd)

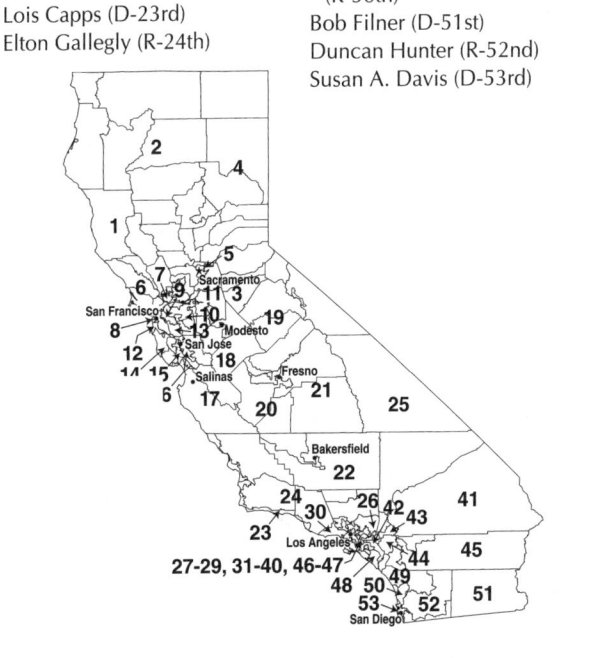

Colorado

2000 Pop.: 4,301,261 **2003 Est.:** 4,550,688
Reg. Voters: 3,098,421 **Rep.:** 36% **Dem.:** 30% **Green:** .2% **Other:** 33%
Caucasian: 82% **African-Am.:** 4% **Nat. Am.:** 1% **Asian:** 2% **Other:** 10% **Hisp.:** 17%

Senators
Wayne Allard (R)
Ken Salazar (D)

Representatives
Diana L. DeGette (D-1st)
Mark Udall (D-2nd)
John T. Salazar (D-3rd)
Marilyn Musgrave (R-4th)
Joel Hefley (R-5th)
Thomas G. Tancredo (R-6th)
Bob Beauprez (R-7th)

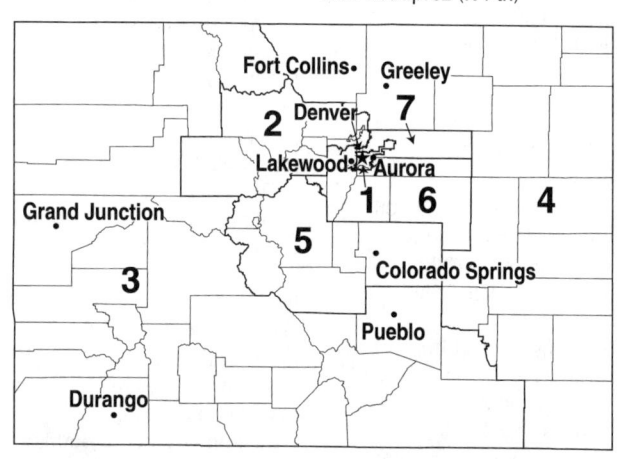

Connecticut

2000 Pop.: 3,405,565 **2003 Est.:** 3,483,372
Reg. Voters: 2,044,181 Party registration not required.
Caucasian: 82% **African-Am.:** 9% **Nat. Am.:** .3% **Asian:** 2% **Other:** 7% **Hisp.:** 9%

Senators
Christopher J. Dodd (D)
Joseph I. Lieberman (D)

Representatives
John B. Larson (D-1st)
Robert R. Simmons (R-2nd)
Rosa DeLauro (D-3rd)
Christopher Shays (R-4th)
Nancy L. Johnson (R-5th)

Delaware

2000 Pop.: 783,600 **2003 Est.:** 817,491
Reg. Voters: 554,377 **Rep.:** 33% **Dem.:** 44% **Other:** 23%
Caucasian: 75% **African-Am.:** 19% **Nat. Am.:** .3% **Asian:** 2% **Other:** 4% **Hisp.:** 5%

Senators
Joseph R. Biden, Jr. (D)
Thomas R. Carper (D)

Representative
Michael Castle (R-At Large)

Due to population, this state has only one district.

Florida

2000 Pop.: 15,982,378 **2003 Est.:** 17,019,068
Reg. Voters: 10,301,290 **Rep.:** 38% **Dem.:** 41% Green: .1% **Other:** 21%
Caucasian: 78% **African-Am.:** 15% **Nat. Am.:** .3% **Asian:** 2% **Other:** 6% **Hisp.:** 17%

Senators
Bill Nelson (D)
Mel Martinez (R)

Representatives
Jeff Miller (R-1st)
F. Allen Boyd, Jr. (D-2nd)
Corrine Brown (D-3rd)
Ander Crenshaw (R-4th)
Ginny Brown-Waite (R-5th)
Cliff Stearns (R-6th)
John Mica (R-7th)
Ric Keller (R-8th)
Michael Bilirakis (R-9th)
C.W. Bill Young (R-10th)
Jim Davis (D-11th)
Adam Putnam (R-12th)
Katherine Harris (R-13th)
Connie Mack (R-14th)
Dave Weldon (R-15th)
Mark Foley (R-16th)
Kendrick B. Meek (D-17th)
Ileana Ros-Lehtinen (R-18th)
Robert I. Wexler (D-19th)
Debbie Wasserman Schultz (D-20th)
Lincoln Diaz-Balart (R-21st)
E. Clay Shaw, Jr. (R-22nd)
Alcee L. Hastings (D-23rd)
Tom Feeney (R-24th)
Mario Diaz-Balart (R-25th)

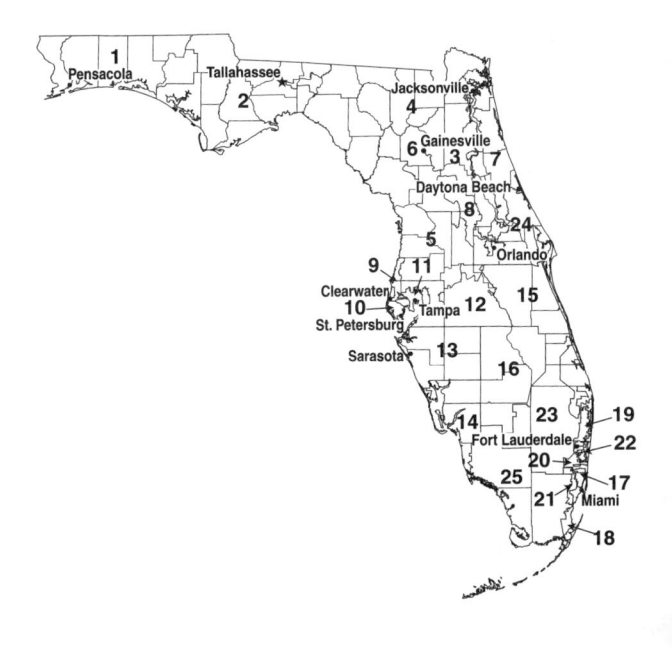

Georgia

2000 Pop.: 8,186,453 **2003 Est.:** 8,684,715
Reg. Voters: 4,967,541 Party registration not required.
Caucasian: 65% **African-Am.:** 29% **Nat. Am.:** .3% **Asian:** 2% **Other:** 4% **Hisp.:** 5%

Senators
Saxby Chambliss (R)
Johnny Isakson (R)

Representatives
Jack Kingston (R-1st)
Sanford Bishop, Jr. (D-2nd)
Jim Marshall (D-3rd)
Cynthia McKinney (D-4th)
John Lewis (D-5th)
Tom Price (R-6th)
John Linder (R-7th)
Lynn A. Westmoreland (R-8th)
Charles Norwood (R-9th)
Nathan Deal (R-10th)
Phil Gingrey (R-11th)
John Barrow (D-12th)
David Scott (D-13th)

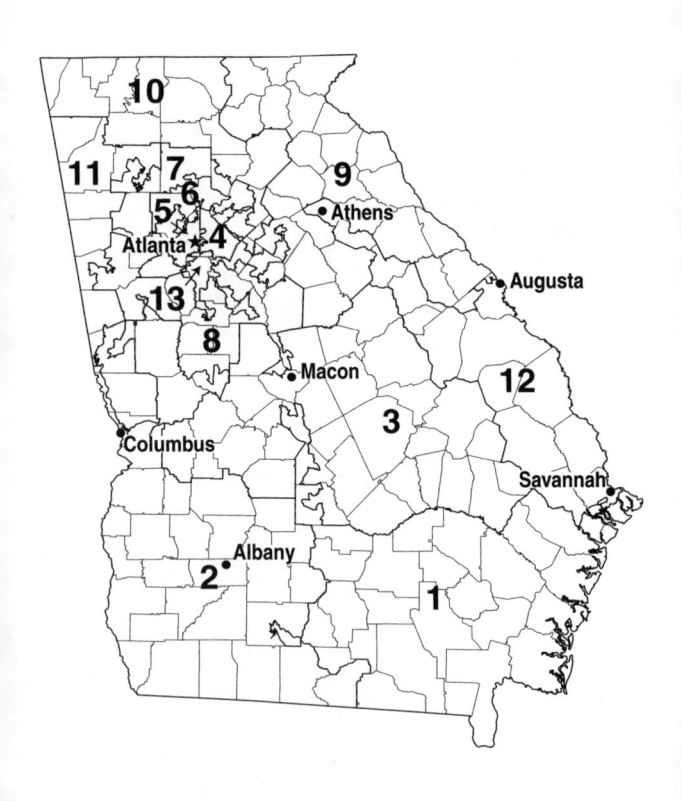

Hawaii

2000 Pop.: 1,211,537 **2003 Est.:** 1,257,608
Reg. Voters: 647,238 Party registration not required.
Caucasian: 24% **African-Am.:** 2% **Nat. Am.:** .3% **Asian:** 42% **Other:** 32% **Hisp.:** 7%

Senators
Daniel K. Inouye (D)
Daniel K. Akaka (D)

Representatives
Neil Abercrombie (D-1st)
Ed Case (D-2nd)

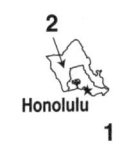

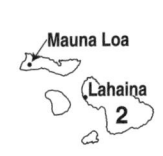

Idaho

2000 Pop.: 1,293,953 **2003 Est.:** 1,366,332
Reg. Voters: 798,015 Party registration not required.
Caucasian: 91% **African-Am.:** .4% **Nat. Am.:** 1% **Asian:** 1% **Other:** 6% **Hisp.:** 8%

Senators
Larry E. Craig (R)
Mike Crapo (R)

Representatives
C.L. "Butch" Otter (R-1st)
Mike Simpson (R-2nd)

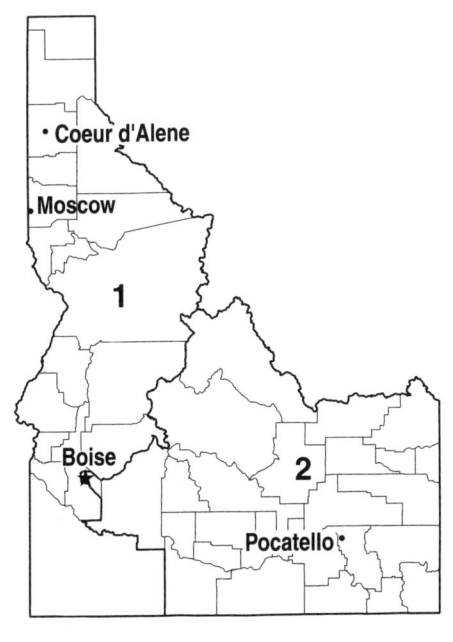

VII

Illinois

2000 Pop.: 12,419,293 **2003 Est.:** 12,653,544
Reg. Voters: 7,025,999 Party registration not required.
Caucasian: 74% **African-Am.:** 15% **Nat. Am.:** .2% **Asian:** 3% **Other:** 8% **Hisp.:** 12%

Senators
Richard J. Durbin (D)
Barack Obama (D)

Representatives
Bobby Rush (D-1st)
Jesse Jackson, Jr. (D-2nd)
Dan Lipinski (D-3rd)
Luis V. Gutierrez (D-4th)
Rahm Emanuel (D-5th)
Henry J. Hyde (R-6th)
Danny K. Davis (D-7th)
Melissa L. Bean (D-8th)
Janice D. Schakowsky (D-9th)
Mark S. Kirk (R-10th)
Jerry Weller (R-11th)
Jerry F. Costello (D-12th)
Judy Biggert (R-13th)
J. Dennis Hastert (R-14th)
Timothy V. Johnson (R-15th)
Donald A. Manzullo (R-16th)
Lane Evans (D-17th)
Ray H. LaHood (R-18th)
John M. Shimkus (R-19th)

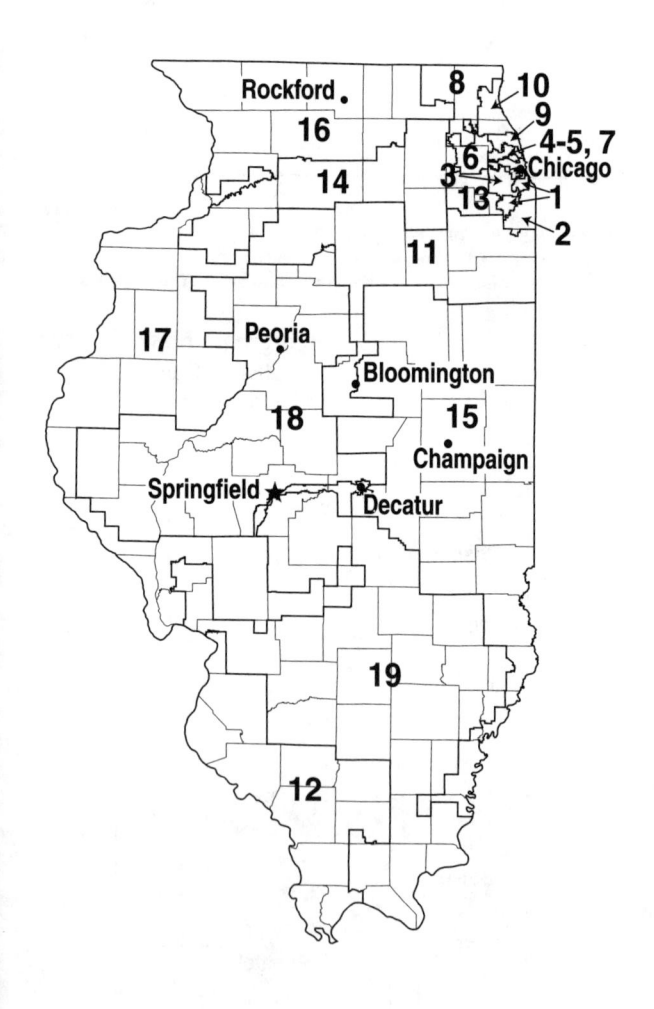

Indiana

2000 Pop.: 6,080,485 **2003 Est.:** 6,195,643
Reg. Voters: 4,296,602 Party registration not required.
Caucasian: 88% **African-Am.:** 8% **Nat. Am.:** .3% **Asian:** 1% **Other:** 3% **Hisp.:** 4%

Senators
Richard G. Lugar (R)
Evan Bayh (D)

Representatives
Peter J. Visclosky (D-1st)
Chris Chocola (R-2nd)
Mark Souder (R-3rd)
Steve Buyer (R-4th)
Dan Burton (R-5th)
Mike Pence (R-6th)
Julia M. Carson (D-7th)
John N. Hostettler (R-8th)
Mike Sodrel (R-9th)

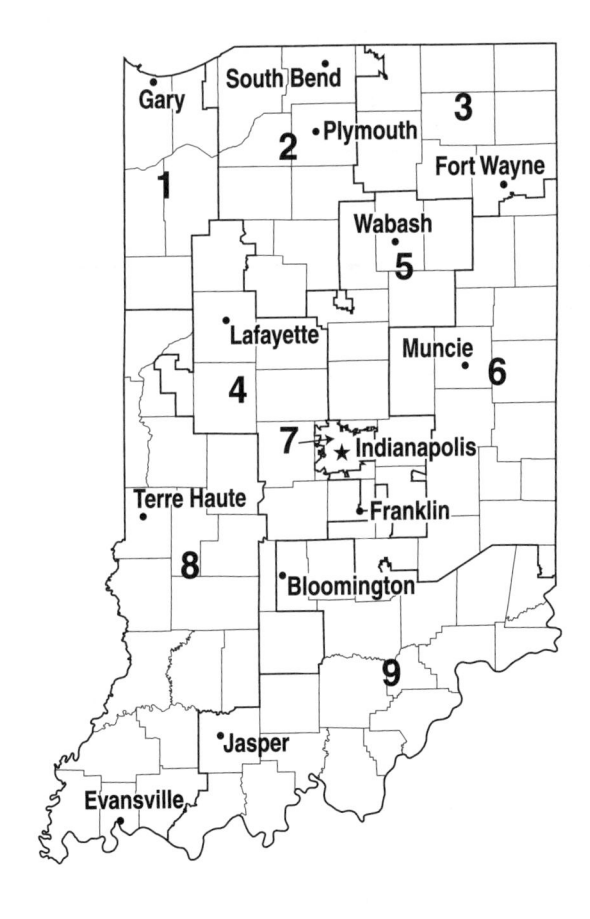

Iowa

2000 Pop.: 2,926,324 **2003 Est.:** 2,944,062
Reg. Voters: 2,138,880 **Rep.:** 31% **Dem.:** 30% **Green:** <.1% **Other:** 39%
Caucasian: 94% **African-Am.:** 2% **Nat. Am.:** .3% **Asian:** 1% **Other:** 2% **Hisp.:** 3%

Senators
Charles E. Grassley (R)
Tom Harkin (D)

Representatives
Jim Nussle (R-1st)
Jim Leach (R-2nd)
Leonard L. Boswell (D-3rd)
Tom Latham (R-4th)
Steve King (R-5th)

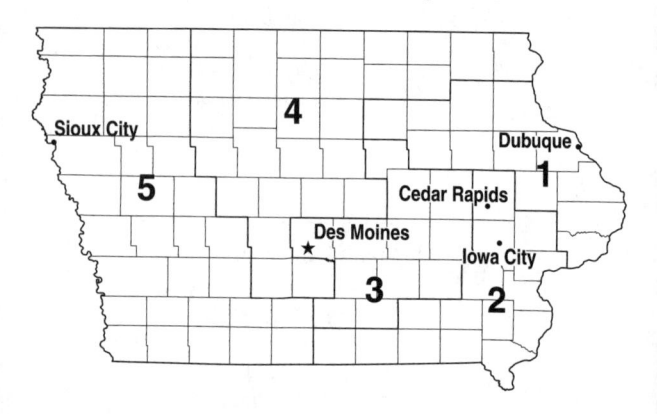

Kansas

2000 Pop.: 2,688,418 **2003 Est.:** 2,723,507
Reg. Voters: 1,591,428 **Rep.:** 46% **Dem.:** 27% **Other:** 27%
Caucasian: 86% **African-Am.:** 6% **Nat. Am.:** 1% **Asian:** 2% **Other:** 6% **Hisp.:** 7%

Senators
Sam Brownback (R)
Pat Roberts (R)

Representatives
Jerry Moran (R-1st)
Jim R. Ryun (R-2nd)
Dennis Moore (D-3rd)
Todd Tiahrt (R-4th)

Kentucky

2000 Pop.: 4,041,769 **2003 Est.:** 4,117,827
Reg. Voters: 2,808,234 **Rep.:** 36% **Dem.:** 58% **Other:** 7%
Caucasian: 90% **African-Am.:** 7% **Nat. Am.:** .2% **Asian:** 1% **Other:** 2% **Hisp.:** 2%

Senators
Mitch McConnell (R)
Jim Bunning (R)

Representatives
Edward Whitfield (R-1st)
Ron Lewis (R-2nd)
Anne M. Northup (R-3rd)
Geoff Davis (R-4th)
Harold Rogers (R-5th)
Ben Chandler (D-6th)

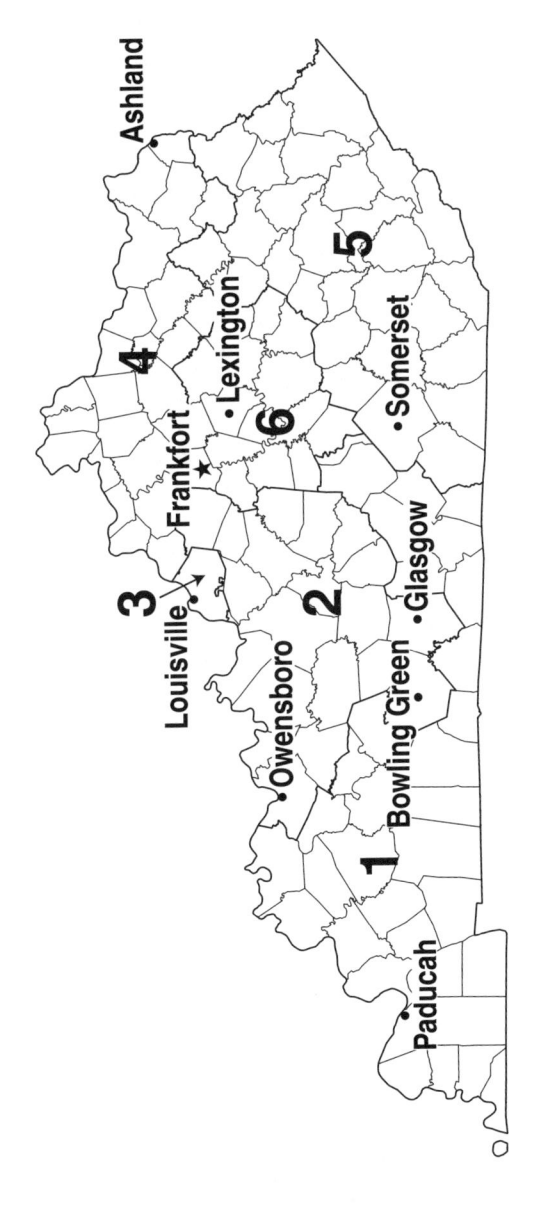

Louisiana

2000 Pop.: 4,468,976 **2003 Est.:** 4,496,334
Reg. Voters: 2,822,427 **Rep.:** 24% **Dem.:** 56% **Other:** 20%
Caucasian: 64% **African-Am.:** 33% **Nat. Am.:** 1% **Asian:** 1% **Other:** 2% **Hisp.:** 2%

Senators
Mary Landrieu (D)
David Vitter (R)

Representatives
Bobby Jindal (R-1st)
William J. Jefferson (D-2nd)
Charlie Melancon (D-3rd)
Jim McCrery (R-4th)
Rodney Alexander (R-5th)
Richard H. Baker (R-6th)
Charles W. Boustany, Jr. (R-7th)

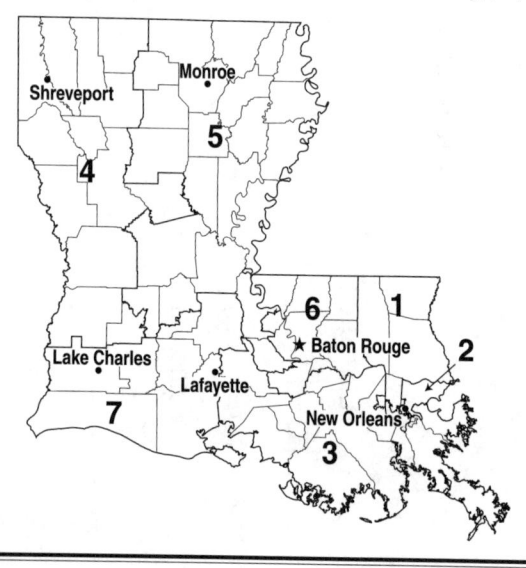

Maine

2000 Pop.: 1,274,923 **2003 Est.:** 1,305,728
Reg. Voters: 957,485 **Rep.:** 29% **Dem.:** 31% **Green:** 2% **Other:** 38%
Caucasian: 97% **African-Am.:** .5% **Nat. Am.:** .6% **Asian:** .7% **Other:** 1% **Hisp.:** 1%

Senators
Olympia J. Snowe (R)
Susan M. Collins (R)

Representatives
Thomas H. Allen (D-1st)
Michael H. Michaud (D-2nd)

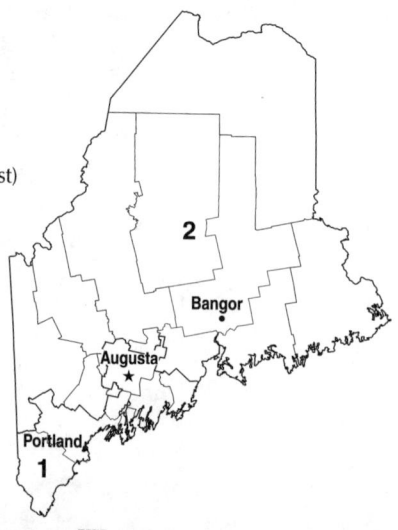

Maryland

2000 Pop.: 5,296,486 **2003 Est.:** 5,508,909
Reg. Voters: 2,939,970 **Rep.:** 30% **Dem.:** 55% **Green:** .2% **Other:** 15%
Caucasian: 64% **African-Am.:** 28% **Nat. Am.:** .3% **Asian:** 4% **Other:** 4% **Hisp.:** 4%

Senators
Paul S. Sarbanes (D)
Barbara A. Mikulski (D)

Representatives
Wayne Gilchrest (R-1st)
C.A. "Dutch" Ruppersberger (D-2nd)
Benjamin L. Cardin (D-3rd)
Albert Wynn (D-4th)
Steny H. Hoyer (D-5th)
Roscoe Bartlett (R-6th)
Elijah Cummings (D-7th)
Chris Van Hollen, Jr. (D-8th)

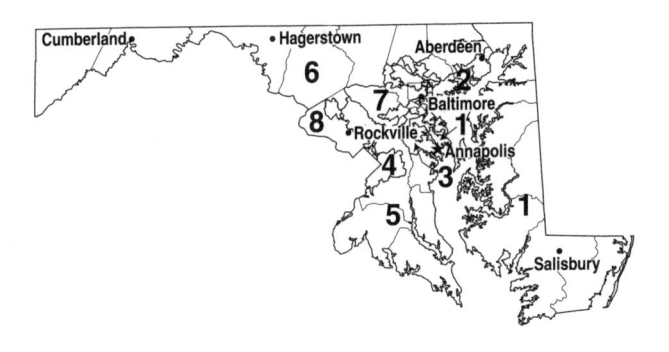

Massachusetts

2000 Pop.: 6,349,097 **2003 Est.:** 6,433,422
Reg. Voters: 4,098,634 **Rep.:** 13% **Dem.:** 37% **Green:** .2% **Other:** 50%
Caucasian: 85% **African-Am.:** 5% **Nat. Am.:** .2% **Asian:** 4% **Other:** 6% **Hisp.:** 7%

Senators
Edward M. Kennedy (D)
John F. Kerry (D)

Representatives
John W. Olver (D-1st)
Richard E. Neal (D-2nd)
James P. McGovern (D-3rd)
Barney Frank (D-4th)
Marty Meehan (D-5th)
John F. Tierney (D-6th)
Edward J. Markey (D-7th)
Michael Capuano (D-8th)
Stephen F. Lynch (D-9th)
William Delahunt (D-10th)

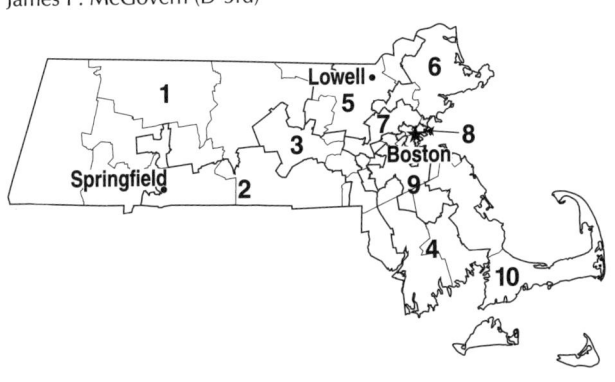

Michigan

2000 Pop.: 9,938,444 **2003 Est.:** 10,079,985
Reg. Voters: 7,164,047 Party registration not required.
Caucasian: 80% **African-Am.:** 14% **Nat. Am.:** 1% **Asian:** 2% **Other:** 3% **Hisp.:** 3%

Senators
Carl Levin (D)
Debbie A. Stabenow (D)

Representatives
Bart Stupak (D-1st)
Peter Hoekstra (R-2nd)
Vernon Ehlers (R-3rd)
Dave Camp (R-4th)
Dale E. Kildee (D-5th)
Fred Upton (R-6th)
Joe Schwarz (R-7th)
Michael J. Rogers (R-8th)
Joseph Knollenberg (R-9th)
Candice Miller (R-10th)
Thaddeus G. McCotter (R-11th)
Sander M. Levin (D-12th)
Carolyn C. Kilpatrick (D-13th)
John Conyers, Jr. (D-14th)
John D. Dingell (D-15th)

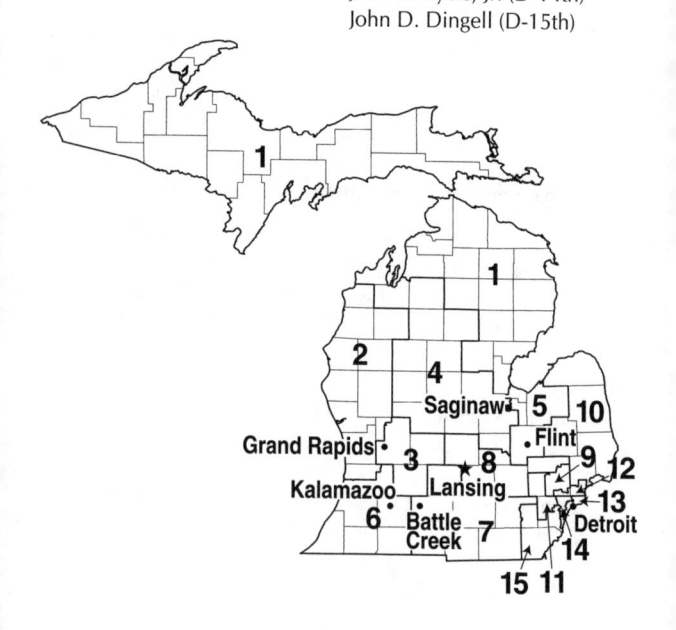

Minnesota

2000 Pop.: 4,919,479 **2003 Est.:** 5,059,375
Reg. Voters: 3,238,386 Party registration not required.
Caucasian: 89% **African-Am.:** 4% **Nat. Am.:** 1% **Asian:** 3% **Other:** 3% **Hisp.:** 3%

Senators
Mark Dayton (D)
Norm Coleman (R)

Representatives
Gil Gutknecht (R-1st)
John Kline (R-2nd)
Jim Ramstad (R-3rd)
Betty McCollum (D-4th)
Martin Olav Sabo (D-5th)
Mark R. Kennedy (R-6th)
Collin Peterson (D-7th)
James L. Oberstar (D-8th)

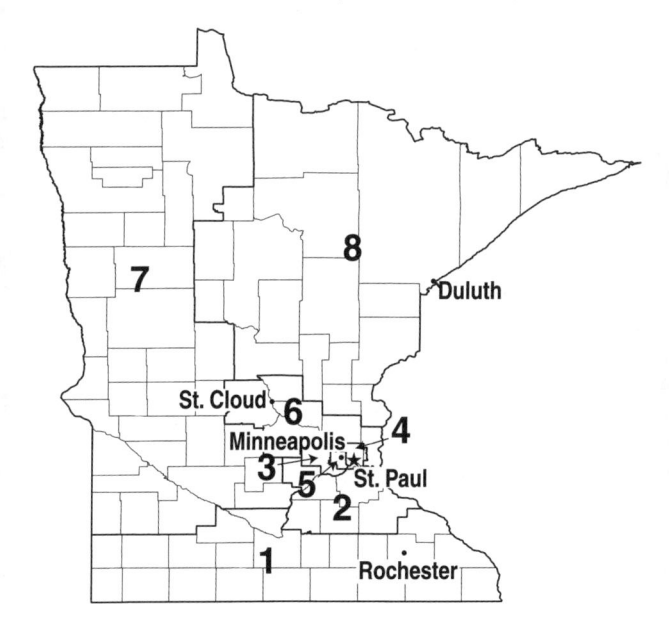

Mississippi

2000 Pop.: 2,844,658 **2003 Est.:** 2,881,281
Reg. Voters: 677,636 (2002) Party registration not required.
Caucasian: 61% **African-Am.:** 36% **Nat. Am.:** .4% **Asian:** 1% **Other:** 1% **Hisp.:** 1%

Senators
Thad Cochran (R)
Trent Lott (R)

Representatives
Roger Wicker (R-1st)
Bennie G. Thompson (D-2nd)
Charles "Chip" Pickering, Jr. (R-3rd)
Gene Taylor (D-4th)

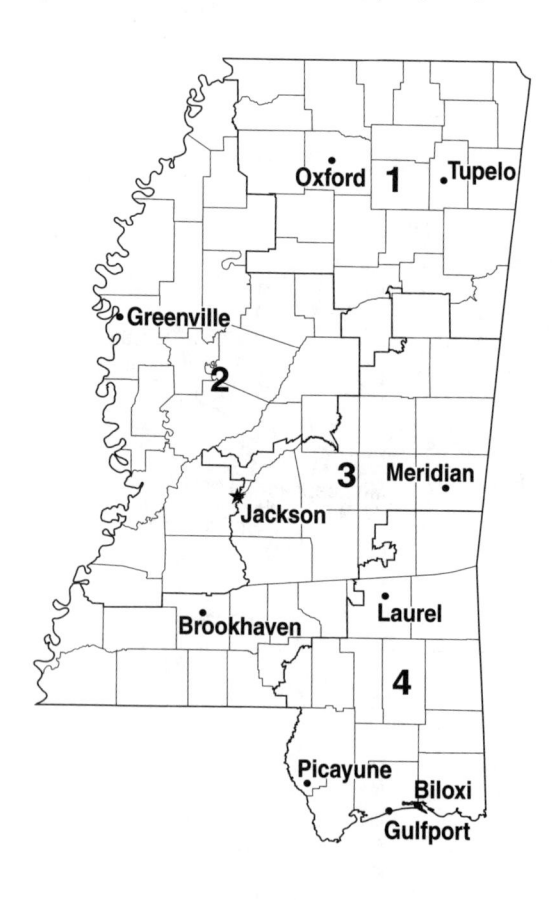

Missouri

2000 Pop.: 5,595,211 **2003 Est.:** 5,704,484
Reg. Voters: 4,194,146 Party registration not required.
Caucasian: 85% **African-Am.:** 11% **Nat. Am.:** .4% **Asian:** 1% **Other:** 2% **Hisp.:** 2%

Senators
Christopher S. "Kit" Bond (R)
Jim Talent (R)

Representatives
Wm. Lacy Clay (D-1st)
Todd Akin (R-2nd)
Russ Carnahan (D-3rd)
Ike Skelton (D-4th)
Emanuel Cleaver (D-5th)
Sam Graves (R-6th)
Roy Blunt (R-7th)
Jo Ann H. Emerson (R-8th)
Kenny C. Hulshof (R-9th)

Montana

2000 Pop.: 902,195 **2003 Est.:** 917,621
Reg. Voters: 638,474 Party registration not required.
Caucasian: 91% **African-Am.:** .3% **Nat. Am.:** 6% **Asian:** 1% **Other:** 2% **Hisp.:** 2%

Senators
Max Baucus (D)
Conrad Burns (R)

Representative
Dennis Rehberg (R-At Large)

Due to population, this state has only one district.

XVII

Nebraska

2000 Pop.: 1,711,263 **2003 Est.:** 1,739,291
Reg. Voters: 1,160,193 **Rep.:** 50% **Dem.:** 34% **Green:** <.1% **Other:** 16%
Caucasian: 90% **African-Am.:** 4% **Nat. Am.:** 1% **Asian:** 1% **Other:** 4% **Hisp.:** 6%

Senators
Chuck Hagel (R)
Ben Nelson (D)

Representatives
Jeff Fortenberry (R-1st)
Lee Terry (R-2nd)
Tom Osborne (R-3rd)

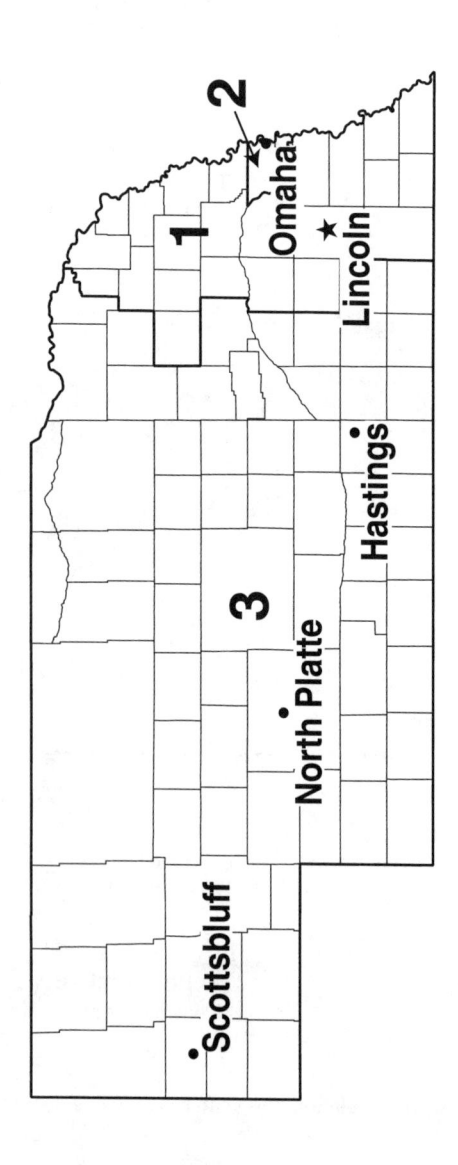

Nevada

2000 Pop.: 1,998,257 **2003 Est.:** 2,241,154
Reg. Voters: 1,103,366 **Rep.:** 40% **Dem.:** 40% **Green:** .3% **Other:** 19%
Caucasian: 75% **African-Am.:** 7% **Nat. Am.:** 1% **Asian:** 5% **Other:** 12% **Hisp.:** 20%

Senators
Harry Reid (D)
John Ensign (R)

Representatives
Shelley Berkley (D-1st)
James A. Gibbons (R-2nd)
Jon C. Porter (R-3rd)

New Hampshire

2000 Pop.: 1,235,786 **2003 Est.:** 1,287,687
Reg. Voters: 447,135 (2002) Party registration not required.
Caucasian: 96% **African-Am.:** 1% **Nat. Am.:** .2% **Asian:** 1% **Other:** 2% **Hisp.:** 2%

Senators
Judd Gregg (R)
John E. Sununu (R)

Representatives
Jeb Bradley (R-1st)
Charles Bass (R-2nd)

New Jersey

2000 Pop.: 8,414,350 **2003 Est.:** 8,638,396
Reg. Voters: 5,009,140 Party registration not required.
Caucasian: 73% **African-Am.:** 14% **Nat. Am.:** .2% **Asian:** 6% **Other:** 8% **Hisp.:** 13%

Senators
Jon S. Corzine (D)
Frank R. Lautenberg (D)

Representatives
Robert E. Andrews (D-1st)
Frank A. LoBiondo (R-2nd)
Jim Saxton (R-3rd)
Christopher H. Smith (R-4th)
Scott Garrett (R-5th)
Frank Pallone, Jr. (D-6th)
Michael A. Ferguson (R-7th)
Bill Pascrell, Jr. (D-8th)
Steven R. Rothman (D-9th)
Donald M. Payne (D-10th)
Rodney Frelinghuysen (R-11th)
Rush Holt (D-12th)
Robert Menendez (D-13th)

New Mexico

2000 Pop.: 1,819,046 **2003 Est.:** 1,874,614
Reg. Voters: 1,091,237 **Rep.:** 32% **Dem.:** 50% **Green:** 1% **Other:** 17%
Caucasian: 67% **African-Am.:** 2% **Nat. Am.:** 10% **Asian:** 1% **Other:** 21% **Hisp.:** 42%

Senators
Pete V. Domenici (R)
Jeff Bingaman (D)

Representatives
Heather A. Wilson (R-1st)
Steve Pearce (R-2nd)
Tom Udall (D-3rd)

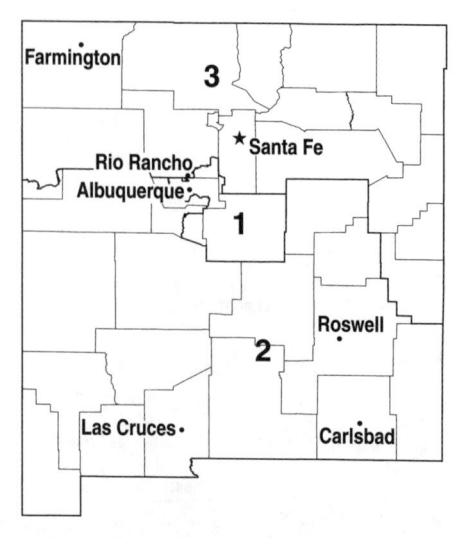

New York

2000 Pop.: 18,976,457 **2003 Est.:** 19,190,115
Reg. Voters: 11,837,068 **Rep.:** 27% **Dem.:** 47% **Green:** .3% **Other:** 26%
Caucasian: 68% **African-Am.:** 16% **Nat. Am.:** .4% **Asian:** 6% **Other:** 10% **Hisp.:** 15%

Senators
Charles E. Schumer (D)
Hillary Rodham Clinton (D)

Representatives
Tim Bishop (D-1st)
Steve J. Israel (D-2nd)
Peter King (R-3rd)
Carolyn McCarthy (D-4th)
Gary L. Ackerman (D-5th)
Gregory W. Meeks (D-6th)
Joseph Crowley (D-7th)
Jerrold Nadler (D-8th)
Anthony D. Weiner (D-9th)
Edolphus Towns (D-10th)
Major R. Owens (D-11th)
Nydia M. Velázquez (D-12th)
Vito Fossella (R-13th)
Carolyn Maloney (D-14th)
Charles B. Rangel (D-15th)
José E. Serrano (D-16th)
Eliot Engel (D-17th)
Nita M. Lowey (D-18th)
Sue W. Kelly (R-19th)
John E. Sweeney (R-20th)
Michael R. McNulty (D-21st)
Maurice Hinchey (D-22nd)
John McHugh (R-23rd)
Sherwood L. Boehlert (R-24th)
James T. Walsh (R-25th)
Thomas Reynolds (R-26th)
Brian M. Higgins (D-27th)
Louise McIntosh Slaughter (D-28th)
Randy Kuhl (R-29th)

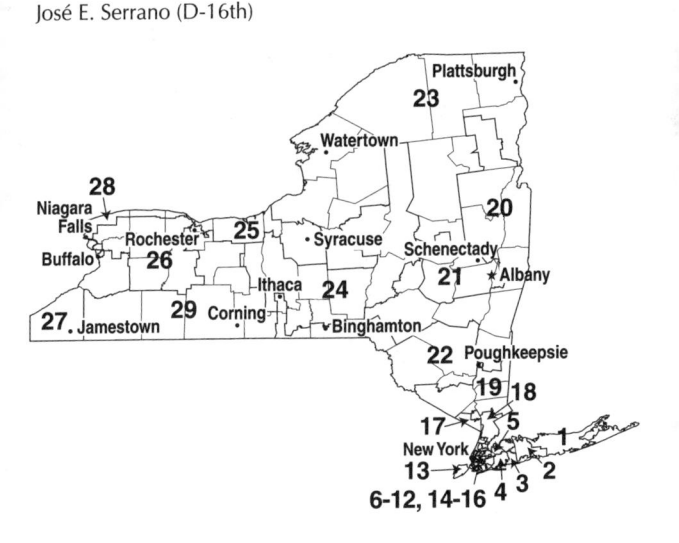

North Carolina

2000 Pop.: 8,049,313 **2003 Est.:** 8,407,248
Reg. Voters: 5,001,522 **Rep.:** 35% **Dem.:** 48% **Other:** 18%
Caucasian: 72% **African-Am.:** 22% **Nat. Am.:** 1% **Asian:** 1% **Other:** 4% **Hisp.:** 5%

Senators
Elizabeth Dole (R)
Richard Burr (R)

Representatives
G.K. Butterfield (D-1st)
Bob Etheridge (D-2nd)
Walter Jones, Jr. (R-3rd)
David E. Price (D-4th)
Virginia Foxx (R-5th)
Howard Coble (R-6th)
Mike McIntyre (D-7th)
Robin Hayes (R-8th)
Sue Myrick (R-9th)
Patrick McHenry (R-10th)
Charles H. Taylor (R-11th)
Melvin L. Watt (D-12th)
Brad Miller (D-13th)

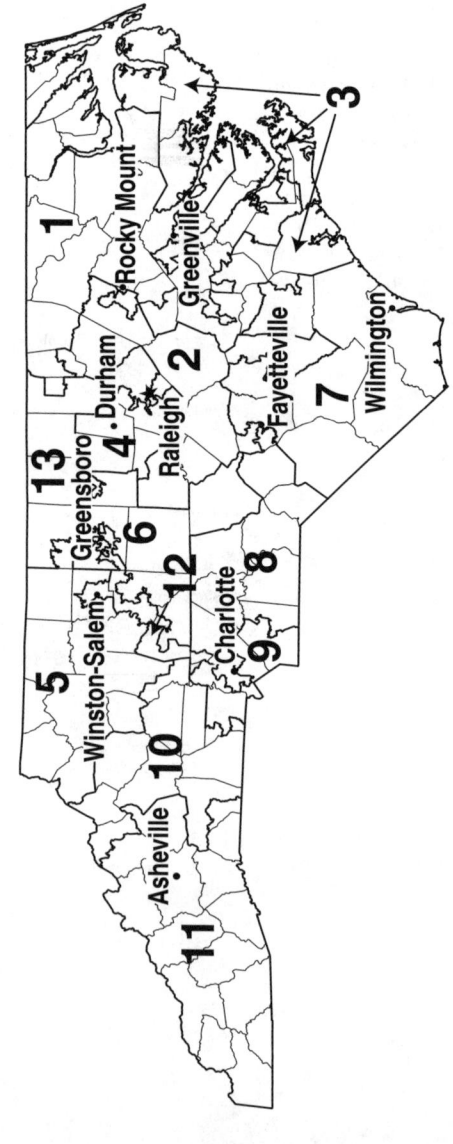

North Dakota

2000 Pop.: 642,200 **2003 Est.:** 633,837
No Voter Registration (487,010 eligible voters)
Caucasian: 92% **African-Am.:** 1% **Nat. Am.:** 5% **Asian:** 1% **Other:** 2% **Hisp.:** 1%

Senators
Kent Conrad (D)
Byron L. Dorgan (D)

Representative
Earl Pomeroy (D-At Large)

Due to population, this state has only one district.

Ohio

2000 Pop.: 11,353,140 **2003 Est.:** 11,435,798
Reg. Voters: 7,974,770 Party registration not required.
Caucasian: 85% **African-Am.:** 12% **Nat. Am.:** .2% **Asian:** 1% **Other:** 2% **Hisp.:** 2%

Senators
Mike DeWine (R)
George V. Voinovich (R)

Representatives
Steve Chabot (R-1st)
Rob J. Portman (R-2nd)
Michael Turner (R-3rd)
Michael G. Oxley (R-4th)
Paul E. Gillmor (R-5th)
Ted Strickland (D-6th)
David Hobson (R-7th)
John A. Boehner (R-8th)
Marcy Kaptur (D-9th)
Dennis J. Kucinich (D-10th)
Stephanie Tubbs Jones (D-11th)
Patrick J. Tiberi (R-12th)
Sherrod Brown (D-13th)
Steven C. LaTourette (R-14th)
Deborah Pryce (R-15th)
Ralph Regula (R-16th)
Tim Ryan (D-17th)
Bob Ney (R-18th)

Oklahoma

2000 Pop.: 3,450,654 **2003 Est.:** 3,511,532
Reg. Voters: 2,249,557 **Rep.:** 41% **Dem.:** 49% **Other:** 10%
Caucasian: 76% **African-Am.:** 8% **Nat. Am.:** 8% **Asian:** 1% **Other:** 7% **Hisp.:** 5%

Senators
James M. Inhofe (R)
Tom Coburn (R)

Representatives
John Sullivan (R-1st)
Dan Boren (D-2nd)
Frank D. Lucas (R-3rd)
Tom Cole (R-4th)
Ernest Istook, Jr. (R-5th)

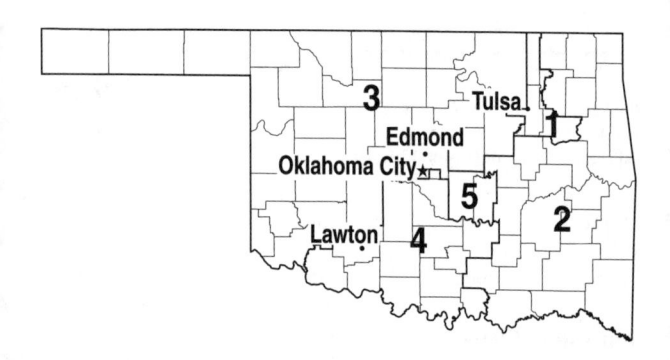

Oregon

2000 Pop.: 3,421,399 **2003 Est.:** 3,559,596
Reg. Voters: 2,141,249 **Rep.:** 36% **Dem.:** 39% **Other:** 26%
Caucasian: 87% **African-Am.:** 2% **Nat. Am.:** 1% **Asian:** 3% **Other:** 8% **Hisp.:** 8%

Senators
Ron Wyden (D)
Gordon Smith (R)

Representatives
David Wu (D-1st)
Greg Walden (R-2nd)
Earl Blumenauer (D-3rd)
Peter A. DeFazio (D-4th)
Darlene Hooley (D-5th)

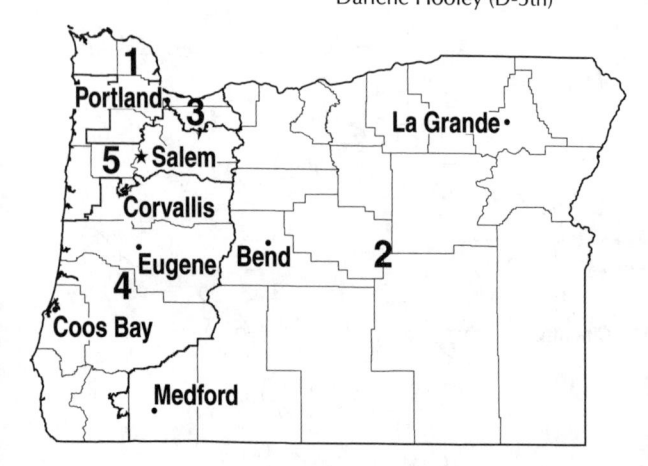

Pennsylvania

2000 Pop.: 12,281,054 **2003 Est.:** 12,365,455
Reg. Voters: 8,346,863 **Rep.:** 41% **Dem.:** 48% Green: .2% **Other:** 12%
Caucasian: 85% **African-Am.:** 10% **Nat. Am.:** .1% **Asian:** 2% **Other:** 3% **Hisp.:** 3%

Senators
Arlen Specter (R)
Rick Santorum (R)

Representatives
Robert A. Brady (D-1st)
Chaka Fattah (D-2nd)
Philip S. English (R-3rd)
Melissa A. Hart (R-4th)
John E. Peterson (R-5th)
Jim Gerlach (R-6th)
Curt Weldon (R-7th)
Mike Fitzpatrick (R-8th)
Bill Shuster (R-9th)
Don Sherwood (R-10th)
Paul E. Kanjorski (D-11th)
John P. Murtha (D-12th)
Allyson Y. Schwartz (D-13th)
Mike Doyle (D-14th)
Charles W. Dent (R-15th)
Joseph R. Pitts (R-16th)
Tim Holden (D-17th)
Timothy F. Murphy (R-18th)
Todd R. Platts (R-19th)

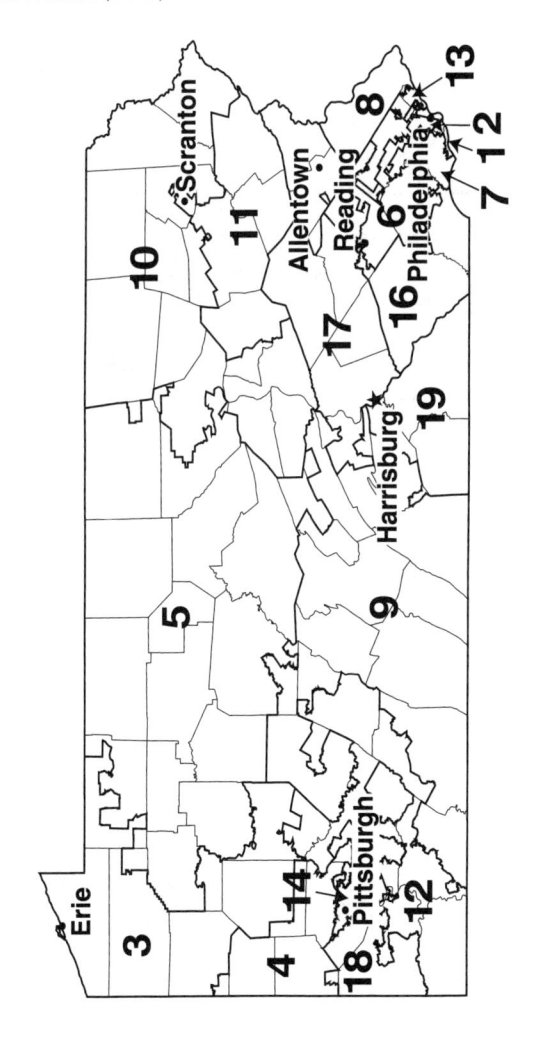

xxv

Rhode Island

2000 Pop.: 1,048,319 **2003 Est.:** 1,076,164
Reg. Voters: 672,950 Party registration not required.
Caucasian: 85% **African-Am.:** 5% **Nat. Am.:** 1% **Asian:** 2% **Other:** 8% **Hisp.:** 9%

Senators
Jack Reed (D)
Lincoln D. Chafee (R)

Representatives
Patrick J. Kennedy (D-1st)
James R. Langevin (D-2nd)

South Carolina

2000 Pop.: 4,012,012 **2003 Est.:** 4,147,152
Reg. Voters: 2,337,052 Party registration not required.
Caucasian: 67% **African-Am.:** 30% **Nat. Am.:** .3% **Asian:** 1% **Other:** 2% **Hisp.:** 2%

Senators
Lindsey O. Graham (R)
Jim DeMint (R)

Representatives
Henry E. Brown, Jr. (R-1st)
Joe Wilson (R-2nd)
J. Gresham Barrett (R-3rd)
Bob Inglis (R-4th)
John M. Spratt, Jr. (D-5th)
James Clyburn (D-6th)

South Dakota

2000 Pop.: 754,844 **2003 Est.:** 764,309
Reg. Voters: 502,261 **Rep.:** 48% **Dem.:** 38% **Other:** 14%
Caucasian: 89% **African-Am.:** 1% **Nat. Am.:** 8% **Asian:** 1% **Other:** 2% **Hisp.:** 1%

Senators
Tim Johnson (D)
John R. Thune (R)

Representative
Stephanie Herseth (D-At Large)

Due to population, this state has only one district.

Tennessee

2000 Pop.: 5,689,283 **2003 Est.:** 5,841,748
Reg. Voters: 3,771,888 Party registration not required.
Caucasian: 80% **African-Am.:** 16% **Nat. Am.:** .3% **Asian:** 1% **Other:** 2% **Hisp.:** 2%

Senators
Bill Frist (R)
Lamar Alexander (R)

Representatives
William L. Jenkins (R-1st)
John J. Duncan, Jr. (R-2nd)
Zach Wamp (R-3rd)
Lincoln Davis (D-4th)
Jim Cooper (D-5th)
Bart Gordon (D-6th)
Marsha Blackburn (R-7th)
John S. Tanner (D-8th)
Harold E. Ford, Jr. (D-9th)

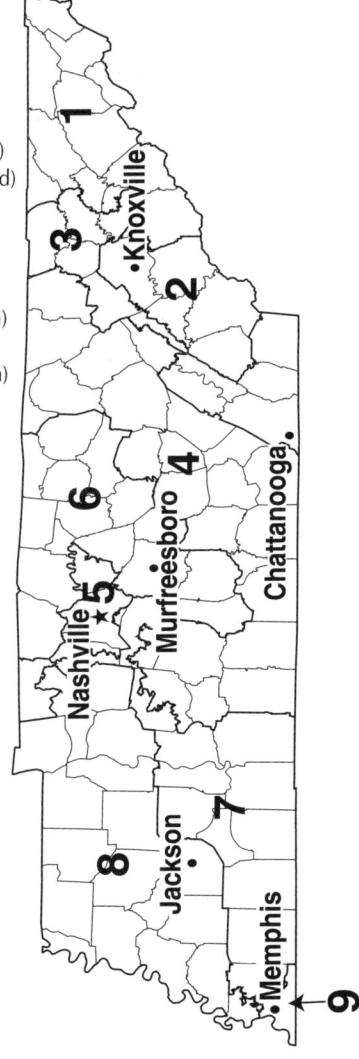

XXVII

Texas

2000 Pop.: 20,851,820 **2003 Est.:** 22,118,509
Reg. Voters: 13,098,329 Party registration not required.
Caucasian: 71% **African-Am.:** 12% **Nat. Am.:** 1% **Asian:** 3% **Other:** 14% **Hisp.:** 32%

Senators
Kay Bailey Hutchison (R)
John Cornyn (R)

Representatives
Louie Gohmert (R-1st)
Ted Poe (R-2nd)
Sam Johnson (R-3rd)
Ralph M. Hall (R-4th)
Jeb Hensarling (R-5th)
Joe Barton (R-6th)
John A. Culberson (R-7th)
Kevin P. Brady (R-8th)
Al Green (D-9th)
Michael McCaul (R-10th)
Mike Conaway (R-11th)
Kay Granger (R-12th)
William "Mac" Thornberry (R-13th)
Ron E. Paul (R-14th)
Rubén E. Hinojosa (D-15th)
Silvestre Reyes (D-16th)
Chet Edwards (D-17th)
Sheila Jackson Lee (D-18th)
Randy Neugebauer (R-19th)
Charles A. Gonzalez (D-20th)
Lamar S. Smith (R-21st)
Tom DeLay (R-22nd)
Henry Bonilla (R-23rd)
Kenny Marchant (R-24th)
Lloyd Doggett (D-25th)
Michael C. Burgess (R-26th)
Solomon P. Ortiz (D-27th)
Henry Cuellar (D-28th)
Gene Green (D-29th)
Eddie Bernice Johnson (D-30th)
John R. Carter (R-31st)
Pete Sessions (R-32nd)

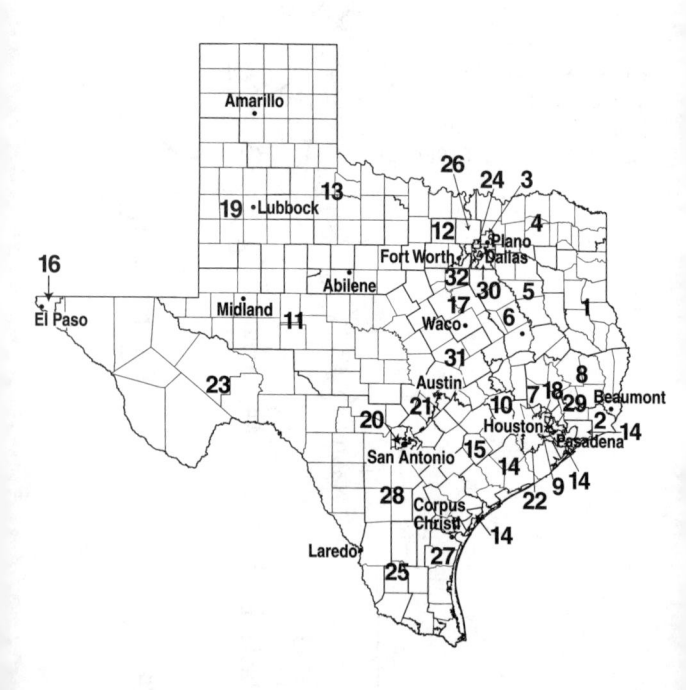

XXVIII

Utah

2000 Pop.: 2,233,169 **2003 Est.:** 2,351,467
Reg. Voters: 1,278,429 Party registration not required.
Caucasian: 89% **African-Am.:** 1% **Nat. Am.:** 1% **Asian:** 2% **Other:** 7% **Hisp.:** 9%

Senators
Orrin G. Hatch (R)
Robert Bennett (R)

Representatives
Rob Bishop (R-1st)
Jim Matheson (D-2nd)
Chris Cannon (R-3rd)

Vermont

2000 Pop.: 608,827 **2003 Est.:** 619,107
Reg. Voters: 444,077 Party registration not required.
Caucasian: 97% **African-Am.:** 1% **Nat. Am.:** .4% **Asian:** 1% **Other:** 1% **Hisp.:** 1%

Senators
Patrick J. Leahy (D)
James M. Jeffords (I)

Representative
Bernard Sanders (I-At Large)

Due to population, this state has only one district.

Virginia

2000 Pop.: 7,078,515 **2003 Est.:** 7,386,330
Reg. Voters: 4,530,902 Party registration not required.
Caucasian: 72% **African-Am.:** 20% **Nat. Am.:** .3% **Asian:** 4% **Other:** 4% **Hisp.:** 5%

Senators
John W. Warner (R)
George Allen (R)

Representatives
Jo Ann S. Davis (R-1st)
Thelma D. Drake (R-2nd)
Bobby Scott (D-3rd)
Randy Forbes (R-4th)
Virgil H. Goode, Jr. (R-5th)
Bob Goodlatte (R-6th)
Eric I. Cantor (R-7th)
James P. Moran (D-8th)
Rick Boucher (D-9th)
Frank R. Wolf (R-10th)
Thomas M. Davis, III (R-11th)

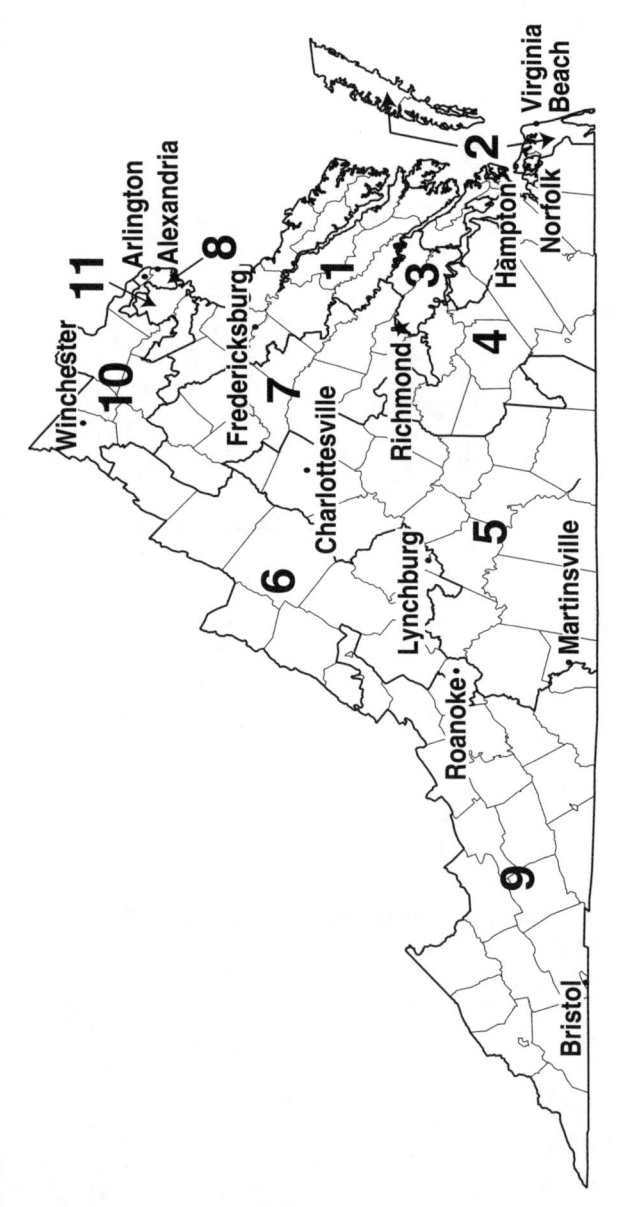

xxx

Washington

2000 Pop.: 5,894,121 **2003 Est.:** 6,131,445
Reg. Voters: 3,508,208 Party registration not required.
Caucasian: 82% **African-Am.:** 3% **Nat. Am.:** 2% **Asian:** 6% **Other:** 8% **Hisp.:** 8%

Senators
Patty Murray (D)
Maria Cantwell (D)

Representatives
Jay Inslee (D-1st)
Rick Larsen (D-2nd)
Brian Baird (D-3rd)
Doc Hastings (R-4th)
Cathy McMorris (R-5th)
Norman D. Dicks (D-6th)
Jim McDermott (D-7th)
Dave Reichert (R-8th)
Adam Smith (D-9th)

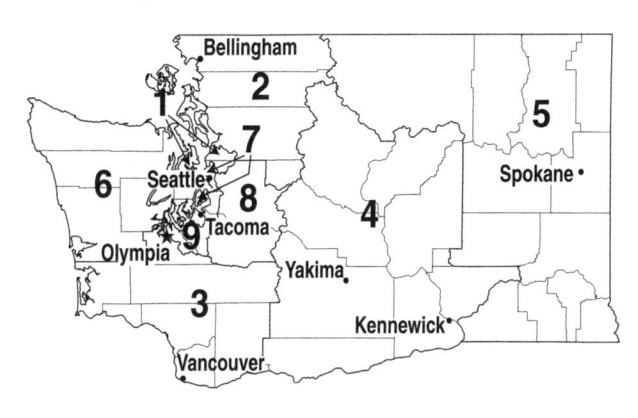

West Virginia

2000 Pop.: 1,808,344 **2003 Est.:** 1,810,354
Reg. Voters: 1,168,694 **Rep.:** 30% **Dem.:** 58% **Other:** 12%
Caucasian: 95% **African-Am.:** 3% **Nat. Am.:** .2% **Asian:** 1% **Other:** 1% **Hisp.:** 1%

Senators
Robert C. Byrd (D)
John D. Rockefeller, IV (D)

Representatives
Alan B. Mollohan (D-1st)
Shelley Moore Capito (R-2nd)
Nick J. Rahall, II (D-3rd)

XXXI

Wisconsin

2000 Pop.: 5,363,675 **2003 Est.:** 5,472,299
Reg. Voters: 1,775,349 (2002) Party registration not required.
Caucasian: 90% **African-Am.:** 6% **Nat. Am.:** 1% **Asian:** 2% **Other:** 3% **Hisp.:** 4%

Senators
Herbert H. Kohl (D)
Russ Feingold (D)

Representatives
Paul D. Ryan (R-1st)
Tammy Baldwin (D-2nd)
Ron J. Kind (D-3rd)
Gwen S. Moore (D-4th)
F. James Sensenbrenner, Jr. (R-5th)
Thomas E. Petri (R-6th)
David R. Obey (D-7th)
Mark Green (R-8th)

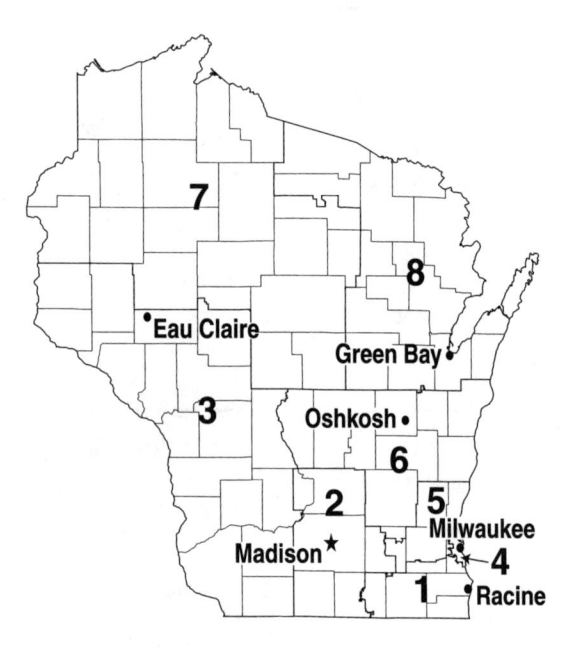

Wyoming

2000 Pop.: 493,782 **2003 Est.:** 501,242
Reg. Voters: 241,200 **Rep.:** 62% **Dem.:** 27% **Other:** 11%
Caucasian: 92% **African-Am.:** 1% **Nat. Am.:** 2% **Asian:** 1% **Other:** 4% **Hisp.:** 6%

Senators
Craig Thomas (R)
Michael B. Enzi (R)

Representative
Barbara Cubin (R-At Large)

Due to population, this state has only one district.